JOSEPH LOSEY

JOSEPH LOSEY

EDITH DE RHAM

ANDRE DEUTSCH

First published in Great Britain
1991 by André Deutsch Limited
105-106 Great Russell Street, London WC1B 3LJ

British Cataloguing in Publication Data

Rham, Edith de
Joseph Losey
I. Title
791.430233092
ISBN 0 233 98723 1

Phototypeset by Falcon Graphic Art Ltd
Wallington, Surrey
Printed in Great Britain by
St Edmundsbury Press,
Bury St Edmunds, Suffolk

In memory of Jill Bennett

Contents

	Foreword	ix
I	La Crosse, Wisconsin	1
II	New York	18
III	Russia and the Roosevelt Years	35
IV	Hollywood and HUAC	52
V	Exile from Tinseltown	73
VI	The Outsider	89
VII	England and The French Connection	104
VIII	All About Eve	125
IX	The Making of *The Servant*	142
X	On Holiday from Harold	161
XI	A Happy *Accident*	173
XII	A Financial *Boom*	185
XIII	Troubled Times and Redemption	200
XIV	Treading Water	218
XV	At Play with Ibsen and Brecht	230
XVI	A Further Exile	242
XVII	Grappling with the Don	255
XVIII	Not Waving but Drowning	271
	Bibliography	287
	Filmography	291
	Index	305

LOSEY FAMILY TREE

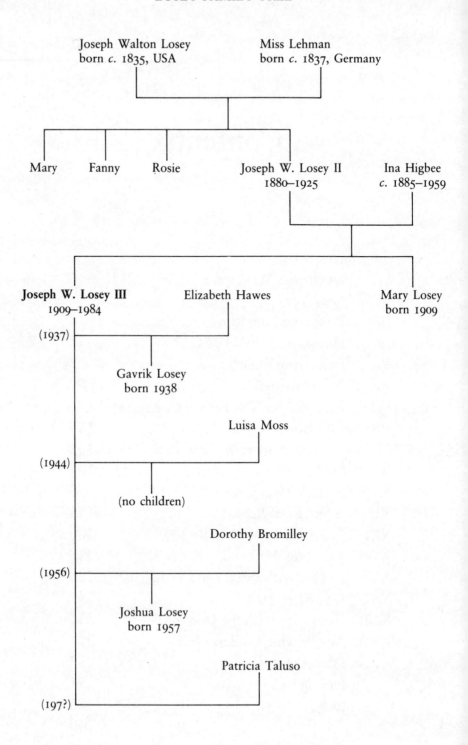

Foreword

Investigating the life of so complex and gifted an artist as Joe Losey was bound to be a rewarding enterprise, but I had not realized how much he would be missed once the work was finished. Ultimately, having thought about and examined every available aspect of a person's career, and enjoyed a varied intercourse over a period of years with many of his friends and colleagues, there is an inevitable sense of loss. Though not physically present, Losey had become a friend who was in some ways better known to me than he was to many of those who actually shared some portion of his life. One of these was Jill Bennett, the actress whose abiding affection for Losey glowed undiminished till the day of her own untimely death on 4 October, 1990.

Joseph Losey not only hoped to explain his life through his films, but used them to rationalize his problems, obsessions and phobias, and to reconcile them with the need to nurture and sustain human relationships, no matter how difficult. The man was a study in polarities, an individual in whom powerful contradictions battled for precedence and never quite came into balance. Many of Losey's classic themes rise from the well-springs of his nature, and the visually stunning interpretations of his dark and claustrophobic world-view flow from the collision between that nature and the effects of his provincial American upbringing and subsequent experience in the large world.

The cinema of Joseph Losey is not merely his life's work, it *is* his life. It has been my intention to celebrate the long and productive life of a great film director, who, being human, had many faults – faults which, even if they had been more numerous, could never outweigh the beauty, quality, and importance of his legacy to the cinema.

I am indebted to many people, all of whom have been incredibly generous, patient and forthcoming. Pride of place must be given to the French academic, author and critic Michel Ciment, without whose comprehensive and conscientious collection of interviews, *Conversations with Losey*, this book would have been impossible to produce, for the vibrant voice of Joseph Losey would have been unheard, along with much of the detailed chronology of his life. My only regret is that Michel's packed schedule of lecturing, teaching and writing limited the amount of time he could spare to talk to me, but his mind is so orderly and precise that an enormous amount of information, analysis and insight was conveyed in a relatively short space of time.

Others in France to whom I am eternally grateful are Mme Charlotte Aillaud, Jack Berry, Marc Bohan, Barbara Bray, Eugene Braun-Monk, Michel Legrand, Jeanne Moreau, Pierre Rissient, Delphine Seyrig, George Tabori, Bertrand Tavernier, Daniel Toscan du Plantier, Alexander Trauner and Robert Velaise. I should also like to thank Darian Leader, studying in Paris to be a psychiatrist, for helping me with much of the more academic elements of research.

For their invaluable help in New York and Los Angeles I would like to thank Henry Bamburger, Ben and Norma Barzman, Alan Bernheim, Eileen Finletter, Foster Hirsch, Luisa Hyun, Evelyn Keyes, John Kohn, Stanley Kramer, Viveca Lindfors, Ruth Lipton, George Litto, Norman Lloyd, Jack Loring, Richard MacDonald, Maestro Loren Maazel, John Mazzola, Alexis Smith, Dean Stockwell, John Van Eyssen and Philip Waxman, with special thanks to Linda Zimmerman for helping me so vitally in Hollywood, where I was a stranger.

In England the list is even longer: Alan Bates, Jill Bennett, Dirk Bogarde, Keith Botsford, Ros Chatto, Julie Christie, Leon Clore, Dr Barry Cooper, Tom Courtenay, Theo Cowan, Wendy Craig, John Dankworth and Cleo Laine, David Deutsch, Gerry Fisher, Eve Forman, Angela, Edward and James Fox, Georgina Hale, Peter Handford, Winston Harold, Doug Hayward, Norma Heyman, Joseph Janni, Evan Jones, Alexander Knox, Joshua Losey, Sarah Miles, Nicholas Mosley, Philippa Murphy, Dorothy Phelan, Pieter Rogers, Douglas Slocombe, Chaim Topol and Moira Williams not only informed and enlightened me, but provided me with a memorable collection of profoundly enjoyable afternoons.

Special credit must go also to Janet Moat and all her excellent and patient staff at the British Film Institute, who were obliged to put up with me for many months. I also thank John Walker for his assistance in editing my manuscript. My sincere wish is that I have done right by everybody, if such a thing is possible.

'Actually, there is a permanent strain of suffering in love which happiness neutralises, makes conditional, procrastinates: but which may at any moment become what it would long since have been had we not obtained what we were seeking – sheer agony.'

Marcel Proust, *A la Recherche du Temps Perdu.*

E. de R. 1991

La Crosse, Wisconsin

The state of Wisconsin is an unremarkable place, even by provincial American standards, and yet within a decade, in the early twentieth century, it spawned three major cinematic talents: Orson Welles, Nicholas Ray (né Kienzle), and Joseph Walton Losey. Even more remarkably, Ray and Losey both came from La Crosse, a small, north-western town, which, at the time of Losey's birth in 1909, harboured no more than 15,000 souls of mostly German, Polish, or Scandinavian origins.

Today La Crosse is transformed. Its population has mushroomed to three times what it was at the turn of the century, and its ambience has lost even such modest charms as it held briefly between the time it was first settled by European immigrants, and the evolutionary era leading up to World War II.

Gone are most of the 'grand' houses built by the new-rich mid-westerners like Losey's grandfather, and also many of the rambling old wooden public buildings, such as the high school from which Losey graduated in 1925. Unmanageable without cheap domestic labour, these places have been torn down to make way for clinics, youth centres and the like, leaving only the most banal domestic architecture, flung up, it would appear, without benefit of anything resembling a pre-conceived plan. Four walls, a porch, and sloping roof designed to discourage lingering heavy snowfalls describes the norm for private houses, in varying degrees of hideousness and lack of distinction. Losey's visual fastidiousness would have been deeply offended by most of the public buildings, which range from the inoffensive-functional-modern to dowdy mid-western. Three vast churches, constructed at the turn of the century in diverse styles, each hoping to suggest majesty, loom on various corners, representing the three principal religious influences in the town: Episcopalian Protestant, which always ministered to the spiritual needs of the rich folk (those of primarily German and English descent), Lutheran, there to comfort the Scandinavians, and Catholic, which ministers to everybody else.

Losey was born on 14 January 1909, in La Crosse. He was christened in the Episcopalian church with the same names as those of his father and grandfather: Joseph Walton Losey. The family was proud of the fact that his grandfather's mother was a descendant of Izaak Walton, author of that immortal work, *The Compleat Angler*. Thereafter, tradition ensured that the name was bestowed upon the eldest male child, until Losey himself became a father, and Gavrik, his son, was given no middle name.

Joseph Walton Losey I was born in Pennsylvania and educated at Amherst College in New England. Family legend has it that, graduating in 1858, he decided to seek his fortune elsewhere and walked westward for nearly a thousand miles until he came to the Mississippi river, whence he turned south until he reached La Crosse. The place was beautiful then, rich in good soil, meadows and forest, so he decided to stay, setting up one of the first law practices in the area, where he subsequently became an important local politician.

Like all the Losey men to follow, he was tall and big-bellied. With his bulk and great, square beard, he projected a formidable presence that proved an asset during his rise to prominence. By the turn of the century he was a tycoon of sorts, having been made a vice-president of the Great Northern Railway, thanks to his association with the president of the company, who had married one of his sisters and was in a position to dispense patronage. Before long, the town named a boulevard after him and a memorial arch was erected at the entrance to the local cemetery.

Now a man of substance, he built a rambling, spacious wooden house to provide a suitable home for his German wife, whose parents had moved to America soon after her birth. They had five daughters in quick succession, two of whom died in childhood. Their only son, Joseph Walton Losey II, was born fifteen years after the last of his sisters. The three surviving girls – Fanny, Rosie, and Mary – were all talented musicians, and their father, a liberal as well as a generous man, sent the string players to study in Berlin. Fanny became a well-known concert violinist before returning to America with Mary, who was an accomplished pianist. Rosie, a

2

cellist, remained in Germany until just before World War II, and married a doctor.

Their brother, who was known as Walt, played guitar and, in the evenings, following a reading from the Bible, the four siblings often provided music in the drawing-room. Walt was tutored privately until the age of sixteen, when he was sent east to Lawrenceville, in New Jersey, one of the many élitist, north-eastern clones of the English public school. He went on to Princeton University, where he became an all-American football player on the celebrated, undefeated team of 1901. He rode well, distinguished himself as an athlete, and became a member of Tiger Inn, which was among the most exclusive of Princeton's college clubs, where he could be found wearing custom-made gloves, shoes, and shirts, according to his son's recollection.

Walt evidently lacked the ambition and drive of his father, being content to settle for a life devoted to enjoying the family fortune. 'He was not educated to be useful,' was Losey's judgement on his father. 'He was not an intellectual, he was an athlete. He hadn't read anything; he was really equipped to know animals, to lead a physical life.' A curious anomaly was Walt, in this thrusting, frontier, enterprise culture.

It came, therefore, as a shock to this carefree young blade when, in 1902 during his second year at Princeton, his father died, and at the age of twenty-three he found himself not only head of the family, but also bereft of an inheritance to maintain his position. In spite of, or perhaps because of, his constant benefactions to town and family, Joseph Walton Losey had spent the fortune he had made and died close to bankruptcy.

Losey's father was disarmingly sanguine about his decline in status, minding it far less than his son in later life. Luckily, the sudden reversal of fortune was limited in its effect, since Fanny and Mary had prudently made extremely good marriages. The latter, always referred to by Losey as 'Aunt Mer', had married into a rich and prominent local family, the Eastons. Losey depicted her life as one of grandeur and luxury: a forty-room house, staffed by seven to ten servants, with carriages and horses aplenty until automobiles came in, when the family acquired a Cadillac. There were fresh flowers all year round, even amid the heavy winter snows, a private bowling alley, and a big farm, run by Aunt Mer, which supplied fresh vegetables, eggs, chickens, beef and milk to the entire family.

When they felt in need of a change, there was a fully appointed houseboat and accompanying paddle-steamer in which they could potter lazily up and down the Mississippi, the children taking their pleasure swimming and canoeing around their floating home. It was a life founded on the fortune made by Aunt Mer's father-in-law who, Losey insists, 'sweated money out of poor tenant farmers, and collected a fortune of five to six million dollars'.

Aunt Mer's husband offered to finance Walt in his remaining years at Princeton, but he refused, being too proud to accept and keenly aware of the need to get a job to impress the girl he loved and wished to marry: the petite and beautiful Ina Higbee, who conveniently lived next door. Through the influence of his father's powerful friends, he secured a modest position as a claims agent with the Burlington Railroad. The job, which involved arbitrating in disputes between the railroad and its aggrieved customers, was far removed from the life he might have enjoyed as a lawyer, had he not abandoned his university career. But it did make it possible to wed the lovely Ina and move into a house in Ferry Street, next door to her parents.

Losey's remembrance of his mother is as confused as his attitude to other aspects of his past. In his more snobbish moments he described her ancestors as having been among the earliest English colonizers of America's northeast, making her eligible for membership in the Daughters of the American Revolution. He maintained that, although she was born in Wisconsin, she was sent to Chevy Chase, a posh finishing school in the east. In another mood he would claim that her family consisted of relatively poor and uncultured farmers.

Ina is still remembered in different ways by many in La Crosse, though all agree she was 'pretty as a picture', with her soft, brown curly hair, and bright blue eyes. Losey's cousin, Mary Higbee Cameron, who now lives at 1612 Ferry Street, in the house where he grew up, says: 'Aunt Ina played the piano beautifully, and definitely had eastern manners. You'd never get a cracked cup in her house, that's for sure. She was born in Arcadia, Wisconsin, which is a really small town, but her father was a lawyer who became a circuit judge. I don't know why Joe ran my family down. They were certainly as good as the Loseys, maybe better. It must have had something to do with his father.' Geneva Ragland, a family friend who is now 101, thought 'Ina was very dignified and very snooty. Always felt she was a little above Joe's father, I think, though he was sure handsome, and a good catch by any standards. She was always trying to keep up with the Eastons.'

The house in Ferry Street lacked the splendours of either Grand-father Losey's establishment or that of the even grander Aunt Mer. Joseph Walton Losey II and his family had sunk to the level of poor relations, which was as galling for young Losey as it evidently was to his mother. Whatever Walt's success as a professional arbitrator, a job he held for the rest of his life, he was unable to keep the peace at home. He and Ina quarrelled almost incessantly. Although Losey always maintained that his mother's ambition was at the root of their disagreements, others in the family insist that his father, with his feckless attitude towards life, gave as good as he got.

'My mother was one of those Ibsenian women who use sex as a kind of threat,' her son recalled later, in conversations with the French critic Michel Ciment. 'The bedroom door would be locked and sex banned when things were not quite right. She was always threatening to leave if she didn't have a servant, which they couldn't afford, so she made him borrow money ... If he didn't arrange for holidays, didn't buy her a new evening dress, didn't take her to Chicago ... luggage was got out, and clothes were packed, and she was moving out, but of course she never did. I don't suppose she really intended to, but it was a constant pressure on him, and we all felt it very much.'

The couple had other problems. Ina was too lively as well as too ambitious to find fulfilment in La Crosse. She tried to make money by importing hand-crafted items and selling them from the house. Prohibition was in effect, and Ina, together with many of her racier friends, took a delight in drinking bootleg liquor, which helped inflame her moods. She attempted to alleviate her boredom by giving parties, at which she played the piano (which she did rather well) and sang the current popular songs surrounded by male admirers, of which there was no dearth. Many rows erupted as a result of Ina's fondness for going for a spin in some fellow's new car, a luxury her husband was unable to afford. Jealousy exacerbated his sense of inadequacy. 'Most of the people with brains got out of La Crosse pretty pronto,' says Fran Burgess, one of Losey's childhood friends who stayed to work as a photographer on the local newspaper, the *La Crosse Tribune*, which was run by her father. 'Ina was too smart for this place. Very frustrated.'

In his early youth Losey had developed chronic asthma, which was to affect the conditions and moods of his life forever, isolating him at home, taking him away from the robust mayhem of school and bringing him closer every day to the semi-invalid artist whom he would come to admire more than any other: Marcel Proust. Feigning an interest in Aunt Mer's *Le Figaro*, which she had delivered daily, Losey persuaded her to help him obtain novels by Proust and Balzac, which were forbidden in his home, on moral grounds. With the help of a French dictionary he even claimed to have ploughed through *Swann's Way*, which impelled him for ever to equate Aunt Mer's opulent household with the highly-charged emotional and aristocratic ambience of Proust's elegant and moribund world. (Whatever the nature and degree of this early introduction to the French language, it seems to have proved fruitless, since Losey died not speaking a single phrase of French, in spite of having lived and made films in Paris during his penultimate years.)

Much to his chagrin, Losey had inherited none of his aunts' musicality, which defect reinforced his linguistic disabilities. Another contributive factor, and one of which he never spoke, was that he was dyslexic, making his difficulties with reading, even in English, that much more daunting. He was not an athletic child, preferring to read or go to the movies. His father, a strong swimmer, had taught him to look after himself in the muddy pools and undercurrents of the nearby rivers, for the Mississippi could be dangerous and had claimed the lives of several of his boyhood friends. But beyond that, the son inherited none of his father's love of physical exercise, particularly if it was in any way competitive.

'He was very quiet and very, very smart,' says Fran Burgess. 'He wasn't a loner, but he was a reader. And fascinated by the theatre. That's what drew us together in school; we were always in the plays.' Losey was less gregarious and outgoing than his younger sister, Mary. She counted among her many friends Nicholas Ray, then known by his real name of Ray Kienzle, who, because of his Norwegian ancestry, tended to be stigmatized as being 'from the wrong side of the tracks'.

Losey's cousin Mary Cameron, then living next door, remembers, 'I liked Joe when he was young, but most people didn't, because he was rather arrogant, a bit of a snob. Not that he was embarrassed about coming from a small mid-western town; more of an intellectual snob. He was so sensitive; he taught me to look at the clouds. Once in New York I said to Joe, "Don't you get tired of it? Not being able to see the sky?" And he said, "There are other things to see here." Most people here didn't appreciate what he'd done. I didn't see that many of his movies, but I know they were wonderful. I read about this fantastic style he had – his taste. He got that at home, of course, from my Aunt Ina.'

His best friends at school, Jonathan Bunge and Robert Lees, were the sons of lawyers. (Reference books on the cinema tend wrongly to describe Losey in similar terms.) All three went to a private school before attending La Crosse's rambling wooden-built Central High School, which Losey claims to have loathed. He attributed his unhappiness to being a 'spoilt brat' who didn't like the way the other children behaved, spoke, or smelled. He felt that his passion for books set him further apart from the others, who admired the sporting Bunge and Lees. While the school team, The Red Raiders, were all colliding happily with each other on the football field, Losey was at home, curled up in a leather chair reading Dickens, Dumas, Scott and Thackeray, as well as such American classics as Twain, Hawthorne and Melville. He was nevertheless able to find common cause with his two athletic chums, because they too were interested in school drama, and excelled in academic work as well.

When he wasn't reading, Losey was at the movies. His aunts disapproved, preferring that their nephew attend the ballet, a concert, or the theatre, where touring companies run by old-fashioned actor-managers performed Ibsen and other dramatists acceptable to local tastes. Nevertheless, by the age of ten, Losey was allowed to see two movies a week, absorbing the varied talents of Chaplin, Fairbanks and Pickford, Buster Keaton, Harold Lloyd, Von Stroheim, and Griffith. He claimed to have seen more films as a boy than he did during the rest of his life, when he was too busy making them.

The 1925 edition of *Booster*, the yearbook of Central High School, reveals a more extrovert youth. Losey was involved in everything literary, musical, or theatrical. He served on the *Booster*'s editorial committee and, despite his lack of musical skills, played the saxophone in the orchestra. He took leading roles in nearly every school play produced during his years at Central High, including Falstaff, and, in a farce called *The New Poor*, a Russian prince fallen on sufficiently hard times to become a butler to a *nouveau-riche* American family not unlike his own. Losey's athletic friend Johnny Bunge, who was president of the drama society in that final year, played one of the Americans with great panache. Losey admired him for having talents equally balanced between the physical and the artistic, as if Bunge combined the qualities of both his father and himself.

Beneath the *Booster*'s graduation photograph of Joseph W. Losey is the verdict: 'Inebriated with the exuberance of his own verbosity'. Even those who loved Losey, and there were a great many, would not have argued with this judgement: 'He was a *monologiste*,' declares a close French friend, 'never a *dialogiste*. He preferred an audience to conversational partners. People must amuse him very much before he will listen.' The pattern was never to change.

Unlike many of his classmates, Losey was given no nickname, although some of them decorated an enlargement of his photo with the words, 'Professor Losey, Head of Goofology Dept'. The most striking aspect of the sensitive, deep-eyed, full-lipped face that gazes out from the picture is its melancholy gravity, its seriousness. Not typically American; more the face of a European.

During his years at Central High, Losey was in constant rebellion against his family. ('He was always talking through his hat,' was Mary Losey's reaction to interviews he gave in later life slighting their mother's family.) He was determined to put as much space as possible between himself and La Crosse by escaping to an eastern university. To hasten his departure, he attended summer school and continued with private tutoring, which had begun during his bouts of illness. His efforts resulted in him achieving the honour roll for two of the three school terms in his final year. As a result, he was able to finish his four-year high school course in two years, and went to university at sixteen, earlier than most of his contemporaries, which was something he later regretted.

Curiously, Losey did not try for Princeton, where his father had studied, although he considered that life would have been relatively easy for him there. Neither did he attempt to enter Harvard, having decided that the entrance examinations would be too difficult. Instead, he chose Dartmouth. Central High's upstanding headmaster, Guildford M. Wiley, was a Dartmouth man, and gave young Losey a good recommendation. Moreover, Dartmouth, a college in the small New England town of Hanover, New Hampshire, was a less daunting place to a young and unsophisticated boy from La Crosse, Wisconsin than those other great Eastern universities.

As Losey's university plans developed during the winter of 1925, and with them the mounting excitement and anticipation of a new and liberating chapter in his life, he received his first serious emotional blow. On 16 February his handsome, life-enhancing father died. The perfunctory obituary published in the *La Crosse Tribune* read:

WALT LOSEY DIES TODAY

J. Walton Losey of 1612 Ferry Street, claims agent of the Burlington Railroad and well-known resident of La Crosse, died at 1:55 this afternoon at a local hospital, where he had been ill since a week ago last Saturday with appendicitis. His appendix ruptured before the first operation could be performed, and a second one was performed during the week.

Losey was plunged into despair. He felt cheated and horrified at the prospect of being abandoned to the quixotic mercies of his mother, who was anyway unable to offer him help of any kind. He was to remain almost accusatory in his attitude towards his dead father, whose untimely departure he came to regard as a betrayal. He dreamt night after night that his father was still alive. For the rest of his life, whenever he was under stress, he was to dream the same dream: he was a youth again and his father had returned from the dead.

By happy chance, he had come into a small inheritance, left to him by his godfather who had committed suicide the previous year, so that there was no difficulty over paying his college fees. He was to augment this minor windfall by washing dishes in the college kitchens and working in the library, with his devoted Aunt Fanny providing him with an additional $25 a month, a beneficence she continued throughout his undergraduate days.

And so it was that, in the autumn of 1925, Joseph Walton Losey III turned his back on his home-town and much of what he thought it stood for, perhaps realizing, even then, that he had already outgrown the attitudes enshrined in *The Ode to the Senior Class* in *Booster*, printed above a picture of a boy and girl holding hands and advancing towards a castle of dreams set high on a hill, haloed by the flamboyant rays emanating from a perfect American sunset:

> *You've found yourselves, Oh, senior class,*
> *You've found yourselves at last.*
> *Bemoan not the years of groping;*
> *Scorn not the struggles past.*
> *They'll help you and prepare you*
> *To make good the lot you've cast.*

Left virtually destitute on the death of her husband, Ina sold the house in Ferry Street and moved to a converted carriage house nearby. The ground floor she rented to Fran Burgess, who, with several like-minded friends, used it as a studio where they sketched and painted, dreaming of the Bohemian life. The neighbours were shocked to discover that Ina was living there with the father of Losey's friend Robert Lees, whose wife had recently died. None was more disapproving, however, than Losey, who prudishly scorned not only his mother's loose living arrangements, but her increasing drinking.

Ina tried to keep her little craft business going from the carriage house, but her customers grew bored and deserted her. When her relationship with Lees' father also collapsed, she went to New York, where she became a salesperson in a department store, a step her son admired grudgingly, secretly ashamed by the loss of status it represented. He was even more dismayed by the discovery that she gave most of her meagre salary to her new lover, a stockbroker who was to lose it all in the Wall Street Crash four years later. Losey approved only of her politics: she had been a Democrat within a hive of Republicans, and had voted for Eugene Debs in the '20s, when, from prison, he ran for the Presidency as a socialist.

Losey left for Dartmouth that autumn accompanied on the train by both Lees and Bunge. Lees was on his way to Williams College in Massachusetts; Bunge was not only joining Losey at Dartmouth, but was also booked in as his room-mate, a circumstance which afforded both boys a certain comfort. Their destination, too, was a small town: sizzling in summer, snow-bound in winter, and inhabited by much the same people they had just left behind, though less parochial as part of a university campus. (Jonathan Bunge did not take to university life in the east, leaving after his first year to go to the University of Chicago, back in the good old mid-west.)

Losey's interests and essential ambitions changed during his time at Dartmouth. He believed that he was 'expected to do something professional', but was determined not to become a lawyer like his uncles and both grandfathers. 'I hated the law. It seemed to me to be complete sophistry, and deadly dull,' he told Michel Ciment. For a while, he turned to medicine, plunging himself into the study of physics, anatomy, and organic chemistry, which he enjoyed, but in which he earned only average grades.

He joined The Players, Dartmouth's drama club, soon becoming its lighting director and then its first student director. Losey's interest in theatre intensified to the point where his extra-curricular activities took up nearly as much of his energies as his studies. His eagerness to learn was intense. The faculty member in charge of drama at Dartmouth, a professional who had trained in the New York theatre, was expert in all areas of stage production. The skills Losey acquired from him in lighting, for which he showed a particular aptitude, had an undoubted influence on the style and mood of his later work in films.

In his new role, he stage-managed Eugene O'Neill's *The Great God Brown*, and a musical, *The Green Peach*. When he was not backstage, he acted, principally in productions of plays by Pirandello. He joined the Cercle Français and played in Molière's *Le Malade Imaginaire* – in French, which makes even more mysterious his unwillingness to develop his spoken French during his years in Paris. (As one of his close friends pointed out, however, he would never have attempted another language unless he could speak it perfectly; ever intolerant of both failure and mediocrity.)

Losey also made his debut as a playwright during this period. Attracted by the prize for winning a one-act play competition, which was the opportunity to stage and direct the work, he wrote *The Gods of the Mountain*, an adolescent piece of blank verse, 'about *Weltschmerz* and the loneliness of the human soul – a horrible piece of romantic shit', Losey recalled in conversation with Michel Ciment. The set consisted of several high platforms, representing the mountains of the title. One evening while checking the scenery, both Losey and his mentor fell from the highest platform. Losey landed disastrously, his back cracking against a thick length of board; when his friend fell on top of him, two of his vertebrae were broken. As a result he spent nearly the whole of his final year at Dartmouth immobilized in hospital.

During the long months that followed, Losey had time to contemplate his future. His academic record in the first three years had been far from brilliant, and he realized that medicine had been a wrongly motivated vocation. Lying in bed with a broken back enabled him to focus on his intellectual life more intensely than he would otherwise have done, and to catch up on studies and artistic pursuits which he'd neglected. He chose to be positive and to regard the accident as a blessing in disguise.

He had perceived that Dartmouth was a place where a man was nobody unless he was either rich or athletic. 'If you were interested in poetry or reading, or films, theatre, or music, it was just not on,' he complained to Ciment. He decided to change his major course of study by switching to art, and to become even more involved in theatre. From that moment he began to achieve top grades, graduating *cum laude*.

Despite its sporting emphasis, Dartmouth was a centre of cultural activity, frequently playing host to theatre companies and musical groups. Importantly for Losey's future, it was visited by the Theater Guild's infant road company. Based in New York, and run with an iron hand by the redoubtable Welsh-born Lawrence Langner, the Theater Guild was to do much to develop such American playwrights as S. N. Behrman, Elmer Rice, Sidney Howard and Eugene O'Neill through its innovatory subscription system. So successful was the system, which enabled people to book in advance for an entire season of plays, that the Guild extended it throughout the country, touring several companies at once, all containing first-class actors.

In Losey's initial year, the Guild's first road company visited to stage Ferenc Molnar's comedy of a marital jealousy, *The Guardsman*, in which Alfred Lunt and Lynn Fontanne had become stars of the Broadway theatre under the direction of Philip Moeller during the season. Not only did Losey attend all the performances but also the rehearsals and it was during this happy time of discovery that he became committed to a theatrical career. No introduction to the professional theatre could have been more fortunate or more inspiring. The Theater Guild's production, again directed by Moeller, featured Florence Eldridge in the lead role and her husband, Fredric March, as stage manager. (March was to assure his place among the greatest of American actors by creating the role of the despotic father in O'Neill's masterpiece, *Long Day's Journey Into Night*, with his wife playing the drug-addicted mother.)

In charge of the sets and lighting was Kate Lawson, the ex-wife of John Howard Lawson, a left-wing playwright destined to cross Losey's path in Hollywood two decades later under far less pleasant circumstances. Pleased to find so keen an assistant, she allowed Losey to help her with the lighting and set dressing throughout the weeks the company was in Hanover. He also became close to Moeller, with whom he would walk for hours in the darkness of the dozing town, talking of the theatre.

Instead of automatically going home for the Christmas or Easter holidays to see his mother, with whom he was becoming increasingly disenchanted, Losey would visit New York and spend his vacation watching Moeller rehearse great stars such as the Lunts in some of the finest plays of classical and contemporary repertoire. Once, on a brief visit to the Theater Guild, he was thrilled to meet O'Neill and ever after claimed that the playwright exerted a major influence over him.

In the summer of 1928, when Losey was nineteen, he managed to visit France under a student tour scheme sponsored by Dartmouth. There, far from the painfully plain, sere, and charmless façades of mid-western American architecture, he rejoiced in the elegantly carved and festooned glories of Paris's baroque and regency buildings. Realizing what the journey meant to their nephew, both Aunt Fanny and Aunt Mer helped with his expenses. Losey lived for the rest of the summer first in the Rue Guy-Lussac and later in the Rue Bonaparte. He attended the Alliance Française, which, on his own admission, did him little good, but he managed to meet many of the literary and artistic expatriates who had gathered around Ernest Hemingway, and who helped him to acquire a limited familiarity with the city. Towards the end of an enchanted time, he went to England for a couple of weeks, but it was with Paris that he had fallen in love.

After graduating from Dartmouth, Losey returned briefly to La Crosse, where his mother was back in residence and in dire straits. He was to remember the visit, in conversation with Ciment, with a ponderous nostalgia: 'I was aware, not of the euphoria of the 1920s, but of a shrivelling, really, because there was a new class. I mean, in La Crosse where various branches of my family were the heads of society, they no longer had any power. There were nineteen new families in La Crosse that were in the millionaire class, and most of them were industrialists and not "socially acceptable" at all. They didn't entertain musicians or literary figures, or bishops! All that remains of my family is the cracking memorial arch and the Losey Boulevard.'

Later in the summer of 1929, Losey apprenticed himself to a small repertory theatre in Boothbay Harbor, Maine. It was not a random choice, but another sentimental journey, for he, Ina and Mary had been taken there in the early '20s for three summers, trading the dusty heat of La Crosse for the fragrant pines and cold, wild, navy-blue seas of the north-eastern coast. The theatre was run largely for the benefit of the 'summer people', rather than the locals, by a seedy, failed actor, whom Losey disliked so intensely that he refused in later years even to remember his name. He was nevertheless grateful to the old ham for taking him on as both actor and stage manager in a production of Jean Cocteau's *Orpheus*. Here, in his first paid theatrical job, Losey began his lifelong occupation as well as an equally impressive career of purloining other men's women. He charmed the one member of the company who was best kept at arm's length: an actress whom his employer loved. It did not make for a harmonious summer, and, in spite of his obvious talents, he was not urged to return the following year.

By this time Losey felt himself increasingly drawn to Harvard, which, in the 1920s, was the centre of university drama. During his years at Dartmouth he had made many happy weekend visits to Boston and Cambridge to stay with a new friend Henry Longfellow Dana in his poet-ancestor's splendid home, Craigie House, on Brattle Street in Cambridge. Together they watched the Harvard–Dartmouth football game in the autumn, or went to a play or a concert by the Boston Symphony. It was a natural progression, therefore, that he chose to spend a year in post-graduate work at the Harvard Graduate School of Arts and Sciences.

It was inevitable that these two should meet, for all that Losey admired and envied was epitomized in Henry Dana, who was a man for all his seasons. An intellectual aristocrat, Dana was the son of Longfellow's golden-haired daughter Edith and Richard Henry

Dana, a renowned Boston lawyer and author of the classic *Two Years Before the Mast*, a personal diary which put paid to the evil practice of impressment of merchant seamen.

Dana, a lifelong socialist and therefore a maverick within the society into which he was born, was during his lifetime (he died aged 69 in 1950) a scholar, author, and teacher of drama at several great American schools and universities. He lived for a time in Russia, where he studied Russian theatre, an enduring passion, as it was to become for Losey, who later worked with Dana for Russian War Relief during World War Two. Two men could not have been more like-minded, Dana serving as mentor and father figure to the younger man.

A pacifist as well as a socialist, Dana had opposed America's entry into the 1914-18 war in Europe, and because of this, and his sympathy with the aims of communism, he was expelled from Columbia University along with Professor James McKeen Cattell for 'disseminating doctrines of disloyalty in the war'. Much to his family's increasing chagrin, Dana did not confine his leftist activities to his own country: in 1927 he presented a motion to a Communist meeting in Paris, advocating a strike in protest against the conviction of Sacco and Vanzetti in his home state of Massachusetts.

Dana's illustrious grandfather was a keen crusader in his time, employing his fame, talent and wealth in the battle for the abolition of slavery in the South. It is not surprising, therefore, that Edith, the most strong-minded of his crusading daughters, should produce such a son nor that he would rank among the most enduring of Losey's idols and influences.

The Harvard drama department was headed by George P. Baker, who had founded the famous 47 Workshop, named after the year, 1847, that Harvard's theatre had been inaugurated. Losey became involved with this group, while simultaneously following selected courses with many of the university's distinguished literary specialists.

In the October in which he began his year at Harvard came the terrible event that was to alter the world and Losey's course in life: the Wall Street Crash, which wiped out the fortunes of many and ushered in the years of the Great Depression. Though he did not know it at the time, Losey and many others among the young intelligentsia were to be caught up in the rush of youthful idealism and political radicalism that followed.

For the moment, it was still a blissful time, marked mainly by Losey's discovery of dark murmurings from his unconscious. He had begun to realize how much he had been disturbed by his father's death, the resulting disintegration of his family, and by the pressure of ambitions he had no idea as yet how to realize. Early in the term, he befriended a bright, charming medical student from the South who lived in the dormitory opposite his own. The young man, who had a self-assurance Losey lacked, aspired to be a brain surgeon (which he indeed became) and was studying psychoanalysis.

One day, during their intense discussions, the aspiring therapist suggested that Losey should undergo analysis. Losey was keen, but lacked the funds, and knew that it was something his rich aunts were unlikely to finance. The student offered to provide his services as an analyst free, on condition that Losey would allow himself to be quoted as a model case. Five days a week for a year he lay on the Southerner's couch, learning about the unconscious mind and discovering how to articulate his obsessions. From that time on, he rarely went long without periods of similar consultation and therapy.

As the academic year progressed, Professor Baker quarrelled with Harvard's academic bureaucracy, and, feeling he'd been shabbily treated, departed to found the Yale Drama School. So incensed were the alumni of the 47 Workshop over Harvard's loss of Baker that they re-established themselves outside the university under the leadership of an equally distinguished man, Alexander Lovejoy. Losey was among a dedicated group of students who attended the revived workshop, determined to sustain and develop the work begun by Baker. Their success was such that those who taught there in the first year included the designers Lee Simonson and Robert Edmund Jones, playwrights Sidney Howard, Philip Barry and Robert Sherwood, and critics such as John Mason Brown, John Anderson, and Brooks Atkinson – all alumni of the original 47 Workshop eager to renew their support. Philip Moeller came as well, giving Losey the opportunity to revitalize their friendship, all of which was to help him when he eventually went off to tackle the New York theatre.

These were stimulating days, particularly when he was joined on his walks by the lovely poet and sometime actress May Sarton, whose father taught at the university. To her, he could speak about what was now dearest to his heart: the theatre. They had met at a poetry reading in Cambridge, and he had been struck by her resemblance to photographs and drawings of Virginia Woolf, save that she was prettier and not so droopy. May, who was two years younger than Losey, came from much the same type of Brahmin family as his friend Henry Dana, and was robust enough to match him stride for stride as the pair took brisk walks through the dazzling patchwork of autumnal leaves. But by the end of the college year, he was ready to relinquish his student life.

With understandable regret, he bade farewell to his gently-bred friends in Cambridge and boarded a train for the tough streets and even tougher citizens of New York City.

II

New York

Losey arrived in New York at an inopportune time for a young and inexperienced graduate to find work in the theatre, where an estimated 17,000 actors, directors and stage managers were desperately scrambling for any job on Broadway. The aftershocks of the stock market crash were still being felt and many were faced with poverty in what should have been a time of plenty. Only a year before, President Hoover had promised voters that they could expect two cars in every garage and two chickens in every pot. Instead, in the wake of Black Thursday, 24 October 1929, when there had been a panic selling of nearly 13 million shares followed by more than 16 million changing hands four days later, fortunes had vanished overnight and there were to be years of emotional and financial depression before the American economy recovered.

For the 'workers of the world', many of whom were busily uniting under the hammer and sickle, life was not so jolly. Their poverty was real and grim, and they found that even here in the celebrated land of opportunity and plenty to which most of them had fled from oppressive European societies, the government would not or could not protect them from those more powerful than they, in particular from the banks. For those labouring in the arts, life was also deprived, materially if not spiritually. It was into this ambience that Losey flung himself, penniless, following the halcyon days at Harvard, 'with nobody to help me and qualified for nothing'.

His first step was to renew the theatrical friendships he had begun at Dartmouth and Harvard. Sleeping on people's sofas and floors, he kept body and soul together by working at the Actors' Dining Club, which paid him in meals, and, later, by apprenticing himself to the eminent producer and director Jed Harris, reading plays and answering the telephone largely for the privilege of watching Harris rehearse. Another inducement was room and board in Harris's home.

Harris, then 28, was among the most flamboyant theatrical directors and impresarios of the day, nicknamed 'The Wonder Boy' because of his youthful success. He had staged *Broadway*, an uproarious comedy of actors and bootleggers that was among the hits of the 1926–7 season, and followed it in 1928 by producing *The Front Page*, Charles MacArthur and Ben Hecht's classic melodrama of cynical Chicago newspaper life. Harris was not, however, known for his amiability. Two larger-than-life villains, Walt Disney's Big Bad Wolf and Sir Laurence Olivier's definitive Richard III, were both based on Harris's acidulous personality and mannerisms. As late as the 1970s Olivier remembered him as the most loathsome man he had ever met: sarcastic, cruel and merciless.

Harris in rehearsal provided Losey with a piquant contrast to watching Philip Moeller at work. Moeller, whose approach was poetic, once instructed the three leading actors in his cast: 'You are a trombone; you are a clarinet; and you are an oboe.' Harris preferred to bully, screaming at his actors, yelling insults and obscenities, sincerely believing intelligence to be a handicap to an actor. Occasionally, they retaliated. During a rehearsal, the tough Ina Claire, maddened by his rudeness, knocked him down and then kicked him in the stomach; Edna Ferber, watching Harris at work on one of her plays, pronounced him 'as fresh as poison ivy'.

An insomniac, Harris developed the irritating habit of telephoning his associates at all hours of the day or night. Only Losey seemed not to mind, for he was developing a tolerance for awkward characters and somehow they became friends. As with his other mentors, Losey walked with Harris late at night talking into the dawn and soaking up theatre lore minute by minute. But eventually his need for money led him to end his apprenticeship to Harris and to make further use of contacts from the Harvard period.

John Anderson, the drama critic of the *Evening Journal*, found him work writing second-night reviews of plays for the glossy *Theatre Magazine*. Brooks Atkinson, the most eminent critic of his era, allowed him a few reviews for his newspaper, the *New York Times*, and from there he procured an entrée to the *Saturday Review* to write an occasional book review. He lived on the meagre remuneration from these jobs and the occasional hand-out from Harris.

Losey's most profitable move was to approach George Haight, one of the first graduates of the Yale Drama School under Professor George Baker, who had just begun his career as a Broadway producer. Haight pointed Losey in the direction of his colleague Herman Shumlin, a boyhood friend of Harris, who was directing *Grand Hotel* at the National Theatre. Shumlin needed extras to play bellboys and hotel guests; Losey joined the queue of hundreds of out-of-work actors looking for bit parts, and was fortunate enough to be chosen, probably through Haight's influence.

The show's star was Eugenie Leontovitch, who was then married to her second husband Gregory Ratoff. Both were White Russians and ex-luminaries of the Moscow stage who had gone into exile after the Revolution of 1917. In her new life, Eugenie had been obliged at first to lower her sights, working as a showgirl in such musicals as *Topics of 1923* and *Artists and Models* while she learned English. When *Grand Hotel* opened in November 1930, she had the largest part in the biggest hit New York had seen for years, and the star was restored to her dressing-room door.

Losey, on the other hand, shared a dressing-room with twenty-five others, but still found it new, glamorous, and thrilling. He also found Eugenie glamorous and thrilling, and before long he was completely infatuated with her. She was 30, beautiful and exotic, in the Garbo mould, with a past that was exciting to a young man also passionate about the theatre. More impressively, she had studied in Moscow with the dynamic Theodore Komisarjevsky, the former director of the Imperial and State Theatres, who had staged Ibsen's *Peer Gynt* in New York at the invitation of the Theater Guild, with Vsevolod Meyerhold, a giant of experimental theatre.

Eugenie seems to have enjoyed the attentions of the tall, sad-eyed, young bit-player, who appeared to have the concession on creative melancholia. On her recommendation, he was promoted to assistant stage manager when the previous incumbent was sacked for incompetence shortly after rehearsals began, and he was invited home most evenings to have supper with her at her sister's apartment. In return, he had some good ideas about how she should look on stage, and suggested various improvements to her costumes. One night during the Christmas season, he took her out for dinner, blowing a week's pay on this idyll. And this was not his only extravagance: instead of buying food, every day Losey provided her with fresh gardenias.

It was only a matter of time before Losey was to incur not

only the ire of the tough and exuberant Ratoff, who had served in the Czar's army during World War I, but the opprobrium of his sponsor, George Haight. Haight gave his erstwhile protégé a severe dressing down, emphasizing that he was merely an extra who had won the position as stage manager virtually by default, and who would do better to mind his own business instead of the leading lady's. Typically, Losey chose to ignore this excellent advice.

He stayed with the production for nine months, not only gaining experience, but using his spare time to write book reviews and to enlarge his circle of acquaintances and contacts. What he later called a 'late adolescent crush' on Eugenie was turning into a serious emotional involvement. The impulsive Ratoff was beginning to throw jealous fits, which could turn threatening at any moment. The situation was a precarious one for the inexperienced young man.

He was saved, however, through his growing friendship with an extraordinary man called John Hammond, whom he met at a theatrical party. Hammond, a graduate of Yale, was the wealthy son and grandson of engineers and inventors. A fascinating and dedicated jazz-buff, he was to influence the course of jazz by his early championing of such talents as the Count Basie Orchestra, which he brought to New York from Kansas City, Billie Holiday, the revolutionary guitarist Charlie Christian and the 'King' of the swing era of the later 1930s, Benny Goodman, whose brother-in-law he became. (Hammond was to remain a prime mover in popular music into the 1960s with his promotion of Bob Dylan.)

Guided by the enthusiastic Hammond, Losey journeyed to the jazz spots of Harlem: the Savoy Ballroom, Small's Paradise, the Apollo and the Lafayette, where they would listen till dawn, then make their way down town to Coven's, a speakeasy bursting with many of the greatest musicians, who congregated there to talk, drink and improvise. Hammond took Losey to hear his latest discovery: a plump 16-year-old black singer named Billie Holiday, whose songs were to be remembered and used in later life when Losey was making his most personal film, *Eve*. It was paradise.

Two years older than Losey, Hammond initiated him into left-wing politics, teaching him, among other things, that rich socialists could be a good deal more effective than poor ones. The two had much in common, especially in their attitudes toward the free-wheeling capitalism practised by their grandfathers. Hammond rescued Losey from his entanglement with Eugenie by suggesting they take a trip to

Europe at his expense. One moonlit midnight in the spring of 1931, John H. Hammond III and Joseph W. Losey III boarded the liner *Homeric*, travelling first-class. It was, Losey recalled later, 'all very Scott Fitzgerald'.

For a time the pair drifted about Europe, enjoying themselves in all the best watering holes. In Munich, however, they decided to part; Hammond wanted to return to New York, while Losey went to seek out a cousin whose address he had winkled out of Aunt Fanny. This European cousin was a successful opera singer, married to a writer called Frank Thiess. Losey had hoped that, with their artistic connections, they might help him find work in the German theatre, which was enjoying a period of vigorous innovation: Bertolt Brecht and Kurt Weill's *The Threepenny Opera* had caused a sensation three years earlier, and in Berlin Brecht had recently staged his dramatic cantata *Die Massnahme* (*The Measure*), with music by Hanns Eisler, who, like Brecht, was to play a significant part in Losey's future life. Moreover the towering Max Reinhardt had been directing plays at three Berlin theatres when not staging epic productions around the world. Times in Germany, however, were bad, with roaring inflation and high unemployment. What is more, Thiess, who was to become a member of the Nazi party, and Losey did not agree politically, especially when it came to left-wing influences in contemporary theatre. Wisely, Losey departed for England.

Once in London, his New York connections began to pay off handsomely, starting with Gilbert Miller, a New Yorker who worked on both sides of the Atlantic. Miller, who had been producing plays on Broadway since 1916 and also controlled the St James's Theatre in London, was busy with *Payment Deferred*, a play based on C. S. Forester's novel of a murderer who escapes the consequences of his crime. It starred the 31-year-old Charles Laughton, the most acclaimed of young English actors at the time, with his wife, the diminutive Elsa Lanchester, cast as his 12-year-old daughter. Miller needed a stage manager and Losey immediately offered his services.

Payment Deferred opened on 4 May 1931, and though Laughton's performance was masterly, it made audiences unprofitably uneasy. After three months Miller decided to cut his losses and try it in New York at the Lyceum Theatre. Laughton and Lanchester, making their first trip to the States, repeated their roles, and Losey returned with the production as stage manager. Broadway's audiences liked the play even less, though Laughton was again praised for his acting. In the final days of its three-week run, one actor fell ill and Losey was asked to take his place, speaking a prologue and epilogue with Laughton. It was a daunting assignment under any circumstances, but rendered even more frightening since Losey had just four hours to rehearse it. He did not enjoy his performances and decided it was an experience never to be repeated if he could help it.

The play went on the road to Chicago and Losey with it, and when they all returned to New York, together with the actress Ruth Gordon, Losey introduced the Laughtons to the tough and ambitious Jed Harris, Gordon's latest consort. This critical meeting took place during one of the many evenings they spent in a friend's small, elegant brownstone house. As Elsa Lanchester recalls in her memoirs, 'There would be light food and drink and theatre talk. Thornton Wilder would be there, reading from his plays. Charles would read and expound. Jed Harris would dominate and sparkle.' Following these evenings, Harris persuaded Laughton to play Agatha Christie's detective Hercule Poirot once more in *Alibi*, which he had done in London in 1928. Harris retitled it *Fatal Alibi* and hired Losey as stage manager for its run at the Booth Theatre, where it opened in February 1932.

During that time, Losey's friendship with Elsa ripened as they discovered politics in common: Elsa's parents were Marxists and she had grown up in an atmosphere of excited political discussion, moving in the literary and socialist circles that had formed around H. G. Wells. She was also intensely fun-loving, her talents as a performer best displayed in cabaret and revue when she had run her own nightclub in London. Since Laughton was often occupied, she and Losey would go out together to relish whatever entertainment could be found: they heard Louis Armstrong playing his dazzling jazz in vaudeville, and spent evenings in Harlem in the company of John Hammond, listening to jazz and visiting the famous Cotton Club. Laughton came with them only once, for Harlem frightened him.

Laughton and Lanchester were an ill-assorted couple, Elsa being tough, vivacious and sharp-tongued. Their marriage had, in fact, run into difficulties after only two years, although it was to remain unhappily intact, until Laughton, large, clumsy, hyper-sensitive and

self-conscious, died in 1962. Inevitably, just before the London opening of *Payment Deferred* came the crisis that created a lasting barrier
between them: Laughton, facing a day in court after a youth had tried
to blackmail him, admitted to her that he was homosexual.

In later years both Losey and Elsa publicly referred to their close
relationship as little more than an innocent friendship. 'Whenever
Charles was deeply unhappy in a play or a film, he often started
to bully me,' she recalled. 'Joe Losey increasingly took my side
after these bitter arguments, and privately sympathized with me.'
Subsequently, Losey confided to Jack Loring that they had enjoyed
a tempestuous affair, and that to his surprise Elsa had pursued him
tenaciously. As Loring confirms, 'He and Elsa Lanchester *did* have an
affair, and she was very provocative . . . very insistent . . . she did
not leave him alone. It was a very *intense* affair to which she was
extremely devoted, pursuing it with all her force.' In later life it was to
be Losey who instigated his affairs with famous and talented women.
However, their love-making was necessarily brief, as *Fatal Alibi* had a
short run, and the affair ended on a note of tragi-comedy: Losey had
caught mumps from Laughton – a painful and worrying illness for
a virile young man, with its side-effects of swollen, tender testicles
and possible sterility.

Elsa always preferred to refer to their fling as an unfulfilled dream:
'If Joe hadn't gotten mumps, we might have become involved, two
lost, angry people floating around, overshadowed by Charles.'
Fatal Alibi closed with Losey still ill in bed, Elsa having already
returned to England and Laughton following as soon as he was
able. Alone in a cheerless hotel room, Losey gave way to his con-
genital gloom. He felt that his illness was a curse, inflicted on him
by Laughton as punishment for trifling with his wife. Throughout his
life his feelings tended to be melancholic and fatalistic, except when
a satisfying and well-received piece of work brought a momentary
elevation and brightening of the spirits.

When Losey and Elsa were reunited on her next visit to New
York, they found that their passion had wilted. 'We met for an
early dinner at his sister's flat,' she wrote. 'Joe cooked oysters – an
elaborate dish served in shells on rock salt. I disliked oysters very
much. Years before, in England, a distinguished old barrister had
patted my knee and said, "If oysters are really fresh, they should
twitch in your mouth". So my meeting with Joe and his oysters in
every way fell flat. A great relief!' Losey's feelings grew sourer with

time. Laughton, he told Michel Ciment after the actor's death, 'had a bitchy streak that was very destructive'. Elsa, he added, 'had an even bitchier one that was more destructive'.

The election of the aristocratic Democrat Franklin D. Roosevelt as President in 1932 brought new hope to a nation still mired in depression, as well as his New Deal, which was a far-reaching programme for recovery and reform. He buoyed up the spirits of all those who laboured in the arts with his life-saving scheme under the Works Progress Administration to aid the unemployed, which encompassed art, music and theatre. The WPA provided funds for young, proven artistic talents and helped to produce a new experimental and socially conscious artistic milieu. Artists were freed momentarily from the crippling necessity to find all the funds to pursue their aims.

The WPA's Federal Theater Project was established in August 1935 under Hallie Flanagan, who later became professor of drama at Vassar College and creator of its Experimental Theater. Its main purpose was to provide relief for unemployed professionals and to preserve their theatrical skills, although it was allowed to employ a percentage who were already in work in order to maintain a reasonable standard of production. In New York, it provided jobs for roughly 5,000 people.

Among them was John Houseman, great-grandson of the celebrated architect of modern Paris, born in Romania and educated in England, who had given up a job in the grain trade to work in the theatre. He was to make his reputation directing Virgil Thomson's opera *Four Saints In Three Acts*, which opportunity Losey claimed to have turned down. Later Flanagan made him co-director of the Negro Theater Project in Harlem, of which Houseman was soon in sole control, since his fellow director, the black actress Rose MacLendon, was dying of cancer. His first act was to bring in Orson Welles, then 20 years old and, like Losey, born in Wisconsin, to direct a sensational voodoo version of Shakespeare's *Macbeth*.

The Federal Theater project was only one of the left-wing theatre groups which were emerging to promote themes of working and lower-middle class life. Harold Clurman and Lee Strasberg, two men who were to be among the most influential figures in

American theatre, together with administrator Cheryl Crawford and other discontented members of the Theater Guild, had formed their own company, the Group Theater, in 1931. They put on their first production that September: Paul Green's play of Southern decadence *The House of Connelly* with a cast that included Franchot Tone and Clifford Odets. Odets was to write the Group's most provocative play, *Waiting for Lefty*, a drama built around taxicab drivers' struggle for a better life, which was staged in January 1935.

Smaller groups came and went as enthusiasms and money waxed and waned: the Theater of Action, in which Nicholas Ray and Elia Kazan, two other future film directors, were involved, and the Theater Union, formed in 1933 by a group of Stalinist and Trotskyite playwrights who were partly financed by Hammond and a few trade unions. The rivalry was most intense between the now old-fashioned Theater Guild, which had become just another conventional commercial production company, the breakaway Group Theater, and the Federal Theater.

'The running joke at the time was that the Group Theater, whose adherents were so filled with idealism and social consciousness, was actually boringly conservative in a lot of what they produced,' writes Houseman in his memoirs. 'That was largely due to Cheryl Crawford, a lesbian who was very conservative. Not politically; she just thought it was better to rock the boat gently, and, I dare say, more commercially, than to throw everybody into the sea. So they did all their shows under the auspices of people like the Schuberts on Broadway. We in the Feds, on the other hand, were totally non-socially conscious and jumped into the local current, doing the classics under the Federal umbrella. I always used to tease Harold about letting Cheryl play it so commercially.'

It was to be the 'Feds' who were to give Losey his first taste of success and the opportunity to make a permanent contribution to the theatre of his time, though for the moment he continued to work in stage management. In 1932, through the influence of a friend, he landed a job as an assistant stage manager of the Radio City Music Hall, one of two new theatres being built by the Rockefellers. (The other one was designed as a cinema and was unsuccessfully converted at the last moment into a stage for lavish musicals.)

The plan was that the Music Hall would save vaudeville, which was then moribund. The opening bill was intended to cater for all tastes and indulged in overkill: it ranged from the jazz trumpet and hoarse vocals of Louis Armstrong to the operatic soprano of Elisabeth Schwarzkopf. There were also dancers, including Ray Bolger, a slapstick act consisting of the Sisters of Skillet (whose antics included pitching mud 'n' custard pies at each other for the better part of half an hour) and a 25-minute ballet – more than could be comfortably fitted into an evening's entertainment. On opening night, following a disastrous dress rehearsal, during which a chorus girl fell to her death through a trap door, the entertainment dragged on until the early hours. The audience left well before the end and the show continued to play to near-empty houses, until vaudeville finally became extinct.

Many of the staff were fired, which resulted in Losey's promotion to stage manager, and the policy changed to a mixed entertainment of movies supported by a few live performers and the high-kicking chorus-line now known as the Rockettes. Shortly after, Losey, too, was sacked and forced back to the patronage of Jed Harris, looking for work in return for room and board.

While reading scripts for Harris he became excited by a new play called *Little Ol' Boy*. Harris was not interested in this tale about reform schools; he was searching for another big Broadway hit, which he was to find in 1938 with Thornton Wilder's *Our Town*. Meanwhile Losey took the other play to Hammond, hoping to involve his friend as its producer. Hammond liked *Little Ol' Boy*, thinking that it might have been designed specifically to appeal to a socially conscious producer-director team. It was an autobiographical work by Albert Bein, a 31-year-old proletarian writer and former hobo from Chicago, who had ridden freight trains across the States until a brakeman had thrown him from one, and one of his legs had been severed under its wheels.

The pair set out to raise enough money to stage *Little Ol' Boy* at the Playhouse Theater. Eager to help, Robert Benchley, theatre critic and humorous columnist for the *New Yorker*, gave $1,000, as did Lewis Milestone, who was about to depict Hollywood's idea of a tramp's existence in *Hallelujah, I'm A Bum*, from a script by S. N. Behrman and Ben Hecht. Hammond also persuaded some of his family to finance the production and put up the rest of the money himself.

The cast was made up of talented young actors, including Lionel Stander, Garson Kanin and Martin Gabel, with Burgess Meredith in the lead role. Mordecai Gorelik, who was among the many Jewish immigrants to influence American theatre and film, designed three vast and ambitious sets. *Little Ol' Boy* opened on 24 April 1933 and was a commercial failure, though enjoyed by many of its audiences. The critics praised the production, and Robert Benchley wrote in the *New Yorker*, 'a word for Mr Joseph Losey's direction: the curtain of the first act, in which nothing is heard but the sullen scraping of knives across raw potatoes, is as effective as anything of its kind in New York this season.' Stark Young, the critic of *The New Republic*, described Losey's direction as 'admirable'. Still, some condemned the play as mere propaganda. Hammond's reaction was to run a newspaper advertisement quoting the reviews under the headline, 'If it's propaganda, you can have your money back', which did not enhance box-office takings, which, even so, amounted to $2,500 in its first week. In his autobiography, John Houseman, acerbic as ever, described it as 'an admired failure'.

What mattered in the longer term was that Losey, at the age of 24, had discovered his true talent, on which basis he and Hammond opened a small office with Hammond's money, so that they could find and stage more new plays. Thus the production company of Henry Hammond came into being. (Hammond used his middle name for this purpose.)

Losey's next important assignment arose from an unexpected call from his old Harvard friend May Sarton. She was understudying the redoubtable actress Eva La Gallienne (who had founded the Civic Repertory Company off-Broadway) and directing the company's apprentice group. When Eva La Gallienne went on an extended tour in 1932, she started a similar company called The Associated Actors' Theater and enlisted the help of Losey's other Brahmin chum, Henry Dana. They suggested that Losey return to the scene of his student triumphs to direct a revival of Maxwell Anderson's *Gods of the Lightning* at the Elizabeth Peabody Playhouse in Boston, with Gorelik designing the sets.

Norman Lloyd, a member of the Associated Actors, who was later to join Orson Welles's sensational Mercury Theater company, knew Losey, who was a year or two older, from an earlier meeting at Harvard. He was delighted to have the opportunity to act under his direction, and became one of his most loyal and enduring friends.

'I liked Joe right away,' he recalls. 'We had great fun in those days, mostly taking the mickey out of some of those snotty Harvard boys. Joe had very little self-confidence then, but you could see he was loaded with talent. I'll never forget how kind he was to me. Later on he began to take himself too seriously, made a lot of people very angry.'

On one of his forays into puritan Cambridge to discuss the project with Sarton and Dana, Losey met the composer Virgil Thomson, who was teaching at Harvard and acting as chief organist in the local church. Thomson suggested that Losey direct Dennis Johnston's musical *A Bride for the Unicorn*, for which he had written the music. They were hoping to produce it at the Brattle Hall in Cambridge, using a combination of amateur actors from the Harvard Dramatic Club and professionals.

Losey was willing, since there were too many obstacles to overcome with *Gods of the Lightning*, not only with casting the eighteen players but with various local political lobbyists and censors. Consequently Losey began to develop his style of working closely with his artistic collaborators. Though he lacked specific expertise, his innate taste and instinct served well. He even helped change Thomson's score, much of which was vocal and written for the Chorus, a major element in the play.

A Bride for the Unicorn was a modern version of *Jason and the Argonauts*. It caused a furore which continued despite a prestigious cast (the Radcliffe students were banned from playing the controversial female roles) and cuts made to the dialogue before opening night. A local critic, George Brinton of the *Boston Post*, gave the production a caustic review:

'The play is composed of a series of insanely devised parables and attempted symbolism. In fact, in view of the many fine productions of new plays done in the past by the Harvard Dramatic Club, the best thing to do under the circumstances is to forget the whole business,' he wrote.

Gods of the Lightning finally reached the Boston stage on 25 November 1935, having been written by Maxwell Anderson some five years earlier with Harold Hickerson. The play mounted a fierce attack on the injustice of the executions in 1927 of Nicola Sacco and Bartolomeo Vanzetti for an armed robbery and murder they did not commit. Anarchists and aliens, the two became martyrs to America's first 'Red Scare', which swept the nation in 1920. The second such 'witch hunt' was to begin in 1949 and would number Losey among its victims, irrevocably altering his life and witnessing his transformation from a good director into a great one. (Anderson returned to the Sacco-Vanzetti case in 1935 in his verse play *Winterset*; it also inspired at least four other plays, many novels and innumerable poems.)

Losey was credited in the programme as 'Jo Losey'. May Sarton says of him at that time, 'I sensed great intelligence, bitterness, and above all fearful intensity'. The production's run was short. 'At the end of two weeks we had to close,' recalls May Sarton. 'The $5,000 Richard Cabot had given me had gone down the drain. That was the end of the Associated Actors Theater, and the next year my first book of poems came out, and I never looked back at the theatre. Nor did I ever see Jo Losey again.'

Explains Norman Lloyd, 'To be part of the establishment theater of the time, you had to be on the left politically. It was ridiculous. It was really the beginning of the break from the English drawing-room comedy tradition, represented by Katharine Cornell and Guthrie McClintic, where actors came out imitating English folk, which was ridiculous.'

Pleased with their work together, Thomson asked Losey to direct *Four Saints in Three Acts*, an opera about St Teresa of Avila and Ignatius Loyola, which he had written to a libretto by Gertrude Stein. It was characteristically eccentric, including a ballet for small angels learning to fly, two protagonists who represented Gertrude Stein and James Joyce, and St Teresa played by a brace of singers. In addition, the Holy Ghost appeared both as a stuffed pigeon and a magpie, and St Ignatius miraculously produced a telescope to view the Heavenly Mansions.

Thomson had written the work seven years earlier, but it was not until 1933 that he found the money to stage it, and it had proved difficult for him to interest any director in such experimental work. Many established figures had turned it down. Losey also spurned the project, claiming that Thomson's ideas, involving a mainly naked all-black cast wearing transparent cellophane, risked being tainted by cliché. John Houseman finally staged it, opting for brightly coloured costumes for its black actors. It was his first theatrical production, and it took nine and a half weeks of frantic work.

At last, news of Losey's activities had filtered through to his hometown, and the *La Crosse Tribune* of 15 April 1934, printed a photograph of him with John Hammond 'at their office in the Empire Theater building in New York City'. It reported that Losey had directed a play by a tramp in the spring, another up at Harvard during the summer, and that John Hammond was the nephew of Mrs Burnside Goster of St Paul, Minnesota. It added that Losey had stayed in Cambridge to direct a play called *A Bride for the Uniform* (sic).

Returning to New York, Losey began once more to search for work and to engage in more intense discussions with his friends over the state of the nation. There was talk of revolution, which no one took very seriously. Norman Lloyd remembers, 'The great drawing-room joke was: "Come the revolution, you'll all eat strawberries!" "But I don't like strawberries . . ." "You'll eat 'em anyway, and like 'em!"'

In was in one such drawing-room that Losey met Elizabeth Hawes, a gently-bred Vassar graduate, from Ridgewood, New Jersey. She had a talent for *haute couture*, and had set herself up as a fashion designer in the Parisian manner. She had become the first American designer to hold annual shows of her seasonal collections of clothes. Four years earlier, in 1930, she had married Ralph Jester, a sculptor she met when both of them were living in Paris. It was not a happy partnership, possibly because she was far more successful as a designer than he was as an artist.

Elizabeth, who was six years older than Losey, dressed superbly, which deflected attention from her somewhat plain appearance. With her large nose and hair cut in the fashionable severely bobbed style of the period, she had the look of a thoroughbred field-hockey coach. Often accompanied by two camel-haired Afghan hounds, she exuded an aura of wealth, glamour and the self-confidence that led her to write in her autobiography, published five years later in 1939: 'I, Elizabeth Hawes, have sold, stolen, and designed clothes in Paris and New York. I have reported on Paris fashion for newspapers and magazines and department stores. In America, I have built up my ivory tower on Sixty-seventh street in New York. There I enjoy the privilege of making beautiful and expensive clothes to order for those who can afford them.'

John Houseman, who regarded her as a good friend, considered that, 'She was very strange, very driven. I remember she'd had a roommate at Vassar called Narcissa Vanderlip. I couldn't believe anyone could really be called that.' Losey, despite the differences in their ages and the presence of her husband, was immediately attracted to her, and drew her into an affair shortly after their first meeting.

Meanwhile Hammond, who was an acquaintance of the novelist Sinclair Lewis, had agreed to finance the production of an historical play *Jayhawker*, which the latter had written with Lloyd Lewis, a Chicago theatre critic. Losey was to co-produce and direct it. Sinclair Lewis, who had become the first American to receive the Nobel Prize for literature four years earlier, was then in decline. His best work, satirical novels such as *Main Street, Babbitt* and *Dodsworth*, was behind him and he was drinking heavily. ('What's the use of winning the Nobel Prize if it doesn't even get you into speakeasies?' Lewis had lamented the year before, sitting on the kerb outside a New York club that had refused to admit him because he was drunk.)

However, Lewis sobered up the following year to write *It Can't Happen Here*, which warned about the possibility of a fascist takeover in the USA. His stage adaptation of that book, produced by the Federal Theater project, was a great success in 1936, opening simultaneously in eighteen cities including New York. It was Losey's misfortune to work with Lewis on the wrong play at the wrong time. In the early months of 1934, when he made many trips to Lewis's home in Vermont to discuss changes in the script, he found himself more often than not acting as a nursemaid to the alcoholic and often bad-tempered writer.

There were problems with the form of *Jayhawker*, which was concerned with raids along the Kansas-Missouri border around the time of the Civil War, and Lewis's recourse to the whisky bottle was not helping to solve them. From the moment the play went into rehearsal in New York in August, disaster was never far away.

It did not help matters either that Losey was always disappearing into the wilds of Massachusetts to oversee rehearsals of *Gods of the Lightning*, which opened three weeks after *Jayhawker*. Nevertheless the first performance in Washington on 15 October 1935 received reasonable reviews before travelling to Philadelphia. Work still needed to be done on the play, particularly to the last act, but Lewis was often too drunk to write well, or at all. Lloyd Lewis thought the changes that were made were not an improvement and, tiring of Sinclair's irascibility, lost interest in the work. Sidney Howard, who had collaborated with Sinclair Lewis on a dramatisation of *Dodsworth*, was brought in to help with its reshaping.

The crisis was not only to do with Lewis's drinking and the play's structure, but also with its casting, which turned out to be problematic. Featuring as rivals were two old-time vaudeville comedians Fred Stone and Walter C. Kelly who, unknown to Losey, had long been antagonists in real life. They spent the play trying to upstage and undermine each other's performance. The situation was exacerbated because Stone, who had been a star of the 1901 Broadway production of *The Wizard of Oz*, had committed his part to memory before rehearsals began and was incapable of remembering either which lines had been cut or which new ones had been added.

Against all odds, *Jayhawker* opened at the Cort Theater in New York on 5 November, and Robert Benchley was the only critic with a kind word to say for it, though his review was hardly enthusiastic. He judged it 'a good job from start to finish'. John Anderson, writing in *The American*, thought that Losey 'had a decided flair for crowd scenes'. Lewis, however, had the last word on the critics' reaction, in his column which appeared inside a black-bordered box in the *New York Times*. 'I have been roasted. I have had the hell roasted out of me. I have been praised, but I have no complaints,' he wrote. The play closed on 24 November.

It is possible that, had *Jayhawker* found an audience, Losey's career might have followed the pattern of his nearest contemporaries, such as his hometown friend, Nick Ray, or Elia Kazan, a more recent acquaintance, who had arrived in America aged four, and worked his way through college and drama school as a waiter. All three moved from involvement in left-wing theatre to become film directors in Hollywood. In spite of his increasing insecurity and disenchantment, Ray continued to work in Hollywood until 1963; Kazan survived by publicly repenting his membership of the Communist party; he subsequently submitted the names of his former comrades to the House Un-American Activities Committee, when it established itself in Hollywood in 1951 to investigate the activities of leftist directors, writers, and actors. As it turned out, Losey's subsequent flight to Europe was to free him from both artistic impotence and moral compromise.

Losey retained an affection for Lewis, whom he found a warm, if sad, man. But wearied by the failure of *Jayhawker* and overwhelmed by that brand of intense disillusion peculiar to the young, he decided he needed a change. Borrowing enough money for a third-class return ticket, he boarded the *Ile de France* and sailed once again for Europe on 5 November 1934, bound this time for Russia by way of Scandinavia.

III

Russia and the Roosevelt Years

This sea voyage turned out to be as dreary and infelicitous as the other with John Hammond had been idyllic. Losey discovered that the producer Gilbert Miller was on the ship, travelling first class, but they had little in common, Miller's style of theatre and living being antithetical to Losey's. Miller, who moved in fashionable New York society, was rumoured to wear white tie and tails with a white carnation in his buttonhole at breakfast. Still, whenever he could, Losey escaped from steerage to drink and talk with Miller and enjoy the luxuries of his first-class suite. Losey, hating the miseries of travelling rough and sharing a room with half a dozen strangers, preferred to distance himself from the realities of poverty.

Although Losey had already moved from the vague liberalism of his Dartmouth days to a tougher, more radical stance, which he henceforth described as Stalinist, his ideas still remained theoretical and idealistic, lacking clarity. He did not, for example, attend political meetings or rallies, nor did he join any political party. He had left New York a political innocent, and returned a Communist in all but name.

His first stop was Finland, where he stayed in Marlebak with Hella Woulijoki, a playwright who had been a friend of the exuberant John Reed, whose celebration of the Russian Revolution in his book *Ten Days That Shook The World* and early death in Moscow had made him America's most famous Communist. Losey's political education continued. It was winter, a season Losey always loved, when he could skate on a nearby lake, pushing Hella around on a sledge, indulging in saunas, followed by a rush to jump into the icy water through a hole cut in the ice. He repaid Hella's kindness by introducing her to Brecht, who later stayed on her estate in 1940 having fled from the

Nazis and resurrected one of her plays as *Mr Puntila and His Man Matti*.

A minor setback had occurred when a stack of 78 rpm records entrusted to Losey by John Hammond as gifts for his jazz-starved Soviet friends was confiscated as he crossed the border from Finland to Russia. But his pockets bulged with letters of introduction to everybody of importance in the Russian theatre, which brought him into contact with its leading theorists and practitioners: Stanislavsky, Meyerhold, Eugenie's former mentor, and Nikolai Okhlopkov. Losey was most excited by the work of Okhlopkov, an actor turned director who was greatly influenced by Japanese theatre; he worked in a flexible space, one that could be changed to suit each production so that it drew the audience into the action. His technique of using the audience and involving them in the production came as a revelation to Losey. 'Theatre in Moscow that year was great,' he said, deeply impressed by the innovative work he saw there.

It was in Moscow that he was able to put into practice what he had learned from Okhlopkov by directing Clifford Odets' *Waiting for Lefty*, a play in which the audience is treated as if it were at a union meeting, harangued by speakers who argue for and against striking for better working conditions. Losey's production followed closely on the play's opening night in New York on 16 March 1935, where Harold Clurman's much vaunted production achieved a total involvement of players and audience. In its final moments Kazan, playing a taxi driver, had raised his clenched fist and shouted 'Strike!'; and the audience had bellowed back, 'Strike! Strike!' As Clurman recalled, 'Audiences and actors had become one. The actors no longer performed: they were carried along by an exultancy of communication that seemed to sweep the audience toward the stage.' Despite staging the play with all its American dialogue intact in front of a Russian audience, Losey rejoiced in being able to create an equal excitement, though one wonders where he found actors sufficiently proficient in the language.

His euphoria was further heightened by the unexpected arrival in Moscow of Elizabeth Hawes. Missing her lover, she had used her formidable powers of persuasion on the Soviet Commissariat of Education and been invited to stage the first-ever fashion show there. This posed unforeseen problems such as finding suitable models to show off her clothes, which she normally designed for America's most elegant women, small-breasted and slender-hipped.

Though such figures were in short supply in Moscow, she managed, and admired the Soviet strategy of inviting the audience to express its preferences by popular vote as to which dresses should be mass produced.

Remaining together after the show, they embarked on a tour of Russia. Though they were frequently exposed to poverty and misery, it hardly dampened their enthusiasm, being so wrapped up in each other at the time. The air was infused with a lethal, negative aura and not only were there rumours, which no one wished to hear, that terrible wrongs were being committed by Stalin and his entourage, but there had been precious little improvement in standards of living. After Hawes' return to America, Losey saw poverty, filth and discomfort everywhere, although those who lived within the embrace of the artistic collective fared better than most, and it was among these that he was sheltered. Losey would often quote Brecht, whose own words would come back to haunt him: 'A man cannot unsee what he has seen.' Though the infamous trials and purges would not start till the following year, the atmosphere was already thick with unease and suspicion.

Losey spent long hours in the company of Russian playwrights and directors, caught in the ferment of their excitement at creating a new theatre. He watched Meyerhold at work, rehearsing a production of *Camille*, and attended classes in the director's system of bio-mechanics in which actors were taught to use their bodies like acrobats. The ageing Stanislavsky was to have an enormous and enduring influence on American film and theatre acting, largely through Lee Strasberg's teaching at the New York Actors' Studio of what became known as 'The Method', but Losey remained minimally impressed by the practice of the technique. He thought the Moscow Art Theatre, which Stanislavsky had founded in 1898, to be old-fashioned and conventional. Losey's interest in cinema, too, remained modest, although he enjoyed the few classes he attended on photography and film given by the Soviet Union's most famous director Sergei Eisenstein.

He was not the only artistic explorer in Russia at this time. Brecht and his musical collaborator Hanns Eisler were visiting, as was Joris Ivens, the peripatetic Dutch director who had filmed the documentary *Song of Heroes* there two years earlier. Erwin Piscator, who, in Germany, had pioneered the epic style of theatre that Brecht was to develop, was there as well and the little group toured under the auspices of Piscator's International Revolutionary Theatre, talking to theatrical collectives across the breadth of Russia. Piscator's innovations were bold, and light-years ahead of their time, incorporating film and newsreels in his expressionistic productions, employing optical, acoustic, and mechanical devices to create an experience of total, all-encompassing theatre – 'mixed media' methods which were strongly to influence Losey's productions on his return to New York.

Imagining that he wanted to stay in Russia to help the revolution, Losey obtained an interview with a member of the Politburo, to whom he offered his services, not as a director, but as one of the proletariat. He explained that he wanted to be in touch with real life, suggesting that he might work as a lumberjack. The Russian's response was unexpected: Losey was told not to be a fool; that his place was not in Russia, but back in the USA. 'He was really like a breath of fresh air because he cut through all of my nonsense, my idealistic nonsense,' Losey admitted to Michel Ciment.

Arriving back home stuffed with new theatrical ideas, he found, to his considerable delight, that Elizabeth Hawes had started divorce proceedings against her husband, which was the best homecoming present he could have had. Buoyed by happiness, Losey set about creating a proletarian theatre on the Russian model, something which he was not the first to attempt in America. Hallie Flanagan wrote after a three-week visit to Russia in 1931, 'There are only two theatres in the country today that are clear as to aim: one is the commercial theatre which wants to make money; the other is a workers' theatre which wants to make a new social order.' She added, 'Unlike any art form existing in America today, the workers' theatres intend to shape the life of this country, socially, politically, and industrially.'

But Losey discovered that the workers' theatre he wished to shape was beginning to splinter. There were divisions between Stalinists and Trotskyites, and differences of opinion and approach between one group and another. There were also rumblings of a growing opposition from the Right to state subsidies being provided for what it regarded as subversive drama.

Losey's first engagement on his return to New York reflected the spirit of his Soviet experiences. He worked without payment with an actors' collective on an experimental production of Paul Green's one-act play *Hymn to the Rising Sun*, an arraignment of life in a black prison-camp, which opened at the Civic Repertory Theater on 12 January 1936. His staging incorporated stark lighting focused on a bare platform bereft of props or scenery apart from a torture box.

In the meantime, Losey's old colleague John Hammond was providing backing for the Theater Union through his friendship with its head Charles Walker, a former journalist. Losey helped the group raise the finance to stage Albert Bein's new play *Let Freedom Ring*, about a mill strike in North Carolina, in return for which Walker lent him books on the 'wobblies' (International Workers of the World), Emma Goldman, Kropotkin and other Trotskyite heroes.

Losey's next production came through Houseman, who, for four months, had been running the Negro Theater Project, which was housed in the cavernous, decaying Lafayette Theater in Harlem. Houseman was as hostile as ever towards Losey. 'We detested each other. He was one of the worst men I have ever known – envious, mean, just awful.' He admitted: 'I was always in direct competition with him so it created a difficult situation,' but 'He was a great expert on negro affairs, he and John Hammond, who was a very talented chap, very powerful. Sort of a pain in the ass, too, but a very valuable man for Losey, all of us, really, since he backed a lot of our independent theatre projects. Joe was a very bright young man, very ambitious. He was a real operator, with one eye always on the main chance. He was habitually suspicious and quarrelsome. He loved feuds, and would invent elaborate ones. In those days, with the black issue and the socialist issue, it was very easy to start these feuds if you weren't tactful.'

The play Houseman asked Losey to direct was a mixture of comedy and mystery, *Conjur Man Dies*, written by the black novelist Rudolph Fisher and starring Dooley Wilson as a detective. (Seven years later, Wilson, in the role of Sam in *Casablanca*, was singing *As Time Goes By* to Humphrey Bogart and Ingrid Bergman.) Losey's direction was as straightforward as the play and gave it great pace and a sense of fun. Nevertheless, the reviewers were unimpressed at its opening on 11 March. Under the headline 'Harlem Mumbo-Jumbo', the *New York Times* critic wrote, 'To a paleface, fresh from Broadway, the new play seemed like a verbose and amateur charade, none too clearly written and soggily acted.' The audience, as he also reported, 'roared at the obese comedian and howled over the West Indian accent of a smart Harlem landlady.' In spite of the critics, Losey had a smash hit.

Three days after the opening of *Conjur Man Dies*, the first of the Federal Theater's Living Newspapers reached the stage. The Living Newspaper, the brainchild of Morris Watson, a journalist who had been sacked from his job at United Press for trying to organize a newspaper union, was an ever-changing, acerbic, aggressive comment on the topics of the day, attacking social injustices. Losey, together with the writer Arthur Arent, was responsible for creating the style and setting the tone of the productions. The project gave him the opportunity to use what he had learned from Okhlopkov.

The Living Newspaper's strength was that it was grounded in fact. Its documentary style used reports from newspapers and magazines of the day, focusing on a particular subject, which ranged from syphilis to flood control, and the founding of California to the history of vaudeville. As such, it was an ephemeral form. As George Jean Nathan wrote, 'The Living Newspaper drama said its effective say and then properly passed into limbo, like yesterday's newspaper.'

Its influence, however, lasted longer and created an appetite for documentary drama that was to be met by many subsequent European writers. In Britain Joan Littlewood and Ewan McColl adapted the form to local needs, and its factual approach was to influence her work at Littlewood's Theatre Workshop in London's working-class East End, which produced such famous plays as *Oh, What A Lovely War!*, that restaged World War I as a seaside vaudeville show.

'This was really one of Joe's outstanding achievements in the theatre, as he was the first and virtually only director of The Living Newspaper,' conceded Houseman. 'He truly created that genre, and he was bloody good at it too.' Norman Lloyd, his actor friend from *Gods of the Lightning*, was one of the leading performers, and among the designers was Elizabeth Hawes, who managed to produce costumes for poor actors at the expense of her rich customers. All those working on the Living Newspaper, actors, directors and backstage workers, received a paltry $30 per week for four 50-minute shows a day.

The productions were controversial from the outset. *Triple-A Plowed Under* was scripted by Arent and dealt with the exploitation of farmers by middlemen taking advantage of the free market economy created by the government's Agricultural Adjustment Act (AAA or Triple A). For this Losey adapted cinematic techniques, with blackouts and spotlights, cutting from one small scene to another, and using a cast of characters that included Earl Browder, head of the Communist Party in America. So far left was the play's orientation that Hallie Flanagan tried to stop it on the grounds that it was Communist propaganda. In response, Losey, Arent and Watson threatened to resign and go public with their reasons. The production went ahead. On opening night, 14 March 1936, members of the American Legion picketed the theatre, and later stormed backstage where they destroyed equipment and beat up stagehands; angry audiences threw eggs and rotten vegetables at the performers.

Losey, Houseman insisted, relished such ructions, while Lloyd remembers his seriousness most vividly: 'There was a joke about Joe among the cast, which was that when he wasn't clear in his own mind as to what he wanted to do, he just sighed. He sighed a lot, and actors took this for despair. He sometimes had problems with actors this way, because it made them feel unloved. He was very sensitive and physically vulnerable. One day he fainted during one of the plays. He had asthma, and got nosebleeds too. He seemed to get ill when people were upset with him.' As one of his closest friends, Jack Loring, was to remark nearly fifty years later, 'For Joe, life wasn't so much a vale of tears as a bridge of sighs, and it never changed.'

In July, Losey directed the more experimental *Injunction Granted* using mime and a score by Virgil Thomson written for trombones, percussion and fire sirens. Among the cast, playing a labour leader, was Nicholas Ray, dubbed 'Joe's best friend and enemy', by Houseman. It was to be Losey's last work for the group, for rehearsals were marked by fierce rows with Hallie Flanagan, who demanded that Losey and Watson 'clean up the script and make it more objective'. After the opening night, on 24 July, she wrote them a long memorandum complaining about the content, which she called 'special pleading, biased', and also the style, objecting to the use of too many devices and 'too much hysteria of acting'. This view was not shared by the critics. Richard Watts Jr wrote in the *New York Herald Tribune*: 'Joseph Losey, the stage director of The Living Newspaper, has a genuine gift for stage movement and for stylized simplicity, and he has made the early sections of the new offering dramatic and striking.'

Four days later, after another row with Losey and Watson, Flanagan told them that, as far as she was concerned, they were through. 'I think you both let me down,' she said. Brecht, then on a visit to New York, came to one performance and was impressed, an event he was to remember later, when he was searching for a director to stage his masterpiece *Galileo*. Brecht wrote in a letter to Piscator, 'You cannot imagine how greedily many people in New York seized on our new methods after realising that traditional theatre and ideology cannot solve the new problems.' But the old ideology proved difficult to shift. Congressman Joe Starnes of the House Un-American Activities Committee denounced the production as 'an attack on our system of courts'. So Losey decided to move on in a search for a more sympathetic platform, since 'Flanagan found my political militancy increasingly inconvenient'.

Determined to distance himself from the opposition of Hallie Flanagan, Losey tried to set up an independent theatre group, Social Circus, hoping that the trades unions which had backed Theater Union would also finance him. Kazan and Ray, who had tried unsuccessfully to form the first Communist collective theatre in New York two years earlier, were also involved, throwing themselves eagerly into the effort. They hoped that Social Circus would develop into something more than a theatre: a meeting place where workers could come and eat, have a beer, play games (such as chess) as well as see theatre.

For his part, Losey envisaged epic productions, using acrobatic actors after the manner of Meyerhold. But there was too much fragmentation between the various groups to achieve any consensus, and opposition to overtly political theatre was growing. Hoping to get backing from the Garment Workers' Union – one of the most thuggish of the lot – he turned his charm on Louis Schaefer who ran its cultural programme and was even more skilled than he at exploiting opportunities. Schaefer, executive director of the Labor Theater, did not care for plays about strikes and revolution; they gave him a pain, he said. The result of the meeting was that Losey was outmanoeuvered: he helped Schaefer raise money for one of the union's own projects, a revue called *Pins and Needles*, which used comedy as its means of attracting support for the workers.

Meanwhile the Spanish Civil War had exploded, and a Theatre Committee for Republican Spain was formed by Losey and some comrades, including Paul Bowles, who used to come to the flat Losey shared with Hammond at 21 East 67th Street to listen to the latest jazz records. The group decided to raise money by staging Kenneth White's agitprop play on the Spanish struggle, *Who Fights This Battle?*. Losey directed it in a resolutely experimental style in a hotel ballroom, creating one of the first productions to present theatre in the round. Bowles, then better known as a composer than as a writer, provided the music, often a vital element in Losey's productions, as it was to be in his films, for he believed it essential in reinforcing the emotional and psychological foundations of any piece of theatre. They raised $2,000, which they sent to Spain. *The Daily Worker*, one of the few newspapers to display an interest in the production, wrote that 'Joseph Losey's direction of the play must be noted among his best work'.

The experience was sufficiently enjoyable for Losey and members of the cast to decide to stay together as The Political Cabaret. They obtained a little money from the powerful Theater Arts Committee, later a major supporter of Roosevelt in his final presidential campaign. The Political Cabaret, which was to occupy much of Losey's energies during 1937, operated from an old firehouse on 55th Street, following, though on a much smaller scale, the precepts of the abandoned Social Circus. On Sunday afternoons, drinks and sandwiches were served to the audience who sat at tables to watch a topical revue both anti-capitalist and anti-fascist. The actors included Martin Gabel, Howard Da Silva and Norman Lloyd, who fondly remembers one occasion when the black folk singer Leadbelly played his twelve-string guitar and sang *Joe Hill*:

> *The copper bosses killed you, Joe*
> *They shot you dead, said I,*
> *Takes more than guns to kill a man,*
> *Said Joe, I didn't die.*
> *Said Joe, I didn't die.*

That year, Losey had other matters on his mind. Marrying Elizabeth Hawes quietly, without much ceremony or ostentation on 23 July in Hoosick Falls, New York, he moved into the comfort of her townhouse at 52 Jane Street in Greenwich Village. They spent weekends at her house in Vermont, where, in the winter, they would wake up in the morning and dash outside to roll naked in the snow before returning to eat breakfast in front of a blazing fire. The following year Elizabeth became pregnant.

Despite the imminent baby, their marriage was not happy: Elizabeth preferred to move only among the rich and fashionable, and although she did occasionally design costumes for Joe's productions, she found many of his theatrical friends and acquaintances objectionable. To make matters worse, Losey was too involved in his work to spare her much attention, and it soon became clear that neither was suited for parenthood. The idea of fathering a child appealed to Losey a great deal; the day-to-day input, not at all. Both he and Elizabeth were ambitious, self-centred artists, each unwilling to offer the necessary time or thought to the other, with inevitable results.

The baby, born on 5 May 1938, was a boy, whom they named Gavrik, burying the 'Joseph Walton' once and for all. Hiring a nanny, Elizabeth went back to designing couture clothes and writing her autobiography. Losey started work on D. A. Doran's Broadway production of *Sun up to Sun down*, a play about the exploitation of child labour, written by Francis Faragoh, a radical playwright who had become a scriptwriter in Hollywood.

It was a conventional work and a conventional production designed to appeal to the expectations of a conventional audience. Its young cast included the 13-year-old Sidney Lumet, later to become a leading Hollywood producer and director. Much to his surprise, Losey discovered he enjoyed working with children and was able to coax fine performances from them, a talent which would enhance his early film career. The play opened at the Hudson Theater on Tuesday, 1 February 1938 to poor reviews, although the critics praised Losey's direction and his skill in orchestrating the young cast. As the audiences stayed away, one of the boys concocted a letter to be signed by the rest of the cast:

'As you all know the show has a great chance of closing on Saturday night. The children have joined together in a plan which they think will help prevent this mishap. The plan is as follows: that every member of the cast turn back his salary as an investment in one lump sum. This in a small way may relieve the strain from Mr Doran's shoulders.

'This is only a gamble, but I think we all can afford to gamble as did Mr Losey and Mr Faragoh, who staked their names and reputations for us.' Their plea went unheeded: the play duly closed, the following Saturday night, after seven performances.

In these changing times, the WPA's arts sponsorship schemes were running into considerable political opposition. In July 1938 Congressman J. Parnell Thomas attacked the WPA's Federal Theater Project. 'Practically every play presented under the auspices of the Project is sheer propaganda for Communism or the New Deal,' he said. His views were echoed by Martin Dies, then chairman of the House Un-American Activities Committee (HUAC). 'All over the United States, the Federal Theater Project produced plays which were nothing but straight Communist propaganda,' he was to write in his book *The Trojan Horse in America*, published in 1940.

HUAC began to investigate the activities of the Federal Theater. Robert E. Stripling, its Secretary, later to be called Chief Investigator, was to cite Losey's production of *Triple-A Plowed Under* as an example of Communism: 'One play which on the opening night required 30 policemen to guard the play and prevent a riot,' he wrote of it in his book *The Red Plot Against America*. 'Such characters as George Washington and Andrew Jackson were removed from the play in order to give a prominent part to the secretary of the Communist Party, Earl Browder.'

The credibility gap between the attitude of the Federal Theater and HUAC is probably best summed up by an exchange between Hallie Flanagan and Congressman Joe Starnes from Alabama when she was called before the committee on 6 December 1938. Starnes read out extracts from her article on workers' theatres, 'A Theatre is Born', written for *Theatre Arts Monthly*:

Starnes: '"They intend to remake a social structure without the help of money – and this ambition alone invests their undertaking with a certain Marlowesque madness." You are quoting from this Marlowe. Is he a Communist?'

Flanagan: 'I am very sorry. I was quoting from Christopher Marlowe.'

Starnes: 'Tell us who Marlowe is, so we can get the proper reference, because that is what we want to do.'

Flanagan: 'Put in the record that he was the greatest dramatist in the period immediately preceding Shakespeare.'

Starnes: 'Put that in the record because the charge has been made that this article of yours is entirely Communistic, and we want to help you . . .'

Starnes and his colleagues helped in the way they knew best: in 1939, after a short life of four years, during which time it had played to audiences of more than 25 million across the United States, the Federal Theater Project was shut down, starved of government funds. By this time war was engulfing Europe. Losey, still working with the Political Cabaret, was offered employment by the Rockefeller Foundation's Human Relations Commission, which was financing a programme of educational films. His task was to edit clips from existing films, creating new works that would provoke discussion in school classrooms.

His opening gambit was to fragment the Oscar-nominated *Alice Adams*, starring Katharine Hepburn and Fred MacMurray, into a series of short films illustrating different aspects of middle-class family life. He applied his scissors to *If I Had a Million* in order to remove the comic sequence of a mild-mannered clerk wrecking a store's china and glass department, which was then shown to young vandals in the hope that it would act as a safe release for their own destructive tendencies. For Losey, the work became a valuable lesson in the techniques of film editing that was to last throughout his life.

Poised on the brink of his new career, Losey's first attempt at direction involved working on a miniature set with marionettes, to make *Pete Roleum and his Cousins*, a publicity film employing animated drops of oil, destined for the Petroleum World Fair Exhibition of 1939. The music was composed by Brecht's colleague Hanns Eisler, who had fled the Nazi pogrom in his native Germany and spent many months in Cuba, waiting for a visa so that he could go to America. Losey was among those who wrote to the American consul in Havana to support Eisler's application. Others included Odets, Clurman, the German-born film director William Dieterle, who had moved to Hollywood in 1930, and Eleanor Roosevelt.

Losey moved on to filming real people through Frontier Films, a documentary outfit occupying the office next to his. The company was backed by some of America's leading writers, including John Dos Passos, Lillian Hellman, Archibald MacLeish and Odets. At its head was Paul Strand, who had worked on some widely admired films, including *The Wave*, a story of Mexican fishermen made in 1936, and *The Plow That Broke the Plains*.

Through Frontier, Losey was offered the chance to direct an 18-minute documentary about an inter-racial, inter-denominational children's camp, taking its title, *A Child Went Forth*, from a poem by Walt Whitman. He hired Joris Ivens' cameraman John Ferno, who also helped with the editing. This time Eisler not only wrote the film score with a grant from the Rockefeller Foundation, but with Losey's help was awarded another grant to write a book on the subject, *Composing for Films*.

Losey borrowed $500 to make *A Child Went Forth*, then persuaded the processing laboratory to give him $2,000 credit before selling it at a profit to the State Department, who regarded it as a guide to dealing with the evacuation of children in the event of war.

Unhappily, while his career moved forward, his marriage was beginning to crumble, the couple's incompatibility showing itself at first in small ways. Although always impeccably dressed when he was older by Doug Hayward, the most renowned of London's show business tailors, in these early days Losey showed little interest in clothes, despite his marriage to a designer who attempted a virtual revolution in men's attire, styling a whole range of comfortable clothes which she could not persuade her husband to wear.

'Joe won't wear my slacks suit, because he says he's averse to being conspicuous. Yet he'll go out in a dark green, plaid jacket, grey trousers, and blue shirt, socks, and tie!', she complained on the publication of her autobiographical best-selling book, *Fashion is Spinach*, in April 1939. Their disagreements were to proliferate and increase in gravity.

Losey had earned little money since his return from Russia, certainly not enough to support a wife and child. He depended on the income 'Lizzy' was making from her fashion business, but that, too, was running into difficulties. In an atmosphere of post-Depression and pre-War financial jitters, her clients were deserting her, and even those who remained faithful were cutting their spending on clothes. Life was becoming too serious to bother about fashion and in January 1940, the house of Elizabeth Hawes was forced to close. Almost immediately she began work as an editor on *PM*, a liberal newspaper started by Ralph Ingersoll, who, contrary to his rivals, carried no advertising. *PM* struggled on until 1948, when, alas, the journal which had provided Lizzy with a platform for attacking French fashion designers and advocating trousers for women also brought her to the attention of the FBI. Some readers began to complain that *PM* was under the influence of Communists, so to defuse the criticism, Ingersoll published a list of Party members and sympathizers on the staff, which included Elizabeth's name. This inevitably resulted in an investigation.

Thanks to the State Department's purchase of *A Child Went Forth*, in 1941 Losey was commissioned to make *Youth Gets a Break*, a 20-minute documentary on the work of the National Youth Administration. Travelling around America to cover all aspects of the subject, he used three film crews which included Ferno and Willard Van Dyke (soon to be a documentary director himself) as cameramen. He completed the film quickly, already developing the skills that were to ensure his future films finished on time and within budget. In a column she wrote for the *World Telegram*, Eleanor Roosevelt praised the film and hoped 'it will be run by every motion picture theater in this country, for it has a deeply moving story to tell'. During the next four years, *Youth Gets a Break* was to be dubbed into twenty-four languages and shown in more than forty countries, where it would be seen by more than a hundred million people.

On 7 December 1941 Losey's documentary career was abruptly ended: the Japanese bombed Pearl Harbor, and America was catapulted into the war. Just before that traumatic event, Hitler's Operation Barbarossa, the invasion of Russia which had begun on 22 June 1941, saw Losey working for Russian War Relief. He staged patriotic dramatizations on a great central stage in Madison Square Garden in New York, as well as in other major cities.

In aid of the suffering Russian allies, he created a unique type of theatre, combining mime with voices amplified by loudspeakers to reach huge audiences, which swelled to as many as 20,000 in the vast auditorium. The scripts were written by Kenneth White, to whom Losey had grown close following his staging of *Who Fights This*

Battle?, and were acted by such performers as Paul Robeson, Paul Draper and Larry Adler, with Martin Gabel providing the narration. Lord Halifax, Andrei Gromyko, Henry Wallace and Joseph Davies, the former US Ambassador to Moscow, were among the politicians who prefaced these entertainments with short pleas for aid. The Russian War Relief was soon incorporated, along with other similar organizations, in the United War Relief, for which Losey continued to work on a small salary.

In February 1942, Losey was suddenly inspired to seek service in one of the armed forces. He volunteered to head a camera combat unit in the Army Air Corps, and asked influential friends for their help in obtaining a commission. Ex-Ambassador Davies provided a letter of recommendation in which he wrote, 'I have been impressed beyond measure by two things – first, his versatility and imagination as to ideas and spectacles; and, second, that which is very unusual in such a situation, an extraordinary ability for executive capacity. In my opinion, in those two respects he is the "tops".' Losey was accepted subject to a medical, during which the examining doctor noted his varicose veins and asthma, but saw no reason why he should not serve. Losey went home and waited, but received no reply.

In June, he tried the Navy. This time, he was sponsored by James Reilly, chairman of the League of New York Theaters, who wrote, 'His Americanism and loyalty to the best traditions of the United States of America are unquestioned. There is no doubt in my mind of Mr Losey's devotion to any naval or other governmental task to which he may be assigned.' Similar letters came from Serge Semenenko, Vice-President of the First National Bank of Boston, with whom Losey had been working on his war relief spectaculars, and the *Journal American*'s theatre critic John Anderson. Again a doctor examined him, noted his disabilities, and pronounced that they should not prevent him from serving. Again, he went home and waited, and again, he heard nothing.

Losey appealed to ex-Ambassador Davies to discover the reason for his apparent rejection. Davies made some enquiries and telephoned him to say there was a long dossier on him that was causing concern to the authorities. He suggested Losey should write him a letter explaining his political views, which he did. Losey never again heard from Davies or anyone else from the armed services.

Opportunities in film and theatre being curtailed by the war,

Losey was bored, and asked NBC radio for work. He began as a production assistant on afternoon soap operas, but was soon offered the opportunity to direct. He worked there for nine months on *Worlds at War*, a series that dramatized new books on great battles, using leading actors such as Helen Hayes, Raymond Massey, Paul Muni and Peter Lorre. Losey's work in what was still a young medium was often experimental, particularly in his productions of two plays by the adventurous radio writer, Norman Corwin, *The Long Names None Could Spell* and *Alexandra Writes a Letter*.

Meanwhile Lizzy had formed the Committee for the Care of Young Children in Wartime with Elinor Gimble, an investor in *PM*, who had also been one of her most loyal customers. The committee's work was thwarted by hostility from the exclusively male leadership of organized labour, who complained that she had no experience as a common worker. Her marriage virtually defunct, Elizabeth answered the attack by working on the assembly line in an aircraft engine factory in Long Island and writing a book about her experiences, entitled *Why Women Cry: Wenches with Wrenches*, which was published in 1943.

Her relationship with Losey had run its course. Although he maintained that he still adored her and admired her considerable talents and accomplishments, the world in which they lived did not seem ready for the combination of career and marriage which they attempted to sustain. Strong-willed and passionately independent, Lizzy was grossly unsuited to motherhood. Little Gavrik, painfully vulnerable, spent more and more time with his grandmother, 'Sam' Lehman, while his parents poured their energies into changing the world.

In her book *Anything But Love*, Hawes made her views on the lives of ordinary men and women balefully clear, announcing:

'This is a study of the relationship between men and women as outlined by the *Ladies Home Journal*, circulation 4,000,000 a month . . . A complete digest of the prescribed female behaviour pattern in the USA . . . Of all the labor-saving devices ever invented for women, none has ever been so popular as a devoted male . . . Most causes of frayed marriage nerves can be traced to a too-intimate knowledge of each other by husband and wife. You must "evoke wonder" by change.'

Her conclusion was, 'Though they speak with the tongues of men and of angels, and they have not love ... they are nothing. And they can speak of anything but love.'

But Hawes' pronouncements remained disturbingly impersonal, her feelings for Losey conspicuously muted, for although she was to write many variously autobiographical books, she failed to mention him in any of them. The final break came in 1944 when she went to Detroit to work in the education department of the United Auto Workers. The FBI investigators followed her there. 'It was a curious marriage,' concluded John Houseman, providing its epitaph. 'She was lonely and bitter, and he was lonely and bitter. So they got married and tortured each other for five or six years.'

Losey seemed deceptively unaffected by the end of their relationship, expressing no deep regrets. 'My first marriage busted up amicably,' he told Michel Ciment. But he was about to discover a new, though passing, love and an obsession that was to last the rest of his life.

IV

Hollywood and HUAC

Disorientated by the disintegration of his small family and with work in the theatre hard to find, Losey answered the siren call of Hollywood. He still had no particular interest in making films, but he needed a new beginning. When he compared himself to his contemporaries, those who had worked alongside him in the Federal Theater or the Social Circus, he was aware that they were becoming far more successful than he and that most had already gone west to work in Hollywood.

Orson Welles's spectacular career had culminated in 1939 with the signing of a contract with RKO that gave him the unprecedented creative control to make two films in the multiple roles of producer, director, writer and actor. He had taken John Houseman with him. Elia Kazan had established himself among the top directors on Broadway by staging such hits as *The Skin of Our Teeth* in 1942 and *One Touch of Venus* in 1943; he, too, had gone on to film *A Tree Grows in Brooklyn*, which was to win Oscars in 1945 for its stars. Even Brecht was there scrabbling, with little success, for work, although the experience was to result in some memorable poems:

> *Every morning, to earn my bread,*
> *I go to the market, where lies are bought.*
> *Hopefully*
> *I join the ranks of the sellers.*

Losey, with many others of his generation, shared Brecht's ambivalence. J. B. Priestley, after a visit in 1937, thought that Hollywood's trade in dreams at so many dollars a foot changed those who worked there. 'The artist begins to lose his art, and the businessman becomes temperamental and overbalanced,' he wrote. It did seem to affect the abilities of many a writer who went there. 'He loses all his erstwhile conception of values, whether dramatic or personal,' considered the critic George Jean Nathan. 'The place for playwrights who spend most of their time in Hollywood is still Hollywood. One can't drink one's swimming pool and have it.'

Nathan cited Sidney Howard as an example of how talent was warped. Howard was a liberal intellectual and graduate of Baker's 47 Studio who had worked with Losey on trying to rescue Sinclair Lewis's *Jayhawker*. Shortly before he died in 1939, crushed to death in an accident on his 700-acre cattle farm, he told the *New York Times* that the lack of an audience and the low standard of taste in Hollywood had affected his writing. 'It's the easy money, perhaps,' he added. Hollywood was 'a dreary industrial town controlled by hoodlums of enormous wealth,' opined S. J. Perelman, who went there to write scripts for the Marx Brothers' early comedies. Perhaps as a result of such feelings of distaste, it was to be Karl, rather than Groucho, Marx who cast a spell over many of Hollywood's richly paid labourers, including Losey.

His opportunity came with a call from the office of Louis B. Mayer, the ruthless patriarch of the greatest of the Hollywood studios, Metro-Goldwyn-Mayer. Mayer could have given Jed Harris lessons in nastiness. The trade paper *Variety* wrote of him after his death: 'One does not remember his achievements so much as his monumental pettiness, his savage retaliation, the humiliation he heaped upon old associates.' He had begun as a ragpicker, working for his father before buying a small cinema, and then moving into distribution and, finally, production in 1918, when Losey was a mere nine years old.

By 1937 Mayer was earning nearly $1.3 million a year, an income greater than anyone else in the United States. He was still the highest-paid individual in the winter of 1943, and at the height of his power when he summoned Losey to a meeting at the Warwick Hotel in New York. Someone at MGM had listened to Losey's radio programmes and had liked what he heard.

Mayer, with as many as fifteen films in production on any given day of the year, thirsted for new talent, particularly as many of his producers and directors were serving in the armed forces. Losey found him in the barbershop in mid-shave, swathed corpse-like in a white sheet and surrounded by his entourage, who were watching the staff working on him: one was at his feet, clipping his toenails; another buffing the nails on his stubby fingers, while a third wielded a razor.

From beneath the lather that covered his face Mayer offered Losey a standard contract at $350 a week, more than Losey had ever earned, although it was not high by MGM's standards. (Mayer was about to try to persuade the writer-director Preston Sturges to work for him at a salary of $6,000 a week.) Such contracts gave the studio complete power over the professional life of those who signed them. Directors and actors were told what films they were to make; if there was nothing suitable, actors were 'loaned out' to other studios, with the fees (usually much higher than their salaries) going to the studio. Writers clocked in each morning like factory workers, to work on whatever script was assigned them. A standard contract lasted for seven years, renewable every six months by the studio. Hortense Powdermaker, a sociologist who studied the workings of Hollywood, decided that it smacked 'more of medieval power relationships between lord and serf than of employer and employee'.

Losey, too, regarded his as 'a slave contract'. He turned it down. But he was tempted, nevertheless, and asked Arthur Lyons, an agent renowned in both New York and Hollywood, to negotiate a deal, one that offered better money and gave him the freedom to work for other studios so long as MGM was not using him at the time. Another meeting was arranged, this time in Hollywood, when Mayer told Losey to take his time, to run whatever films he wanted to see, to go on to sets and watch other directors at work, to talk to producers and to try to find a story he wanted to film.

Needing somewhere to live, Losey found lodgings with Jack Moss, a producer with Paramount, his wife Luisa and young son Michael. An ambitious and beautiful blonde actress under contract to Paramount, Luisa was stuck at the starlet stage of her career. Losey settled into a routine of devouring movies, but his interest was soon concentrated mainly on Luisa, who indicated that she was also attracted to him. Losey soon became accustomed to hearing voices raised in anger and distress, accompanied by the sound of slamming doors and splintering china, for he had walked into a marriage on the point of disintegration. Moss often struck Luisa when he was displeased with her and Luisa sought comfort from Losey, who was happy to provide it, and so began the process of divorcing Elizabeth.

Their affair was less than a month old when Losey received an unpleasant surprise in the morning mail. He was being called up to serve in the infantry. The notion, once so attractive, now filled him with horror. Thinking that, with his varicose veins and asthma, he would never survive the tough training, he was determined not to go; the war, after all, was almost over. The night before his medical he took two kittens to bed with him, for cats had always triggered asthma attacks. On this occasion they failed to do so; the army doctor passed him as fit, and four days later he was on a troop train, depressingly darkened in accordance with the blackout regulations in operation throughout the war, heading for North Carolina. The camp itself, however, turned out to be rather a winner, located in an area with majestic pine trees, rich, red earth, sparkling-clean air, and most astonishingly of all, good food. Even the gruelling discipline was not overly daunting, and after sixteen weeks of basic training, which included forced marches carrying a forty-pound pack, and night-time reconnaissance missions, the reluctant soldier was still in one piece, feeling duly proud of himself, and fitter than he'd ever been.

He lost weight, gained muscle and discovered, having hitherto never handled a gun before, that he was a crack shot. Fortunately, friends he had made in Hollywood had not forgotten him and pulled strings, as they had done for many stars and directors. Three days before the rest of his unit was shipped out to serve in the Pacific, he was transferred to the Signal Corps in Long Island which was making propaganda films for the army. It was a haven for inmates of Hollywood. Anatole Litvak, who became a Colonel, was there working under the command of Colonel Frank Capra, who was directing such documentaries as *War Comes to America* rather than the sentimental comedies (*Mr Deeds Goes to Town*, *Mr Smith Goes to Washington*) which had made him rich. Losey was assigned to direct a couple of basic training films, which was not without its problems. A private, he was outranked by nearly everyone with whom he worked: his cameraman, who was a captain, his operator, who had achieved the rank of sergeant, and even his first assistant, who was a corporal. Hating the atmosphere of the camp, he asked for permission to live outside it and, when it was granted, moved to a flat in Greenwich Village, with Luisa Moss, who was by now divorcing her husband.

Losey was living at a hectic pace; trying to keep up with a frisky fiancée in her mid-twenties, and rising in time to be at the camp at 6.30 a.m. was taking its toll. His asthma returned and the veins in his legs swelled until he was hospitalized and, only six months after arriving at Long Island, in November 1944, he was discharged from the infantry because of his health. Virtually his first act as a civilian was to marry Luisa at a Methodist church in Bucks County, Pennsylvania.

Throughout the many hours of interviews Losey conducted with Michel Ciment between 1976 and 1979, Losey is callously dismissive of Luisa, generally referring to her as 'the woman' and never dignifying her by her name. She perceives events rather differently, recalling a neurotic and insecure young man with a 'hurt mouth' pursuing her doggedly, occasionally even violently. She recalls him, emotional and out of control, falling to his knees in tears, begging her to marry him and to forgive his many past love affairs, and, in the next breath, warning her not to succumb, lest he destroy her. 'Joe said it was my New England look: untouchable, but a victim at the same time. And incidentally, I knew everybody in Hollywood who could help him, so he really needed me then. He was so terrified of failing there, or anywhere, in anything,' she says.

The best man at their wedding was John Wexley, a left-wing playwright turned scriptwriter, who had befriended Losey during his month in Hollywood. Taking Wexley with them in Luisa's Lincoln convertible, the happy couple headed back to Hollywood, stopping in Palm Springs, Nevada on the way. It was there that Luisa received the first intimation of what lay ahead. 'I heard my brand new husband say to Wexley, "I wonder what it's going to be like married to a woman with no talent?" Why I didn't tell him to shove it then, God only knows. I was utterly destroyed,' she says.

Losey went back to MGM at the beginning of 1945, and was given an office and a secretary, but no film to direct. Once again he spent his time watching movies all week. Then he and Luisa would leave for Palm Springs, where they stayed with various friends until Monday night, mingling with the rich and powerful, hoping that someone might provide him with work as a director.

It was during this period that Losey became a member of the Communist Party, an act of political commitment that arose partly from his feeling of utter uselessness. But there were other reasons. His visit to Russia had left him temperamentally inclined to communism, and there was a core of talented Communists in Hollywood with, at its centre, John Howard Lawson, whose former wife Kate had given Losey his earliest experience of stage management when he was at Dartmouth. Lawson, who had organized the first Hollywood writers' union, The Screen Writers Guild, in 1933, became a Communist in 1934, when he publicly announced his membership. Wexley, another early member of the Party, had been earning $1,500 a week in the spring of 1942 when he worked (and quarrelled over screen credits) with Brecht on a movie about the assassination of Reinhard Heydrich, the Nazi Protector of Czechoslovakia, which became *Hangmen Also Die*, directed by the Austrian-born émigré, Fritz Lang.

Two of MGM's highest paid writers, Lester Cole and Dalton Trumbo, were Party members. So was Ring Lardner Jr, who had won an Oscar in 1942 for his work on the story and script of *Woman of the Year*. The director Edward Dmytryk joined in 1944, preceding Losey by a year. Francis Faragoh, whose play Losey had staged in New York, was another member of the circle. Hanns Eisler was also working in Hollywood, and through him Losey renewed his acquaintance with Brecht and met many other European refugees.

Losey was influenced, too, by an incident which occurred at a party to celebrate Wexley's 38th birthday in the winter of 1945, when Wexley had been attacked and badly hurt by two young men who lured him outside on the pretext that they had damaged his car. 'Tonight, we kill us a Jew,' one of them had barked, waving a knife. Wexley had only been saved from serious injury by the arrival of a police car, which had coincidentally been patrolling the area. At their trial, his assailants' attorney defended them on the grounds that they were ex-servicemen who had fought in the war for freedom, which apparently included the freedom to hate Jews. (Wexley magnanimously suggested to the judge that their punishment should be an obligation to read books on Jewish history.)

Losey was stupefied and bewildered by what had happened. Was Hollywood not virtually populated and animated by the talents of hundreds of Jews who had been forced by the Nazis to leave Europe? Clearly, Fascism had a long and deadly reach, and Losey decided impulsively that the most effective action against it was to join formally with the opposition, which was the Communist Party.

It was at this time, too, that the Federal Bureau of Investigation began to take an interest in his activities. In July 1945, the FBI's Los

Angeles bureau received a letter claiming that Losey was an agent of the NKVD, the Soviet Secret Intelligence Service. During the next three years, FBI agents tapped his telephone, opened his mail, and tailed him around Hollywood and New York, noting the names of the people to whom he talked – 'for the purpose of determining the extent of his activities on behalf of the Soviets and for the additional purpose of identifying espionage agents', as the FBI's director J. Edgar Hoover explained it in a memorandum for the Attorney General.

The FBI's files on Losey, obtained under the Freedom of Information Act, run to nearly 800 pages, although most of the information they contain has been so heavily censored that many pages consist of nothing but blacked out text.

On April 9, 1946, an unknown woman contacted ■ and advised her to tell JOE LOSEY that the meeting is for Thursday at 8:15 P.M. at 8625 Wonderland Road, Laurel Canyon and her telephone number is GRanite 8625.

On April 16, 1946, ■ advised that JOE LOSEY contacted ■ a Communist, and JOE advised him of the housing project in the valley in which he ■ intend to buy. JOE stated that this project is progressive and there will be no racial restrictions. The name of the project is the Community Homes, Inc, Encino, California.

On April 21, 1946, ■ sent a telegram of hasty greetings to ■ On the same date she sent a telegram to Senator SHERIDAN DOWNEY protesting the house bill on O.P.A. and urging "REAL CONSUMERS BILL TO PREVENT INFLATION".

The FBI sent an agent to his home at La Crosse, and involved other bureaux across the country in their investigations at a cost of $72.95 a month. One of its early reports notes that 'Losey was well-known in Communist circles for being extremely dramatic and unreliable'. The Los Angeles Bureau closed its investigation in 1948, noting that it 'did not substantiate the allegation but it disclosed that Losey was a close associate of Communist Party members, some of them highly placed, as well as being a Communist Party member himself'. The FBI continued to report on his activities during the 1950s and was to cause him difficulties in obtaining a passport and other travel documents.

Work was still slow in coming his way, although Losey tested two children, 13-year-old Elizabeth Taylor and 9-year-old Dean Stockwell for parts in *Now That April's Here*, a sentimental film that was soon dropped. He shot another screen-test with Elizabeth Taylor for the producers of *National Velvet*, but the direction of that was entrusted to the veteran Clarence Brown. Had he been chosen for this historic Taylor classic, his career might have assumed a very different character, with Success holding out her hand to him a good deal sooner.

Wexley's party proved significant in another way, for among the guests was George Tabori, a Hungarian writer who would become one of Losey's most cherished friends and collaborators. Tabori, who admits that he was attracted by Losey's interest in his latest novel, *Companion of the Left Hand*, spent more and more time in the Loseys' low, wooden ranch house in the Valley, where Gavrik was also in residence, having been retrieved from his grandmother to complete the family and provide some company for little Michael.

Much to his dismay, the first film that Losey was asked to make for MGM was a 19-minute movie entitled *A Gun In His Hand* as part of a series called *Crime Doesn't Pay*. Since he had been contracted exclusively to make feature films, he at first refused, and was told that if he did not make the film, his contract would be terminated at the end of the year. He started work under the guidance of Jerry Bressler, a producer he soon came to despise. 'He was a really awful, vulgar, tasteless man,' he told Ciment. Shooting was disrupted by a violent strike caused by the struggle between the militant left-wing CSU (Conference of Studio Unions) and IATSE (International Alliance of Theatrical Stage Employees), which was not only controlled by unsavoury racketeers but also had the covert backing of the studios, culminating in battles in which the CSU pickets were attacked by IATSE strike-breakers armed with baseball bats and tyre irons. These street fights held up filming and Losey was forced to shoot his night scenes in broad daylight (day for night) using filters and underexposing the film, a technique he hated.

Worse was to follow. When he handed the completed film over to Bressler, the producer complained that Losey was so incompetent that the film was impossible to cut. Losey recalled years later to Ciment, 'I got so emotional I burst into tears. I felt thoroughly ashamed of myself.' As a result, he was allowed to cut the film, which was later nominated for an Oscar.

Losey's new marriage was already problematic, since he was hardly earning enough to support two children and a wife accustomed to luxurious living. 'He was furious with me, because I'd simply walked away from that very rich marriage and asked for nothing,' says Luisa. '"How could you do that?" he kept saying. With custody of my son, Michael, how did I think he could support us? He'd been sure I'd keep the house, the acre in the San Fernando Valley, and a nice fat settlement, plus child support. I compounded the problem by needing expensive dental work. I still have the letter that he wrote to Jack stating flatly that he had no idea I had such an expensive dental problem when he married me, and that he felt Jack should pay for it!'

Among the powers whom Losey met at Palm Springs was Dore Schary, a man of leftish opinions who had risen from being a writer at MGM to overseeing the studio's low-budget B pictures before resigning in 1943 to work with David Selznick as an independent producer. (He was to return triumphantly to MGM in 1948 as vice-president in charge of production, eventually ousting the legendary Louis B. Mayer.) He asked Losey to organize a star-studded memorial to Roosevelt at the Hollywood Bowl (which, with his old friend Nicholas Ray acting as his stage-manager, was a great success). Swift to recognize Losey's organizational abilities, Schary invited him to co-ordinate the Academy Award ceremony in Grauman's Chinese Theater in Los Angeles, with Ray again serving as stage manager.

This new friendship was to bring Losey the opportunity to direct his first feature film, since Schary had accepted the job of production chief at RKO Studios, and was soon to give both Losey and Nicholas Ray their first assignments as directors. One of Schary's first acquisitions at RKO had been *The Boy With Green Hair*, based on a story by Betsy Beaton, which he wanted Losey to film, in collaboration with one of Hollywood's hottest producers, the 35-year-old Adrian Scott. Scott's work at RKO had already included such thrillers as *Farewell My Lovely*, from Raymond Chandler's novel; *Cornered*, based on a story by Wexley; and *Crossfire*, which was among the first films to attack racism. All three had been directed by Edward Dymytryk.

Schary offered Losey a seven-year contract and added that he would willingly release him if the urge to bolt became overpowering. The terms, which began at $50,000 for his first film, were an improvement on those offered by Mayer, who did not seem sorry to let Losey go.

This was an offer which Losey could not refuse, and he proposed to begin work on the picture straightaway, which he would have done but for the creeping rot of politics. Starting almost immediately after the war, the insidious activities of the House Un-American Activities Committee – acronymed HUAC – began to blight the lives of so many people in the entertainment industry as to bring, not only individual projects, but entire careers and lives to a complete standstill. One could scarcely expect someone with Losey's political background to escape, and thus it was that, having been lured west by Hollywood's tempting sirens, Losey was doomed to fetch up on the murderous, sunken reef of the Blacklist.

In the meantime, another irresistible project was offered to Losey: the staging of the English-language premiere of Brecht's *Galileo* which was to become one of the most important in twentieth century theatrical history. Losey admittedly played a subservient role to both Brecht and Charles Laughton (the leading actor), but without his involvement the play would never have reached the American stage, for it was Losey who found much of the finance, recruited key members of the team, and acted as a buffer between the often bad-tempered Brecht and the rest of the cast.

Brecht had written the first version of *Galileo* during a hectic three weeks in Denmark in 1938. He sent a copy to Ferdinand Reyher, a friend who was also a Hollywood scriptwriter, who tried, and failed, to sell it as a movie.

On his arrival in Hollywood Brecht met Laughton at the home of Salka Viertel, another writer and a mutual friend. The two men were at once attracted to one another; indeed, the homosexual Laughton may even have been in love with Brecht. They decided to create a new version in English, and with this in mind, Laughton commissioned two writers working at MGM's studios to prepare a draft script. Then, working in the small library of his house above the Pacific, he and Brecht together wrote a new version, making many changes to the original.

When it was finished in December 1945 Laughton read it to a few friends at home, among whom was Orson Welles, who

agreed to direct it. But Welles and Brecht had different approaches
to theatre. Six months later Welles dropped out altogether when
Laughton and Brecht appointed, as producer, Mike Todd, a totally
commercial animal whom Welles disliked. But Brecht soon became
unhappy with Todd's ideas, so he too was seen off.

Beating the bushes for another director, the pair approached
Alfred Lunt, Vincent Sherman, Elia Kazan (who said he didn't
know how to stage it) and Harold Clurman, who Brecht considered
unduly spellbound by the Stanislavsky mystique. Reyher, who had
been asked by Brecht to do some rewriting of the play, suggested
Losey. 'He knows casting, has the feel for it; he knows what to
do with actors; he can get a crowd sense without numbers, and
movement that isn't just confusion, and keep the whole of a play
in mind,' he attested.

Brecht had known Losey since their meeting in Russia and
had admired his work for the Living Newspaper. Losey, in turn,
revered Brecht and held certain attitudes in common with him. As
he once said of the playwright, 'he ate very little, drank very little
and fornicated a great deal'.

Brecht and Laughton took their time getting *Galileo* into production, mainly because Laughton had committed himself to several
film roles. Taking advantage of the hiatus, Losey journeyed to New
York, where he directed Arnold Sundgaard's *The Great Campaign*,
an uncommercial play with music by Alex North that opened at the
Princess Theater on 30 March 1947.

A political drama about an Ohio farmer who runs for President
and is cheated out of victory, *The Great Campaign* received respectful reviews as a piece of experimental theatre. 'Thanks to Joe Losey's
freehand direction, Mr Sundgaard's discursive drama is as lively as a
vividly coloured lithograph on stage,' wrote Brooks Atkinson in the
New York Times. But the play closed within a week of its opening.

The project was to prove important in Losey's life, however, in
that he formed a close working relationship with the set designer
Robert Davison as well as the choreographer Anna Sokolow, and
became a friend of the play's producer, T. Edward Hambleton, an
inordinately rich young man with a passion for the theatre.

Having agreed to work as the director of *Galileo* and knowing
that there was no guarantee of money to stage it, Losey approached Hambleton, who offered $25,000 towards the costs. Laughton
matched this sum from his own pocket, which produced just enough

money to mount the play providing that all salaries were kept low. Laughton was to be one of five actors receiving the highest payment of $40 a week for rehearsals and performance, with the others on $20 or less a week.

In the meantime, Norman Lloyd had persuaded John Houseman to join him in setting up Pelican Productions, whose aim was to bring good theatre to Los Angeles, and whose venue would be the Coronet Theater, a beautiful little building, which they rented, on La Cienega Boulevard, which bordered on Beverly Hills. Losey's old mentor, Kate Lawson, was appointed the executive director of the theatre, whose financing was implemented by what Houseman admitted were 'certain underworld elements' who wanted to launder the money they were making from their Las Vegas casinos. The two agreed to produce *Galileo* at the Coronet, following the theatre's opening with an all-American Thornton Wilder play, as Houseman had judged *Galileo* to be too controversial to offer as their first production.

In a fortnight Hanns Eisler, Brecht's old collaborator, wrote the incidental music, scored for harpsichord, orchestra and an unaccompanied choir of three boys. This sufficiently impressed Igor Stravinsky, another Hollywood émigré, to come several times to hear it in rehearsal. Losey involved Davison as the play's costume and set designer and recruited Sokolow to help in choreographing the crowd scenes. Rehearsals began on 15 May with an opening planned for 1 July.

From the beginning, the atmosphere was tense and Losey was working on his reputation for being difficult. 'Integrity was his big thing. In the name of integrity he would have these monstrous quarrels, saying that everyone else was lacking in integrity. It was the integrity thing that kept him from the big studios, where people get rich. The independents always have a much tougher time, no doubt about that,' said Houseman. 'He'd have never done anything just to make himself rich, in spite of his love of the opulent lifestyle. In a way he enjoyed being poor, and complaining that everyone had done him down. This was part of his act.'

Laughton and Brecht hardly needed a director. As they worked on the play, Brecht would act it in his muddled Anglo-German, then Laughton would play it back to him, trying different readings until they were both satisfied, taking it a sentence at a time, with Laughton writing each one down in longhand. By the time they had finished, they had a clear idea how the play would look and sound, so that much of a director's habitual task had already been done.

Laughton even hired John Hubley, an artist who had worked for both Walt Disney and Losey, to make sketches of the play scene by scene, with the characters arranged in artistic groupings on the stage. Losey's role was more akin to a traffic cop than a director, or as Elsa Lanchester uncharitably put it, 'a dumb director', as in dumb waiter.

Brecht was not only determined that his play would be staged as he wished, but in a style reflecting his vaunted 'alienated' approach, far removed from Hollywood or Broadway's concept of the dramatic. When a group of actors asked what their motivation was in a scene they were finding difficult, Losey, prompted by Brecht, answered, 'What's the motivation of a tightrope walker not to fall off the high wire?' Brecht wrote in his notebook, 'The actors were incidentally asked on no account to prove their suitability for the part by putting something "impressive" into it,' adding that 'the portrayal of Galileo should not aim at rousing the audience to sympathy or empathy'.

Losey perceived Brecht's staging methods as basically film technique transferred to theatre, and he accepted that working with Brecht and Laughton was an unforgettable learning experience that more than compensated for his subsidiary position. ('Brecht and Charles were the real directors, and everyone knew it,' said one of the actors, Stephen Brown.)

On 22 November 1946, the Los Angeles office of the FBI, ever alert for subversive activities, reported to J. Edgar Hoover that Losey was involved in a stage production 'written by BERTOLDT BRECHT, a refugee German writer', adding: 'There is also some indication that the play, itself, which is entitled "Galleleo" (sic), may be a Communist propaganda medium.'

Laughton had worked himself up to a highly nervous condition: it was thirteen years since he had last acted on the stage and he fretted about his ability to sustain the role. As the first night approached he became almost hysterical, throwing tantrums when it came to contemplating his own performance although he continued to work quietly and carefully with the other actors. He developed a worrying mannerism, clawing at his genitals so much that Brecht's wife Helene Weigel sewed up the pockets of his trousers. 'You're just being a big baby,' Losey would tell him. 'Yes, I am,' Laughton would reply, pouting.

The large cast numbered over fifty, including singers, dancers and musicians in costume, and rehearsals had begun badly, partly because the actor playing Andrea, the second lead, was inadequate. But there was no question of replacing him, since he was Laughton's latest lover, a situation Brecht preferred to ignore. Houseman remembered Brecht's behaviour as appalling. 'He was harsh, intolerant and often brutal and abusive.' Tempers frayed dangerously. Complaining that her staging of the street scenes was 'a lot of Broadway commercial shit', Brecht fired Losey's chosen choreographer Anna Sokolow. One member of the cast, Eda Reiss Merin, walked out after Losey persisted in finding fault with her performance, although Brecht persuaded her to return and be helped by Helene. Near the end of the rehearsal period Laughton barked at Brecht's mistress Ruth Berlau, who was busy photographing the rehearsals, screaming that he would kill her if she ever reappeared in the theatre.

Soon after rehearsals began, HUAC, under the chairmanship of J. Parnell Thomas, arrived in Los Angeles to begin its investigations of Communist infiltration in Hollywood. The Committee's Chief Investigator, Robert E. Stripling, explained their purpose in his book *The Red Plot Against America*: 'Our primary task was to uncover and subpoena Hanns Eisler. With Eisler served and heard in a short executive session, we began calling in key Hollywood figures.'

It was perhaps inevitable that HUAC would pounce on Hollywood. As one of its best historians, Victor S. Navasky, explains in *Naming Names*, his book on the investigation: 'HUAC chose Hollywood for its glamour ... HUAC saw a chance to bask in the publicity glow of Hollywood's stars. And, as Edith Tiger, current director of the Emergency Civil Liberties Committee, observes, "They were our royalty and if you want to scare a country you attack its royalty".' The playwright Arthur Miller had a shorter explanation. HUAC's members, he said, 'were cheap publicity hounds'.

By the same token, HUAC's investigation had undeniably been encouraged by many Hollywood luminaries, including Sam Wood, a leading director at MGM who became so obsessed with subversion that he insisted in his will that his beneficiaries should not inherit until they had sworn an affidavit that they 'are not now, nor have they ever been, Communists', a form of words similar to that used by the Committee when examining witnesses.

In February 1944 Wood had founded the Motion Picture Alliance for the Preservation of American Ideals. He explained its aims at an inaugural meeting which included members such as Clark Gable, Robert Taylor, Gary Cooper, Walt Disney, John Ford and John Wayne: 'The American motion picture is, and will continue to be, held by Americans for the American people, in the interests of America, and dedicated to the preservation and continuance of the American scene and the American way of life.'

When not organizing the MPA's monthly meetings, which were always addressed by prominent anti-Communists, Wood noted down in a little black book the names of all those he considered to be subversive. He was one of its first 'friendly' witnesses when its sessions began in private at the Biltmore Hotel in Los Angeles in May 1947. (He was to die two years before HUAC returned for its second session in 1951.) Thirteen friendly witnesses were called by HUAC, who leaked their testimony to the waiting journalists. They included the Russian-born writer Ayn Rand and actors Gary Cooper, Adolphe Menjou, Ronald Reagan and Robert Taylor. Ginger Rogers' mother Lela told the Committee how her daughter, playing a wartime worker in *Tender Comrade*, had refused to speak a line written by Dalton Trumbo ('Share and share alike – that's democracy') because it was Communist propaganda.

The Committee needed little help in identifying members of the Communist Party, since the Party's Los Angeles secretary was an FBI informer. HUAC's chairman J. Parnell Thomas announced, to no one's surprise, that public hearings were necessary, claiming that many highly paid writers were using the movies for propaganda purposes, that many of their films subtly lauded the Communist Party while the Communists prevented the making of films showing the American way of life, and that pressure from the White House had brought about 'some of the most flagrant Communist propaganda films'. As Walter Goodman notes in *The Committee*, the standard history of HUAC's activities, not one of the charges was ever substantiated, 'but the publicity which these coming attractions received bespoke high success for the feature event'.

HUAC had targeted Hanns Eisler after a lengthy investigation in February 1947 of his brother Gerhart, who had been denounced by their sister Ruth, as having served as head of a network of agents of the secret Russian state police in America since his arrival in the country in 1942. Oddly, the Committee's session with Hanns, which finally took place in May, lasted no more than an hour. Eisler had, Thomas told reporters, 'sought to evade and confuse the issues', which obviously saved him, at least for the moment.

Those working on *Galileo* included Communist Party members other than Losey, who could not fail to see a resemblance between HUAC's activities and those of the Inquisition who forced Galileo to recant his beliefs on pain of punishment and torture. 'They showed me the instruments,' says Galileo, explaining his recantation. HUAC threatened the loss of well-paid livelihoods that was to bring many they accused to change their opinions and to name others as Communists.

The event that gave *Galileo* its greatest resonance was the bombing of Hiroshima and Nagasaki two years earlier in August 1945. As Brecht wrote in a poem addressed to the American audience – 'respected public of the way called Broad':

> *If you won't learn from Galileo's experience*
> *The Bomb might make a personal appearance*

Against the background of HUAC's much-publicized investigations, the stormy rehearsals continued. Faced with the continually abusive playwright, Losey finally lost his temper, flung the script at Brecht, walked out and went home. As Losey worked in his garden, Laughton telephoned him and, using all his actor's honeyed powers of persuasion, begged him to return. Losey agreed to do so, providing Brecht apologized. Laughton called back to say that Brecht had said please would he return – and that he should know that Brecht never apologizes. Losey went back, nevertheless.

It soon became obvious, however, that the production would not be ready by 1 July. Opening night was postponed until 30 July as interest in the play intensified, and every seat had been sold for its four-week run. The first night was so hot that buckets of ice were placed at the sides of the stage with electric fans blowing the cool air towards the tiny, 300-seat auditorium which was packed with celebrities including Charlie Chaplin, Charles Boyer, Ingrid Bergman, Gene Kelly, John Garfield, Billy Wilder and Frank Lloyd Wright.

At the dinner which followed, Chaplin sat next to Eisler and told him that he felt that the play should have been mounted differently. 'When I told him that Brecht never wants to "mount" things, he simply couldn't understand,' Eisler lamented.

Many in the audience and certain critics shared Chaplin's bewilderment. Patterson Greene, the critic of the *Los Angeles Examiner*, described it as 'a harangue – and a fussy, juvenile harangue at that', adding a line that may have frightened Laughton, who was increasingly nervous of associating with Communists, 'Mr Brecht's corn is red'. *Variety* declared, 'it doesn't make the grade'. There were some favourable reviews, such as that by Edwin Schallert of the *Los Angeles Times*, who thought it would 'capture the imagination of those who want to see drama put on a technically freer basis.' The *New York Times* saw Losey's influence in its 'episodic *Living Newspaper* technique'.

Brecht took *Galileo*'s critical failure philosophically. 'Given the way the American theatre was organized in those years, it was impossible that such plays and such productions should reach their audience,' he wrote. 'Productions like this one, therefore, should be treated as examples of a kind of theatre that might become possible under other political and economic conditions. Their achievements, like their mistakes, make them object lessons for anyone who is looking for a theatre of great themes and rewarding acting.'

Towards the end of *Galileo*'s Los Angeles run HUAC again summoned Eisler to appear before it in public session on 24 September 1947. This time, the Committee questioned him relentlessly, describing him as 'the Karl Marx of Communism in the musical field'. Soon after, he and his wife left for Czechoslovakia. Five days before Eisler's summons, HUAC had issued its pink subpoenas to nineteen Hollywood figures whom it wished to question on their political affiliations. Of these, only eleven were to take the witness stand in 1947, and only one – Bertolt Brecht – was to answer the Committee's questions. The other ten, including Adrian Scott, who was still waiting to produce *The Boy With Green Hair* for Losey, refused to co-operate and questioned HUAC's right to investigate their political beliefs. Apart from Scott, another producer Herbert Biberman, and Edward Dmytryk, the accused were all writers: Alvah Bessie, Lester Cole, Ring Lardner Jr, John Howard Lawson, Howard Malz, Samuel Ornitz, and Dalton Trumbo.

Following their refusals to name names, the group was cited for contempt of Congress and the hearings were suspended until their appeals were heard and they were sentenced to terms of imprisonment. HUAC was to resume its investigation of Hollywood, with even deadlier purpose and effect, in March 1951. By that time it had a different chairman, for, a year after these first hearings, J. Parnell Thomas was serving an eighteen-month sentence in the same prison as Ring Lardner Jr and Lester Cole, having been convicted of padding his payroll with phantom staff and pocketing the wages.

Once HUAC had issued its subpoenas, the first reaction of many was to support and defend the Hollywood Nineteen, as they were then known. Two directors, John Huston and William Wyler, together with writer Philip Dunne formed a Committee for the First Amendment. Losey was one of hundreds who crowded into that first meeting, at the home of lyricist Ira Gershwin, packed with such stars as Humphrey Bogart, Rita Hayworth, Katharine Hepburn, Groucho Marx, Judy Garland, Frank Sinatra and Fredric March.

On 26 October, while HUAC was hearing the public testimony of its friendly witnesses, Huston's committee broadcast a radio programme, *Hollywood Fights Back*, that was transmitted across the nation, while Losey followed this success by organizing a protest meeting at the Shrine Auditorium in Los Angeles. The next day Huston flew to Washington with a group of celebrities in an aircraft supplied by Howard Hughes, then boss of TWA. Huston made one stipulation: no Communist Party members were to go, for he had wangled an invitation to dine with President Truman at the White House the day after they arrived.

Together with Bogart, Lauren Bacall, Danny Kaye and Gene Kelly, Huston made a speech at the airport to sympathetic journalists. 'It was exciting,' Lauren Bacall was to remember. 'I couldn't wait to get to Washington. Wouldn't it be incredible if we really could effect a change – if we could make that Committee stop?' Once there, they delivered a petition and filed into reserved seats at the hearing to watch the first of the unfriendly witnesses, John Howard Lawson, give evidence. As with other of the Hollywood hearings, the session was broadcast live across America. It was a stormy occasion. Lawson shouted his defiance while Thomas pounded his gavel as he tried to obtain answers to his questions. It ended with Thomas, still pounding, yelling at Lawson, 'Stand away from the stand', to which Lawson retorted, 'I have written Americanism for many years, and I shall continue to fight for the Bill of Rights, which you are trying to destroy'. To a mixed response of applause and boos, Thomas ordered officers to take Lawson away and, again pounding his gavel, added, 'There will be no demonstrations. No demonstrations for or against.'

But the performance by Lawson and the witnesses who followed lost them enough public support for Truman to withdraw his invitation to lunch. 'I disapproved of what was being done to the Ten, but I also disapproved of their performance,' said Huston. 'Before this spectacle, the attitude of the press had been extremely sympathetic. Now it changed.'

Another member of Huston's committee, the actor Paul Henreid, wrote in his autobiography, 'Our brave campaign had become a disaster.' The committee's supporters began to fade away. Henreid was never to forgive Bogart for giving an interview in Chicago on his return from Washington in which he claimed that he had been duped, adding, 'I didn't know the people I was with were fellow travellers.'

Struggling against the backlash of the political drama, Losey tried to concentrate on the transfer of *Galileo* to New York. Apart from Laughton, the cast he had to rehearse was new. But he dropped everything when the moment came when he and Hambleton went to accompany Brecht to Washington for his appearance before the Committee on 30 October. It was a curious occasion. Brecht's answers were evasive, but the Committee seemed reluctant to press him on his views. At the end of his testimony, the Chairman thanked him for being 'a good example' to the other witnesses. Afterwards, on the way back to his hotel, Lester Cole recalled, 'Brecht grieved; he wondered whether any of us could ever understand and forgive him.' The next day, Losey took him to New York. There was a brief meeting with Laughton, who was worried that his career would be damaged if he were now to appear in *Galileo*, but who was reassured by the fact that Brecht had been praised by the Committee. Losey took Brecht to the airport that evening and put him on a flight to Paris. After he had gone, Helene Weigel, who was to join her husband later, gave Losey a present and a message that Brecht had left for him. The message was, 'You must relax!' With it came an exquisitely carved opium pipe that Brecht had acquired in China.

Laughton, clean-shaven in California, had grown a beard for the New York production to match the change in his performance. With the departure of Brecht, the play had changed, too. In response to Hambleton, who was pressing for a style of production more in tune with conventional theatre, Losey called in his friend George Tabori to help reshape the script and they, together with Laughton, made changes in accordance with notes that Brecht had left behind.

With Scott, who would never work in films again, cited for contempt and on the way to prison, Losey feared that *The Boy With Green Hair*, and his chance of becoming a movie director, were lost: the climate of opinion was turning against him and his friends. Lloyd and Houseman dissolved Pelican Productions. 'The truth is that no vital theater could have prospered in the atmosphere of suspicion, anger and fear which prevailed in Hollywood,' wrote Houseman. Losey was cheered, however, when Dore Schary told him the filming of *The Boy With Green Hair* was to go ahead as soon as he was free.

Galileo opened in New York on 7 December 1947, to a considerably less friendly critical response than in Hollywood. The most powerful critic, Brooks Atkinson of the *New York Times*, denounced it as 'stuffed with hokum' and its run lasted a mere three weeks. Brecht tried to set up a film in Italy, with Laughton as Galileo and Losey directing. He had found a producer, Rod E. Geiger, who had funds in Italy derived from his involvement in Rossellini's film *Open City*. But Laughton was a frightened man; he was beginning to panic over his association with left-wingers and without his participation there was no film. Brecht wrote a bitter and premature obituary for the actor:

> *Speak of the weather*
> *Be thankful he's dead*
> *Who before he had spoken*
> *Took back what he said.*

It is possible that Laughton went even further in his desire to appease the gathering hostility. Certainly Losey thought so. 'Charles Laughton turned my name in to the Committee,' he told the *Los Angeles Times* in 1975. 'He went to them and denounced Brecht and me. Why? Why did anybody talk to the FBI? To save their own necks!' Losey's evidence was based on Kurt Singer's biography of Laughton, in which Laughton claims that he had been duped by Losey and Brecht. Laughton's widow Elsa Lanchester denies that Singer's statements were either authorized or accurate. 'Some people are more comfortable feeling hurt and betrayed,' she wrote in retrospect.

Losey never met Brecht again after their farewell at the airport, although he continued to write to him, but he ceased communicating with Laughton once the plans to film *Galileo* had collapsed. Laughton, however, remained wary of any association with Brecht, however slight. When Brecht died in 1956, Laughton and Losey were among those invited to the state funeral staged by the East German government. Losey was unable to go because his passport had expired and there was no time to renew it. At first Laughton did not reply to the invitation, wounding Helene Weigel, who rang Losey and asked for his help. Losey sent a cable to Laughton, who contacted his lawyer, who in turn called in the FBI. Only after he was officially reassured that there would be no repercussions did Laughton send a telegram of regret.

But all that was to come. Losey's immediate concern was to get *The Boy With Green Hair* on the screen.

V

Exile from Tinseltown

Losey was fortunate to be working for Schary, who was one of the few Hollywood executives to oppose blacklisting during a secret meeting at the Waldorf-Astoria Hotel in New York on 27 November 1947, the day that Congress decided to cite the Ten for contempt. In the crowded, smoke-filled room, where lawyers outnumbered the twenty or so film-makers by three to one, the mood was one of surrender. Despite his misgivings, Schary was a member of the committee that issued a statement declaring that the Ten's actions had been a 'disservice to their employers and have impaired their usefulness to the industry'. The studio bosses seemed fearful of arousing HUAC's virulent antisemitism and, in response to urgings of Eric Johnston, president of the Motion Picture Association who had organized the meeting, also agreed that they would not knowingly employ Communists.

Schary refused to fire Edward Dmytryk and Adrian Scott, the two RKO employees among the Ten, although he did nothing to prevent another executive from carrying out the task. By the beginning of 1948 the script for *The Boy With Green Hair*, which Losey and producer Scott had roughed out, was polished and finished by Ben Barzman and Alfred Levitt and presented to Schary, who wrote to Losey on 12 February saying that he liked the script, which he was certain would make a successful film, and he was pleased for Losey that after all this time he had finally got his hands on the wheel. Schary was shrewd enough to replace the disgraced Scott with Stephen Ames, a producer of pronounced right-wing views: the American Legion was already threatening to picket films that bore credits of those it considered subversive, and he wanted to avoid confrontation. Losey's worries that he would not be able to work happily with Ames proved groundless, for the producer turned out to be both generous and helpful.

The Boy With Green Hair concerns Peter (Dean Stockwell), a young war orphan who lives with a series of relatives in a small, mid-western town until he is cared for by Gramp (Pat O'Brien), an avuncular ex-vaudeville conjurer who is more or less permanently marinated in kindly Irish bonhomie. One morning Peter wakes up to find he has green hair, an event which transforms him into a pariah, shunned and mocked by his schoolfriends and the community at large. *Nature Boy*, the film's hit theme song (for which its composer eden ahbez [sic] received $10,000 more than the author got for the film rights to her story), reinforces Peter's discovery that green is the essential hue of nature and the symbolic colour of peace.

An imaginary encounter with the ghosts of some fellow war orphans, whose pictures Peter had seen on posters at school, clarifies his understanding: he must spread the gospel of brotherhood among the less enlightened adults, stressing that 'war is bad for children'. Finally, Peter is bullied into having his hair shaved off; even Gramp reasons that it is bound to grow back a normal colour so that the boy will once again be ordinary. But Peter's sense of mission has overcome his desire to conform, giving rise to his triumphant culminating line: 'And when my hair grows back, it'll be green!'

While the film was being made, RKO was taken over by the eccentric Howard Hughes, who paid $9 million for the studio and its cinemas. The result was disastrous, both for the studio and for Losey's film. John Houseman, who had been hired by Schary to produce Nicholas Ray's first film, thought Hughes' influence was sinister and found that the usually relaxed atmosphere had changed to something 'unpleasant and unproductive'. Hughes, who saw most of RKO's staff resign within months of his arrival and would lose $40 million on the studio in the next six years, devised a means to test employees' political affiliations by asking them to direct an hysterical Red-baiting script called *I Married a Communist*. Losey turned it down and advised Nick Ray to do the same when the two met at night to walk the deserted sets and talk together without being seen. Rumour had it that even the dogs who regularly roamed around the studios were fitted with bugged collars; you couldn't be too careful. Even so, Ray reported that Hughes had phoned to ask him why he was talking to Losey.

Hughes hated the pacifist message of *The Boy With Green Hair*, and did what he could to sabotage it, firing off frequent directives to Losey and others, written on long sheets of yellow scrap paper. Barzman recalls: 'I remember the day Hughes called Pat O'Brien and Dean Stockwell into his office. The kid was terrified. He said to Dean, "Now listen, boy. You know where the orphan kid says to you that war's no good for children?", and Dean nods, and Hughes says, "Well, I want you to say, 'And that's why America has gotta have the biggest army, and the biggest navy, and the biggest air force in the world!' You got that, boy?" The kid thought about it for a couple of minutes, and then he said, "No, sir."

'No, sir! A twelve-year-old kid, to one of the most powerful men in the industry! Hughes couldn't sway him, and started to scream. O'Brien would have been willing to do anything, but not Dean. He damn well knew what this film was about, and he believed in it. Joe was furious, but in the end he just ignored the whole incident. We had a lotta fun pretending we were responding to these dictats that Hughes was bombarding us with, but Joe shot the picture in such a way that there wasn't much possibility for change. A few lines were stuck in here and there to soften the message, but that was about it.'

Losey's problems were mounting at home as well. Luisa became incensed after Losey refused to give her any credit for some additional dialogue she claims to have written for the film, and when her son Michael was recruited to work without pay or recognition: 'He wouldn't have his wife's name in the credits. God no! I was a damned good actress too, but he'd never have me in any of his pictures. He had to put me down all the time to feel superior and in control,' she concludes. Luisa's responsibilities now included Gavrik, whose mother had decided to leave for the Virgin Islands for some liberated love among the natives. (Elizabeth Hawes was to die in poverty in Los Angeles a few years later.) 'All of a sudden I had two sons,' she says. 'Joe was cruel – cruel with both of them, not just mine. I tried to leave him twice, but he fell apart – broke down and cried – so I didn't go.'

Whatever his domestic difficulties, Losey enjoyed working with children and especially Stockwell, whom he found 'truly adorable', regretting that he had to be cruel to the boy in order to get him to cry on cue. Stockwell, then the leading juvenile actor in Hollywood earning $40,000 for his four weeks' work on the film, remembers, 'He did what was necessary to get me to do the right thing in the scene, and I understood this. I think what he did, actually, was to get me to remember the saddest thing that ever happened to me, and that was the death of my kitten. It's interesting that Joe felt he was being cruel. It shows the warmth, the sensitivity of the man. Joe was so keen to be understanding he even let me express ideas of my own on the set, even though I was only twelve. How many directors would do that?'

At the outset Losey was less adroit with adults. Barzman recalls getting a call from the production manager Rupert Rosenberg complaining that Losey's inability to delegate was driving everyone mad. 'I said, "Listen, this is Losey's first picture!", so Rupert says, "O.K., look at this!", and there was Joe showing a man who was supposed to wield a mop on a plastic runway, which we had to include in the film to show off the Technicolor, and the crews and everybody are standing watching this. There was Joe, waving the mop in a certain way – the guy had taken the mop and thrown it at him, saying, "Here! You do it!", and so Joe was mopping the goddam runway. So I go over and I say, "Listen, Joe. Take a break for a minute. I got something to say". He says, "No. I gotta do this", and I say, "You better listen to me, because the feeling on this set is not good for you or the film", and he wasn't able to take this kind of thing – criticism, or even suggestion.'

Losey shot the film in thirty-four days, which was the fastest anyone had made a film in colour. He did not have to learn to be fast; it was instinctive, an attribute which remained with him throughout his long career. Hughes remained unhappy with the result, spending $100,000 in an unsuccessful effort to get the line that Stockwell had refused to speak inserted into the film. He gave the film a token release, and then withdrew it, shelving it for six months, thereby undermining the entire publicity campaign for the movie, a tactic he also used with Ray's film *They Live By Night* which he withdrew for two years. Hughes sent Losey a message reminding him that he had a seven-year contract, adding: 'You'll stay here seven years, and you'll do nothing!'

Even though in February 1949 *The Boy With Green Hair* won an award in the US for Best Picture of the Month, its reviews reflected the difference in levels of sophistication between eastern and western America. Schary wrote to tell Losey about an exuberant letter from Jesse Lasky, the producer. Lasky had been so profoundly affected by *The Boy With Green Hair* that he had felt compelled to write to Schary immediately after seeing it. He would, he said, have been immensely proud to produce it himself. In his view, *The Boy With Green Hair* represented a real test for American audiences. If they did not like it, then the problem was not with the Hollywood that had made the film, but with the American public that had not accepted it.

The *New Yorker* critic, reviewing the film's sentimental message from the more urbane heights of that eastern city, wrote, '*The Boy With Green Hair* was produced by Dore Schary, and it's good he doesn't approve of people going around killing each other. Maybe, however, he could have summed up his views more interestingly in a commercial.'

During the next eighteen months Losey did not work, since Hughes was as bad as his word, keeping him to his contract but offering him no films to direct. Losey felt as if he had been blacklisted, and loathed this period of inactivity. Once again, Schary came to his rescue, for he had returned to MGM soon after Hughes's arrival at RKO and offered Losey a job as a writer. Glad to get rid of a troublemaker, Hughes agreed to let Losey go. Work began on *Man on the Train*, a film about Abraham Lincoln which was to feature Lena Horne as Lincoln's maid. Losey became infatuated with her, for she seemed to have everything – looks, talent and fame – which for Losey was the most powerful aphrodisiac of all; but she showed as little interest in the film as she did in him and the project was shelved. Next he worked with Richard Brooks writing a mystery, *Murder at Harvard*, which never saw the light of day either.

During this time Losey became friends with a former journalist Daniel Mainwaring, then a successful screen-writer and novelist, who persuaded two of Paramount's B movie producers, William Pine and William Thomas, to let Losey direct *The Lawless*, a film he had written about a liberal journalist who champions the cause of a young victim of racial bigotry. Excited by the movie's theme, Losey asked for a temporary release from MGM, which Schary granted though he was distinctly displeased by this, and from that time onwards their friendship cooled, a process quickened by Schary's need to distance himself from known Hollywood left-wingers. Twelve months after their parting, Schary was under attack as a Communist sympathizer in popular magazines such as *Hollywood Life,* which published an article that claimed, 'Schary has associated himself with numerous dangerous communists and red fellow travellers. It is said, often, that Schary from time to time favoured his "Red Boy Friends" with many studio writing and acting jobs.' Losey, reading personal danger into such references, realized that his future was already in jeopardy.

The Lawless starred Macdonald Carey as the journalist. To play the victim, Losey discovered a young Mexican, Lalo Rios, in a church in Los Angeles, providing him with yet another opportunity to exercise his penchant for artistic, as well as psychological, paternalism. Losey's independence, inevitably viewed by many as a kind of arrogance, led him into a good deal of trouble, and it was now that he began to acquire his reputation as a lover of discord. He was soon on shouting terms with the producers, who insisted on a musical score that he thought cheapened the film. Once he walked off the set after throwing the script at Thomas during a meeting, and was fired in turn after another row. On both occasions it took all of Mainwaring's persuasion to keep the peace. In view of all this, perhaps Houseman's assessment of Losey's Hollywood persona is not so misshapen after all. The author, Keith Botsford, one of Houseman's oldest friends, puts it this way: 'Not many people would say good things about Joe relative to that period, the general feeling being that he was something of an "affairiste" . . . He was eager, obsessional, compulsive, self-advancing, not very firm in his personal relationships, and not a particularly loyal friend, a treacherous man. If John (Houseman) said Joe was a troublemaker, this would reflect John's instinctive distrust of creative people taking over. Don't forget, John, as a producer, was generally t'other side – the commercial side, with his eye on the balance sheet.

'John doesn't even mention Joe in his memoirs . . . but if there was jealousy there, it would have been on Joe's part. John was engaged to Joan Fontaine in the early '30s – a big star. Joe would have been impressed . . . No, the enmity probably dates from the hearings, when John was playing the aristocratic businessman, and not popular, because he wasn't as left-wing as he should have been to please Joe and that whole gang. Norman Lloyd and Carl Foreman were much more deeply into that leftist cabal than John, who was merely a liberal, and that wouldn't have been strong enough for them.'

Losey shot *The Lawless* in twenty-one days, thanks mainly to his director of photography, Roy Hunt, who worked at a hectic pace, running off with the camera as soon as one scene was filmed to set up the next — an example that Losey was to emulate in his subsequent movies. He also worked again with John Hubley, the illustrator who had made production sketches for *Galileo*, using him to draw storyboards for the film's most complex sequences.

Now HUAC was ready to turn its attentions once more to Hollywood, where it could be guaranteed more valuable publicity. In the wake of its first investigations, many middlemen had appeared, acting as intermediaries between the Committee, the studio heads and those accused of Communist sympathies.

Ben Barzman remembers how he got a call from a lawyer called Martin Gang who told him that for a payment of $16,000 a congressman would prevent his name from being added to the blacklist. About sixteen more people had been approached in this way. 'If they all paid up, that would be around $150,000 just for that congressman. What a bunch of crooks! The big producers were preparing for the advent of the Cold War. And they were preparing the American public to accept it.'

There was to be one brief victory for Hollywood's liberals and left-wingers before the Cold War froze them out. Cecil B. DeMille, who had set up a foundation to compile dossiers on directors he regarded as subversive, wanted every member of the Screen Directors Guild to agree to an oath of loyalty along the lines of the Taft-Hartley Act, passed in 1947, which required that officers of unions sign non-Communist affidavits. The Guild's president, Joseph Mankiewicz, objected but, while he was on holiday after making *All About Eve*, DeMille persuaded the rest of the board of directors to pass a bylaw that made the signing of a loyalty oath mandatory.

On his return, Mankiewicz insisted that members should discuss the matter in an open meeting. DeMille retaliated by secretly organizing a faction to have Mankiewicz removed as the Guild's president. Losey, together with John Huston, Fred Zinnemann and some others, discovered DeMille's plans and decided to petition for a special meeting to challenge Mankiewicz's removal. To succeed, they needed to obtain without delay twenty-five members' signatures and accordingly set up their campaign headquarters in Chasen's, which, as Hollywood's most famous restaurant, was the likeliest place to find sympathizers. On the advice of Martin Gang, the petition contained a clause stating, 'Each of us hereby swears for himself alone that I am not a member of the Communist Party or affiliated with such party and I do not believe in, and I am not a member of, nor do I support any organization that believes in or teaches the overthrow of the US government by force or by any illegal or unconstitutional methods.'

Losey, Nicholas Ray and others objected on the grounds that the inclusion of such a clause was precisely what they were fighting against. Losey was shocked when Gang, advocating expediency, pointed out that the petition had no legal standing so that it was unimportant whether or not the statement was true. 'It's not perjury,' the lawyer said. So sign they did. Huston's was the first name, with Losey following at number seventeen and his friend Ray as the twentieth.

Every member of the Guild attended the acrimonious showdown which was held on Sunday, 22 October 1950 in the ballroom of the Beverly Hills Hotel. DeMille launched a violently personal attack on the twenty-five signatories, accusing them of being members of subversive organizations and adding that many of them were foreign-born. For four hours the debate raged until the most respected of all the directors present stood up, announced 'My name's John Ford, I make Westerns' and moved that DeMille and the board of directors resign and that Mankiewicz be given a vote of confidence. The motion was passed with only four abstentions.

Five days later, Mankiewicz, in an apparent recantation of his earlier views, issued an open letter to the members of the Guild urging them 'to set aside whatever reservations you may have concerning any aspect of the oath or its method of adoption, and sign it now.'

With the rise of Senator Joe McCarthy and the intensification of HUAC intervention, Losey seemed to realize that his time in America was running out, and worked as though possessed, making three films in 1951 while HUAC continued its investigations: *The Prowler*, *M* and *The Big Night*. *The Prowler*, which was to become a classic *film noir*, partnered Van Heflin and Evelyn Keyes, then married to her second husband, John Huston. Shortly before filming began, Huston asked Losey to lunch and offered him one piece of advice: never to forget that the screen had three dimensions. It was an enlightening remark that Losey never forgot. Its effect is manifest in many aspects of his films, especially the sets, which, regardless of whom he chose as designer, are always rich in depth and perspective.

An uncomplicated story about an unhappy and dissatisfied wife in love with a policeman who, motivated by passion and greed, murders her husband, *The Prowler* was scripted by two of Hollywood's best writers, Hugo Butler and Trumbo, though neither could be mentioned in the credits because they were blacklisted. At some risk to himself, the producer Sam Spiegel arranged for both to work on the film, Trumbo providing the radio voice of the cuckolded husband in the story, for which he received $35. It took Butler five years and a lawsuit against Spiegel, however, to obtain the last payment due on the $7,500 owed for the script, a problem which Losey was to experience with Spiegel shortly thereafter.

Although neither Losey nor Luisa was prepared to admit it, their marriage was effectively in its terminal stage. Luisa, hoping that a child might help to keep them together, had become pregnant, but soon after, she miscarried, plunging the couple into a deep despair. Losey had his work to distract him from grief and disappointment; Luisa had nothing to fill the void or dull the pain. For weeks she could speak only of her lost baby, and inevitably Losey's patience, never his strong suit under the best of circumstances, was exhausted. He came home less and less, just when Luisa needed him most, and before long, she discovered that he was having an affair with Keyes, an actress whose nickname, 'Treasure Chest Keyes', had been bestowed upon her because her bosom was insured for $1,000,000.

According to Keyes, the troubled and resentful Luisa was 'dragging out her sorrow too long after the miscarriage' at a time when Losey was getting tired of her. Something which Keyes did not know, however, was that Losey's alcohol consumption was causing his sperm count to be dangerously low, and Luisa considered that she had been extremely lucky to become pregnant at all.

In Losey, Keyes had discovered not only someone to mother, but a consummate artist, who offered her the kind of working environment she had rarely experienced. She speaks of rehearsing scenes for two or three weeks before they were shot, including camera angles, which was not then common practice.

Losey had already begun to pre-design his films, which became

increasingly rich in symbolism. Where other directors offered physical direction, movement, and a style of delivering the lines, Losey
demanded a deeper and more subtle reading of character and motivation. The fact that *The Prowler* is less loaded with psychological
undertones than some of the subsequent work is one of its strengths,
ensuring that the film endures as one of his most powerful. Again
Losey worked closely with John Hubley. Sharing the same vision,
he and Losey created an atmosphere of claustrophobia that was to
become endemic in Losey's films.

Black and white, which was always Losey's preferred medium, is
used by Hubley to maximum dramatic effect in the wedding scene,
for example, where the forms are etched in an intensity of light and
shadow reminiscent of a Caravaggio painting. The down-shot of the
couple in a blazing, Death Valley sun seems to be observed from
the point of view of some wrathful deity, already brooding on their
punishment, lurking in the dark shadows of the buildings. Another
church, in shadow on the street opposite, has a funeral in progress,
foreshadowing the death of the policeman and the denouement of
the marriage. The scene was shot in one take from a crane atop
the high steps of the wedding-church in a technical *tour de force*,
uniting the Hubley/Losey imagination with the photographer, Arthur
Miller's, immense skill to create a masterpiece. Negative criticism
of this developing style now often included the word 'baroque' to
describe the theatricality which characterized such camerawork.

Though flawed, and by no means Losey's favourite film, *The
Prowler* was viewed by its maker in retrospect as very accomplished.
He judged both Van Heflin and Evelyn Keyes to have given excellent
performances, and that Heflin, who he knew was a good actor, had
taken his first chance to prove the extent of his talent. He found
Keyes 'pure delight', with a keen intelligence. That was one of the
reasons for falling in love with her, the other being that both she
and her husband were very big stars by whom Losey was dazzled.

Losey was beginning to make a reputation for himself. He was
negotiating a contract with a small production company set up by
Stanley Kramer and Carl Foreman to make three movies including
a Western entitled *High Noon* and a film with Marlon Brando,
called *The Wild One*. But first another producer, Seymour Nebenzal,
working for Columbia Pictures, asked him to remake *M*, the classic
thriller about the hunt for a child molester and killer, originally
made in 1931 by Fritz Lang. Neither Losey nor Fritz Lang much

liked the idea, but as always, Losey needed the work for his soul
and the money for his belly.

David Wayne, who played the psychopath, created few subsequent roles to match the brilliance of his performance as the
tormented child-molester Martin Harrow, upon whose back a daring boy chalks the letter M for 'murderer' in order to identify him.
Losey was able to find a part for his friend Norman Lloyd, as well
as some others whose names have become as familiar through the
blacklist as through the screen, such as Howard Da Silva, Luther
Adler, and Martin Gabel. Ernest Laszlo's magnificent photography
initiates that circular style which was to become a Losey trademark,
the camera literally slinking around the nooks and crannies of the
city (portrayed as San Francisco but shot in L.A.), and creeping up
winding staircases.

Losey developed a full psychological history for Harrow, right
down to establishing a complete social and family background for
him, and giving him a full clinical history of paranoid-schizophrenia.
This method of building a character from within was to become his
usual *modus operandi*, which served him well on many subsequent
films. For the first, but not the last, time in his films he introduced
a sub-theme of homosexuality, implicating Harrow as a repressed
homosexual.

There is no suggestion in Lang's *M* of homosexuality, repressed
or otherwise; Losey deliberately introduces it in his own version, in
an attempt to probe his own psyche for nuggets of insight into his
relationship with his parents and his developing creative gift, which
he had by now identified as 'feminine'.

Losey's fundamentally puritanical, mid-western morality ensured
that he would regard such a manifestation in himself with a mingling
of abhorrence and fascination. More liberal-minded in this regard
towards others than he was towards himself, Losey, like all those
involved in the arts, had scores of homosexual friends and colleagues,
whose sexual proclivities failed to affect his respect and affection for
them. He simply had difficulty in reconciling the sensitive, feminine
aspect of his own nature with the conventionally 'macho' image
displayed by his late father. After the latter's death, someone who
had known him well confided to the distraught young Losey that
his father had been very proud of him. This surprised Losey, who
always thought that his father had wished that he would be more
athletic and less bookish, a view shared by many middle-American

parents at the time. 'Maybe I've gone too far the other way with my own sons,' he later confessed to a French interviewer, unaware, perhaps, of the damage he may have done to them in other competitive areas.

Although the reviews of M were generally positive, Losey's film inevitably suffered from comparison with Lang's. Lang's ability to create and intensify atmospheres with his renowned contrapuntal use of image and sound was unsurpassed; whereas Losey was still an apprentice, Lang was an acknowledged master. Losey's contribution, however, was considerable, for he brought the psychological assumptions behind the character up to date, and, while Lang's use of the idea of the individual being pursued and 'tried' by the gangster-mob was reminiscent of Hitler's Germany, Losey's mob echoes the erosion of personal liberty represented by HUAC.

While at RKO, Losey had been approached by Martin Gang with a plan: Losey's contract, which was for three films on a progressive scale starting at $50,000, stipulated that, if he were implicated by HUAC, the studio would sever the contract, paying him an indemnity of $10,000. For the promise of $10,000, Gang would guarantee that Losey was not implicated, and would thus be able to fulfil his contract and pay for his safety. Gang suggested that Losey should have a private hearing before HUAC, but Losey refused, fearing that he would be tricked into having to bear witness against his friends. Gang said he was a fool and that he would be netted sooner or later, when it would be too late to make any deals.

Losey was ultimately fingered by another of Gang's clients, Leo Townsend, who agreed to a private session with HUAC which lasted all day on 18 September 1951, during which he named thirty-seven people as members of the Communist Party, including Losey and Luisa, Ben and Norma Barzman and John Wexley. Townsend, a mediocre scriptwriter who praised Warner Brothers for promising to continue to employ him, said he had joined the Communist Party in 1943 for two reasons: Russia was then an ally and his wife, Pauline, was a Party member. He later defended his testimony on the grounds that he had not implicated anyone who had not already been named, apart from Losey. (Townsend's testimony did him little good, since Warners fired him two weeks later and it was to be two years before he found work, writing for the Perry Como Show. Even then he had to sign an affidavit stating that he was not a Communist.)

*

1 Losey and the boys from *Sunup to Sundown*, including Sidney Lumet, fourth from the left, top – 1938

2 Dean Stockwell instructing his elders (Samuel Hinds, Pat O'Brien, and Barbara Hale) in *The Boy With Green Hair* – 1948

3 Losey wins the Best Picture of the Month award for *The Boy With Green Hair* – 1949

4 Evelyn Keyes and Van Heflin over her husband's dead body in *The Prowler* – 1951

5 A murderous posse forms in *The Lawless* – 1950

6 John Barrymore Jr., Joan Lorring, Howland Chamberlin, and Mauri Lynn in *The Big Night* – 1951

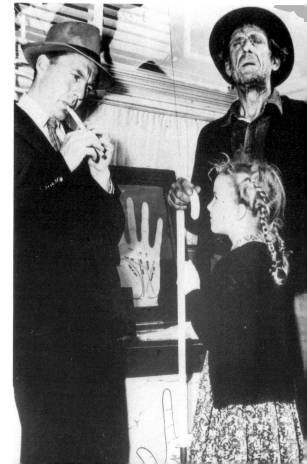

7 David Wayne as the psychopath, 'M', enticing a potential victim with a balloon – 1951

8   *Stranger on the Prowl (Imbarco a Mezzanotte):* Paul Muni and Vittorio Manunta

9   Glyn Houston, Alexander Knox, Dirk Bogarde, and Alexis Smith in *The Sleeping Tiger* – 1954

10   Richard Basehart and Roger Livesey in *The Intimate Stranger* – 1956

11   Ann Todd with Michael Redgrave, who comforts Alec McCowen as his doomed son, in *Time Without Pity* – 1957

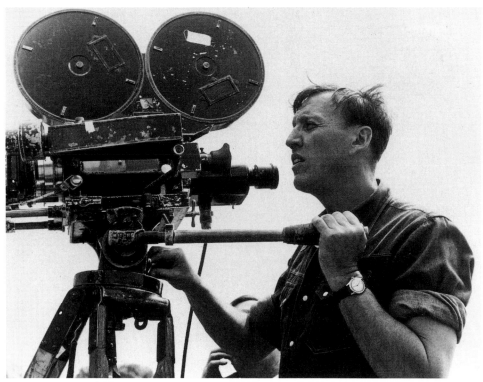

12   Losey – 1957

13   Losey showing Keith Michell how to subdue an assailant in *The Gypsy and the Gentleman* – 1957

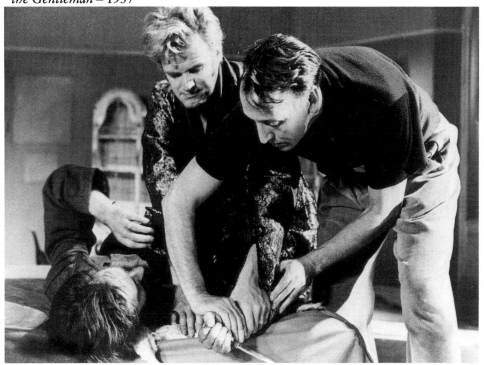

14 Stanley Baker examines the
evidence in *Blind Date*, as
John Van Eyssen and
Hardy Kruger look on – 1959

15 Melina Mercouri, Keith
Michell, and Patrick
McGoohan in *The Gypsy and
the Gentleman* – 1957

Losey's last film in Hollywood, *The Big Night*, which was produced by Philip Waxman for Columbia, tells of an unhappy and
disillusioned New York City boy in his late teens: his mother has dis-
appeared, as has his father's mistress, of whom he was very fond. The
father, a hard and undemonstrative café proprietor, cannot express
his affection for the boy, insisting, furthermore, on treating him like
a child. One evening a powerful newspaperman comes into the bar
with a brace of minders, and forces the father to submit to a savage
beating. The boy, shattered and ashamed, spends the rest of the night
attempting to discover the reason behind his father's humiliation and
hoping to avenge him by killing the newsman, whom he tracks down
at a boxing match in Madison Square Garden.

He befriends a kind but seedy journalist, as well as the sister
of the journalist's mistress, who shelters him after he has attempted
to shoot his father's attacker. Much to his consternation, he learns
that his father's mistress, who committed suicide when he refused
to marry her, was the evil newspaperman's sister. Back in the café,
the father reveals that he could not have married her because he had
never been divorced: his wife had abandoned him and their son, and
not been sent packing as the boy had believed. An emotional reconciliation takes place and, in a baffling sequence, the police arrest the
father, who has apparently decided to take the blame for his son's
attempted crime.

Losey's involvement was particularly revealing of his own character and obsessions. He did not like the novel, Stanley Ellin's *Dreadful
Summit*, on which the film was based, although there were elements
that interested him, particularly the relationship between the boy
and his father. He also looked forward to working again with the
film's scriptwriter Hugo Butler, with whom he collaborated on *The
Prowler*. Most importantly, he had met John Barrymore Jr., who
was to play the boy.

Barrymore, then 17, was obsessed with his father, America's
most famous actor and alcoholic, whom he had seen only a few
times in his life. He watched his father's films over and over again.
'He wanted to be a Barrymore,' Losey told Michel Ciment, 'and
being a Barrymore was to drink and take drugs, and to have a
temperament, and generally be a character. So he became a cari-
cature in a kind of sad love affair with a father he never knew.'
Losey persuaded himself that it was necessary for him to spend all
his time with the boy. He did not want to take him home, because

85

Gavrik and Michael might be jealous, so he took a suite for them both in a hotel and rented a small beach house at Malibu. There he and Barrymore could spend quiet and uninterrupted hours with the actress, Frances Chaney, Ring Lardner Jr.'s wife, who had been brought in as an acting coach for the boy, who showed little acting ability.

There were tremendous pressures on Losey: the budget was an insulting $300,000, and, shortly after they had begun work on the script, Butler was blacklisted and forced to disappear into the wilds of Mexico. Ring Lardner Jr., who had by now served his jail sentence for contempt, was enlisted to finish the script, working under a pseudonym. Eventually Losey had to pose as the author, since neither of the other two men's names could appear in the credits. Ironically, by the time the film came out, Losey could not be credited with authorship either.

In spite of the efforts of people like Losey in soliciting help for the Ten, most of them went to prison or were forced to leave town. Nevertheless, so grateful were they for this kind of support from one who, after all, had not yet himself been blacklisted, that they banded together with seven others and signed a curiously clumsy letter of thanks before they went.

'Dear Joe Losey,' it began. 'We cannot leave our home town without expressing to you our gratefulness for the unselfish and effective work you have contributed to the common defence of our Constitution and our industry.

'You have launched a counterattack from which our whole people will profit.

'This is small thanks, but you don't need any anyway.'

It was signed by Alvah Bessie, Lewis Milestone, Edward Dmytryk, Herbert Biberman, Lester Cole, Richard Collins, Larry Parks, John Howard Lawson, Dalton Trumbo, Albert Maltz, Gordon Kahn, Irving Pichel, Samuel Ornitz, Ring Lardner Jr., Adrian Scott, Waldo Salt and Bertolt Brecht.

Many of the flaws in *The Big Night* sprang from Losey's intense personal involvement, not only with the actors but with the characters they play. Losey, working closely with Frances Chaney and Barrymore, to the exclusion of his own family, had achieved his preferred domestic arrangement: a claustrophobic triangle, with himself at the fulcrum of love, admiration, and inspiration. In spite of all efforts, Barrymore's acting was clumsy and painfully melodramatic and it is difficult to assess the balance between Losey's need to have Barrymore's name to attract the production's financing and his desire to help him to 'become a Barrymore'. Certainly, Losey allowed his affection to cloud his judgement, for it would have taken a lot more than Frances Chaney to help the young Barrymore to approach the talent possessed by his illustrious relatives.

Luisa remains convinced that there was more to her ex-husband's relationship with Lardner's wife than the grooming of young Barrymore: 'He was sleeping with Ring Lardner's wife when Ring was in jail, which I thought was really tacky. She lived four houses down the street, so Ring's kids would say to mine, "Hey, your old man's down at our house more than he's up at yours", and mine would say, "Yeah, he sure is".' It was only a matter of time before Lardner himself would hear rumours about the affair, and he was reported to have said, shortly after the film was finished, that if he ever got his hands on Losey, he'd murder him. But the two never met again.

'My father also died when I was very young, just like Joe's,' Lardner confides. 'And my brother was killed in Spain fighting with the Lincoln Brigade, so I understood a bit what went on inside Joe, and why he cared about this film. He was very good to work with – a man of impeccable taste, at least in his work.'

Somehow, in the midst of all his other intense relationships, Losey also found time and energy for an affair with Joan Lorring, the 25-year-old Russian-English actress who played the girl who looks after Barrymore – and to whom Barrymore was also attracted. Lorring, a voluptuous, dark-browed 'blonde', was sometimes described as an Evelyn Keyes look-alike, which may explain Losey's attraction. An unmanageable tendency to hurt those who meant most to him was beginning to emerge in Losey's behaviour. It blighted one of the most important friendships forged during the filming of *The Big Night*, with Robert Aldrich, one of the top production assistants in Hollywood, who had been seconded to Losey as a sort of gift from the Spiegel organization. Aldrich, a great athlete with a colossal appetite for women and drink, was the kind of man Losey had always admired, benefiting from his immense energy, good humour, discipline, honesty and authority. Among the cruising sharks and con-men of Hollywood, Aldrich was someone Losey could trust, and who would help him perfect the techniques which he was still learning. Aldrich was given to terrible rages, Losey to monumental sulks, and inevitably the two clashed. Losey criticized Aldrich over some minor point, Aldrich overreacted, and they parted on bad terms.

Before his work was actually finished on *The Big Night*, Losey was offered a project in Italy, which he would, under normal circumstances, have postponed until he had finished supervising the final cut of the film. However, the day he had been dreading for so many months finally arrived: he had heard through the grapevine that he and Luisa were both about to be subpoenaed to appear before HUAC. Pat O'Brien offered them his beach house to hide out in, but Losey decided it was time to cut and run, or spend the following year languishing in jail.

Philip Waxman describes the final hours: 'The day we finished shooting, we had a wrap party, and we all got drunk. That night, at about three o'clock in the morning, I get a phone call: "Get over here as soon as possible." Click. That was it! But of course I recognized the voice. I couldn't comprehend this. I thought he was dying, I swear to God. I mean, what could this be, to give me this kind of dialogue? I don't remember if I even put on a pair of pants. I must have gone over in my pyjamas. I lived in Beverly Hills at the time, and I drove over the hill at breakneck speed to the valley, where Joe was living, and – we're talking three thirty in the morning, right? – he says, "Phil, there's a subpoena out on me, and I'm leaving the country in an hour or so, and here's the way I want you to cut the picture."

'Now, this is the first picture I ever produced. By now I'd just about found out which end of the camera you point at the actors! That's how green I was. And here was Joe Losey telling me how to cut the picture!' Losey wanted the film told as one long flashback, but it was changed, to his dismay, to following a chronological sequence. 'I know he didn't like it,' admits Waxman. 'He said so. Every day *I* was saying, "Godammit, I wish Losey was here to do this".'

But Losey wasn't there, for, within a matter of hours of the dawn briefing, he had committed himself to an exile which was to last the rest of his life, using a ticket paid for, in spite of everything, by Robert Aldrich.

VI

The Outsider

Luisa drove Losey to the airport, where he handed her as much money as he could afford, which amounted to no more than $200. She waited while he caught a plane to Rome to begin work on *Stranger on the Prowl* (*Imbarco a Mezzanotte*), a film set up by two Americans, John Weber and Bernard Vorhaus, who also wished to absent themselves from America during HUAC's investigations in Hollywood. The script was by his old friend Ben Barzman, another victim of HUAC, who had also left the United States. Losey ensured that his exile would be as painless as possible by insisting that his new lover, Joan Lorring, play the female lead opposite Paul Muni, then in the twilight of his career and dying from cancer of the throat.

Losey had escaped, but Luisa was having serious problems, having been left with the two boys, Gavrik and Michael, and little money to support them. On her return from the airport, she discovered that half the furniture and Losey's Jaguar had been taken away by removal men acting on instructions from Losey's business manager Henry Bamburger, who explained that he had been given them in lieu of the money Losey owed him for his services.

'Losey was hopeless, of course,' says Bamburger. 'Rarely under regular contract. Worked week by week, until he went to MGM. He was always short of money, but so choosy! He never let his need for money affect his judgement, and I admired that. When everyone else was buying a Ford or a Chevy, Joe had one of the first Jaguars ever seen around here, so he was always somebody who saw himself as something a little different. He liked to eat in fancy restaurants, and tried to live well, though it wasn't easy.

'With these people it's always difficult, because they make money intermittently, but spend it all the time. He worried about this a lot

– about debts and the people he owed money to. He left in an awful hurry, but years later he ended up sending me some money, saying, "please pay some of these old bills", like some doctor whom he went to for his asthma.'

Bamburger, who remains fond of Losey, had inherited the director as a client when he set up his own business. 'My boss said, "Take Joe along. You have plenty of time, you need clients, and he's a person who needs nurse-maiding." Joe led me to Robert Ryan, and to Barbara Hale because of *Boy With Green Hair*, and they became clients, so you could say I owe him quite a lot. I saw him some years later – in the '60s I think, in Rome. I was so glad to see him working again, making good pictures. He was living in the most beautiful apartment in the Via Gregoriana – like a stage set. He had an eye for beauty and grandeur, that's for sure. God knows *how* he paid for it. In Paris he lived on the Left Bank in a flat in one of those lovely old courtyards.

'Over the years he'd say, "Be sure you pay yourself, Henry", but he didn't say how I was to pay myself. From time to time he'd send me some money, and I'd pay the postage, or I'd keep the little life insurance policies going, or his membership in the union. There was a period when he didn't have enough money to even file a tax return, then there'd be money again and tax problems. Joe had what all great artists have to have – he was an innovator; he had incredible integrity, and his films have an endurance, a universality. I thought he was great.'

Frantic, Luisa turned for advice to her lawyer, who suggested she join Joe in Rome and attempt, at least, to settle their financial affairs. When she telephoned him, Losey told her that it was bad timing because he was totally involved in the film and could not afford to pay for her fare. He suggested that she go to New York and persuade Sam Spiegel to pay the $4,000 he was still owed for his work on *The Prowler*. Having found friends to look after Michael, Luisa flew to New York with Gavrik, arranging for him to spend a night or two with his mother in the city.

She rang Spiegel on her arrival, and was shocked by his suggestion that she come up to his apartment that evening and join him and another blonde for a romp in his satin-sheeted bed, when he would give her a cheque. Luisa demurred, but Spiegel paid her some money anyway. On returning to the Algonquin Hotel, where she and Losey always stayed in New York, she was phoned by Elizabeth Hawes, who told her that she was keeping Gavrik. The reason for her action, Hawes added, would be made clear when Luisa arrived in Rome.

Luisa discovered the truth at Rome airport, where there was no sign of her husband; instead she was greeted by George Tabori, who explained that there had been a break in shooting, and that Losey was in the South of France with Joan Lorring. She was not to mind, Tabori said, 'You know Joe. He'll come back. He always has. We both know there have been other women.' Losey later explained to Luisa that, although he loved her, he was *in love* with Joan Lorring, expecting her to be understanding and resigned to the situation.

The making of *Imbarco a Mezzanotte* was troubled. Weber and Vorhaus, who were denounced as Communists to HUAC during the filming, had obtained most of their finance from Italian fascists, causing a destructive tension on the set. This was exacerbated by Losey's dislike of Muni, who was not only terrified of being involved with people who might be Communists, but was being made even more irritable by his illness. Muni also hated working with children, and his co-star was a 12-year-old boy Vittorio Manunta, an Italian orphan with considerable natural talent, who had been adopted by a rich Bostonian couple and brought back to his motherland to make the film.

Unfortunately, Barzman was refused entry to Italy because of his blacklisting, and Losey was therefore unable to work with him on improving a script which satisfied no one. *Imbarco a Mezzanotte*, based on a short story by the French novelist, Noël Calef, held an attraction for Losey similar to *The Big Night*. He was intrigued by its central relationship between two fugitives, a murderer (Muni) and a boy (Manunta) who thinks a mob are after him for stealing a bottle of milk.

Losey formed a close relationship with Manunta, who instinctively understood what was expected of him, and coaxed from him an impressive performance. Losey disliked Muni's arcane, mechanical approach, which involved rehearsing his part in front of a mirror and using a tape recorder so that his performance was worked out in detail before he faced the camera. Muni turned all his frustrations against the character, portraying him as a spiteful, bitter, and ultimately hateful man, instead of the sympathetic victim he should have been. Losey could not control him, and without Barzman there to help (he maintains he would have suggested that Muni be replaced), the result was disastrous. Also, Losey again had a musical score he disliked imposed upon the film by its producers.

Neither Losey nor Calef cared much for the final result, and Barzman, who saw the film during its brief release in Paris, hated it. United Artists were equally indifferent, particularly as most of the major participants had been blacklisted. The studio shelved it for a time and finally released it, after cutting its length from 100 to 80 minutes, under the new title of *Stranger on the Prowl*, hoping to cash in on the success of *The Prowler*, although there was no indication that Losey had directed that film. The names of all the blacklisted people were removed from the credits: both the director and the scenarist were listed as Andrea Forzano, who was the son of one of the film's backers, and Noël Calef assumed the role of producer.

Losey's time in Italy ignited a more enduring love affair, a passion for the Renaissance and the Baroque – for cypress trees, for all the forms, textures and splendours with which Italy was laden. His relationship with Joan Lorring ended with the conclusion of the film. Losey sent for Gavrik, now aged 13, and, together with Luisa, left for a fortnight's holiday in Menton. When they tried to return to Italy, they were turned back and unceremoniously dumped on the French side of the border by an armed guard. Losey, who had little money, refused to report his problem to the American consul, knowing that if he did, his passport would be seized.

Luisa decided that she had finally had enough and returned to New York with Gavrik, who was deposited once more with his grandmother, like a wayward parcel. Luckily, Calef and his wife offered Losey the life-saving hospitality of their home in Paris for a few weeks, after which, at the end of August 1952, he set off for England alone.

London had already become a refuge for other victims of HUAC, including the scriptwriter Howard Koch who, though never a member of the Communist Party, had nevertheless found work impossible to obtain, and the writer Carl Foreman, who had reason to feel aggrieved at Losey's sudden departure from Hollywood. They had had an agreement for Losey to direct three films for a company Foreman had set up with Stanley Kramer. 'Joe simply didn't want to take the stand [before the Committee]. So I was left without a director. My arrangement with Joe preceded the subpoena, so I feel he should have honoured our agreement. But I understand now. This thing was hitting everybody, and I don't blame him for going.'

Foreman boosted Losey's morale immeasurably by meeting him when he arrived at London airport with no more than a few hundred dollars in his pocket. Had it not been for his kindness, Losey's situation would have been bleak, utterly alone and without hope. The two exiles strolled at length in Hyde Park among the Sunday crowds, surrounded by gambolling children and dogs, and discussed the situation. Foreman knew of an available flat and had a few ideas about getting Losey some work which would help him to survive.

The contrast between the life-styles and atmosphere of California and those of post-war Britain undoubtedly came as a shock to Losey. Although many thousand young American men were lost in the European conflict, they were never obliged to fight and die on their own soil, nor, apart from the rationing of meat, sugar, butter and petrol, were the lives of their families at home greatly altered or disturbed.

England by comparison presented a bleak and crippled facade, her cities scarred, her economy in ruins, shortages everywhere, as the Empire lurched towards the final watershed of Suez. The apparently immutable social hierarchies had been shaken to their foundations too: vengeful and confiscatory taxation became the order of the day for the rich (the upper crust still attended each others' dinner parties in vast elegant houses, where they sat at long tables glittering with family silver and crystal, but precious little food), while the lower orders, who never had much anyway, were now worse off than ever, with only the National Health Service to look forward to. The weather, too – grey, damp, and dark – stood in cold contrast to that of balmy Hollywood, bathed in semi-tropical heat and brilliant colour.

Losey was much cheered by the unexpected arrival of John Barrymore Jr., flush with money. For ten days, Barrymore entertained Losey, footing the bill in pubs and nightclubs and resuming their old relationship as they walked the London streets at night, talking endlessly. It was not until they met again, nine years later in Rome, that Barrymore revealed that he had been pressured by his family into going to the FBI after Losey's blacklisting and that the FBI had planned and paid for his visit to London so it could obtain a detailed report on Losey's political opinions and activities.

Losey found a little work writing documentary films, although it paid no more than £75 per script. One assignment, under the auspices of Shell Oil, took him to Spain, where, to his horror, he found himself involved in a film demonstrating how police dogs were trained to attack demonstrators. He vowed never to return to that country while it remained fascist. Finding it difficult to settle, and believing that his future still lay in America, he took what little money he had left and returned to Hollywood briefly, in spring 1952, hoping to find a job there, in spite of his political history; but he discovered that he could not escape either his circumstances or the effects of his past behaviour.

Then came the hope of directing Arthur Miller's new play in New York, when the potent theatrical partnership of Miller and Elia Kazan (as director) had come to an abrupt end in April of that year. Kazan appeared before HUAC to reverse his earlier stand, and not only named former associates in the Communist Party, but also took an advertisement in the *New York Times* urging others to follow his example. It was an incident that shocked many at the time – the blacklisted actor Zero Mostel always thereafter referred to Kazan as 'Looselips' – and it was to have repercussions twenty years later, when Losey was president of the jury at the Cannes Film Festival, and Kazan's *The Visitors* was among the favourites to win an award.

Miller had tried to persuade Kazan not to testify and, when he failed, had gone to Salem to write *The Crucible*, a play ostensibly about the witch hunts of the seventeenth century but containing obvious parallels to Senator McCarthy's activities: 'I saw men handing conscience to other men and thanking other men for the opportunity of doing so,' Miller wrote. The play's producer Kermit Bloomgarden was looking for a director, and Losey thought he might be given the opportunity. But Bloomgarden decided not to risk employing a blacklisted director and, instead, hired Losey's old mentor Jed Harris, whose direction of his play Miller found unsympathetic.

Losey then asked Bill Fitelson, a lawyer who shared his political views, to help him recoup the rest of the money owed to him by Sam Spiegel. Fitelson was successful, but kept a quarter as his fee. Losey remained in New York until the night of the presidential elections, and as the country celebrated the triumph of General Eisenhower over Governor Stevenson, he flew back to London.

This became his most testing time: now aged 44, Losey felt that his achievements were no longer valued and that his career was over. His asthma attacks increased and became more severe. Foreman was again on hand to help him, introducing him to Edward and Harry Danziger, two American-born brothers who ran the New Elstree Studios outside London, where they churned out cheaply-made 'B' movie thrillers and episodes for television. The series which the Danzigers were currently producing needed supervision, with a little directing on the side, and they offered to slip Losey £100 a week to perform the task. Losey agreed, but his situation remained precarious, for he had been granted a visa that limited his stay to thirty days, and whenever he came to renew it, difficulties arose that he only later overcame with the aid of influential British friends.

Losey became a patient of Dr Barrington (Barry) Cooper, a deeply cultivated man with a particular interest in cinema and music, who not only looked after Losey's physical ills but, in his capacity as psychologist and guru, also tended to the demons which assaulted his spirit. Dr Cooper, who became Losey's most valued friend, probably delved deeper into Losey's mind than anyone else, though even he would not claim complete understanding. Cooper concluded that Losey possessed a 'phobic personality': compulsive, addictive, tormented by fear and, frequently, paranoia.

Considering the question of whether Losey was ever able to genuinely love any of the people who filled the landscape of his complicated emotional life, Cooper replies that he could only answer such a question using his own definition of love as a reference point: a total acceptance of another person's needs. Given the fact that Losey's own emotional needs were so staggering, it was difficult to see how he could find the time or inclination to address himself to those of anyone else. Losey was therefore not always as charitable as he would have liked to be. On one occasion Nick Ray turned up in London in great difficulties, and Losey's response to his oldest friend, after a rather cursory interview, was to hand him and his problems over to Dr Cooper.

Soon after he arrived in England, Losey met Olwen Vaughan, who ran The French Club, or *Le Petit Club Français*, a watering hole in St James's frequented by many involved in the arts. Though much older than him she became his mistress for a brief time, and remained devoted to him all her life. Being something of a 'fixer', she was able to throw a great many people and opportunities Losey's way. There are many who say that Losey used people mercilessly, but by the same token there were many who were only too happy to volunteer their services, and Olwen was among them. It was at the French Club that Losey met the painter Richard MacDonald, who would play an increasingly important part in his life, as designer for most of his greatest films.

MacDonald, a portrait painter in his spare time, 'loved the look of him, that sensitive, Indian face', and the two hit it off immediately. Though he was a serious and gifted painter, MacDonald worked as creative director in Europe and New York for the American advertising agency BBDO. Making films with Losey was treated as a luxury, something that was fun.

At last, in 1953, after a great deal of hardship, Losey was offered his first British feature film, thanks to the efforts of Carl Foreman. While Foreman's motives towards his beleaguered compatriot were consistently generous, the film's English producer, Nat Cohen, saw certain advantages in employing Losey: he was experienced; he was inexpensive because of the blacklisting; he knew how to make films that would succeed in America and he would also attract transatlantic stars. The movie was *The Sleeping Tiger*, based on a novel that Losey found tedious, and scripted by another blacklisted writer, Harold Buchman. Losey was to be paid a mere £1,000 as director, the film's budget being small, but the money was not as important as the work itself, which revived his spirits and his sagging self-esteem.

Losey had been fortunate in finding Pieter Rogers as his secretary and general factotum. He was a bright, kind and openly homosexual young man, fresh from drama school. Among other attributes, Rogers had an exceptional gift for casting, which Losey was quick to exploit, and it was he who suggested that Dirk Bogarde might be suitable for the leading role of handsome young delinquent.

As Losey knew little about Bogarde, one of Britain's most popular actors, he asked Rogers to arrange a screening of Bogarde's last picture, *Hunted*. He had been told, however, that under no circumstances would Bogarde consider doing a low-budget picture with a blacklisted director, nor would he be prepared to accept any reduction in salary, which at the time was high by English standards. Losey adored the film, emerging from the screening room determined that Bogarde should be his star.

He rang the actor, saying that though he knew he didn't want to do the film, would he come and talk about it? Had Bogarde declined the offer, the history of the two men's careers might have been quite different. Losey told Bogarde of the problems, inviting him to come and see one of his films, *The Prowler*, at Pinewood Studios. While Bogarde watched on that bitterly cold evening, Losey, too nervous to sit inside, paced up and down the car park until Olive Dodds, who worked for Rank and was an early admirer of Losey's work, invited him in. 'She'd said he was exciting and new,' Bogarde recalls. 'She said there was no money, and reckoned they'd hired Joe because he was cheap, but that she thought it would amuse me. So Olive became very much a part of our lives, though Joe never really liked her. Maybe because he owed her a lot – right from rescuing him from that arctic car park.'

Bogarde's participation not only doubled the film's budget but guaranteed the presence of an excellent cast that included Alexander Knox, Hugh Griffith, and the American star Alexis Smith, who only discovered that her blacklisted countryman was to direct the film after her arrival in England. One incident that she and Bogarde found hilarious occurred on the first day of shooting, when they saw Ginger Rogers and her daunting mother, both indefatigable Red-baiters, walk into the foyer of their hotel.

'It was positively dangerous for Joe,' Alexis Smith confides. 'At that time it could have cost him his job, so we had to take him out immediately. Dirk and I bundled him outside, and stuck him in the back of Dirk's car – on the floor, with a blanket over him – and whisked him away to another hotel. I was worried. I had been told nothing about Joe and the blacklist at all, until after I signed for the film. Had I not already had a contract, I wouldn't have gone. The people who hired me just said that this guy called Victor Hanbury was directing it, and that there was this writer, who was helping on the picture. Of course the writer turned out to be Carl Foreman, and he was blacklisted as well. Joe was a gentleman, though. He said he'd try to get me out of the contract, if I was really leery about it, but I thought, "What the hell?"

'I was impressed with the light-hearted way people spoke in England about Communists and Communism, and joked about it on the set – not in relation to Joe or Carl, but generally. I remember one day coming on to the set wearing a red robe, and one of the grips from up high shouted, "Oh, Senator McCarthy wouldn't like that", followed by a big laugh. In England people were saying, "Who is this silly ass, McCarthy?" I used to go to Hyde Park on Sundays – one of my favourite things to do – and listen to the Communist speakers, and it gave me a totally different perspective. That, and reading the English papers. I was struck by how much freedom there was by contrast to "the land of the free", from whence I had come. I wasn't very politically orientated at the time, but this came as a big shock to me.'

The Sleeping Tiger tells the story of a young delinquent (Bogarde) under the care of a psychiatrist (Knox) who believes that with proper counselling, the boy can be put straight. The boy, brought to live at the psychiatrist's home, begins an affair with the doctor's wife (Smith), with unhappy results for both. The film strives to demonstrate how rarely people, including professional analysts, understand themselves and their own motivations. Losey called in MacDonald to help with the design, but recognized that the film was not destined to be judged one of his greatest works. Filming was further hampered by the occasional appearance of journalists on the set, precipitating the suspension of shooting, often for the rest of the day, while Losey hid from them. The film was not a great success, but led to the enduring friendship between Bogarde and Losey; both vowed that they would work together again as soon as they could find a suitable subject, a search that would last a decade.

One balmy evening in the spring of 1953, soon after Losey had finished work and was enjoying the comforting confines of the French Club, a 22-year-old blonde swept in with a band of acolytes. Olwen Vaughan converged upon them, in the manner of old friends, and Losey was introduced. Her name was Jill Bennett, an actress grieving over the death from cancer of Godfrey Tearle, one of Britain's best-loved actors, with whom she had been deeply in love, despite a difference in age of more than forty-five years.

Compared with some of Losey's other encounters, which might

be termed *coups de foudre*, the liaison with Jill developed in a leisurely manner. On their first night out, they went to the theatre, then walked till dawn in St James's Park. 'I was so young,' she said. 'And I'd been through a ghastly experience with Godfrey dying. Compared to him Joe didn't seem old at all. He was feeling dodgy too, having just left a difficult marriage. He was intoxicating to look at. Like an Indian. In a really sort of corny way, he looked like a typical American film director. He had a wonderful style and class; I had a bit of style and a bit of class too – shades of the old jolly hockey sticks. He liked that, and we simply fell in love.'

The affair lasted over nine months, during which time there was much love and a few rows, mostly attributable to Losey's chronic possessiveness. 'He wanted to get married, but I couldn't commit. We were very much in love, but I was very ambitious, and Joe had to have one's total attention. I mean, there were times when I was working and Joe wasn't. He could never have tolerated an equal or greater success than his, and I was a young actress on the way up. I never asked about his past; that's why he liked me so much. I was so unpossessive. This has been a bit of a bane in my life, because people think I don't care. I do care, but I don't need to own people. Joe needed people around who cared only about him, which I did, but I cared about my career too, I'm afraid.

'Having been so long with a much older man, I'd never really sown my wild oats. I wanted to go out to nightclubs, have fun, dance. Joe loved to dance, and was a wonderful dancer. I know people say he was gloomy; well, he was never gloomy with me. We are what other people bring out in us, and this was especially true of Joe. He treated me like a queen. Did all the cooking, which he loved. I never lifted a finger.'

Luckily, Jill's devotion and generosity during this period extended to more material considerations; taking pity on Losey's forlorn sartorial state, she bought him six suits and two pairs of shoes so that he could appear in society dressed in a manner suitable to a gentleman-artist.

At the height of the affair, in 1954, Losey received an invitation to direct an American play, Edmund Morris's *The Wooden Dish*, starring Wilfrid Lawson as a geriatric father, and, playing his granddaughter, Dorothy Bromilley, a fresh young actress from Manchester. The play itself, a depressing tale describing the tribulations suffered by people obliged to care for an ageing and troublesome relative at home, was nothing exceptional, but for Losey it was good to return momentarily to the theatre, which had bred and nurtured his talent. Dorothy had just returned from a stint in Hollywood, which had not set her career ablaze, although it had ironed out her north-of-England accent. Losey felt initially that her voice was still wrong for the play, and told her that her presence was conditional upon her making a special effort with the accent. Despite his attitude, he had already taken a fancy to this malleable and attractive young woman.

It was not a happy production, due largely to the fact that Lawson, an alcoholic, was usually drunk, a condition that resulted in frightful scenes with Losey, who was going through a relatively sober period at the time. Losey exerted a rigid self-discipline, and never drank on the job, expecting others to follow his example. Towards the end of his life, this rule was sometimes waived, but drink, for which he had an astonishing capacity, rarely interfered with the quality of his work.

Jill Bennett did not welcome the attentions Losey bestowed upon Dorothy, but was philosophical about the affair: she was not prepared to commit, Dorothy was, and so was Losey. He also very much needed the vital work permit. His position was still in jeopardy, and whenever his passport expired, he had to leave the country, never knowing whether or not he would be re-admitted. Carl Foreman and a sympathetic MP, Sir Leslie Plummer, helped him, taking the view that he was a political refugee and a positive addition to the country's cultural life. However, marriage to a British subject was the easiest and quickest way of acquiring a permit, though Dorothy never felt that this was the reason for Losey's interest in her. Those who saw them together had no doubt that the two were genuinely in love, and, as Dorothy said, 'There were others who could have been more useful to him, so why pick me?'

And so, with a liberal sprinkling of tears on both sides (Losey was ever an unabashed weeper), accompanied by vows of enduring and devoted friendship, the affair with Jill Bennett ended without bitterness; their mutual devotion continued until Losey's death with a constancy which would be the envy of most married couples. 'He was a constant and loving force,' Jill testified with passion, 'an intellectual force too, always there if I needed him. In that way we always loved each other.' She emphasized how kind Losey had been to her mother and how he paid her a special visit to explain why he and Jill were parting and to say his fare-wells.

Dr Cooper's view of this relationship is most perceptive, considering that it was the liaison about which he had learned the least: 'For Joe, as for many of us, constancy and commitment were antithetical to contract. Constancy stays hot, romantic love does not. Whereas others complained about his drinking, Jill matched him jar for jar. Such commitment as was between them was one of common need – a non-phobic commitment.'

Ironically, one of Losey's more phobic non-commitments turned up in the form of his 75-year-old mother, Ina, as *The Wooden Dish* went into production. Weary of flitting from one American city to another, none of which ever felt like home, she had decided to join her son in England and spend her remaining years in a place where he and his sister, Mary, could better afford to keep her.

It was not Losey, however, who took charge of her, but the loyal Rogers: 'I'm the only person who really knew Joe's mother. She was a lovely old lady, a very good woman, quiet and sweet, and very intelligent. But Joe seemed embarrassed by her, because she'd done so many humble jobs, many of which were for *him*, after all, when he was growing up. He made out she was an alcoholic, but he always put on to others those faults he had himself, putting her down, as he did all those who were important to him, as though he was ashamed he owed them so much. He farmed her out to Torquay, and it was I who took her down there when she arrived. She was a sort of distressed gentleperson, not ill-bred at all, or ill-educated. Joe hardly ever went to see her, he was so busy and so fraught. I felt very sorry for her. Dorothy was always terribly kind to her, though, which she appreciated.'

The Wooden Dish opened at the Phoenix Theatre in London on 27 July 1954, but failed to find an audience for long. But it led to an offer to direct another play in London, Michael Burn's *The Night of the Ball*, which opened in January 1955, at the New Theatre. This was financed by Ethel Linda Reiner, an overpowering American lady with bows in her hair ('The tougher they are, the more bows they sprout,' Jill observed), and in its way marked the end of an era, opening as it did not long before the Suez crisis. The cast was positively dazzling: Wendy Hiller, Gladys Cooper, Robert Harris, Tony Britten, and Jill Bennett, but it received discouraging reviews and closed within six months.

The play proved to be a milestone for Losey, however, since his friendship with the author led him to the all-important work permit. Michael Burn's father, Sir Clive Burn, was in close contact with Lord Monckton, then Minister of Labour, and the two of them, together with Sir Leslie Plummer, expedited Losey's application. He and Burn remained friendly correspondents for many years.

Losey's next film was a half-hour *divertissement* called *Man on the Beach*, set up by Michael Carreras of Hammer Films and starring Donald Wolfit, an actor of the old school whom Losey found even more difficult than Muni. The film's only distinguishing feature was that it was the first on which Losey dared place his own name since leaving America.

Nat Cohen, a man of tremendous energy and ambition, had become a major British producer by 1955, and one of his subsidiary companies, Anglo-Guild, was scheduled to produce a series of low-budget movies. Remembering Losey's imaginative treatment of *The Sleeping Tiger*, Cohen offered him the job of directing three films at a salary of £1,000 per film, plus a small percentage. Losey agreed to the minimal fee providing he could choose his own material and actors. Cohen raised no objection, and Losey suggested a thriller called *Intimate Stranger*, which had been scripted by Howard Koch (the co-writer of *Casablanca*), with whom he was then sharing a house. Cohen, who was again taking a risk in employing a blacklisted director and writer, hid Koch's contribution under the name of Peter Howard, the author of the novel on which it was based, while Losey used a pseudonym consisting of his first two names, Joseph Walton.

The film starred Richard Basehart as a movie executive, suffering from amnesia, who is blackmailed by a girl who claims to have been his mistress. Losey, working with a budget of $125,000, shot the film in twelve days, relying again on Richard MacDonald's ability to transform second-rate material through his brilliant designs. MacDonald borrowed works of art, including sculptures by Henry Moore, from rich friends and indulgent art galleries to create a suitably sophisticated ambience for Basehart portraying a wealthy film producer. Problems arose, however, due to the fact that MacDonald was not a member of the appropriate union, so that he was credited as 'design consultant'.

Meanwhile Losey's romance with Dorothy Bromilley thrived, and in 1956 they were married in a quiet registry-office ceremony in Kensington: 'The morning we were married,' Dorothy says, 'he gave me a ring and said, "For my child bride." Then everyone called me the child bride, and I was very angry about it. Not that our marriage was a marriage of equals. He didn't consider me a challenge. He played the role of the father figure with me, and I think everybody saw us that way. I was twenty-one years younger, after all, and pretty naive about a lot of things.

'I remember once when we were living in Montpelier Square, Kenneth Tynan came to see us. Joe had met him at the French Club, as he did so many people. We had a large kitchen on the second floor, with a sort of wagon for the drinks. Joe offered Ken a drink, but didn't have one himself, explaining that he was "on the wagon", an American expression I'd never heard. I thought it had something to do with that wagon. I felt such a twit! There's no doubt that I was in love with him, and I think he was in love with me too. I'm sure of it.'

With Dorothy's enthusiastic consent, Gavrik came to live with them in England. Since Gavrik was more often away at school than at home during this period, tensions between father and son were reduced to a minimum for the time being.

VII

England and the French Connection

Losey made his next film, *Time Without Pity*, during the summer of 1956, although it was not to be released until the spring of 1957, when the presence of stars such as Michael Redgrave and Ann Todd, coupled with splendid reviews, brought about a quantum leap in his career. Calling upon his old collaborator Ben Barzman (who was living in France) to write the script, Losey crafted it into one of his most personal films, working out themes of particular concern to him: homosexuality, fathers and sons, alcoholism and English class attitudes. The whole cast was distinguished and included not only Redgrave and Todd, whose participation guaranteed the money, but also Leo McKern, Peter Cushing, Alec McCowen and the very young Joan Plowright.

The story, based on a play by Emlyn Williams, concerns a father's love for a son wrongfully convicted of murder. Losey transformed Williams' whodunnit by showing the murder of a young girl at the very beginning of the film and then concentrating on the effects of the crime, rather than the search for the criminal. The killer is a rich businessman (McKern), but the blame is made to fall upon one of his employees, a young man (McCowen) who is convicted and sentenced to hang. In a race against time, the boy's estranged and alcoholic father (Redgrave) tries to prove his innocence, so that he can prevent a miscarriage of justice and effect a reconciliation between them.

The film's producer Leon Clore had met and liked Losey soon after his arrival in England: 'Dorothy was charming, and Joe was always very nice to her in front of me. Always maintained a kind of avuncular air towards her – like a sort of patriarch. I can remember him carving the Sunday roast with great pomp and ceremony. He loved that. Said it reminded him of his childhood days in Wisconsin. Don't know how they lived as they did – anything Joe bought had to come from the best places, and damn the expense.

'I never worked with people I didn't like, so I had to feel positive about Joe. I knew he was difficult, but all good directors are difficult. They have a point of view, which they must carry through. In those days he didn't drink that much, not like later. This project was important to him. This was a film of "firsts": a first movie for Joan Plowright, and the first time Joe'd had his name in the credits of a feature film since he was blacklisted. *Time Without Pity* didn't make much money for anybody except the distributors.'

Dorothy was happy for a time, especially when she discovered she was pregnant. She felt that with a baby in the house, a prospect which delighted Losey, perhaps he would begin to treat her as an adult. Many have said that, for Losey, producing children was largely a matter of reasserting his manhood, but Dorothy insists that when Joshua was born on 30 October 1957, he 'was delighted, especially since he was nearly fifty at the time, and felt it might be his last.'

His paternal feelings towards Joshua bore the same uncertainties, however, as his relationship with Gavrik. 'Both boys have had a rough ride in different ways,' Dorothy admits, 'but I don't think either of them would say that Joe had been a rotten father. Difficult, yes. Joe's main drive was work, and those around him learned to recognize that priority. Even the boys knew that there was a time when they were to be seen and a time when they were not. I think most creative people are like that; it's one of the hazards.'

A recent letter from Joshua Losey confirms this assertion: 'I loved my father. I still love my father, although it was an ambivalent relationship. I don't blame him for anything. He gave me many things, and there were many things he was unable to give me – nature of the man.' Ambivalent is the word which best describes Losey's own feelings about fathers and father-figures, with his penchant for being paternal towards various young men, and his difficulty in doing so with his own two children.

Losey and his family were now living in considerable comfort in Montpelier Square in Knightsbridge, tended by a cook, a maid, and a nanny. When asked how he managed to pay his domestic staff, Dorothy merely replied: 'God knows, but he paid them.' He was less punctilious with his office staff; Pieter Rogers recalls: 'I wasn't paid for months on end. I'd be doing his drinks bill – £150 to £160 a month, but I wouldn't be paid. I was always broke, but I wanted to work for Joe, because I was learning such a lot. Anyway, he always paid up in the end – a bit late, that's all.'

Soon after *Time Without Pity* was released, Bogarde and Olive Dodds managed to persuade James Archibald, then head of J. Arthur Rank, to offer Losey a contract. This seemed a good move, since Rank dominated British film production, but the resulting experience was not happy. Since Bogarde was one of Rank's major stars, it seemed likely that he and Losey would be able to work together, but that was not to be: either the right material turned up for which Bogarde was the wrong actor, or the material offered was so dreadful that neither of them wanted to touch it.

Losey had only just joined the studio when there was a re-shuffle in top management: out went Archibald and in came John Davis, a difficult and autocratic man, who sent him one dreadful script after another to direct. In desperation, having turned down several, Losey agreed to make *The Gypsy and the Gentleman*, a romantic melodrama about a Regency rake who marries a gypsy, starring Keith Michell and Melina Mercouri, which he began filming in June 1957.

It was an expensive production, budgeted at more than one million dollars, and was Losey's first film in Technicolor since *The Boy With Green Hair*. He and MacDonald based the film's look on Thomas Rowlandson's cartoons of Regency high-life, insisting that the cast wear their costumes for weeks before their scenes were shot so that the clothes looked lived-in. Innovative at the time, all this came under the heading of 'pre-designing', which is now, as MacDonald admits, general practice: 'I was perhaps the first to draw a lot of pictures in planning for the same shot. You've got to do a lot of them to build the shot up.

'Joe could be very difficult, very hyper-sensitive, but all creative people are like that to a certain extent. I just couldn't take it very seriously. The fights were part of the fun, I think. I remember once Joe said, "I don't know how you put up with me. I'd put up with *you* anyway, because you always come back – don't just sort of wander off into the blue or something. You just come back and tell me off and don't take me seriously." Well, you couldn't take him seriously half the time. I mean, he had more moods than one thought were possible.'

Davis became unhappy with the footage Losey was producing; he expected a costume movie in the style of *The Man in Grey* and *The Wicked Lady*, which had been box-office hits in the 1940s. There were those who did appreciate what Losey was trying to achieve, including the film's associate producer David Deutsch: 'Sometimes films that are very bad, like that one, show up a director's contribution to it more than the good ones do, because when the whole thing's good, it's difficult to separate one contribution from another. In *The Gypsy and the Gentleman* Joe showed an absolutely sure touch rarely seen in England in those days. For the first time I came into contact with someone who truly re-created the Regency period, visually. And he did this within the framework of a very conventional major studio, in which everyone was under contract to do a specialized job, including the producer and the director. You started on a Monday and finished in six weeks, and started another picture, just like any other job, a pedestrian approach.

'Joe was a lonely figure there, because they weren't used to people doing things that way. The cameramen were delighted – they'd always been dying to do things his way – all the technicians, those who weren't stuck in a mould. I hadn't worked with a director of Joe's calibre before, as there had always been these contract directors at Pinewood. Joe was a perfectionist. His interest and concern with every detail was something incredible, admirable. He'd come in and comment on the colour of the painted surfaces. Joe was my first *real* artist, and it was thrilling.'

Davis grew more displeased as filming continued. By the end, Losey had lost control over the cutting and the music which had been promised him. Once again a musical score, written by Hans May, was imposed and which he thought was too slow and lugubrious. He was so dispirited that he left the picture before the final mixing was done, feeling bitter, frustrated, and physically ill with exhaustion. Davis terminated his contract. 'After *Gypsy*, Joe left, and I did too. We were all fired,' says Deutsch. The film opened in London in February 1958, reaching America in the summer of that year with seventeen minutes cut from it to bring its running time down to the conventional hour-and-a-half.

Although Losey characteristically blamed most of what went

wrong with the film on the producers, he himself was far from guiltless. The casting of Melina Mercouri, for example – with her heavy Greek accent – to play a Regency beauty was nothing if not ill-advised, especially since it meant having the love-struck Jules Dassin lurking droopily around the set for the duration, so loath was he to be parted from his beloved. But Mercouri was bankable and had allure, and Dassin was an old friend and comrade, so Losey was stuck with the situation.

Needing to earn more money following the *Gypsy* fiasco, Losey was initiated into MacDonald's world, and began directing commercials for television, from which he learned a great deal. From March to August of 1958 he busied himself making advertisements for washing-up liquid, lime juice and Horlicks. None lasted more than forty-five seconds on-screen, although some took days to shoot, but he found the experience invigorating. Over the next three years he was to make more than two hundred of them, which earned him a considerable amount of money.

A gap of two years ensued between *Gypsy* and the next film, during which Losey suffered a prolonged 'phobic' attack – panic, paranoia, asthma, the 'certainty' of an impending stroke, which precipitated frantic visits by Dr Barry Cooper. During this hiatus, however, something vital to Losey's future occurred: he was discovered by the French. In fact, this Gallic appreciation had begun, unbeknown to himself, some years earlier with the appearance of an interview with none other than Jules Dassin.

If it may be said that the mid-1950s was the golden age of French cinemania, then its holiest temple was certainly the Cinéma MacMahon located in the Avenue MacMahon on Paris's Left Bank. Here the faithful convened on Sunday mornings, deaf to the tolling of the bells of Notre Dame, to worship at the altars of largely American film-makers, and thenceforth to argue blissfully into the afternoon about the relative merits of their creations. The high priest presiding over these occasions was Emile Villion, owner and manager of the theatre, and cinemaniac *par excellence*. Even Albert Camus in his *American Journals* suggests that Paris was *the* place to swot up on Hollywood, the greatest purveyor of twentieth-century myths, starting with *le Western*.

MacMahon was not a place which attracted the ordinary movie-goer, catering rather to the aesthetic film buff and the intellectual, for whom the cinema was viewed as a major communicator of ideas through art. Although the general post-war mood in France had been intensely anti-American, American cinema was vital and very much *en vogue*. Villion had, in fact, been showing American and some British pictures of artistic stature since 1945 with French subtitles, because he believed they should be available to French audiences.

One day in the early '50s, two young cinephiles paid a call on Emile Villion, who received them with warmth and curiosity. The purpose of their visit was to establish their credentials as educated acolytes, and to persuade M. Villion to show more films by Preminger, Max Ophuls, and others. These two were Pierre Rissient and Michel Fabre, both in their mid-teens, and studying for the Baccalaureat.

Rissient recalls that 'Villion was a man who liked to speak with people, and find out what they thought. We fascinated him, because we were perhaps more literate than he. He was proud of his theatre, and wanted to show the best of the élite. We persuaded him to bring Dassin's *Night and the City*, which was ignored when it opened at the Studio Parnasse, but is now considered one of Dassin's best. The interview with Dassin in *Cahiers du Cinéma* asked about blacklisted American directors, and he mentioned John Berry and Joseph Losey. Dassin said that Losey was a director of particular interest because of a film called *The Prowler*, so we got Villion to show it at MacMahon in December of '55, where it was a huge success. That was the beginning.'

In June 1956, following the triumph of *The Prowler*, Villion managed to discover that a print of *The Lawless* was on its way to Dakar, and asked Paramount to delay the film long enough for it to be shown in Paris. It was not long before Losey's films were to be seen, discussed and fought over by the most knowledgeable and influential people in French cinema.

Between the making of commercials, Losey visited Paris, yielding to the pleas of his two most ardent French admirers Fabre and Rissient, who had discovered that Barzman was living in France and made contact with him. With Barzman's encouragement, they wrote to Losey, telling him what they were trying to do. Cheered by their enthusiasm, Losey then flew to Paris to meet them, taking with him the first print of *Time Without Pity*. Fabre and Rissient arranged a special screening for friends such as Nissim Calef and many black-listed expatriates, including John Berry and Michael Wilson, who the year before failed to receive any credit for his work with Carl Foreman on the Oscar-winning script of *The Bridge on the River Kwai*.

Losey took the opportunity to consult with Barzman on a project they were planning called *SOS South Pacific*, which was to be produced by Sydney Box, one of the most successful postwar British producers, and financed by Columbia Pictures. For this melodrama about the evils of the atomic bomb Box wanted a star for the lead, preferably Hardy Kruger, a stereotypically blond German actor, who had just enjoyed success in Britain playing an escaping prisoner-of-war in *The One That Got Away*.

Losey subsequently travelled to Cambridge, where Kruger was filming *Bachelor of Hearts*, and the two got on so well that Kruger immediately agreed to do the film without even having seen the script. Box, however, abruptly backed out, on the grounds that Columbia wanted nothing to do with a film which had both Barzman and Losey in the credits. Losey was furious, because Box had signed contracts with both of them; so, by way of recompense, Box offered the team another project: *Blind Date*, a thriller scripted by Eric Ambler from a novel by Leigh Howard. The budget was small, but it did not need the approval of Columbia. There was a problem, however, in that Losey hated Ambler's script and shooting had to begin in four weeks' time. Losey's solution was to split the rewrite between Barzman and another blacklisted writer and old friend, Millard Lampell, who happened to be visiting London.

A tale of deception and disillusion, the movie concerns an intense triangular relationship between Jan, a young Dutch painter, Jacqueline, an older French woman with whom he is having an affair, and Morgan, a puritanical policeman investigating the murder of a woman found dead in Jacqueline's flat. With Lampell writing the love scenes and Barzman doing the rest, the script was finished in time. The role of the police inspector had been written for Peter O'Toole, currently making a reputation on the stage of the Bristol Old Vic, but the financiers vetoed him because he was not yet well enough known and suggested three other young actors for the part. From this bunch Losey chose Stanley Baker, with the role of Jan's mistress going to the French actress, Micheline Presle.

Blind Date became a milestone in Losey's career, as it inaugurated his fruitful and powerful relationship with Baker, a dark and aggressive actor, the son of a poor Welsh miner. In his teens he understudied his boyhood friend Richard Burton on the stage; they were, he said later, 'like wild animals, let loose to enjoy the birds and the booze'. Baker was closer in style to the American tough-guy actors than most of his British contemporaries, a quality that had been recognized and used by another American expatriate director, Cy Endfield, in *Hell Drivers*, a melodrama about lorry drivers which had been made the year before, in 1957.

Toughness was Baker's most obvious characteristic. In an obituary following his death from cancer at the age of 49, Burton wrote of his friend: 'He was tallish, thickish, with a face like a determined fist prepared to take the first blow but not the second.' But Baker's outward masculinity masked insecurities – of class and education, and perhaps even sexuality – that Losey recognized and was quick to exploit in *Blind Date*, and in their subsequent collaboration, *Eve*.

'I'm going to act that little German off the screen,' Baker announced to the film's executive producer David Deutsch. 'It was a bit odd,' Deutsch recalls. 'Hardy had a crush on Micheline Presle and Joe had a crush on Stanley – not at first for his acting, though. After the first day's shooting, Joe said, "God, we've made a mistake – should have stuck with O'Toole". Then it stopped, and Joe was able to communicate totally with him, the same as with Hardy and Micheline. Stanley wanted to work in better films, and Hardy and Micheline presented him with a challenge which he took up with a vengeance. He was wonderful, and a very nice man.' Though never intimate with Losey, Deutsch perceived that Bogarde and Baker represented the Janus head of Losey's own character, a view shared by many who knew him much better.

Deutsch was not alone in speculating as to who had a crush on whom in this set-up. On 16 June 1959, the *Daily Mail* reported bitchily, 'While French star, Micheline Presle, has been filming in Britain, a doctor has stood by to give her constant sprays for a streaming cold. Co-star Hardy Kruger spent a day in romantic clinches with her without collecting as much as a sniffle. But last night, director Joseph Losey was sneezing all over the place.'

Losey shot the film during the eight weeks of March and April 1959 for £140,000. Says Deutsch: 'I made a deal with a German distributor, who put up £40,000 for the German rights, then Sydney, who was an extraordinary salesman, went to America and sold the American rights to Paramount Pictures for a sum which was nearly twice what the picture cost, so it was instantly in the black. Joe had a piece of the picture, so he made a bit on that one too. I was able to get married on what I made from it, so I wasn't complaining.

'I never found Joe the most congenial person; we're not the same kind of people. But when you've worked together on a success, it warms you, and a kind of friendship is sustained. Joe's experience of life had left him very scarred, suspicious to a degree, paranoid. What I found a bit difficult to come to terms with was his enormous personal vanity, about himself and his artistry. He was very much into giving serious press interviews at the drop of a hat, things like that. He needed me to keep protecting him from the studio, keep the pressure off him, but it was worth it because he was bloody good.'

Of all the new alliances Losey had formed while making *Blind Date*, Ruth Lipton had the greatest impact on his emotional life. She was an American publicist hired to promote the film. Everybody had warned Ruth that Losey was impossible, arrogant and awful, but she met him a few weeks before the shoot began, and they never stopped talking: 'We got on like a house on fire. I drove him home – he didn't drive, you know. Ever. Never did anything, in fact, if he could get someone else to do it for him – and we became really good friends. I'd been involved with a lot of these blacklisted people, and had come to England with my son to recover from the death of my husband, which hit my boy very hard. He was only ten, so you can see where Joe and I had a lot in common.'

Ruth had also worked in film advertising, so there was little about Losey's work with which she was not familiar and informed. 'Then I actually went off and married someone else, and Joe and I just had a terrific bond and a working relationship in those days. People say he never listened to anybody, but he did. He listened very hard if he respected your opinions, and he respected mine. Unfortunately, my marriage didn't work out, so I was back in England before long.'

Rank, the distributors of *Blind Date*, disliked the film's treatment of the police; Davis tried to have changes made, and the British censor, John Trevelyan, insisted on the removal of an important nude love scene, modelled on Rodin's *The Kiss*. But the film was a sufficiently critical and popular success when it opened in London in August 1959 that an executive of Paramount Pictures subsequently called at Losey's home to offer him a deal to make three pictures with Kruger, on the understanding that Losey would have complete control once Paramount had agreed on the choice of subject. Characteristically, Losey had a project ready to go: *Israeli Love Story*, starring Kruger as a German who has an affair with an Israeli dancer.

Unfortunately, however, the trade paper *Variety* ran a story about Paramount buying *Blind Date* which described Losey, Barzman and Lampell as 'alleged Reds' and Kruger as an 'ex-Nazi', and Paramount lost interest in the deal. Neither did the company exhibit any interest in distributing the film in the States although it was well reviewed under its new title, *Chance Meeting*. One American reviewer, Eugene Archer, defined Losey's gift most clearly: 'No one is likely to deny his flair for visual movement, his neat sense of pace, or the incisive cynicism of his approach to an overpopulated genre.'

Lampell, writing in the *New York Times* in 1966 about his experience of being blacklisted, recalled what happened next: 'When the first publicity came out, a few weeks before it was to open on Broadway, a Long Island post of the American Legion threatened to picket the theatre. The film corporation hastily abandoned plans for the premiere. But they had half a million dollars at stake, and their lawyers met with Legion representatives to work out a deal to protect their investment. The film would have no official opening. A few months would be allowed to pass, to let things cool off. Then the picture would be quietly sneaked into the neighbourhood theatres as part of a double bill with a Cary Grant comedy.'

Following the débâcle of the film's American release, Losey received two further blows. First his psychiatrist, Joe Sharvan, and then his mother, died. In great distress, suffering from another serious bout of asthma, he wrote to Barzman, who says 'He was really low, very depressed and insecure. The letter went on to say that his asthma attack was probably psychologically induced. And then he said, "I just want to tell you – I can't repress it any more – that I think you're one of the most arrogant, unfeeling people I know."

And that was right after this picture was successfully launched, and had been an enormous success in Japan, where he became a big idol too. I couldn't believe it. Then the phone rang, and it was Joe saying, "Tear up my letter," and apologizing, explaining that he'd resented me calling the film a small, commercial movie – after I'd broken my back over that script! There must have been other things he resented about me, God knows what. But that's how he was.'

The death of Losey's mother released within him a residue of guilt. Ina, who had been moved to a nursing home in Hampstead, had died suddenly, with neither of her children at her bedside, a circumstance which was to cause much remorse within the family. Mary was told in America and flew to London at once, arriving at Montpelier Square, where she embraced her brother, who also burst into tears. Dorothy, too, had been saddened by Ina's departure, although she recalls, 'She was a bit of a pain, really – a moaner. Nothing was ever good enough, and she complained a lot. She was deaf, and going blind, poor thing. She was sad, and Joe couldn't face that. Didn't want it as a problem, as it got in the way of work.'

One of Ina's nurses commented: 'It was so sad. Pathetic really. She kept calling out, "Joseph! Mary! Hold my hand." Well, of course the hospital staff all thought the poor old lady was making some biblical reference . . .'

Early in 1960, needing the money, Losey made a 12-minute commercial for Ford, *First on the Road*, which was produced by Leon Clore. Then his young French admirers Fabre and Rissient succeeded in persuading a local distributor to release *Time Without Pity*. It opened in Paris at the Cinéma d'Essai, provoking a ferocious battle between Losey's admirers and his detractors. Most of the critics were negative, but the ones in favour were euphoric. François Truffaut and Jacques Rivette were especially anti-Losey, pronouncing that he was not as good as Nicholas Ray. 'It was all about coteries and cliques,' says Rissient. Because the film had become such a *cause célèbre*, the two were able to convince Eric Rohmer, the publisher of *Cahiers du Cinéma*, that they should edit a special issue of the magazine devoted to Losey's work.

Stanley Baker had gone from *Blind Date* to acting in a war film, *Yesterday's Enemy* for Hammer Films, a British company which had created a successful niche for itself turning out low-budget movies, many of them horror films. Michael Carreras, the film's executive producer, wanted to make another film with Baker and sent him the script written by one of Hammer's regular writers, Jimmy Sangster. *The Criminal* was the story of a gangster who comes out of prison after serving a long sentence for robbery, and attempts to recover the stolen money. Baker agreed to do it if Losey directed.

Losey hated Sangster's script, so Baker suggested that it should be rewritten by Alun Owen, a Welsh Liverpudlian writer of a much-admired television play called *No Trams to Lime Street*. Carreras, who wanted much more overt violence in the film than Losey did, lost interest in the project and the film was picked up by Nat Cohen of Anglo-Amalgamated. In order to obtain authentic background information, Baker introduced Losey and Owen to a friend of his: Albert Dimes, a gangster who controlled a sizeable chunk of London's underworld. Losey had been impressed by the notoriety Dimes had acquired following a daytime fight in a Soho street with a rival gang leader in which both men wielded lethal switchblades.

Losey was completely captivated by Dimes, an old-fashioned criminal, a big, head-man figure, who wore expensive suits and drove around in large, ostentatious cars. He invited Dimes to his home, to Dorothy's displeasure for she found the gang leader 'loathsome and terrifying, like a creature from another planet'. Dimes introduced Losey to several crooks, recently released from prison, who told endless stories about their life inside. Losey also made contact with various prison governors and visited several British prisons with Owen and Richard MacDonald. MacDonald's set was copied from an existing prison, built in Victorian times, which on-screen looked bigger than it actually was, thanks to the director of photography Robert Krasker's creative use of mirrors to reflect passageways and other cavernous spaces.

Owen's script and Baker's performance were both based on Dimes, transforming him into Bannion, a petty criminal who stages a daring robbery on a race-course and manages to hide the money before he is arrested and sentenced. It becomes clear that prison is the only place where Bannion has any real status. The governor (Noel Willman) is a weak and ineffectual liberal, while the sadistic chief warder (Patrick Magee) is as corrupt as his charges. Inside and out, all values are selfish, bourgeois and materialistic. Bannion is allowed to escape, so that he can lead the authorities to his colleagues in the underworld, who are only interested in recovering the money. But he discovers, to his doom, that organized crime is now run like any other business, where the headstrong individualist places himself in serious jeopardy. Bannion is not clever enough to see that his kind of free-wheeling individuality has no further role in the modern underworld, and he dies at the hands of his former colleagues, praying for his lost soul in a desolate snowscape.

The robbery of the tote, one of the most accomplished scenes, was shot during an actual race meeting at the Hurst Park racecourse. During the chase sequence, filmed live in a single take (a typical piece of Losey bravura), Baker ran across the course, dodging the hooves of the stragglers, right under the noses of the Queen Mother and Princess Margaret.

For the musical score, Losey commissioned the jazz saxophonist, John Dankworth, who at that time had written the music for two films by Karel Reisz, *We Are the Lambeth Boys* and *Saturday Night and Sunday Morning*. It was to be the beginning of another fruitful collaboration, not only with Dankworth but with his wife, the singer Cleo Laine. Their initial meeting, recalls Dankworth, was not auspicious: 'Cleo and I were living in a tiny flat, the one Cleo had when her marriage broke up, and I moved in with her. We were very disorganized at the time, but Joe really exaggerated the sleaziness of it. It was only an interim thing anyway, but Joe hated anything down-market. He was about to arrive for the meeting, and I realized that we had no drink in the place. Here we were about to receive this big American film director, and we hadn't got any drinks. So I rushed around the corner and got some, and when I got back, there was Joe on the doorstep, amongst the dustbins, looking dubious.

'I'd left my keys inside, so Cleo threw hers out the window, and we came up. I sat Joe down on this put-me-up bed we had there, put a glass of gin in his hand, and began the song I'd written for Cleo. She'd no sooner started, than the settee collapsed with Joe in it, and next thing we knew, there was Joe on the floor, covered in gin. What a beginning! But Joe adored the song, and so we went on from there without further incident.'

Losey began filming in December 1959 and, as it was winding down in January, Luisa appeared unannounced, purportedly to work with Howard Koch on a screenplay based on an original story of her

16 Stanley Baker and cellmates in *The Criminal* – 1960

17 Macdonald Carey saving the children in *The Damned* – 1961

18 Robert Hakim with Losey, Jeanne Moreau and Stanley Baker on the set of *Eve* – 1962

19 Losey and Jeanne Moreau
on the set of *Eve* – 1962

20 Jeanne Moreau reflects on
her fractured life in *Eve* – 1962

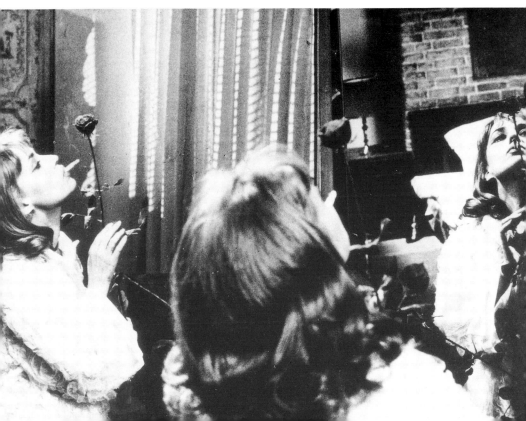

21   Dirk Bogarde and James Fox contemplating their distorted relationship in *The Servant* – 1963

22 Director (Losey), designer (Richard MacDonald) and producer (Norman Priggen) discuss plans for *The Servant* – 1963

23 Dirk Bogarde arrives for his fateful interview with James Fox in *The Servant* – 1963

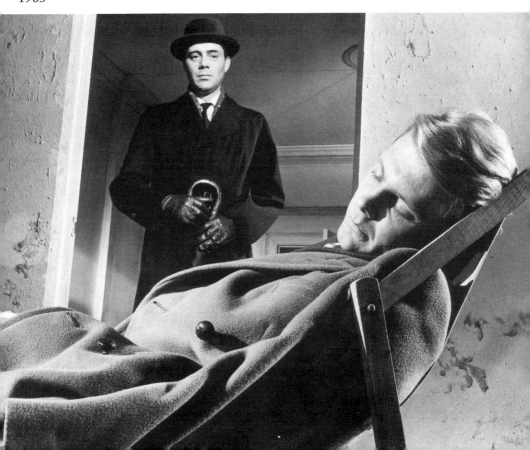

24 Harold Pinter (in 1971)

25 Dirk Bogarde administers the 'coup de grâce' to Tom Courtenay in *King and Country* – 1964

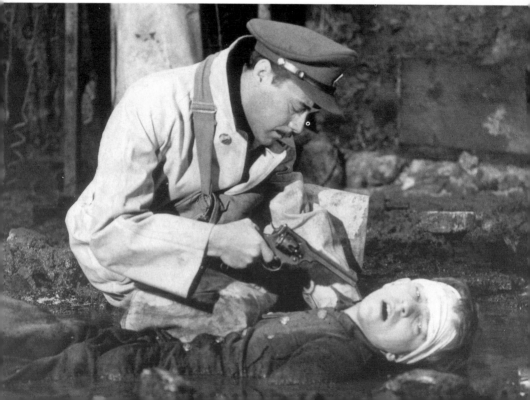

26   Dirk Bogarde looking uncomfortable in wig, trendy 'shades' and parasol,
though not as much so as his wife's latest victim in *Modesty Blaise* – 1966

27　Monica Vitti and Terence Stamp fending off the opposition in *Modesty Blaise*

28　Losey looking to a bright future in 1964

own, which had been sold to producer Victor Saville. According to Luisa, she saw her ex-husband only once during this visit, but managed to establish contact with Dorothy, 'this little actress from Northern England'.

More surprisingly, Luisa also befriended Ruth Lipton, who views them both as victims: 'Joe seems to have gone for two kinds of women, and often said so. One was the strong, horse-faced Hawes type, with whom he associated me, and the other was the Luisa type: chocolate-coated, candy-box type, pretty, young. She was gorgeous. She and Dorothy were both kitten faces. The kittens were more easily dominated by Joe, and were invariably much younger.

'He treated Dorothy with such contempt. I used to say, "No one should treat another human being that way, it's disgusting." He spoke to her as if she was an idiot, and the tone of his voice! He treated her not so much as a daughter, as a not very good servant. At least Joe had the grace to recognize this phenomenon, even though he never quite came to grips with it or made his peace, as it were.'

Howard Koch, who watched the disintegration of the relationship between Losey and Dorothy, refused to be interviewed on the grounds that he had so often witnessed unkindness towards Dorothy that it had seriously affected his opinion of Losey, about whom he would now prefer not to speak.

Losey's private life was growing increasingly complicated. Brian Phelan whom Losey cast in *The Criminal*, an intelligent man and a good writer, who became a friend, was often invited with his wife to Montpelier Square for drinks or dinner. He and Losey would talk the night away over balloons of brandy. It became clear to Phelan, as it was to many of the Loseys' friends, that although Dorothy adored her husband, she was neither happy nor contented with her situation.

Dorothy found that her husband, always demanding, could be petty as well. He would come home, sometimes running his finger over the window sill and complaining if it was dusty. 'Nissim Calef always said Joe ruined my career,' she confided to a friend. 'I was supposed to be in *The Gypsy and the Gentleman*, but I was pregnant. Then, by the time *The Servant* came around, I was too old.

'Joe was overpowering. He took you over, and your life. I wasn't even a housewife, because we had a cleaner, a cook and a nanny. He surrounded himself, always, with support from all sides.

And he so often felt ill. But this thing about the dust wasn't just about his asthma; he was obsessional about order. This is why he didn't like children around that much. He made lists. His inner life was so chaotic that he could only ease his passage through life by maintaining the external order.'

Joan Robson, his principal secretary during the making of *The Criminal*, also explains how difficult Losey was to live with. 'He'd come back from the studio, take his little pill to wake him up, then he'd work till 2.00 a.m. Then he'd take a pill to make him sleep, and he'd pay me to go home in a taxi. He was a fascinating man to work for, very stimulating. Everything he wrote was trying to knock some chip off his shoulder. I used to find a bottle of scotch in my briefcase sometimes – a little bribe to come in and look after little Joshua on Sunday, so he could take Dorothy out. It was a bad time when I was there, and the marriage was already going wrong. It was a great love affair in the beginning. I always thought he'd wanted a daughter, and Dorothy was the substitute. He spent hardly any time with her, and she was very busy with Joshua.

'He had tremendous vitality and dedication, and expected every-body else to, as well; but on the other hand, he could be very kind and thoughtful – when he realized what his regime was doing to people. A mixed up sort of man – just fell short, somehow, of his own ambition. I really left because I couldn't carry on this regime; it was just too tiring.'

Reflecting on the marriage, Dorothy admits that it suited her for a long time: 'He taught me most of the things I hold precious. He had so much integrity. You know, it takes two to tango; if you allow yourself to be manipulated, you're an accomplice. I agreed to the separation, because I knew he was unhappy, but I think it was the most unselfish thing I've ever done, as I didn't want the relationship to end. So we separated, and he started the affair with Ruth, and for a long time I was very angry about it. But I think now she's grown into her wisdom, and is a much more interesting person than she was twenty years ago.'

After the divorce on the grounds of incompatibility, Dorothy citing Losey's adultery with Ruth Lipton, she and Brian Phelan fell in love and eventually made a home together. For a time, however, Dorothy stayed on in Montpelier Square with Joshua, who was a little over five, while Losey found a temporary flat in Markham Street, before moving to Lowndes Square. Although Joshua would go to his father every weekend, it was not often that the weekend's activities were organized around him. He remembers mainly being taken to the sets and locations where his father happened to be working, and finding it all very exciting and demanding of his curious attention. Even on Sundays Losey would work on scripts, with the boy playing nearby, looking forward to having a story read to him as a reward for being quiet.

Joshua recalls that Gavrik, who, at 20, had decided to follow his father into the film business, was very independent, and not much in evidence: 'Since he came over from New York at seventeen, Gavrik had a harder time than I did, in the sense of being the immediate son, and being in my father's shadow. There were bound to be clashes of personality, which damaged both of them, not just my brother. As brothers we really only met with my father on three or four occasions – not even at Christmas. I'd be with my mother, then Gavrik would be with his own family after he got married, which was when he was thirty. Maybe they just expected too much from each other.'

Ruth was happy with Losey not only for herself, but for her son, Peter, who had grown very close to Gavrik. But she became uneasy about the extraordinary way in which Losey seemed to favour Peter, whilst treating Gavrik with contempt. 'He adored my son,' Ruth testifies, 'as if his own children weren't good enough – didn't live up to expectations. Gavrik is a couple of years older than Peter, and he was around a lot. When he was twenty-one, they wanted him in the US Army, to virtually deport him, so I got him a green card. We were very fond of each other. He said I was the most stable woman in his life. But Joe was always saying, "Why can't he be more like Peter?", and I said, "Look, Gavrik's going to end up hating Peter if you go on like this." He wanted Gavrik to be a scientist, up at Oxford – like Peter – and I was always trying to make him see Gavrik's good qualities, and point out that he was perhaps his father's son, after all. He was absolutely no help or support to Gavrik in his life and career, including films.

'I remember one New Year's Eve, they both came down to the drawing room. We both spoke simultaneously, and I said, "Doesn't Gavrik look gorgeous?", and he said, "Doesn't Peter look marvellous?" Well, Peter didn't have to worry – he knew I loved him, but for Gavrik it was part of a pattern. I felt so sorry for him, because he didn't deserve it. What kid does?'

The Criminal was first shown at the Edinburgh Festival in August 1960. The advertising campaign featured a menacing photograph of Baker over the legend 'WANTED! by the girl who loved him, the gang who hated him, and the police who pursued him.' The critics, in general, hailed the film's realism, although there were some who had reservations, notably Frank Lewis of the *Sunday Dispatch*: 'I could have forgiven much of the film's preposterousness in the cause of X-citement, but NOT the crime of casting Jill Bennett – one of our most intelligent, sensitive actresses – in a role of total imbecility.' Mr Lewis could not, of course, have known of the close friendship existing between Miss Bennett and her director, which inspired her to accept a 'signature' role just to work again with one of her favourite people. The critic of the *Guardian* found fault with Losey for 'seeing British criminals through U.S. glasses'. The magazine *Today* called it the toughest film made in Britain: 'No film of our times has thrown such a harsh, white light on the evils of our prison conditions. Those who believe that our penal system aims at redeeming the criminal should see this film. They might be shaken.' It was not to be released in America until May 1962, when it was cut by eleven minutes and given a new title, *The Concrete Jungle*.

In September, the special issue of *Cahiers du Cinéma* devoted to Losey was published, Rohmer making clear that the views expressed were those of the contributors and not necessarily endorsed by the magazine. Losey, while appreciating the French interest in his work, thought that it was admired for the wrong reasons and was unhappy about becoming a cult figure. 'I couldn't do anything they didn't approve of without somehow being a betrayer. I felt I owed them a good deal, as indeed I did, and I tried as much as I could to respect this obligation and help them. That was a mistake, and I'm through with it,' he told critic Tom Milne in 1968.

Rissient feels that he was betrayed by Losey: 'I think you'll find that all the people from the '50s – all of them – Albert Maltz in New York, Barzman in Hollywood, we in Europe, including Dan Mainwaring – all felt betrayed by him. He behaved very badly against Mainwaring, against Adrian Scott even. Joe tried to get Barzman off some scripts because Joe was a big snob, you know, and Ben wasn't "in" among the snob-coterie of chic screenwriters.'

In conjunction with the MacMahon cinema, there developed a private preview club, the Cercle MacMahon. Its first exclusive showing, in the winter of 1961, was of *Blind Date*, which, according to Rissient, marked a major turning point that converted still more *cabalistes* to the art of Losey, who flew in for the day, returning to London after a *grande bouffe* in his honour. Michel Ciment indicates that the Cercle's members were 'aesthetes, very refined people, who spoke only of camera movement, lighting, etc. And, though I'm sure Pierre Rissient would disagree with me, they were largely apolitical, and actually rather to the right, but loved Losey, in spite of his socialism. And though their interests were aesthetic, they were very much interested, too, in the economics of films – how a film is made, how you write a script, the process of film-making. It went above and beyond politics and chauvinism. I mean, MacMahon used to have the *Carré d'As* (four aces) on the wall inside the cinema: Preminger, Walsh, Lang, and Losey.'

Filmwriter Evan Jones remembers an occasion on which he was sipping coffee in a Left Bank café and overhearing a clutch of French film buffs discoursing on the deeper meanings in one of the films *he* had written for Losey: 'I listened to them and thought, "My God, that's extraordinary! Isn't that marvellous? Is that in it? I didn't mean that, and I'm sure Joe didn't either." One chap went on and on, until finally, I couldn't resist it, and said, "Well, we actually made the film, and I think you're a bit over the top," which made all of them furious, because they thought I was trying to put them down – I mean, by saying things like, "the reason we ended there was because we ran out of money, actually." That sort of thing made them even angrier. It's a game they play. They enjoy their little intellectual games, the French.'

Nevertheless, it was the French who made Losey 'respectable'. 'When he made that first film under his own name, and Pierre Rissient arranged for its release, they virtually coached the critics as to what to say,' Ciment confesses. 'There were very few press agents in France at that time, so MacMahon really created the fashion for Losey. If you read *Sight and Sound* of the period, Joseph Losey gets maybe three lines, such as, "A pot-boiler", "crude melodrama", that sort of thing. He had absolutely no recognition to speak of from the Americans either.'

Early in 1961, Michael Carreras of Hammer approached Losey to direct *The Damned*, a film based on H. L. Lawrence's science fiction story, *The Children of Light*, about a group of children specially reared to survive an atomic holocaust. Since none of the plethora of projects which Losey was trying to develop – from a film of Owen's, *No Trams to Lime Street*, to *The Assassination of Ben Barka* and *They Shoot Horses, Don't They?* – were able to attract financing, he accepted Carreras' offer.

The subject of the film attracted Losey, providing another opportunity to examine English class attitudes, particularly towards the young and their education, and he had always enjoyed working with children. He was also drawn to the two locations, hand-picked in Dorset: Portland Bill, a strange, bleak peninsula, and Weymouth, the old-fashioned seaside town. Although interior violence interested Losey much more than the overt variety, *The Damned* examines all forms, from the savageries of King (Oliver Reed) and his gang of Teddy Boys, to the more subtle manipulations of Bernard (Alexander Knox), the very correct civil servant whose pupils are a group of radio-active, brainwashed children. Even Freya (Viveca Lindfors) displays her own form of violence in her powerful, craggy sculptures of wingless birds (actually the work of Elisabeth Frink) which punctuate the landscape.

Though it will hardly be remembered as one of the more sparkling examples of the Losey *oeuvre*, *The Damned* did include three innovations for the beleaguered director: it was the first time he used rock music in a film – which he exploited as a reinforcement of the underlying violence – and the first occasion on which he went into CinemaScope. Most significantly, it was the first time anyone featured a helicopter as a 'character' in a film, as well as the ultimate instrument of insensible destruction, a device he liked so much that he was to employ it again in a film nine years later.

The film began badly. Unhappy with the script produced by Ben Barzman, Losey approached another writer, Evan Jones, a fortnight before he was due to begin shooting the film. Losey showed Barzman's script to Jones and asked his opinion. Jones, who would subsequently write another three films for Losey, explains: 'I very arrogantly said I could do better than that in two weeks. He said: "You're on," and so I did it, revising it as we went along, which was always the way with Joe. All that was left of Barzman was the story slant.' But that did not solve their problems. 'Hammer was very unhappy,' Barzman recalls, 'because they said Joe had changed my script completely, and they wanted to go back to the old one. He gave interviews saying that I was arrogant – too strong a personality for the co-operative kind of close work required.'

By the sound of it, Barzman was unaware that Losey had actually solved the problem of his frustrations over the project by hiring another writer behind his back, without explaining the real reasons for doing so. What is striking is the contrast between Barzman's openness in admitting that he was temporarily working for another team, and Losey's stealth in dealing with the matter. Many were to complain that Losey felt 'betrayed' whenever they had the temerity to work for someone else, but that *he* was not beyond turning his back on them when he felt *they* had outlived their usefulness. As Richard MacDonald points out, it is difficult enough to make a living in films working for *everybody*, and no one can afford to sit around waiting for a particular director to get his act together and sound the rallying call. What is undeniable, on the other hand, is that those who did choose to entrust their talents exclusively to Losey, such as the late Pamela Davies, his continuity and script girl, enjoyed his unwavering trust, loyalty and support.

Alexander Knox, who had known Losey in New York and worked with him on *The Sleeping Tiger*, pinpoints the problems with the film: 'There was no money again, so Joe was pushed, as usual. Evan did his best, but it still fell between two stools: a bang-bang thriller and a serious message. Viveca [Lindfors] tried to introduce even a third element with all this psychological carry-on. I remember a scene that should have taken twenty-five minutes to do, took three hours, and here we were going against the clock and the budget. She was a "method" actress, you see. She was very beautiful, though, and damned good in the right part, in the theatre or film. Joe was too kind and sympathetic with her, but if he'd been brusque, he'd have killed it. He handled her more gently than anyone would have expected.'

It is doubtful if Lindfors would agree with this assessment. She says: 'He was more comfortable with men, and had to control women. He accepted things from a man he would not accept from a woman. Didn't feel equal with women. I have to feel a complete equal, or I don't work well. I liked the role, but felt he didn't like the feeling I was his equal. I am a great actress, let's face it.

'He was very destructive – didn't just accept the performance, kept fussing around with it. I wonder how he makes love? Does he tell the woman exactly what to do, or what? He was very insecure about women, and maybe that's why he had so many love affairs. Maybe the best way to work with him is to be having an affair of which he was in charge. Joe hated anyone who would not let him be in control. This may have been his downfall and why he didn't live up to his promise.'

Knox adds, in total agreement: 'Joe could have been one of the very great directors, but Viveca is right. He was carrying around too much negative psychological baggage from the early days, and from the blacklist, and having to adapt to the "old school tie" style of movie-making in England, and in the society as well. He could have been a Billy Wilder, a Visconti or whatever, but something held him back. He was always on the brink of commercial success, pulling back at the last minute.'

Carreras did not like what Losey had done with *The Damned* and the film was shelved for two years before being cut to eighty-seven minutes and released in May 1963 as part of a double-bill with *Maniac*, another unsuccessful Hammer film directed by Carreras himself. The film had another ten minutes removed before being released in America in July 1965 under the title *These Are The Damned*.

Clearly, nobody felt that *The Damned* had been a great success, but much to the astonishment of the producers, it won the top prize in Trieste at the first science-fiction film festival. Basically, the film was just too depressing for critics and audiences alike. In his *Biographical Dictionary of the Cinema* (Secker & Warburg), David Thomson refers to Losey's 'heavy misanthropy', and quotes Freya's remark about the 'hero', Simon: 'He doesn't like the world; it's a good beginning' – which rather sets the tone for many Losey films.

It was a quality of which Losey was only too aware, prompting him often to relate the story of an older cousin who once asked him why he was so apprehensive. He did not have an immediate answer, but it caused him to brood about his insecurity in childhood, self-doubt at school, the exaggeration of the basic insecurities of life in Hollywood by the blacklist, the trauma of two wars, and not least, the usual uncertainties related to sexuality at a certain point in his life. 'All these things,' he confessed to Michel Ciment, 'tend to make me a character who always anticipates some kind of catastrophe as a way of not suffering so much from it ... It's like the fear I have when I receive a telegram.'

VIII

All about Eve

While busy filming *The Damned*, Losey received an unexpected telephone call from Robert Hakim, a producer unknown to him, asking if he would be interested in directing a film based on James Hadley Chase's thriller, *Eve*. Losey had heard neither of Robert Hakim nor of his brother Raymond, who was the other half of the production team, but when Hakim revealed that both Jeanne Moreau and Stanley Baker had already been signed for the picture, he realized that it was probably Baker who had suggested him as director.

Baker was then Losey's favourite British actor, and he greatly admired the work of Moreau, so he sent someone out to procure a copy of Chase's book, which he read back in his hotel in Portland Bill, late at night, having returned, exhausted, after the day's filming. He was disappointed in the novel, which was about an affair between a detective and a prostitute, and he hated the setting – Los Angeles. Still, there were aspects of the hero's relationships that intrigued him, reminding him of his own dealings with wives and lovers. He determined that he would not, and probably could not, make the film in Hollywood and rang Hakim to tell him so. Hakim assured him that there was no problem: the locale could easily be changed to Europe, and Losey agreed to begin work as soon as he had finished with *The Damned*.

Losey discovered that the Hakim brothers were Egyptians, born in Alexandria, and had worked in film production since the mid-1920s when in their teens. They had produced *Pépé le Moko*, the classic French thriller of the 1930s, starring Jean Gabin as an engaging jewel thief eluding the police in the Casbah, the Arab quarter of Algiers. They had run their own company in France since the 1940s, and had even worked for a while in the States. Their most recent productions had won prizes at the last two Cannes Film Festivals: Michelangelo Antonioni's *L'Avventura*, which had made a star of Monica Vitti, and Henri Colpi's *The Long Absence*, which had taken the prize for Best Film; they were currently producing Antonioni's *L'Eclisse*, which was to be another award winner.

As soon as he was free, Losey flew to France to talk to Jeanne Moreau. Her chauffeur met him at the airport and drove him in a silver Rolls Royce through fragrant French countryside, cloaked in the darkness of night, to her rented home, a hunting lodge in Brittany. The rapport between the director and the legendary French actress was instantaneous. They dined in the light and warmth of a crackling fire, while Losey reminisced about Billie Holiday, a singer they both admired, and whose albums were scattered over the living-room floor. He revealed that he planned to use Holiday's records, songs heavy with loss and sadness, as an essential element in the film, counterpointing and commenting on the action. Losey decided to set the film in Rome against the background of the Venice Film Festival. He envisaged a confrontation between two people – one a rich and famous Welsh screenwriter and the other a French prostitute, who, cut adrift and separated from their familiar surroundings, become involved in a savagely destructive relationship.

'I don't think I ever got along as well with anyone so immediately,' Moreau says. 'I thought he was wonderful from the beginning. We talked until God knows what hour that night, about who might do the script, but mostly about the character of Eve. The subject of this film was very important for both of us, because, apart from anything else, it spoke a great deal of our own psychological problems. I am very attracted to people who have problems and who use films for working them out. In that sense, *Eve* was the biggest film for Joe, with more of himself exposed than in any other. The only one which was as personal for him was *Time Without Pity*; he always said it.

'*Eve* meant a lot to me, because it was about the freedom of women, and how they get trapped by money, how they are the victims of convention – especially marriage. This was one of Joe's big preoccupations as well, of course. He worried about his need to dominate women, and realized that he – and any man – can only do this within bourgeois marriage. He loved femininity in women, but didn't understand what it really was, in its largest sense, except as sexual power over men. This comes up all the time, and of course is central to the character of Eve, who has little but contempt for men, and uses sex as a weapon.'

Moreau saw Eve as a woman who used the lure of her sexuality to torment her men and to reap material benefit from them – Venus borne upon a wave of acid. Her mastery of the role was to be devastating in its effect, especially if the onlooker's perception of women – married or unmarried – would be that they are all fundamentally commercial. Losey realized that he could make use of Stanley Baker's own Celtic division of character to animate the insecure writer, Tyvian: the faux-machismo masking a keen sensitivity and latent puritanism, the Don Juan propping up his basic lack of self-confidence, the aggressiveness surrendering to gentleness, and the street-wisdom battling against relative lack of education.

Tyvian turns out to be a professional as well as an emotional fraud, revealing, in his cups, that he stole from his dead brother the book which made him famous. The only real difference ultimately between Eve and Tyvian is that his soul is irretrievably corroded by guilt, while hers is not. When Tyvian succumbs to Eve, who taunts him cruelly and remains infuriatingly beyond his reach even when she agrees to sleep with him, he is soon 'punished' for his betrayals: his wife Francesca (Virna Lisi) blows herself up in a speedboat, and, having seduced and utterly degraded him, Eve abandons him for another, richer client, saying only, as she departs, 'Don't forget to feed the cat', one of the many lines cut from the final version of the film.

Losey's reasons for ending with these words are indicative of his profound personal confusions. He explained in his long interviews with Michel Ciment that he wanted to make it unmistakable that he was talking about a 'marriage': 'He's going to go on living in her flat, and, as one might speak to one's husband, she says a totally domestic thing.' To view the relationship of Eve and Tyvian as a 'marriage' is to tragically distort an institution in which Losey clearly believes, but cannot accommodate. Eve is a prostitute, whose humiliation of Tyvian includes sleeping with other men for more money than he can provide. There is no reason for them to be together, no commitment, which is essential to any union that may be described as a marriage. Losey's concern with the flaws of bourgeois marriage is hardly evident from the finished film. Much of the reason for its ultimate failure was because it left its audience in a state of confusion as to principle and philosophy.

In the course of that first night at Moreau's home, Losey and she took the character of Eve apart, and reconstructed her from childhood. 'By the time I arrived in Venice for shooting I *was* Eve,' she says. 'The film is also about exiles: Eve is an exile in Italy, as is her Welsh lover. Joe was in exile and Billie Holiday too, in a way, was exiled by her blackness, which made her obsessive about self-destruction. It was that black way she sang, which struck a chord in Joe – her songs full of loneliness and longing for harmony. And Eve is a woman who is trapped in her skin as well: by the need to remain young so she can go on attracting the men who pay well for her services. That is why, when Tyvian asks her what she hates most, she replies, "Apart from men? Old women."'

To write the script, Losey approached Hugo Butler, an old friend and fellow victim of the blacklist with whom he had worked on *The Prowler*. For several weeks they laboured together in London, but Losey was once again unhappy with the result. He was trying to work out the problems of his own sexual relationships and the difficulties of his exile, but Butler was unable to work the material into such personal terms.

Losey brooded during their sessions together on the failure of his first marriage and the damage that the breakup had caused to his son Gavrik. His own love-life was a mess and he was trying to discover why. His intermittent affair with Ruth Lipton was 'off' again, and he was missing her. He had also agreed with Dorothy to take the three-year-old Joshua with him to Venice so that they could spend some time together. Dissatisfied with Butler's script and despite some niggling feelings of guilt towards his old friend, he replaced Butler with his former colleague, Evan Jones, the scriptwriter on *The Damned*, who he thought might be more in sympathy with his approach; Jones's marriage was then heading for the rocks as well.

Then he pleaded with Ruth to return. 'I got a call from him one day, saying the script was terrible, and I had to come back to help him decide what to do,' she remembers. 'Eventually I did go back to England. We had agreed that I would not go to Rome, as we both needed a breather, and I didn't want to be involved in this film, and I knew he'd have Joshua with him. Four times I got desperation calls from him, saying I had to come.

'As soon as I arrived, his problem would go away, including the asthma, but each time, also, I had to pay, because I'd "betrayed" him, and he couldn't bear that. Then he'd weep at me, and I'd cave in. You've never seen anybody who needed so many support systems and blind devotion than Joe. He was that insecure – and selfish. Nobody else's life was as important as his.

'At this point he kept saying he wanted to marry me, and he wanted us to have a baby. I wrote him a letter and said that I wouldn't marry him because he was anti-semitic, and had never had a Jewish wife. It was a joke! I said that at the age of fifty-three he should be having grandchildren, not strewing babies around, which he didn't know how to take care of anyway. Look how he treated Gavrik and Joshua. The next time I saw him he took out that letter, and he'd marked all the things he wanted to discuss with me. For a start, he said he wasn't fifty-three, only fifty-two, but I still said, "No babies!"

'His jealousy would have killed a marriage if nothing else. Whenever we'd been apart, he'd give me the third degree about who I'd been with, and at the same time confess to his own latest peccadillos. Funnily enough, I wasn't jealous, and he couldn't stand that either. Both things – the jealousy and the Don Juanism – stem from his own insecurity, of course. He didn't think he was good enough for a woman to be faithful to. Everybody, including the men he loved in a platonic, but still very emotional way – Dirk and Stanley – had to be only for him, but he could be for everybody. Who could live with that? I'm very glad I didn't marry him; it would have been a disaster.'

Jones did not seem to mind Losey's way of working, for reasons which were best explained by Richard MacDonald to the French magazine, *Cahiers du Cinéma*: 'Joe always arranges to leave the script open to as many contributions as possible. Once we've agreed that we've seen the story in the same way, or that we agree on the characters, we go back to the script and study the scenes more closely. What always annoys us in the scripts is the habitual minuteness with which the writer describes the décor in which he thinks the characters must be placed. More often than not, he is totally incompetent. Generally, on my copy of the script, I cross out all these annotations.'

Losey believed that the writer should discuss his script as precisely as possible with the director in the initial stages and then go off and write it alone. After that, the script could be altered in consultation with the writer but the basic material would remain the same. Most importantly, it had to be understood that it was the director who controlled the film. 'Sometimes, especially in Hollywood, the script is written in such a detailed fashion that the writer is tempted to claim such authorship as is due to the director,' Losey complained when interviewed by *Cahiers du Cinéma*. 'The scenarist who thinks he is transformed into a director by writing a super-detailed scenario is very much mistaken.'

Having secured Jones to write the script for *Eve*, Losey decided that they should retreat to Italy together and work at Hardy Kruger's house in Lugano. But there was one considerable obstacle: Losey had been *persona non grata* in Italy during the ten years which had passed since the worst time of the blacklist, and had been refused entry to the country on several occasions.

He decided that, since the politicians and government officials with whom he was dealing were no better than gangsters, he would solicit the services of Albert Dimes, his shady new comrade from the London underworld. Dimes duly introduced Losey and Stanley Baker to a colleague, an enormous American Jew who, over Sunday brunch at the Queen's Elm pub in Chelsea, said, 'Don' worry. I can fix it. I can get you inta It'ly. But if you an' Stanley do any more pitchers together, I wanna percennage.' And fix it he did.

Luckily, Jones produced a script which pleased both Losey and Moreau, but then began the trouble that no one could have foreseen: the Hakim brothers hated it. 'The Hakims had originally wanted to make a thriller about an L.A. detective, who gets involved with a whore,' explains Jones. 'The Moreau character hardly existed in the Chase novel, so I had to create her totally, Joe having changed everything to suit his private world-view.'

One scene, in which Stanley Baker weeps as he confesses his literary fraud to Moreau, provoked another major confrontation. The Hakims announced that never in a Hakim film had there been, nor would there ever be, a man who succumbs to tears. This attitude struck Losey painfully and deeply, as he wept frequently and shamelessly, and had very deliberately bestowed this trait upon the character of Tyvian as part of his expanding self-portrait.

The production moved to Rome while the combatants argued over the story; Hugo Butler was recalled to add his contributions; and, once again, Losey's personal life complicated an already confused situation. Dorothy became so concerned about the possibility of a schism developing between Joshua and his father that she sent the boy out to Rome so that they could be together. Losey's assistant Liz Caldwell, who had taken over from the exhausted Joan Robson, was expected to help look after Joshua in addition to her other duties, which included running around to the shops at three o'clock in the morning to buy coffee for the 'night shift'. So taxing was this regime that she finally suffered a nervous breakdown, ending up at St Bartholomew's hospital in England where she took a long time to recover.

More complications lay ahead in the form of Patricia Taluso, who appeared in response to Evan Jones's request for a secretary to type the pages of dialogue as they were produced or altered. Patricia, an extremely pretty girl, turned up wearing a mini-skirt over black, fishnet stockings which encased her exceptionally fine legs. When Losey met her, he must have experienced some frisson of jealousy, thinking how lucky Jones was going to be, seeing this charming creature on a daily basis.

Patricia, the daughter of a Free Church English minister, had left school (where she had revealed a natural aptitude for languages) to become a secretary. One of her first jobs was with the author Raymond Chandler, but she finally decided to escape the strictures of family and middle-class England to explore Europe. In Rome she was unable to find much secretarial work at first, but after meeting and marrying her Italian husband Signor Taluso, she was more readily employed. By the time she went to work for Jones, she had a two-year-old son and was again pregnant, which accounted, no doubt, for the particularly radiant glow which so captivated all who beheld her.

Relations with the Hakims continued to deteriorate and the starting date for shooting the film kept being advanced. In the Roman heat, tempers quickly reached boiling point. Finally, at a meeting which included the Hakims, Losey, Jones, MacDonald and Moreau with her agent, the script was gone through line by line, all signing their names at the bottom of each page to signify their agreement. But even then, the difficulties continued: the Hakims were running short of finance for the film.

Losey, feeling low and desperate, pleaded again with Ruth to join him in Rome. She arrived to find him fractious and sighing, wheezing like a bellows under an attack of asthma, provoked by the endless frustration and bickering. It was only a matter of days, however, before they too were quarrelling again; Ruth departed, and moved in with a friend. Then, moved by Losey's pleading, tearful phone-calls, Ruth agreed to accompany him to Positano during a short break in the filming.

They stayed for a week in the bridal suite of Positano's most luxurious hotel. On his best behaviour, Losey was affectionate and kind, even solicitous of Ruth's welfare, worried that she would fall off her water-skis or suffer painful sunburn. They were both very happy, and had a marvellous time. On the train back to Rome, however, pressures began to build up again, and a quarrel broke out which sent her packing once more, back to New York.

Once Jones had finished his script, Losey claimed Patricia as his assistant, replacing Liz Caldwell. He told the Hakims they were fortunate to have Patricia working on the film since she was both reliable and fluent in several languages. Throughout all the dramas, and with Losey stopping and starting on the film, flying back and forth between Rome and London to wheedle more money as they periodically ran out of funds, Patricia was there to assist and to be supportive. So was Richard MacDonald, who says: 'So much did Stanley [Baker] believe in this film that I think he put some of his own money into it. Evan said we were like a real team, a repertory company, and the loyalty to Joe was there, though he'd say we all screwed him at some time or other. Everyone's private life was unbelievably mixed up then, but Joe believed that he was only thinking about keeping the picture together. Of course, Patricia made herself more and more indispensable, with her Italian and everything.'

And so they soldiered on with the filming, flirting, and fighting interspersed with an unacceptable amount of warring with the Hakim brothers, who – far from being supportive, once the script had been agreed – persistently attempted to impose their will on the production. Jeanne Moreau attests to one occasion, corroborated by Ruth Lipton: it looked as though Robert Hakim was about to attack Losey physically, prompting Moreau to threaten them both with a knife if they did not desist. Luckily, however, the diminutive Hakim was saved by the belle, who, with eyes and blade flashing, sent the combatants fuming back to their corners.

By the time Losey had come to make *Eve*, he had outgrown his penchant for 'message' films, having become much more interested in making 'pictures of provocation', in which the mind of the beholder is opened and encouraged to examine situations and attitudes, before drawing one's own conclusions. The narrative had become psychological rather than anecdotal, tracing the nuances of mind and feeling over and above action and behaviour. Losey's work was steadily evolving from action-drama to psycho-drama, building on the solid foundations laid by 'M'.

Ironically, the star, Jeanne Moreau, was utterly charming, professional and amenable during filming, whereas Virna Lisi, playing the good wife, often turned fractious and uneasy; she was chaperoned almost constantly by her mother, who came on the set acting on behalf of Lisi's husband, a man given to extreme jealousy.

The intricate technical plan for the filming of *Eve* had been thoroughly worked out as early as October 1961, when Losey had taken a small unit to Venice for two weeks for some pre-production shooting, which had to be done during the actual film festival. He remembered this brief interlude as near perfection: the shooting schedule had been well organized, Moreau and Baker were marvellous, Losey got all the co-operation he had hoped for from his cast and crew, and everybody had had a great deal of fun. This was what might have been called the honeymoon period, before the production was plagued by troubles with the Hakims, money worries, and illness, which periodically befell both Moreau and Losey, interrupting the work. The only hiccup, and this a minor one, was that he had had to begin with a temporary cinematographer, because Gianni Di Venanzo, the great Italian cameraman, was still finishing a film for Antonioni.

Losey presented Di Venanzo with many problems, not the least being the photographing of reflected surfaces: mirrors – one of his most cherished symbols – and water, in baths, fountains, canals and the sea. Venice, with which Losey was now eternally in love, had made 'visually specific' his preoccupations with mirror vision, left-handedness, sexual reversals (or, more accurately, ambivalence or polarity within the same individual), and the fragmentation of water. He shows the sultry face of Eve, magnified and distorted by her brandy snifter in a Roman nightclub, and Francesca reflected in Eve's sunglasses when she discovers her rival sitting on the beach reading Tyvian's novel. Jeanne Moreau believes that Losey loved mirrors because they allowed people to express their vanity, and because, aided by mirrors, he could watch people without them knowing his eye was upon them.

Losey credited Moreau with the idea of the eggs that swamp Eve's apartment, seeing them as a symbol of both male and female: of bisexuality. He explained that he wanted Eve to be like a magpie, somebody who acquires things and hides them away without any sense of their value or style, collecting for the sake of collecting. Moreau began with her own Fabergé egg, then Losey and Richard MacDonald began to see eggs everywhere. Both Losey and MacDonald enjoyed dressing the sets, sniffing out fabulous objects, including an enormous and quite gratuitous gilt lobster. Beverly Pepper, a dynamic American sculptress for whom Losey developed a typical infatuation, loaned them sculptures and pictures from her own collection, as did many others among their expanding circle of friends.

Having suspended production for a month at the end of the film festival, the team went back to Venice to recommence in earnest. Losey was delighted to note that Venice in the winter was virtually colourless and thus an ideal setting for filming in black and white, which he preferred. They were even blessed by snow to help sharpen the chiaroscuro. Losey's use of black and white photography was due in part to the example of Antonioni – then the acknowledged master of the medium. There was a conscious rivalry lurking there – a feeling, as Evan Jones put it, of the little boy from La Crosse taking on the big boys from Europe. Losey was determined to shoot Venice as nobody had, not even Antonioni and Visconti: 'He had strange, conflicting feelings of inferiority and conceit,' Jones says. 'He reminded me constantly that if I got credits on his films, I could have a big career, and that it didn't matter that I didn't get much money because I'd get it later working for other people, which was perfectly true. After that I got twice as much for *Funeral in Berlin* than I did for the four films I did for Joe, though generally there was more job satisfaction with Joe, because he was such an artist.'

The film opens as it ends, with the camera prowling in a steady, circular motion around a church, whose corner sculptures reveal Adam and Eve in the Garden before the Fall. Here Losey perfects the revolving technique, so effectively introduced in *M*, often swinging the camera 360 degrees, isolating the subject in the centre. The breathtaking down-shot which follows Eve and Tyvian up the Danieli staircase cleaves to this movement, as does the shot where they fall onto the heavily patterned carpet, the camera circling around him as he confesses his fraud, recording his despair in the fractured images of the surrounding mirrors.

In order to implement these effects, Losey imported various bits and pieces of technology from London at considerable trouble and expense, including a new centrifugal device to mount on tripods used in boats, and places where there is movement and vibration. Another was a gyroscope fitted to a camera which, rather than being mounted, was hand-held in order to absorb some of the more violent movements of gondolas and boats. Most of these miraculous gadgets were never to be deployed. The temperamental Di Venanzo, who had arrived fresh from his labours on Antonioni's *L'Eclisse*, flew into a violent rage at the sight of the imported technology, and virtually stomped all over them. Though he taught Losey many things about the camera, Di Venanzo treated his crew like slaves, screaming and shouting abuse, reducing many of them to tears of frustration – although minutes later all would be forgiven and forgotten.

Di Venanzo's work, together with that of his cameraman, Pasqua-lino de Santis, is undeniably brilliant, responding totally to the initial imaginative input that was Losey's. One of the scenes which best illustrates their collaboration is when Tyvian and Eve stroll past an ancient church protected by a massive door. Tyvian holds his hand playfully over the large keyhole; when he takes his hand away and they move on, the eye of the camera looks through to the church behind, a tiny cameo in a cinematic *trompe l'oeil*, indicating perhaps the distance that has grown between the religious world and these two scarred and ruined people.

According to Jones, Di Venanzo was not alone in losing his temper. Lying awake in his bed at night, Jones wondered whether Losey, working at his own pernickety snail's pace, was ever going to finish the film. Shots that in the script were over in a few seconds were being extended until they lasted for several minutes. 'The first day of shooting I was in despair, because we were shooting half a page of script a day,' Jones says. 'There were twenty pages, and we figured eight minutes a page. We were thinking, how are we going to get this within two and a half hours, even? I think the original print was more like three and a half hours.

'Both Richard (MacDonald) and I were worried about this, and one day in Rome, during a two-day Christmas break, we did a storyboard for Joe for the next day's shooting. Joe grabbed it, and threw it down on the table in contempt. He hated people doing anything he hadn't ordered or created. He had to dominate.'

Losey made no attempt to conceal his adoration of his leading lady, and did not at all mind being teased about it by his old friend Robert Aldrich, who was one of the few to see the only screening of *Eve* before the film began to be drastically cut. Yet, as Jones and others observed, Moreau represented everything that Losey both loved and feared in women. Similarly for her, Losey was 'kind and witty, using language so well, but able to destroy with a word.'

However, the 'phobic' *alter ego* was once moved to admit to Michel Ciment: 'There was a period after *Eve* when I felt a bit betrayed by her [Moreau], but she and I have a kind of permanent love which came out of that film.' Further admissions of an astonishing clarity and candour were to follow, which can only be the result of years of self-questioning in and out of analysis:

'I think people who are searching for parents are also searching for a very particular kind of love in any sexual, heterosexual or homosexual relationship. And this is necessarily a love-hate relationship, because whenever such a person enters into it, it is always with the expectation of being betrayed, and the hope that they won't be. Therefore, before you can be betrayed, you aggress and you test the person that you are attaching your affections to by humiliation and cruelty and brutality . . . In my opinion, people who are searching that way – as I am – are to a certain extent incapable of either giving or receiving the thing they want. If you want love more than anything else in the world, it's more than likely that when it's given to you you don't know how to receive it.' Losey had come via a circuitous route to the realization that, in any love affair, it is the one who loves the least who is always in control.

The music for *Eve* was perhaps more important to Losey than that in any of his other films, becoming the most acute source of conflict between him and the Hakims. He had not only planned to use many of Billie Holiday's songs, but also those of the modern jazz trumpeter, Miles Davis. Davis, however, was asking a high price – $50,000 – for his contribution. Robert Hakim haggled, as usual, over the fee and Davis turned him down. An extremely angry Losey sent a one-word telegram of protest to Hakim: 'Merde', which henceforth became a byword in Losey's correspondence. Nor was Hakim able to secure the rights to the Holiday songs that Losey wanted. He had hoped to use thirty; in the end, the film featured only three. According to Ruth Lipton, there would have been more, had it not been for Losey's attitude. 'Just as we were about to get some more, it was stopped by Holiday's last husband, a white guy, who Joe antagonized so much that he didn't want to give us anything,' she says.

Finally, Michel Legrand was hired to write the score, with John Dankworth and Cleo Laine producing a song in collaboration with Jones. It did not survive, but its message is interesting in hindsight:

> *Adam and Eve's a story*
> *But it ain't the story you believe*
> *God made Adam from the woman's rib*
> *That ain't scripture, but it's God's own truth*
> *Man runs from woman till his dying day*
> *Hallelujah, God's a woman!*
> *Hallelujah, Woman's a man!*

Legrand saw Losey's rough cut using the Holiday songs and produced a score to reflect their passion. It was good enough to reconcile Losey to the loss of Davis's frail-toned trumpet and he regarded it as the best music composed for any of his films.

It is difficult, at this remove in time, to discover what went so wrong with the editing of *Eve* that the version screened for the critics as well as the public was one that Losey loathed and virtually disowned. His first cut was two hours and thirty-five minutes long. He worked hard on it so that it would be ready to be shown in September at the 1962 Venice Film Festival, as the official Italian entry. But the Hakims withdrew it, on the grounds that it was simply too long.

Losey was shocked and upset by this decision, but he agreed to cut the film by twenty minutes. By the time it was shown in France to the first critics it had lost a further nineteen minutes and now stood at 116 minutes. Another sixteen minutes were removed before it went on general release in France, although the US version was to remain at 116 minutes, while the British cut was pared to 111 minutes.

Losey had relinquished control of his film hoping that he and others would receive some of the money that the Hakims still owed them for making it. The Hakims had turned down the prestige of the Venice Film Festival partly because they wanted to arrange for the immediate distribution of the film in France, explaining to Losey that unless the film opened in Paris and returned a profit they could not pay the money that was due him. They further insisted that they could not get the print from Rome to Paris without Losey's waiver on what he was owed and his right to control the negative in Italy. With classic innocence, Losey agreed to this, much against Patricia's better judgement, and signed a release of the picture. And so it was that eight major scenes were cut from the film and Virna Lisi and Giorgio Albertazzi re-dubbed by American actors, with ridiculous results.

Losey claimed that these changes were made without his approval. But Pierre Rissient, whose relationship with Losey had already soured by the time *Eve* opened in Paris, claims that Losey wrote a letter to Robert Hakim which reveals that not only the first cuts had been agreed by Losey, which he admitted, but many of the later ones, which he did not. 'One of the reasons our relationship deteriorated was that he knew that I knew a lot of things that he wanted not to be known,' Rissient declares. 'I am one of the people still living who remembers some of the strange and bad things about Losey.

'There was pressure on Losey to shorten the film. He came to Paris for a private screening at the Club Publicis, which Jeanne Moreau, among others, attended. He was disappointed that not many French critics came. After the screening, Moreau went to Losey's hotel, and she suggested Joe cut more of the film. She had realized that the audience of thirty people had not responded to the film, and suggested some cuts which, despite Evan Jones's and my own objections, Losey did himself – the positive cut, not the negative, which he asked Robert Hakim to cut. So these cuts were actually suggested by Moreau and Losey, and done by the Hakims. Then, when the picture opened and was not a success, Losey regretted it, and blamed everything on the Hakims. Something like three weeks later, he wrote a long letter to Robert Hakim asking him to reinstate the cuts. Hakim was not going to suffer the expense, and was fed up with the whole thing anyhow.'

The gala opening of *Eve* (retitled *Eva* in France), which took place at the Cinéma Publicis in Paris, was an unqualified disaster.

Jeanne Moreau found it 'very depressing'. Bob Parrish, the American director, was invited to the opening by Stanley Baker, with whom he had worked previously on a film written by Irwin Shaw. 'It was heavy with heaviness,' he says. 'A bit of an embarrassment. Stanley had decided to take Irwin to *his* opening to see this new acting departure. A girl came up and asked "Who are you?", which annoyed Stanley, because he very much wanted to be recognized as a star. So Stanley said "Stanley Baker", and the girl said, "I know, but who are you?" Irwin said, "He's the star, and I'm his guest, the writer, Irwin Shaw." And the girl said, "Well, there seems to be two screenings, one upstairs and one down, and you're at the downstairs showing."

'It was true. All the bigwigs, Joe and the rest, were upstairs. This really destroyed poor old Stanley, who was nice. Joe was the star that night with his huge French following. Downstairs people started walking out. Stanley, Irwin, my wife and I stayed on. We heard movement around us, and looked to see the whole centre section of about two hundred seats with only twelve people left. We went upstairs to see what was happening there. Stanley was desperate, but as we came up the stairs, there was a burst of applause as that showing ended, and they were chanting "Lo-sey, Lo-sey", so upstairs, they'd loved it. Weird.'

The critics agreed with the downstairs brigade. 'Losey, flattered by a coterie of international snobs, seems to have allowed himself to get trussed up in a skein of efflorescent chic,' wrote the critic of *France Observateur*, adding 'Why not admit, once and for all, that a director, far from being a god, is a fallible person?' Only his admirers at *Cahiers du Cinéma* remained faithful, with Fereydoun Hoveyda writing, 'Losey has achieved not only his best film, but also a work of very great importance for all cinema. It is an aesthetically revolutionary film. For the first time in cinema, the essence is found entirely in the form.'

It also found support when it opened in America. As the *Newsweek* critic wrote, 'Whatever cutting and rearranging the Hakims may have done, the fragment that remains is still one of the most interesting, lively and exciting films to have been released in the past two or three years.' But the British critics were more hostile when the film opened in London in the summer of 1963. 'Something is always happening to Mr. Losey's films . . . and this knowledge is fast creating a climate in which the reviewer's function is subverted, by compassion and the fear of making a fool of himself (do we owe that enigmatic cut to Losey or alien scissors-men?), into a pussy-footing enumeration of the film's best bits, and here Mr. Losey comes to our aid by throwing up bits galore,' wrote the *New Statesman*'s critic. 'Enough of Mr. Losey's original *Eve* is surely left to prove to anyone that the cripple was never really healthy.' The *Financial Times* expressed regret that Losey's work 'has been seized on by the vocal, eccentric fringe of French intellectual criticism, not for argued appreciation but for dogmatic eulogy, for making a cult figure of Losey.'

Worse was to come from the Italians, where most critics expressed pleasure that it had been withdrawn from the Venice Festival – 'a good thing for everybody,' wrote *L'Unità*'s critic. *Corriere della Sera*'s critic concurred: 'One shudders to think that *Eva* was part of the programme and that some of us were disappointed when it was not shown,' he wrote, adding dismissively that the film was 'a rehash of Fellini, Antonioni, Visconti sewn together with Resnais gut.'

After the Paris opening, Losey and his collaborators wrote to Robert Hakim asking for their names to be removed from the film and for this demand to be given publicity. Hakim's reaction was to point out that their contracts forbade them from making any public statement that might damage the film. Later, Losey offered to restore the film to its original condition for nothing, but claimed that the Hakims said that the episodes cut from the film were lost. Robert Hakim has refused to make any comment on the matter.

Jeanne Moreau vowed never to work for the Hakims again, explaining that though she would be prepared to play even the smallest role for Losey, anywhere, any time, she would refuse even the greatest role offered by his betrayers. It is a pledge she has kept.

Losey's feelings of total betrayal by the Hakims over *Eve* were so deep that he subsequently fought above all else for absolute control over all his future projects. Even when working again for major American studios, he insisted on total control without compromise to studio insecurity or whim; moreover, in his view, he had earned the right to make these demands.

He summed up his feelings in *Movie* magazine of January 1963:

'Twenty-five minutes had been removed from the version that I think should have been *the* version of the picture. There were a great many things in the script from beginning to end which the producer didn't agree with, didn't like or didn't understand. He made it so difficult to shoot these sequences by not making locations and other facilities available, that the conditions of shooting finally made the results inferior in quality, at least so far as I was concerned. Having seen these sequences as shot, inferior as they were, he wanted them in the picture. I did not, so they are not in the picture, even though I think they should have been in, in terms of the original conception if they could have been shot right. There has been another kind of censorship exercised in relation to *Eve* and which is perhaps the bitterest of all. That is the post-synching of the Italian and French versions, which was done without any reference to me, the cutter, the writer or any of the actors concerned, excepting Jeanne Moreau in her own role in French. Whatever the producers didn't like or didn't understand they either left out or distorted or changed or added to, and this was true also with the sub-titles in French over the English version.'

Losey came near to being destroyed by the fiasco; his health suffered, as did his self-confidence, and it was to remain forever a bitter memory: 'One of the biggest opportunities of my life to make a personal statement was destroyed by a couple of peanut men.'

Happily, the setback was to prove only a temporary one, as Losey was about to embark on his most productive period to date, and to make a film that established him for all time among the first rank of film directors.

IX

The Making of *The Servant*

The initiation of Losey's next film began with another voice at the end of a telephone. One April evening, while he was still working on *Eve* in Rome, the phone rang in his hotel room. On the line was Dirk Bogarde, who was also filming in Rome. The two had remained friends since working together on *Sleeping Tiger* ten years earlier and had tried many times to find another, better project on which they could collaborate. Early on, Losey had suggested that a suitable subject might be *The Servant*, a novella written by Robin Maugham, nephew of Somerset Maugham. Telling of a young aristocrat being seduced and corrupted by a manservant, the book had caused a minor sensation on its publication in 1949. Maugham, heir to a viscountcy, admitted that it was in part autobiographical, and that his family had tried to persuade him not to publish it. But both director and star had been side-tracked by other films, and nothing more had come of the suggestion.

Now Bogarde was ringing to say that the British playwright Harold Pinter, currently famous for enigmatic stage plays, had written a film treatment of *The Servant*. Neither Losey nor Bogarde had any commitments after terminating their work in Italy, and the opportunity to work together on a project they both favoured seemed too good to ignore. Losey offered to ring a few people to see whether the rights were available and called back to say that Pinter's script had been commissioned by Michael Anderson.

Anderson, the British director of *Around The World in 80 Days* and *The Dam Busters*, had been unable to find any actor willing to play the lead or anyone prepared to finance the film, which he had budgeted at £250,000; he was willing to sell the script if the price was right. He and Losey agreed on a payment of £12,000, which was considerably more than he had paid Pinter.

Losey said that if Bogarde was really serious, he would start negotiations immediately on the basis that Bogarde would play the manservant, which would mark a departure from his usual young and glamorous roles. By September, Bogarde was sitting by the bay of Cannes with the script in his hands: 'The sand was hot, the beer iced, the rattan shades slatted shadows across the pages and made it difficult to read,' he writes. 'It was difficult enough anyway (I had never read Pinter before), but I knew instinctively, which is how I have always worked, that what I presently held in my sandy hands on the hot morning beach, was not merely a script, but rather a key. The key to a door in my long corridor, which only awaited the courage of my turning.'

The film was to mark a turning point in the lives of both Bogarde and Losey: they were to spend much of the next four years making four films together, each one of which, according to Bogarde, 'was a bitter, exhausting, desperate battle.' The beginning of *The Servant* was all of that, and more. No one wanted to finance the film. Bogarde's manager and lifelong companion, Tony Forwood, was concerned about the film's homosexual theme. Losey and Pinter were to have an abrasive first meeting over tea at the Connaught Hotel. There were difficulties in casting the two other main roles: the young, corruptible aristocrat and the sexually voracious girl, the manservant's mistress, who first seduces him.

Losey needed the stimulus of work to assuage the nagging pain of exile that still troubled him. This, and the relentless pressure of his normal paranoia, contributed to his belief that he would always feel a foreigner wherever he was; as Salman Rushdie expresses it in his *Satanic Verses*: 'Paranoia for the exile is a prerequisite of survival.' He had returned to London and his little house in Flood Street profoundly unhappy and defeated. *The Servant*, with its overtones of the legend of Faust and its dissection of the English class system, excited him. Yet, at his gloomiest, alone in his home, he felt at one with Mephistopheles in Christopher Marlowe's *Dr Faustus*, crying in anguish, 'Why, this is hell, nor am I out of it.' Angela Fox, the wife of his agent Robin Fox, perceived two distinct sides in Losey: 'To dine with him was to be with a dull, groaning, humourless American; but on the set he was a creative, authoritative, brilliant and positive director.'

He had already interested Norman (Spike) Priggen, with whom he was to work many times again, in producing *The Servant*. Though believing unswervingly in the talents of both Losey and Bogarde, Priggen had dire misgivings about the commercial possibilities of this strange and moody story of class and moral corruption. The enterprise seemed fraught with doubts and potential pitfalls. Bogarde speaks now of 'wrestling' *The Servant* to the screen. Amid all the uncertainties, however, a series of coincidences gave them hope and encouragement.

Losey was exceptionally close to Robin Fox, who was both his and Bogarde's agent. Although their backgrounds were vastly different – Fox was an elegant, upper-class old Harrovian Englishman – both were compulsive womanizers. Angela Fox admits that she and Losey never liked each other. Finding her neither sexually nor professionally interesting, he treated her dismissively, as he tended to do with the wives of men he adored. In turn, she found him heavy, gloomy, and physically unattractive. This, however, has not inhibited her ability to perceive, appreciate, and admire his professional qualities. 'My husband, Robin, loved all his clients, but he and Joe literally adored each other, so Joe was always around. Robin always had faith in Joe's absolute brilliance, but to me, he was a pompous, overbearing bore – a real provincial horror. Not a glimmer of humour, and for me, no charm.'

Fortunately, Fox was a partner in the Grade Organisation with Leslie Grade, one of three brothers – the others were Bernard Delfont and Lew Grade – who between them controlled much of British showbusiness, from theatres to cinema and television. Leslie Grade had begun to involve himself in films through the production company Elstree Distributors. He first boosted the career of Cliff Richard in two locally successful musicals, *Summer Holiday* and *The Young Ones* (which earned back its cost in its first three weeks), and then helped finance *Sparrows Can't Sing*, which Joan Littlewood directed, based on her successful stage production for Theatre Workshop. Grade offered to put up the money for *The Servant*, provided it cost no more than £150,000, of which Bogarde's salary would be around £7,000. Now all Losey had to do was to find the rest of the cast.

Everyone involved knew that, if the film was to have any chance of success, a bankable actress was needed to play opposite Bogarde. With his quite extraordinary gift for sniffing out the right talent at the right moment, Losey decided that the ideal choice was the eighteen-year-old Sarah Miles, who had caused a sensation as the flirtatious schoolgirl who tries to seduce Laurence Olivier's schoolmaster in *Term of Trial*. Bogarde was also well aware that Sarah Miles (who was to become the epitome of London's 'swinging sixties') was the ideal choice, but doubted – following her triumph with Olivier – that she would accept as modest an assignment as the one they were offering. But they had one factor in their favour: Fox and Leslie Grade were her agents, too.

Then, switching on the television one night to see the news, Bogarde by chance tuned in to the wrong channel, and found himself watching a one-act play of minimal interest, except for the sudden appearance of a young man who instantly struck him as the one actor they must have for the third member of their dramatic triangle: the aristocratic Tony. The actor was tall and golden-haired, with a diffident charm and dazzling smile. His name, according to the cast list, was Maurice Oliver.

Bogarde immediately phoned Losey, who also tuned in and agreed that he was ideal. The next day Bogarde rang Robin Fox to announce the good news. After a long pause, Fox said, 'I can't let you do it. The boy can't act.' Bogarde disagreed, saying that both he and Losey had seen him on television and were determined to have him. 'I can't let you go on,' Fox interrupted. 'You see, Maurice Oliver is actually my son, James.'

When it became clear that his two clients were quite determined, Fox acquiesced. Losey had some doubts as to whether the relatively inexperienced James would be able to cope with the subtle and difficult role of Tony. As William Fox (he is still known to those close to him as 'Willie'), James had been the child star of the forgettable Ealing comedy *The Magnet* in 1950, and had played a small role as an even smaller child in *The Miniver Story*, the sequel to that treasured wartime classic, *Mrs. Miniver*. But his adult acting experience was limited. Having left the Coldstream Guards to study at the Central School of Speech and Drama, he had appeared in only one movie, playing a minor part as a public-school boy who wins the race in *The Loneliness of the Long Distance Runner*.

The next coincidence came with the discovery that James Fox was involved in a three-and-a-half-year-old affair with Sarah Miles, and was actually living with her. At the premiere of *The L-Shaped Room*, one of the movies which, at the time, seemed to mark a new maturity in British cinema, Bogarde and Losey found themselves sitting just behind the two lovers. Bogarde, who had not wanted to come to the opening, having been dragged there by Tony Forwood for diplomatic reasons, testifies that if he'd had any lingering doubts, they were totally dispelled on seeing them together at the theatre. He approached the pair after the showing, and invited them to meet Losey at the Connaught the following day.

During that meeting, all the problems which had hitherto beset the production melted away, although Fox found Losey grumpy, full of tales of woe, and still complaining to anyone who would listen about the way the Hakim brothers had massacred *Eve*. He looked, Fox recalled later, like an asthmatic, intellectual Red Indian Chief without the feathers. Sarah disabused Losey and Bogarde of their belief that she had not liked the script and was otherwise committed; she declared, on the contrary, that she was mad about it, adding, 'and wouldn't he (Fox) be super as Tony?' In fact, Sarah, who was ever a strong-minded girl, convinced of the reliability of her instincts, said that she would only accept the role of Vera if Willie was offered the part of Tony. A jubilant round of Bloody Marys was had by all to celebrate the triumph of faith over economics.

It only remained to cast the part of Susan, Tony's fiancée. Bogarde quickly suggested Wendy Craig, an actress he much admired and had worked with a few months before on *The Mind Benders*, a thriller about political brainwashing. Miss Craig had already achieved an impressive list of stage credits and plaudits from such acerbic critics as Kenneth Tynan, who pronounced her 'one of the six best young actresses in the Western world'. She was to add an unmistakable lustre to the film, though Losey was to blame her, quite unjustly, for some of its failings.

'I think it's fair to say,' muses Willie Fox, 'that Dirk really cast that film and set it all up. I certainly wouldn't have met Joe had it not been for that evening and being with Sarah. I know some people must think that my father – who, after all, was acting as agent for all these people at the time – must have been the one who set me up, but quite the reverse is true. He didn't even think I had that much potential. That's why I was using another name for work.'

*

With the aid of Robin Maugham, Losey plunged into the world depicted in the novella: that of the slightly seedy but indubitably upper-class *demi-monde*. This introduction to another stratum of English life came at a time when he was open enough to absorb it. He had been away nearly two years working on *Eve*, and when he returned it was with a much greater assuredness and insight about the people he studied. Gradually, he had to admit to being less of a stranger in England. Somehow, London was beginning to feel like home.

The film was shot in a house in Royal Avenue, Chelsea, opposite Maugham's and minutes from Losey's own, which Richard MacDonald decorated in the style of a London club, with leather armchairs and a homocentric atmosphere. They hung some of Maugham's own paintings on the walls to create a suitably aristocratic ambience.

Once they got down to business, Losey found that working with Pinter was as rewarding as his relationship with MacDonald, and for much the same reasons. He had always maintained that MacDonald's pre-designing could almost supplant the contribution made by a first-class screen-writer, throwing him back on himself and his visual imagination. He found that having to do without words was enriching to the visual sense, and he came to welcome cinematic situations where they could be eliminated, except for use in extraordinary ways. With Pinter, words were few in any case, and when used often meant the reverse of what they seemed to mean. He quickly learned how to give Losey a 'frame' where the words evoked a whole series of images, precipitating them one upon the other.

Reginald Mills, Losey's shrewd and skilful editor, was not so happy with Pinter's work. In an issue of *Isis*, which was devoted to examining *The Servant* in great detail (an indication of the film's intellectual importance at the time), he said: 'Scripts are not usually so thorough these days, because they're so often written by people who, with all due respect, are like Harold Pinter, whose script was more like a story with dialogue. I think that Pinter should write the libretto for an opera. He repeats everything about six times. Think what he could do with "I love you". I cut out a lot of his lines, and I'm sure he never knew: it just meant one repetition less.' Pinter's riposte to Mills' article was virtually unprintable.

Losey approached the making of *The Servant* in a mood of panic. The failure of *Eve*, combined as it was with what seemed the end of his always stormy relationship with Ruth Lipton, had left him depressed. He was filled with doubt about his abilities as a director. What if *The Servant* failed, too? His self-confidence – always shaky – had sunk. He asked Patricia to come back to work with him after she'd had her baby, confiding to her that he really didn't have the slightest idea how to make a start, let alone what he was going to do with the movie. Patricia said that she would come as soon as she was able to leave the child. He also decided to ask Ruth to return for one last attempt at picking up the pieces and making things work out between them.

The winter of 1962–3, when the filming of *The Servant* began, was the coldest that London had endured for a decade, and Losey was soon overcome yet again by his asthma. Feeling both morally and physically destroyed, he began to miss Ruth's strong and reassuring presence. Knowing, however, that he had probably exhausted her reserves of compassion and forgiveness the last time around, he cajoled someone else to ring her with horrific tales of his sufferings. The impression given was that he was on his deathbed. Since Ruth was not only still in love with Losey but convinced that his illnesses were inevitably brought on by her frequent attempts to terminate their relationship, the ploy worked, and she took the next plane from New York to London. When she arrived, she was met at Heathrow by one of the film crew who told her that Losey was too ill to make the journey to the airport, and within days of beginning to shoot the film, he had succumbed to bronchial pneumonia and was unable to get out of bed. Ruth arrived to find him thoroughly weakened by the stressful months of battles, raised hopes and crushing disappointments.

Ironically, his pneumonia was contracted not as a result of Ruth's defection, but during a pre-Christmas romp with John Dankworth and Cleo Laine at their house at Wavendon in Bedfordshire, an outing which combined a favourite venue with fond company. Having enjoyed a good lunch, and lulled into the belief that they had miraculously regained their youth, they had romped around the snow-covered grounds of Wavendon where they had engaged in a snowball fight. Losey declared that he had never felt better in his life; several days later, he lay at death's door.

*

Dankworth's moody and evocative music represents a considerable advance over *Blind Date, The Criminal,* and *Eve* in Losey's use of jazz in his films. Here the music not only establishes the general atmosphere of the film in the haunting, opening saxophone sextet, but defines and reinforces character as well, with each character having his or her own theme associated with a particular sound or instrument.

The music is integrated into the film by punctuating the action with Cleo Laine singing, in different styles, a song called *Leave It Alone, It's All Gone,* for which Pinter wrote the words. Dankworth complained bitterly that Pinter was no lyric writer. 'Luckily, Harold didn't try to write any lyrics for *Accident,*' he says. 'His lyrics for *The Servant* were virtually incomprehensible. I tried to get him to amend them so that it could work as a commercial song later on, independent of the film, but he wouldn't.

'Joe wasn't really very musical. He'd use the word "atonal", but I doubt he really knew what that meant. I recorded the theme of *The Servant* and Joe said, "Well, I can't be sure I like it because I've never liked Hammond organs." So I said, "That's not the instrument you're going to hear it on in the film, and that's not a Hammond organ, but a violin." He had no ear at all, which I guess is why he was never much good at learning languages. Good thing he had Patricia around.'

As important as choosing the right actors was the next stage – finding the best cinematographer. Losey chose one of the greatest, Douglas Slocombe, who had learned his craft at Ealing Studios, where he worked for seventeen years, filming such comedy classics as *Kind Hearts and Coronets, The Lavender Hill Mob,* and *The Man in the White Suit.* The two had never met, and Slocombe swears that he had no idea where Losey came upon his name. The previous year, Slocombe had worked in Munich for John Huston on *Freud,* starring Montgomery Clift, and many of his techniques turn up in both films. Slocombe was delighted to be offered *The Servant,* because he believed that Losey was one of the greatest artists in black and white, his own favoured medium – 'More art in it,' he explains.

Wendy Craig describes Slocombe's vision as being possibly the closest to Losey's own. 'He seemed to actually see through Joe's eyes, as if he was standing behind him, looking through the back of his head.' However, Bogarde felt that Slocombe was at his wit's end half the time, because of the extraordinary technical demands

Losey made upon him, and remembers the cameraman raging and stamping on the set, wailing in his stuttering voice, 'I'm being directed by a l-l-lunatic! I'm being asked to do things no one can do,' tears of frustration pouring down his face. By the end of the film, he thought that working for Losey had been the most extraordinary experience of his life, that he'd done things he thought he couldn't do, and had survived the challenge a wiser man.

'Well, Dirk tends to exaggerate a bit now and then,' Slocombe counters. 'I won't deny that Joe was demanding but I understood him, and loved the challenge. I found him very meticulous, very careful, first in describing the script, pointing out all the inner meanings he hoped would come out. He was very strong on atmosphere, and tried to imbue me with a feeling for it. In *The Servant*, he concentrated on the house being claustrophobic, like a womb, with people literally locked together without really understanding each other.'

The effect was achieved by tracking shots, in which the characters appeared overwhelmed by their surroundings; the shifting movements of the camera conveyed the moral ambivalence in which they moved. Losey liked to film scenes in one uninterrupted take without resorting to editing: chopping it up with long-shots, mid-shots, close-ups and so on. Slocombe believes that this is one of the areas in which Losey's theatre training came into play: 'Most importantly for his cameramen, Losey never cut a film in such a way as to put their work in jeopardy. He had the courage of his convictions, even though he would sometimes appear to be slightly slow, even laboured. But this was an integral part of his particular style of story-telling. He had the guts to allow the camera to linger, to let a mood communicate itself to the audience. Losey's films often demanded especially slow pans by the camera, perhaps around one or more empty rooms, which helped to create a mesmeric, sinister atmosphere.'

Typically, Losey's commendation of Slocombe bears that occasional, slightly patronizing reserve, claiming, as usual, that he rescued Slocombe from 'bad times', and put him back on his feet. He also contended that, although Slocombe was a first-class cameraman, who understood perfectly what he was after 'in terms of mirrors that reflect mirrors that reflect the camera, and of big, circular shots', there was nothing in *The Servant* to compare with the difficulties that Di Venanzo had faced in *Eve*.

Losey's confinement to bed, a few days after beginning work on the film, terrified him. Telephoning frequently, Bogarde became increasingly alarmed at hearing the weak, agonized voice whispering down the phone, pathetically worried that the illness would cause a fatal delay in the shooting, and perhaps even precipitate cancellation by the producers. There was only one solution, the voice rasped: Bogarde should take Losey's place until he was better, phoning every day to receive instructions.

So Bogarde assumed control of a fiercely loyal cast and crew, while Ruth acted as secretary-cum-nurse at home. During much of this time, Patricia flitted back and forth between Rome and London, but stayed away from the house itself while Ruth was defending the territory.

For ten days Bogarde directed the film, with almost hourly calls to Losey's bedside for explicit and detailed instructions, which he never failed to give, however ill. Neither Bogarde's authority nor his decisions were ever doubted, nor did he stray from Losey's style, and the work proceeded at a good pace. The cast and crew threw themselves into the job of saving the work of a man they respected to the point of reverence, which Bogarde declared to be one of the most extraordinary expressions of loyalty and devotion he had ever witnessed in what he calls 'a sometimes tawdry profession'.

When Losey – gaunt, grey and painfully weak – staggered back to work far too soon and against Dr Cooper's express wishes, the heartfelt applause which greeted his arrival deeply moved him, though he was not normally a sentimental man. Lying on an iron bed, smothered in blankets and a long woollen scarf which Wendy Craig had knitted for him, surrounded by hot water bottles, he proceeded to get on with the job. The only concession he made to his state of health was that the smokers among them were asked to refrain, since the smoke made him cough.

Losey hired stage director Vivian Matalon to coach and support the inexperienced James Fox so that he could feel more confident among the others, though both Bogarde and Wendy Craig were immensely generous with encouragement and advice. He also had Fox's hair bleached very blond. Immensely protective, he began film-ing the first scene in which Fox appears with a circular movement of the camera behind Tony's chair, concealing his face until they were well into the long, seven-minute sequence. Fox attributes this to Losey's sensitivity to his nerves, his youth, and general greenness: 'He didn't really talk to me all that much,' Fox says. 'It was more intuitive with him. I wouldn't say that he profoundly influenced my understanding of the role, but it was the sheer artistic commitment to me, and to the piece in general, the ideas behind what he was saying – and that was through his talking. He was so passionately convinced of what this story meant – the parable, the metaphor.

'Where Joe stimulated me was in this extraordinary view, this particularly American view. After all, I came from this theatrical family and a very British background, Harrow and all that. Then he came along and exposed me to all these political, psychological, sociological and sexual things – through this story – which was truly enriching. We English aren't brought up or educated to know about these sorts of things. Sort of embarrassed by it, you know.'

Bogarde explains that Losey never told an actor whose talent he trusted what to do, or how to do it – only what not to do. 'He preferred to watch the actor as he developed a character: encouraging or modifying, but always taking what was offered and using it deftly. No one knew whether what they had done was to their director's ultimate satisfaction, however, until he said, "Print!" at the end of a take. There was no waste of chatter, no protracted, in-depth discussions about motivation, identification, soul, or truth. That would have been dealt with well beforehand, if necessary. On set they were allowed to simply get on with the job.'

Bogarde summarizes the perceptions and feelings of a great many actors and actresses who have grown and prospered under Losey, highlighting the vast differences in style and approach between Losey and almost everybody else: the speed at which he worked, without denying time for inspiration and developing emotion, the liberality and trust he showed for his actors: 'No frantic cry from the Script Girl that a scene, a speech, a move even, had overrun its time; it was a sublime luxury,' he wrote in his first volume of reminiscences, *Snakes and Ladders*.

Losey understood that each of those who depended on him for guidance needed to be handled differently, and would respond differently. They were allowed to guard their individuality; no one would ever be described as a 'Losey actor'. The majority of those who thrived, however, under Losey's unique, laissez-faire methods had one important thing in common: they were experienced and established professionals, upon whose craft and expertise Losey relied as much as they did on his. He could be very different with those who fell somewhat short of this description (as Jacqueline Sassard was to discover during the filming of *Accident*).

Ostensibly, *The Servant* is about the tortured relationship between a well-born man of property and his manservant. But, upon this deceptively simple tale of class antagonism, Losey and Pinter construct a multi-layered allegory with social and psychological implications that reach well beyond the metaphor of the British social system.

Like Pinter's plays of that era, *The Birthday Party* and *The Caretaker*, the film's basic theme was a struggle for power. To this he added a brooding sexual menace that was to surface in his later plays. The novel by Maugham had been based on an attempted homosexual seduction of him by a manservant and a youth who claimed to be his nephew. The boy became Vera, the servant's supposed sister, in the retelling of the story, with the battle over the indolent upper-class Tony (James Fox) being fought between the servant Barrett (Bogarde) and Tony's fiancée Susan (Wendy Craig).

Barrett, obsequious and attentive, becomes indispensable and introduces Vera (Sarah Miles) into the house so that she can seduce Tony and thus consolidate Barrett's power over him. When Tony and Susan return early from a weekend in the country and find Barrett in bed with Vera, Tony orders them both from the house.

Left on his own, Tony is helpless. His withdrawal from Susan is almost total. Then he meets Barrett in the local pub. In a scene which represents some of the subtlest, most skilful acting in Bogarde's distinguished career, Barrett pleads successfully to be allowed to return. Tony's degradation has begun. He drinks heavily and Barrett introduces him to drugs. The pair play terrifying games of domination, conquest, and submission.

Susan and Vera each make one final visit to this increasingly inverted household, where a strong element of homosexuality has developed, liberated by the drink and other toxic substances, and surfacing in some of Barrett's games. Susan, hoping to stake one final claim to Tony, turns up at one of the late-night parties which Barrett has taken to staging. Finally Barrett expels Susan along with the other guests, but she asserts her place in the social hierarchy by smacking Barrett across the face as she goes, leaving him and his ruined ex-master alone in sole possession of the house.

From today's perspective, the final 'orgy' scene (as it came to be known), which establishes Barrett as a satanic purveyor of immorality and decadence, is relatively tame: a bunch of over-dressed sybarites, either too drunk or too stoned to be able to talk, ogle each other blearily and blow smoke into one another's faces, presided over by the evil Barrett. *The Servant* was, nevertheless, only the second British film to deal frankly with homosexuality before the de-criminalization Act of 1967. The first had been *Victim*, made two years earlier by Basil Dearden, which again starred Bogarde, as a distinguished QC who falls prey to a gang of blackmailers because of his latent homosexual leanings. Maugham had been assured by the film censors, when he initiated the project with Harold Pinter, that a film of *The Servant* could never be made in his lifetime. As it was, the homosexual overtones were oblique when compared to the novella, where Barrett is blatantly gay.

Those were the 'square' years in America, when many of Losey's contemporaries, such as Nick Ray, had been making movies like *Bigger Than Life*, (featuring James Mason, Barbara Rush, and the budding talents of young Walter Matthau), in which men worked themselves into an untimely grave for the loyal and homely family, and the 'little woman' stayed at home with an apron shielding her ballerina-length skirt, to bake a pie for her devoted hubby and cute, wholesome kids. The happy ending, moreover, was virtually obliga-tory, whereas *The Servant* – hardly designed to lift the spirits, though an unexpected masterpiece – was one of the earliest films to break the mould.

With hindsight, and enjoying the maturity and sophistication acquired over the twenty-five years since *The Servant* emerged, James Fox distrusts some of the assumptions formed through Losey's typically American, psychological approach. He doubts, for example, that Tony was from the start a latent homosexual just waiting to be discovered, which Losey linked to the young man's education at an English public school.

Fox, a public schoolboy himself, believes that Losey exaggerated this point in the film: 'My view is that what appealed to Tony was simply having someone to provide for him, wait on him hand and foot. Let's face it, Barrett is not attractive, and you can't see a Tony getting off with someone revolting like that, unless he's bent in a certain way or wants to be abused by ugliness. No, he was into Vera

– into screwing the maid. I mean, that's classic! Joe remained what I've always imagined to be the typical American Puritan. None of us can actually overcome our background, can we?'

Once Losey was back, there were no further serious problems, apart from a clash between him and the strong-willed Sarah Miles. She objected to the costume James Fox was wearing in their most notorious love-scene; a short dressing gown and a pair of Losey's fur-lined boots, which had made the rounds, having been worn by Stanley Baker in *Eve*. Sarah thought her lover looked ludicrous, and refused to play the scene; Fox felt a bit foolish in the boots himself, which reinforced his prevailing sense of insecurity to no good effect.

Losey was furious, both at having his authority questioned and at having Fox's confidence undermined. He ordered Sarah to her dressing-room to reconsider. While she fumed, Losey called in Robin Fox to mediate, which the latter found awkward, since they were all his clients, and one was his son. Eventually, it was agreed that James should play the scene barefoot.

'I suppose Sarah can be a bit naughty,' says Wendy Craig, 'but Joe was normally not what you would call unkind and certainly never to me. I did see it once, but only to get the performance.' This was the last scene of the film, when Losey insisted on putting painful drops in Fox's eyes, over her strong objections, because Tony had to be crying and in pain at that moment. But Fox had accepted the situation with grace, as had the twelve-year-old Dean Stockwell so long ago in Hollywood, when Losey was as green as the boy's hair.

Wendy Craig had been drawn to Losey from their first meeting – tea at the Hyde Park Hotel – but she'd been a bit disappointed by his appearance, which was rendered shabbier in contrast to their surroundings and belied Losey's sartorial reputation. 'Everything he had was very expensive,' she noted, 'but I think he wanted mainly to be comfortable. And he was very serious.' It was not until twenty-two years later, when she read Michel Ciment's *Conversations With Losey*, that she discovered that Losey had not been entirely satisfied with her performance. 'Wendy Craig was miscast,' Losey said. 'I must say that, considering she was miscast, and that I tried to revise the script to suit her miscasting a little bit, she did very nobly. She should have been very upper class.'

Wendy was hurt and upset by these remarks. 'I feel betrayed,' she said. 'I loved working with Joe, respected him greatly, and was very fond of him. And I know he was very fond of me too – that's why these remarks hurt.' In Losey's world betrayal was always an option, but Wendy was able to see beneath the surfaces into the reasons: 'I felt that he was constantly battling: between his body and his mind, the body so ill and the mind so active. There was a terrible struggle going on, which I found very moving. I felt very protective towards him; he brought out the maternal in one. When you see someone gasping for breath all the time, and the tremendous effort he put into his work – there's a very special quality there that needs boosting and protecting. I knitted him an incredibly long, woollen scarf, and he was so pleased with it. Wore it all the time, wrapped around his poor throat and trailing right down.

'I always tried to be cheerful, pleasant, and helpful, and get exactly what he wanted, but obviously I didn't. "Did nobly"! That's an absolute put-down to me. He only had to tell me what he wanted, and I would have done it. I am, after all, a perfectly competent actress. Perhaps he was confused himself about how to direct the role.'

The problem is not with Wendy Craig's performance but with Pinter and Losey's treatment of the character. As the critic Penelope Gilliatt pointed out (she commended Losey on having more insight into the awful intricacies of the English class system than any American), the character wavered 'between a confident, Pont Street loudmouth,and an outwitted provincial'.

Losey later cited *The Servant* as 'the beginning of a career for Sarah Miles and for James Fox, the first real recognition for Richard MacDonald, and a turning point in the career of Dirk Bogarde'. Though no one denies the truth of Losey's evaluation relative to the last three, Sarah Miles may be forgiven for calling him to account. 'Good Lord! He was cheeky to say that. I'd just done *Term of Trial* with Larry Olivier, and I got all the reviews! They said I wiped him off the screen. So, not only was I quite heavily initiated into stardom from that first film, but Joe was certainly not doing me any favours.'

It was one thing to get *The Servant* made; it was quite another to get it shown. Leslie Grade hated it. 'I thought it was revolting,' he said after attending a preview. No one was prepared to give it a showing, finding it obscure and even obscene, and naturally, too uncommercial. It was left on the shelf to gather dust. It seemed as though the entire endeavour had been in vain.

Losey, though, was not prepared to let his work languish. Whenever he met anyone who showed the slightest interest, he would take the film off the shelf to screen it at private cinemas which he hired. The reactions from these audiences gave him so much confidence that he grew bolder and carried his packages to Paris, where he had an influential friend in Florence Malraux, who had worked as script consultant on *Eve*. As the daughter of André Malraux and the wife of Alain Resnais, she was able to set up screenings for influential people, who began to gossip enthusiastically about the film.

The Servant was shown at the Venice Film Festival in September 1963, where it met a lukewarm reception from continental critics. Two weeks later it was shown at the New York Film Festival, but still no distributor showed any interest in it.

Then Losey got lucky. Arthur Abeles, head of Warner Brothers in Europe, had a gap to fill at the company's London cinema in Leicester Square. He examined the pile of previously rejected films, chose *The Servant* and soon became one of its most enthusiastic supporters.

The Servant reached the British cinema at a fortuitous moment, being released in November, just after the scandal had broken surrounding the Profumo affair, in which a top-ranking Conservative politician admitted that he had lied to the House of Commons in denying his affair with the young model, Christine Keeler. As *The Observer*'s critic Philip French observed, '*The Servant* was being privately screened as the Profumo affair emerged in public view. When it opened in 1963, the film uncannily echoed the obsessive themes and occasions of the preceding months.'

Patrick Gibbs wrote in *The Daily Telegraph*, 'Many of the Continental critics were so set against Joseph Losey's *The Servant* after its showing at the Venice Festival that I wondered if I had not been over-enthusiastic in my notice. This second view leaves me sticking to my guns.' The *Financial Times* concurred, 'It is interesting that Joseph Losey, whose most enthusiastic supporters are found among those critics who tend dogmatically to rate *mise-en-scène* over argument in films, should have made his best film from the best-composed screenplay he has been given for a long time. This is not, all the same, to underrate his virtues as *metteur-en-scène*. Each shot is firmly composed, both for its decorative values and dramatic values in a way that Eisenstein could applaud.'

Philip Oakes, in *The Sunday Telegraph*, pulled out all the stops, and declared that *The Servant* was 'the best film of the best director now working in Britain – a work of steady and composed brilliance in which every asset . . . has been made to declare a dividend . . . In the past Losey's problem has been how to inject life into dull, contracted subjects. His solution has usually been to decorate the surface to make it look interesting (*Eve*). *The Servant* has no need of this . . . but habit, like indulgence, is hard to break, and the last quarter hour of the film (the 'orgy' scene) is given over to a virtuoso display of camera angles and special effects as irritating as they are superficial . . . the other Losey . . . must learn to keep this Losey in check.'

Bogarde threw a lavish party at the Connaught to celebrate their success. Looking across the crowded room, he thought that Losey looked like a weary sage on Speech Day as he stood surrounded by congratulating acolytes, glass held tightly in both hands, head bowed to listen to constant questions and praise.

At the height of this evening of triumph and hyperbole, Basil Dearden suddenly sank to his knees in homage to Losey, and asked the secret of making a masterpiece. 'I can't answer when you are down there,' Losey had replied. 'First of all you take your son away from Eton, sell all Melissa's furs, get rid of the house and the pool, get rid of the cars, pack a couple of suitcases and move into a small flat and think things over. No overheads, Basil; just the films.'

Theo Cowan, who had been Head of Publicity at Rank when Bogarde had begun his career and now acted as press agent for both Bogarde and Losey, was asked what he thought *The Servant*'s chances were outside London. This was his first assignment as an independent publicity man, so the success of the film was important to him. 'Slender,' he had managed to say, between mouthfuls of smoked salmon, and with his usual devastating candour. They all knew that what pleased the critics and the sophisticated urbanites often bored or offended provincial audiences, who could make the difference as to whether a film ultimately succeeded commercially or failed.

'We didn't do a lot of hype on *The Servant*,' Cowan explains, 'because it was a special, elite audience anyway, and there wouldn't have been any point. The film was its own best publicity. Joe was an ideal client; there was a lot of mutual respect. He was a good friend too, a good mix of both. I knew that he was quality, even though I'd never make my fortune with him. Unlike a lot of Losey's other films, *The Servant* gave him a piece of the action, so for once I guess he made some money.'

Not everyone was equally enthusiastic. Sarah Miles's parents saw the film at a preview and threatened to disown her, though they changed their mind after reading the reviews. James Fox's mother Angela was appalled to see her son playing a weak and degenerate playboy, and phoned Losey with hysterical abuse. 'You're just being stupid. That's the guy he is,' Losey retorted.

James views it all as rather a joke. 'My mother was outraged. Went out and kicked the dustbins or something. But she learned a lesson too, and accepted it eventually. Well, she was also an actress in her time.'

'I was furious about James's role,' Angela admits, 'and I bloody well did kick the dustbins! But when I confronted Joe about it, he said – and I now know that he was absolutely right – that James couldn't have played that part so convincingly if there hadn't been some of it in him. I was livid at first, but as his mother, I didn't know James at all. Saw what I wanted to, like most mothers. But, you see, this is exactly what happened when James finally went out to Hollywood, what he became for a time. Joe had this great talent for seeing into people, and that's why he could get these great performances out of them. I consider that both my sons owe their present success to the fact that the only person who absolutely recognized whatever gifts they may have, the depths and the extent of their talents, was Joseph Losey.

'I went to a party that Joe gave after *The Servant* was finished. I didn't want to go, but Robin insisted. It was one of those studio things, you know, fairly scruffy, champagne out of tooth mugs – that sort of thing – and for the first time I absolutely got the entire message of Joe Losey. He was utterly worshipped by all his people. He knew them all, and he was relaxed and his own man. He became a dynamic and attractive person when in his own, professional environment. That's when I most admired Joe: when he was working. He was magic then, a near genius.'

When the film reached New York, the American reviews were

as enthusiastic as the British. Richard Roud, in *New York* magazine, called it a masterpiece and, after praising Bogarde's and Fox's
acting and Pinter's script, added 'but the film belongs to Losey'. The
New York Times picked up on its social relevance. 'If you think the
Profumo scandal sheds a seamy and shocking light on what is said
to be a rather general crumbling of the British upper crust, wait until
you see *The Servant*,' wrote Bosley Crowther. 'There are here some
shattering implications of many dismal things that have taken place
in British and Continental society since World War II, and Mr. Losey
and his cast convey them in vivid and subtle terms.'

The French were predictably ecstatic, with Gérard Legrand of
Positif raving that, with the emergence of this *chef d'oeuvre*, Losey
had now been decisively adopted by Europe once and for all, while
France Observateur pronounced *The Servant* Losey's best film ever
– a wonderful culmination of intentions after the crippling failure
of *Eve*. Paul Mayersberg and Mark Shivas devoted ten pages in
Cahiers du Cinéma to *The Servant*, including an interview with
Losey, weighted with nuance and analysis.

The Servant went on to be celebrated as the best British film
of 1963, and Losey and his three stars shone brightly in the cinema
firmament. He was now one of the most highly paid, and highly
regarded, directors in Britain.*

---

*By early 1991 the gurus of cinema had demonstrated their belief in the im-
portance of Losey's work by including a display of memorabilia relative to
The Servant in the general historic collection at MOMI (Museum of the Moving
Image) at London's South Bank. Very few individual directors are so honoured in
this unique museum, a fact which would not have been lost on Losey himself, and
would surely have brought him deep satisfaction.

There, in a glass case which includes costumes from *Lawrence of Arabia* and *A
Room With a View*, may be found letters between Losey and Pinter on the script,
and indeed an early draft of the script itself, with annotations by the two men, as
well as a model of the famous convex mirror which reflected the tormented images
of Fox and Bogarde in the most famous of all the available still photos.

X

On Holiday from Harold

Gripped by terrible fears whenever he wasn't working, Losey continued to ponder the dozens of projects in the planning stages, being discussed, which he championed unceasingly. He reckoned that for every ten films he initiated, one actually got made, with more than seventy aborted in the later stages of development during his thirty-seven years as a director. 'He was never just sitting around,' affirms Ros Chatto, the theatrical agent who worked for Robin Fox from the beginning. 'Joe was completely active all the time. He literally created work. There were always several secretaries typing away. Joe was a compulsive letter writer. If he had one major fault, it was that he was an intolerant man, because his own standards were so high. If something displeased him, there's no way he wasn't going to say it, then follow it up with a letter saying it again. He simply wouldn't step down, or lower his standards.' As a result, during the years of his exile from 1951 to 1984, the longest period he languished between films was three years, and that came towards the end of his career. Between the making of *Don Giovanni* in 1979 to *The Trout* in 1982, his vitality began to flag, as illness engulfed him.

The end of Losey's affair with Ruth Lipton was echoed in the final scenes of *The Servant*; their conclusive argument resulted in Ruth storming out of the house into the snow, just as Susan had done, and returning to New York for good. However, during the two years between the start of his work on *Eve* and the final triumph of *The Servant*, Losey had become increasingly dependent upon, and enamoured of, Patricia Taluso, whose own marriage had come adrift, due in part to her husband having become violent, often beating her so badly that she was hospitalized. The sculptress Beverly Pepper remembers visiting Patricia's sickbed after one attack which had been provoked by Taluso's discovery of his wife's unprofessional attachment to Losey. Patricia literally feared for her life, so when she felt secure in Losey's affection for her, she fled, even though she was obliged by both circumstances and the law to leave her two babies in Rome with their Italian father. Arriving in London with a limited number of possessions, and committing herself to Losey's love and care, she moved into Flood Street.

In the summer of 1963, exhausted from the combined exigencies of *Eve* and *The Servant*, Losey decided to decamp with Patricia to a characteristically grand hotel on the beach at Cabourg, an ancient village on the Brittany coast, taking along Dr Cooper, Cooper's daughter Vicky, who was a friend of Joshua's, and George Tabori, with whom he hoped to work on a screenplay. Cooper remembers how appalling the holiday was: 'Wind, sand, boredom, booze, and arguments – everybody arguing with everybody else: Patricia and Joe argued silently, George and Joe overtly, I with everybody in general, because I was so bored and pissed off.' Losey wanted to collaborate with Tabori on a screenplay based on *The Intruders*, a novel by Georges Simenon. But Tabori, more interested in pursuing women and wine, failed to carry it off with his usual easy brilliance, and the script was pronounced a disaster by Losey, provoking another series of arguments. The holiday ended in total fiasco.

Undaunted, Losey set out for America to present *The Servant* at the New York Film Festival and to discover whether he could end his long exile by directing a film derived from William Faulkner's *Wild Palms*, a novel dealing with subjects close to him: the Depression, the Mississippi River, Chicago and the daunting Mid-western winters of his own youth. He wrote copious notes, scribbling ideas down in minute detail, but he failed to find a writer, and the project was abandoned. Following the success of *The Servant* he recognized that he would do well to concentrate on further cultivating the combined talents of Pinter, Bogarde, and himself.

While casting about for a suitable subject, he came upon a John Wilson play, based on a true story by James Lonsdale Hodson, an Army officer who had defended a shell-shocked soldier executed in the First World War for deserting his regiment. Compared with most of Losey's other work, the tale of the tragically doomed soldier, Hamp, is simple and straightforward, though critical of the Establishment, the British class system and the idiocy and evil of war itself.

The film was brought to him by Danny Angel of British Home Entertainment, a company that made low-budget films for cinema and television release. The cost was £86,000 and Losey filmed it at Shepperton Studios in under three weeks, with the sound stages reeking with imported mud, rats, and fabricated rain. Evan Jones wrote a fine, taut script, while Losey gathered around him actors with whom he had worked before, including Bogarde, Alexander Knox and Leo McKern, although the leading role of the doomed Hamp was played, magnificently, by Tom Courtenay. Other familiar faces turned up on the production team, including Spike Priggen, who, buoyed by the success of *The Servant*, served again as co-producer with Losey. As always, the reliable Richard MacDonald achieved more verisimilitude with the take-away mud and artificial rain than most people would have done with the real thing.

In the opening moments, Denys Coop's camera pans along the heroic reliefs of the Royal Artillery war memorial at Hyde Park Corner, which commemorates the gallant men who gave their lives in that terrible conflict, and carries the legend that they died 'For King and Country', which lent the film its title.

King and Country was more a critical success than a commercial one, serving as a reminder that Losey's artistic aim was the promulgation of ideas, reinforced by powerful and complex images, rather than entertainment or expectation of financial reward. Bogarde noted in his autobiography, *Snakes and Ladders*: 'Although we once again reaped a generous harvest of accolades and awards galore everywhere, and even sold it to television all over the world, it never made a profit, and the film is, to this day, apparently still in the red.'

Courtenay, whose performance won him the prize for Best Actor at the 1964 Venice Film Festival, says of Losey, 'I expect he could be difficult with people he didn't think had talent, but with me he was always sweet, warm, and considerate – on or off the set. Once he asked me to dinner at Royal Avenue with Tennessee Williams. Both were very drunk, and Tennessee was going on about how I wouldn't pull at the box office like Taylor and Burton. I guess they were discussing *Boom!* at the time. Joe actually rang me the next day, very ashamed and apologetic, almost courtly. He didn't want me to think ill of him, that he'd failed somehow in his manners. One was very touched by that sort of thing, and I'm always amazed when people talk about how rude he could be.

'The impact of that film was tremendous, very draining to do, as well as to watch, believe me. I remember when I was learning the part, an old carpenter, about seventy, came to my flat to put in some pine panelling – that was all the rage in those days. I'd acquired this fantastic tape recorder from somewhere, and was using it to record my lines and my cues, and some scenes with Dirk. The old man asked if he could hear it, and so I played it for him. Well, he cried at the end; he'd been in those trenches when he wasn't much more than a kid. I had to give him a drink.'

The film was shown at the 1964 New York Film Festival, where it was well reviewed. Eugene Archer of the *New York Times* wrote: 'Dirk Bogarde and Joseph Losey, whose *The Servant* gave the first New York Film Festival a resounding hit, have come up with another powerful drama for the second annual event. Their *King and Country*, presented last night at Philharmonic Hall, is a savage attack on war and the bestiality it engenders. It represents an impressive achievement, not only for the expatriate American film-maker and his gifted British star, but also for the remarkably talented young Tom Courtenay.'

Even with this praise its release in the United States was delayed for two years. When it did appear in January 1966 Bosley Crowther, the powerful *New York Times* critic, ventured that 'It may be assumed on the evidence that it is not for any lack of quality or power of articulating what it has to say that Joseph Losey's *King and Country* is so late in being released in New York following its production in England. But it is probably because it is so smashing – so stark and unrelenting in the way it exposes the cruelty of military justice and the filthiness and inhumanity of war – that its distributors, Ely Landau and Oliver Unger, have been cautious in putting it on view. Make no mistake about it. It is not an easy film to watch. It is full of nauseating squalor and depressing futility. Mr Losey has spared no feelings.'

King and Country's London opening at the Carlton Cinema in 1964, as part of the eighth London Film Festival programme, received excellent reviews. Penelope Gilliatt probed deepest: 'The things that transform the picture are two, and both of them seem to be extensions of Losey's temperament. One of them is the sarcastic kick-back in the emotional line of the film. The other piece of steel in the picture is Losey's sense of form. The scheme of *King and Country* is as stiff as a grid, a shape that you could lift off the story like a motif imprinting wet cement. One image recurs, of writhing flesh mimicked in dead matter.'

John Trevelyan, the British film censor, was worried about the offensiveness of the scene where Hamp receives last communion from the priest, and vomits immediately afterwards; he fretted about the possibility of giving offence to war veterans whose shibboleths were being vilified. All the way from America, Ely Landau, who distributed the film there, became increasingly unhappy: films with rats, he moaned, were never successful.

In France the ever-faithful Pierre Rissient successfully lobbied for its showing under its original title of *Hamp*. In January 1965, Losey agreed to journey across the channel and lend his support to its opening in Paris, but only on condition that Patricia would be offered a ticket as well. This was not merely motivated by the desire for her company; he also needed her skills as secretary and linguist, to help him communicate with the French, especially when it came to dealing with the finer points. The critics provided their customary eulogies: 'Losey at the summit of his talent in the mud of Passchendaele,' trumpeted *Jeune Cinéma*; and Nissim Calef, in the *Canard Enchainée*, wrote him the best review he'd ever given his old friend. In Italy the reviews were universally glowing, culminating in an award for Tom Courtenay.

Back in London, he was particularly touched by a letter from Derek Partridge, who had played one of the smaller parts as a soldier. In it Partridge thanked Losey for providing him with an opportunity to watch the director at work, which he had found a rewarding experience, and for his understanding, his warmth and gentle approach that guaranteed actors would give their best possible performance. It was an unexpected and welcome tribute to Losey's unobtrusive skills in creating an atmosphere in which his players could flourish.

So enamoured had Losey become of Royal Avenue in Chelsea and the house in which *The Servant* was filmed, that he and Patricia set about trying to buy a house for sale on the opposite side of the square. Thanks to Robin Fox's skills, both Bogarde and Losey earned a percentage of the gross earnings of *The Servant* which, added to earnings Losey still had from his extensive advertising film-work, and some beggings and borrowings, enabled him to buy 29 Royal Avenue, which was to remain his home for the rest of his life.

*

Losey's next film, *Modesty Blaise*, was the nearest he got to providing popular entertainment. It was based on the antics of a heroine
in the James Bond mould, featured nightly in a strip cartoon published
in the London *Evening Standard*. However, the film had originally
been part of an ambitious programme announced by British Lion in
February 1961, and was to have been directed by Sidney Gilliat, best
known as a writer and director of comedies. Its producer was Joseph
Janni, an Italian who had worked in the British film industry since
the late 1930s, and who had been trying to interest Monica Vitti,
the enigmatic star of Antonioni's films, in another project. During a
meeting at her apartment, he had accidentally left a copy of the script
of *Modesty Blaise* behind. Back in his London flat, Janni was woken
at three o'clock in the morning by a phone call from Vitti, telling
him that she was only interested in playing Modesty Blaise.

A few weeks later, Janni gave a cocktail party in Rome, inviting
Vitti and various others he hoped to interest in the film. Someone
had told him that it was her birthday, so he appeared from behind a
vast bouquet of roses, which she swept from his arms, crying, 'But I
don't want roses, I want a contract!' Having met and observed Vitti,
Gilliat wanted nothing more to do with the project, and Janni, who
by now had got backing for the film from 20th Century-Fox, received
a letter from Losey, who had read a story about the production in the
trade press, saying that he would do anything to direct the picture,
so besotted was he with the idea and with Vitti. Janni agreed.

Losey began to gather his regular team around him: MacDonald to
design, Jones to rewrite Gilliat's script, and Bogarde to star opposite
Vitti as the villainous Gabriel sporting a silver wig. Gavrik, now aged
30, was hired as his father's first assistant director.

Modesty Blaise might have been a success had it not suffered an
identity crisis in mid-shoot. Later, Losey insisted defensively that the
film was way ahead of its time. 'There's hardly anything in *Modesty
Blaise* that hasn't been copied and done less well,' he said in 1976.
'I'm perfectly convinced that if the film were released again it would
be a success. It wasn't then, because in one shot a woman would be
sitting at the table and she'd be blonde with a green dress and then,
in the next return shot, she'd be brunette and wearing a white dress.
The film was just a fraction too early for high camp.'

Though Losey must accept most responsibility for the film's
failure, the unpredictable and volatile behaviour of Vitti was an
extra unforeseen problem. One thing is certain: on this occasion

Losey could not blame his producer, for Jo Janni was an urbane and life-loving man with an irrepressible sense of humour which would be greatly needed during the coming months.

One of the few who enjoyed working on *Modesty Blaise* was MacDonald, who had a field-day, using many of his own paintings to decorate Gabriel's walls and copying Bridget Riley's Op-Art style to create the extraordinary, mind-bending chambers of optical deception and dimension-warping décor. He was able to liberate his wildest and most eccentric fantasies with spectacular results. Who could forget Dirk Bogarde and Clive Revill drinking pastel-tinted, noonday libations from goblets with metre-long stems? Or the colour of the giant lobsters, singing in the pain of their boiling grave, as they prepared to become lunch? MacDonald found it all, including the inevitable rows, the best fun in the world.

For once Losey had money and an excellent cast. The film's budget of around one million pounds was big by British standards. Its stars included not only Vitti and Bogarde, but Terence Stamp as Modesty's Cockney boyfriend Willie, with Harry Andrews and Alexander Knox representing MI5 and the Establishment.

But even before filming began in July 1965, there was trouble. Vitti felt insecure and unhappy. In May, writing to Losey, in her stilted English, she appealed to him to postpone the start of shooting. Her recent work had left her tired, she said, and she needed time to recover her spirits. She had every confidence in Losey – whom she considered an exceptionally good director – but she was concerned about some aspects of the film and about herself. This was a big opportunity for her to show that she could do other things, but it would not be easy for her and she had to be in the right frame of mind if she were to do herself justice. She had read the revised script and thought she detected a weakening in the character of Modesty, who now seemed to have lost some of her personality and humour. Since humour must be international, she was convinced that a comic story had to be funny in any language. She begged Losey for a little more freedom to believe in herself. She had always played inhibited characters, now she desperately wanted to invent, to improvise, to do whatever came into her mind at any particular moment. Above all, she concluded, she wanted to have fun playing a role she believed in.

Once filming began, the problems proliferated. Bogarde had

difficulty finding motivation for his part and loathed his wig; Stamp, who acted only with Vitti, declared that his part 'was practically cut out' as a result of the friction between Losey and Vitti; Vitti hated some of her costumes so much that, according to Losey, she destroyed them. She also refused to be photographed in profile. An added difficulty was that her English was practically non-existent. Losey's solution was not ideal: to serve as a dialogue coach he hired Moura Budberg, a Russian friend who spoke English with a heavy accent. (Losey adored and admired her, and she needed the money.) Losey was without Patricia, who was unable to accompany him because she feared her husband would make trouble if she returned to Italy. (In fact, he subsequently took their two children away to live in Brazil, and it was to be many years before she saw them again.)

At the outset Losey followed Jones's script. Then he changed his mind half-way through shooting the film, and rewrote most of it himself, without either consulting or informing the long-suffering Jones, an action that was to end the long and fruitful association between the two men.

Vitti, who had acted in films so much under the direction of Antonioni, felt utterly lost without him, for this was also the first film in which she was required to speak English. She, who had acted in stage comedies in Italy, was in despair over what she perceived as the loss of humour in the role brought about in the revised script. In an attempt to give her some help, Losey recruited his American friend, Beverly Pepper, whose Italian was fluent, to advise and to interpret. But the two women were temperamentally unsuited, and before the end Vitti was complaining bitterly about her presence.

Vitti spent most of her spare time, in fact, on the telephone to her beloved Antonioni. So agitated did she become, and so much in need of his reassurance, that he flew to her side, prompting Losey to insist, in hindsight, that Antonioni's constant presence was one of the principal causes of his difficulties with the film and its star. He vowed, then and there, never again to work with an actor or actress who was tied to another director, a vow he had already made and broken in similar circumstances in *The Gypsy and the Gentleman*, during which he had Jules Dassin mooning around his Mercourial star. Indeed, when it came to working later with Delphine Seyrig in *A Doll's House*, he fervently wished he had not weakened a second time.

Losey so disliked the performance of Annette Cavell, who had been hired to play the sadistic Mrs Fothergill, that he replaced her with Rossella Falk. Feeling shattered, Cavell told Losey that she had wanted him to talk to her about her performance but had been too nervous to ask him. She had thought Losey seemed less concerned after seeing the rushes, and even if she had been wrong about that, playing Mrs Fothergill had meant more to her than she could say. She was simply unable to understand why her performance had not worked, and she was desperately sorry to have disappointed Losey and Bogarde.

In reply, Losey thanked her, saying he hoped they would be able to work together another time. The fact was, however, that having originally asked all sorts of other people, including Viveca Lindfors, to play the role, Losey simply fell for Rossella Falk, who was hitherto unknown to him. So much was he enamoured of her portrayal, in fact, that he expanded her role considerably.

Losey's first choice for director of photography was Douglas Slocombe, who, under contract to 20th Century-Fox at the time, rather resented Losey's surreptitious efforts to persuade Fox to release him. When this ploy failed, Losey hired David Boulton but the two men were not compatible. Boulton, who normally functioned as a 'stills' photographer for MGM, turned out to be insufficiently adept with the movie camera, and so, without telling him, Losey hired Jack Hildyard, who brought along a young man called Gerry Fisher as his camera operator. Boulton was now left to deal with the publicity photographs, which he did brilliantly.

If Rossella Falk had been a good discovery, Fisher – who was to photograph eight of Losey's fourteen future films – was a great one, and worked particularly well with MacDonald. Fisher was grateful for the space that Losey provided: 'The great directors are like this, though some will play God, expecting people to perform whatever they're specifically asked. But a really good director will use the creativity of the people he hires. To do otherwise diminishes the breadth of his own work, since no one person can possess all the special talents necessary to make a great film.'

The film brought many complaints from the censors about the 'blunt sexuality' and violence in the script. But Losey, ever paranoid about censorship, responded by poking fun at the censor, holding Terence Stamp to the obligatory 1940s 'one-foot-on-the-ground' rule in a scene where he made love to one of the movie's expendable bimbos. 'Presumably,' ventured the American censor, 'the audience will be unaware that the whip used by Mrs Fothergill is "made of the dried, stretched penis of a bull".' (Far from being a figment of the writer's lively imagination, Evan Jones reveals that such whips were used on slaves in nineteenth-century Jamaica.)

Unusually, Losey and Jones had conflicting notions about the kind of film they were making. Jones, who saw it as a movie featuring the female equivalent of James Bond, says, 'I saw it largely as an action film, given texture by a few ideas. I guess Joe's view was the opposite.' Losey, who always denied any attempt to exploit the popularity of the Bond movies, was determined that it should be 'high camp', whatever that may have meant to him.

Both genres come together in the knockabout final sequence: Modesty and Willie, having escaped from their op-art prison cells, stand back to back on the rocky beach, pistols in hand, singing John Dankworth's cutely satirical duet for all the world like Fred and Ginger. Meanwhile, the Sheikh and a thousand or so of his wild, Arab horsemen ride whooping up to their rescue, having been alerted to the crisis by the MI5 team. As Modesty and Willie croon cornily about their unexpected yearning for domestic bliss, waves of sheeted Arabs, on thundering horses, on foot, in inflatable, motorized dinghies, hit the beach and save the day.

The troubles continued even after the film was finished. Representatives of the *Evening Standard* complained bitterly about the transformation of their Amazonian heroine into a nymphomaniac adventuress, and listed twenty-two ways in which the screen Modesty had gone to the dogs.

Although there is no evidence that Losey set out deliberately to make a commercial picture, everyone connected with the project expected the film to be a box-office hit. Its world premiere at the Cannes Film Festival in April 1966, however, began badly: Princess Margaret, the guest of honour, turned up an hour late for the screening. Having been to lunch in Nice with the British Consul General, she had left too late and ran into appalling traffic. The only line that had the restless audience laughing was Modesty's dictum that lack of punctuality was the prerogative of royalty. The French critics were not enthusiastic. Losey, said *Positif*, 'had placed on a cushion of air what Cannes has waited for on a plate of gold'.

Laments Jones, 'The script was completely different in the finished film, and I disliked almost everything Joe did with it. It was upsetting, because my name went on it. I wrote to him about this, of course, but there was just a long silence. I guess it's become sort of a cult film, but in terms of my work, *Modesty Blaise* was a mess, and a lot of things which were funny or meaningful to me were neither in the end. When I saw the film at the Odeon Kensington, and nobody was laughing, I wanted to get up on the stage and say, "Something different was supposed to be happening here; let me explain what you should be getting from this".'

The film opened in Paris on 19 October 1966 with a concerted publicity campaign that began with a launching party conceived under the sign of Scorpio. All the special guests invited to the Marbeuf Theatre, who included Petula Clark, Abel Gance, Pierre Dreyfuss, president of Renault, and three members of the Académie Française, were chosen because they too were born under the sign of Scorpio. Twenty-three top French cover girls formed a guard of honour on the staircase, each with her thigh decorated with a scorpion created by a famous designer or painter. Four newspapers gave the film coverage on their front pages the following morning, with only *Le Figaro* disliking it. The only person 20th Century-Fox's publicists failed to invite to the opening was the director.

Although Losey had been in Paris at the time of *Modesty*'s opening there, no one had bothered to inform him of the event, or take advantage of his presence for publicity purposes. Curiously, on this occasion he failed to become either furious or upset. 'It just fascinates me,' he told Robin Fox, adding that, though the film seemed to be doing well in France, Italy and Japan, the US and the UK remained immune to its charms. In the States, the opposition was led by *Time* magazine which called it 'less a spoof than a limp-wristed kind of fairy tale, utterly cluttered up with homosexual malice'. Antonioni's immodest judgement was simply that Losey could not make films with women. 'I know all about women,' he declared to the *Guardian* on 6 February 1967. 'Losey knows all about men. He makes better films with men than with women,'

Ever ready to rationalize, if not to accept his own responsibility for the flaws in his work, Losey acknowledged the mistakes he made with *Modesty Blaise*, considering that he had tried to satirize too many things in the film.

When asked if, in the last analysis, he had enjoyed working with Losey, Joseph Janni chuckles: 'You could never really enjoy making a film with Joe, because he was always so tense. He could never relax for ten minutes. He complained all the time, about everything, about money, about me being too rich, which I wasn't, about Monica, about nobody being serious enough about the work. He hated anything to do with authority, with power, with money, and producers were a symbol of power.

'He loved one thing: the work. I tell you, if he was working with somebody, and someone came in and said, "Listen, there's a fire in the building, the staircase is collapsing, you have to move", Joe would say, "Let's finish the scene." I had a tremendous admiration for Joe, his total dedication. We had our rows, but that's normal. I loved the film; like Joe, it had terrific style.'

XI

A Happy Accident

Of all the prospects jostling for position in Losey's thoughts, working again with Harold Pinter was uppermost. Among the carefully chosen guests invited to one of the early private screenings of *The Servant* was Sam Spiegel, who was so deeply affected by the film that when next they met at the New York opening, Spiegel sent a messenger to his old friend, bearing the gift of a story. What Spiegel offered, by way of breaking the ice which had formed during the fifteen years since they last worked together, was *Accident*, a novel by Nicholas Mosley, the son of Sir Oswald Mosley, founder of the British Union of Fascists. Fortunately for the future of Mosley's relationship with Losey, he shared none of his father's political or social views.

Losey was impressed, perceiving that it could be the ideal vehicle for his 'top team', which included Pinter, Bogarde and Baker, but not MacDonald, who had maddeningly accepted another job. Losey had urged Pinter on during the making of *Modesty Blaise*, writing to tell him of his great excitement at the script and how much he was looking forward to reading the latest version that Pinter was writing. When the new version was finished, Losey braced himself and took Pinter to meet Spiegel. This was not a total success, even though both Losey and Pinter emerged with contracts.

Spiegel wanted changes made to render the script more conventional. He told them expansively that 'a picture seen by 80 million people is not a success. It has to be seen by 800 million to be a success.' Having done his time in Hollywood, Losey was accustomed to this definition of success; and it represented the attitude which he most loathed. Spiegel invited them to another meeting on his yacht in the South of France where, with much reluctance, they went. 'You call this a script?' Spiegel opened. 'It doesn't begin. Nothing happens. People won't understand it. The cinema is a popular medium. You just come into an accident. Who are their fathers? Their mothers? You don't tell people anything.' Not only was he disenchanted with the screenplay, but Spiegel was also unable to imagine why they wanted Dirk Bogarde, when they might have Richard Burton. 'Who ever heard of Bogarde?'

Losey, who by now could afford to challenge the Eagle of Hollywood, rose to the occasion by accepting an expensive Havana cigar proffered by Spiegel after lunch, lighting it and chucking it overboard after two puffs, pronouncing that it was too dry. This gesture upset Spiegel a great deal – not for the expense or the waste, but because the cigars were especially hard for Americans to obtain now that the government had imposed severe sanctions on all Cuban products. Mention has often been made of the pitiable look of pain on the sun-baked, hood-eyed face of their sybaritic host, mocked by the crude and atypical ungraciousness of one of his guests. It is said that Spiegel came as close at that moment to a heart attack as he had ever done, until he suffered the one which killed him on New Year's day, 1986. From Losey's point of view it was merely 'one in the eye' of the Enemy – the Money, the producers.

Without the agreement or approval of his partners, Spiegel approached Burton to star, only to discover that the turbulent Welshman would not be available for a year. Determined to regain control, Losey and Pinter bought the rights from Spiegel, who made a profit on the deal, receiving slightly more than he had paid: $30,000, and a percentage.

Again Losey brought Spike Priggen in as producer and filming began on American Independence Day, 4 July 1966, underwritten by the usual small budget imposed by its thrifty producer. Priggen, a blunt, humorous Londoner, who began his career in films as a tea-cum-messenger boy, decreed that the film would be shot in ten weeks, aware that Losey prided himself on his ability to do good work on a tight schedule.

Accident describes a series of contests of will and endurance between three competitive men: Stephen (Dirk Bogarde), a forty-year-old philosophy don at Oxford, William (Michael York), one of Stephen's young aristocratic students, and Charley (Stanley Baker), an old friend of Stephen's, a popular novelist as well as a don. The object of their rivalry is Anna (Jacqueline Sassard), an Austrian student whose every movement seems to arouse both lust and insecurity in the men. The story begins at the end with the eponymous accident, a car crash which kills William, and spares Anna; Stephen then recalls the events leading up to this dreadful night. The society portrayed in the film is sex-coded, the men playing according to their set of rules, and the women according to theirs. The men seem to understand one another, while the women have their secrets and pass their time manipulating their instinctive understanding of the men, the underlying assumption being that the women possess a superior perception.

Nevertheless, both Losey and Pinter have been accused of presenting women in a narrowly emblematic way, either as fatal temptresses or destroyers – a view of which *Eve* is the perfect example, as is the bloodless Anna in *Accident*. She hardly utters a word, and even when she does, it is of no consequence. She is merely a cipher, a catalyst. Only Rosalind, the conventional wife and mother, comes close to being real, a defined, rounded personality, even though she is basically representative of all women in her limited circumstances. Essentially, all four women in the film – Anna, Rosalind, Charley's wife Laura, and Francesca, Stephen's former lover, are seen as adjuncts to the men, or projections of masculine fantasies.

In the way of many great directors, Losey had by now accumulated a solid team of talented technicians and actors to support him in his creative ventures and deliver the quality he cared about so passionately. Evan Jones, who wrote more of Losey's films than any other single writer, never thought of taking his talent elsewhere during the periods when he was involved with Losey. Equally, MacDonald remembers how betrayed Losey felt that he could even consider working for another director, though having developed a taste for eating well and regularly, he was not always prepared to sit out the gaps between one of Losey's films and another.

On this occasion Losey gathered together as many familiar faces as he could, including Pinter's wife, Vivien Merchant, a highly gifted actress whom he much admired. Contributing to the camaraderie, Pinter also played a small part in the picture, as did Nicholas Mosley and old friends such as Brian Phelan, Alexander Knox and Ann Firbank. Since MacDonald was busy elsewhere, Losey employed Carmen Dillon, whom he had met while working for Rank.

Once again, John Dankworth wrote a wonderfully simple score, interpreted almost entirely by the harp, an instrument he had recently rediscovered. Doug Slocombe, still under contract to 20th Century-Fox, was succeeded by Gerry Fisher, who was promoted to the position of lighting cameraman for the first time in his career, which caused one of the few real problems on the film. Many camera operators who were older than Fisher would not have relished working under his guidance, so Losey found himself having to employ someone less experienced, which resulted in a visible mistake at the end of the film, when the camera pulls back exposing the tracks on which it had run.

The newcomers were Michael York, a recent graduate of Oxford, where most of the film takes place, and Jacqueline Sassard, a rising French starlet described in the publicity material as having been 'discovered at the age of fifteen by an Italian director, Alberto Lattuada, and swept off to Rome' to make a string of films in Italian. Although English was listed as one of Miss Sassard's languages, it was not good enough, which led to many of her subsequent problems with Losey.

Revealing his own feelings about the film, Losey wrote: 'This was a very demanding picture, and repeatedly, technicians and actors said it was the hardest picture they have ever done. The film is about the complicity each of us has in the other's life – and, of course, the horrible co-existence of complicity and loyalty must lead to conspiracy. It is not an easy film to bear, because these elements are so much a part of everyone's life from the time of first friends at school through, and beyond marriage. But then, why should it be easy to bear?'

In accepting an award on television in October 1988, Dirk Bogarde pronounced *Accident* to be 'a perfect piece of work', an opinion with which many critics concurred at the time, and which stands as a glowing tribute to all involved. Carmen Dillon's eye for detail, which was every bit as pin-sharp as Losey's own, managed a tonality so unobtrusive and so beautifully reconciled to Gerry Fisher's that Losey's conception was entirely satisfied.

Both Losey and Mosley accepted Pinter's script as a masterpiece. Losey told the press that it 'is a sort of poetry, extraordinarily lyrical and evocative. It could be likened to a thriller, where the victim paves the way to his own murder, often to the irritation of the reader, or gets into situations which are obviously suicidal, only to be rescued miraculously at the eleventh hour.' Baker declared that Losey had changed his whole attitude to acting, and indeed his attitude to life; York revelled in Losey's lack of compromise; Vivien Merchant, never one to go for lengthy pre-discussions about a part, relaxed into a performance which was a marvel of naturalness.

All 'family' members were excited and energized by the general atmosphere of spontaneity on the film, though it was not always entirely welcome. Baker could probably have done without the 3.00 a.m. call, in which Losey informed him he'd found the perfect location for a particular sequence, and insisted he get up at once to see it. However, it was one of these impulses which produced one of the best scenes in the film, in which Stephen goes to comfort and counsel the demented Laura, whom he finds watering her garden in the rain. The film had been plagued by bad weather from the outset, making it necessary for the actors to jump in and out of the outdoor scenes, dodging the frequent showers, then dashing back out onto the lawn when graced with five minutes of sun to take up where they'd left off. When Losey came to shoot the scene, he had been waiting for days and, deciding he could wait no longer, shot it with Laura in oilskins, watering her garden with rain pelting down, which had the effect of reinforcing the impression of misery and distraction.

The cast was almost unanimous in its enthusiasm for Losey's methods. As Dirk Bogarde explained, Jacqueline Sassard was not strong enough to survive Losey's abrasive direction: 'He completely ruined her career and her performance. How? By bullying her to death. He was appalling to her – pushed her about and told her what to do – didn't want her to utter a word. She didn't really speak English, poor girl. If you were a moron, you were out. He didn't suffer fools gladly, or at all, really, although he was a bit of a fool himself, but that's normal. He could be pretty hard on Vivien too, at times, but she knew how to come back at him, being a wonderfully good actress, which he appreciated.

'The difficult side of Joe was very difficult indeed, especially if he decided that somebody had to be sacked, because he rarely had the guts to do it himself, so it would have to be one or another of us, who'd have to deal with the unfortunate person. It happened on *King and Country* and it happened on *Accident*. Sassard managed to escape, but somebody else got the chop – one of the smaller parts.

It was usually because Joe had seen somebody sipping a drink in a certain way, or whatever, and hired them on the spur of the moment, impulsively. Then on the first day's shooting, he wouldn't like them any more. It didn't happen with anybody major. He was careful about that.

'I never walked off a set in my life, except once – with Joe, on *Accident*. We'd waited all night, till two in the morning, because he'd wanted a particular shot with the sun coming up. So we were sitting about, as he got drunker and drunker. He drank a hell of a lot, I don't know why, frustrated about the weather, I guess, but it didn't seem to impede his ability at all, except on this occasion.

'He came out into the pre-dawn cold. We were all together. I saw a child's bicycle lying in the path in front of the house and for some reason I just pushed it with my foot into the grass. Well, Joe came down on me like a torrent of bricks – this great drunken bull – and said, "For Christ's sake, can't you ever act professional?", and I went back and stood with the others, and Alf, one of the prop men, said, "You know, the bugger meant what he said." Now the one thing I've never been is unprofessional, and he really did mean it. I thought of hitting him. Then I thought, "No, I'll leave it, and I'm leaving." So I got in my car, and drove home, just as I heard Joe's voice say, "All right. Everybody stand by", and I went, and he didn't get the shot. He saw my car going off through the cornfields, and said, "Where's he gone?", and Alf said, "Well, 'e's fuckin' well gone 'ome after that remark", and I didn't go back for a week.

'We made it up, of course. Joe was quite good about apologizing. So at the end of the week, he called, in floods of tears, sobbing. I'd never heard such a terrible noise. And I said, "No, I'm not coming back till you've apologized", which he did. I said, "Give me a couple of days to get over it, and I'll see you on Monday". It was never mentioned again, and I've never done it again, and I certainly didn't enjoy it. He behaved very differently towards me from then on.'

It did not end there, however. Losey's next victim was the little girl who played Bogarde's daughter. Losey's direction on the last shot of the film was that Bogarde should emerge from the house, calling to the child and the dog, at which point the child would run towards her father, and fall over, slightly hurting herself. The problem was that the girl was having difficulty falling convincingly. Losey, losing his patience, instructed the dutiful Alf secretly to string a nylon fishing line across the path, and hide nearby so that he could pull the line taut as the child ran across, thereby tripping her. The ploy worked to perfection, resulting in the child executing a perfect fall, accompanied by wonderfully credible screams. When it was finally discovered why the scene had suddenly gone so well, various members of the 'family' voiced their disapproval, the continuity girl Pam Davies going so far as to slap him across the face with her heavily annotated script. Much to everybody's astonishment, Losey just grinned, while Davies retired from the set, fuming.

Losey's ambivalent view of the English class system is most palpably conveyed in the scene in which Stephen is appointed goal-keeper during the mock rugby game in William's imposing family house. Stephen is painfully aware of being a middle-class outsider, not a member of this game-playing tribe. Both Mosley and Pinter clearly intended the game to serve as a metaphor for the aristocratic inclination to battle and death. Its other purpose was to demonstrate the principle of enclosure, which dominated Losey's perception of society. 'Accident is confinement,' Losey concludes.

The scene was shot in Syon House, Middlesex, one of the great properties belonging to the Duke of Northumberland. It has frequently been observed that Losey, perhaps inspired by Antonioni, often allows the camera to linger in a place before the characters appear, as in *The Servant*, or long after they have departed the scene, as in the final shot in *Accident*. For Losey, places didn't possess or lack character, they *were* characters as much as the people – characters whose functions are very much influenced by their atmosphere, by what had happened in them in the past, and what would happen in the future.

Bogarde remembers that on the day of the shooting at Syon House, the Duke and Duchess received Losey and his crew most graciously, in spite of having just heard that one of their daughters had been in a serious car crash, a grim irony under the circumstances. 'Joe didn't really understand the upper-class mind at all,' Bogarde observes, 'and that day, at Syon, he couldn't believe the apparent lack of concern on the part of the Percys about their daughter. He thought them callous, because they didn't show their feelings, and that's because he never understood this type of person – the degree to which they kept their feelings under control – not wanting to share their grief with strangers, or, worse still, impose it, which would have not been the "done thing" at all. They had promised us the room for the shoot, and they were not going to let the side down by disappointing us. Stiff upper lip. Everything was laid on, sandwiches, scotch, even vodka for Joe. They even got that right. Superb.

'They had a magnificent Holbein over the fireplace, which just had plain, brown paper behind it. Joe couldn't work out why they didn't "get it fixed". After all, they had plenty of money. It turned out that they were finding it terribly difficult to replace the antique silk which had originally backed the picture, which, like everything else in England, was taking time. For a man of such immaculate taste and knowledge, he had these incredible blind spots.'

For the first time in *Accident*, Losey encouraged Fisher to use a zoom lens, a device he had hitherto mistrusted. And he had got his two favourite male actors together in the same film. As Bogarde is the first to admit, Baker was important to Losey long before he himself was. The two men were diametrically opposed in temperament and acting technique, but Losey loved them both, and they in return had great affection and respect for him. Losey did not much care whether they liked each other or not, especially when he saw that the natural tension between them worked to enhance their interaction in the film. Baker was, like the character he played, a brash, extrovert, anti-intellectual, physical man, which, set against Bogarde's contrasting personality, became a major thematic focus.

Accident was made on a budget of £299,970, Losey receiving £17,500, Pinter £15,000, and Priggen £7,500. An almost unqualified success, it was selected as the official British entry for the Cannes festival in May 1967, where it won the Special Jury Prize. Bags of letters appeared on Losey's doorstep, saying that it was his best yet and congratulating him on the splendid reviews from virtually the entire British press.

Among these was a telegram from Gavrik and his recent bride Sally, who were in Dublin, and 'many congratulations and lots of love' from Dorothy and Joshua. Alexander Knox, writing from Northumberland, wished Losey a commercial success as well, in order to 'increase the opportunities to do what you want to do.' As Knox says, 'There's a lot of nice, normal people, who are pleasant to work for, but the trouble is they can't make films. Then there's Joe, a terrible man, who manages to make each film better than the one he did before.'

29   Dirk Bogarde rescuing Jacqueline Sassard from the *Accident* – 1967

30   Jacqueline Sassard, Dirk Bogarde and Stanley Baker form the eternal triangle in *Accident* – 1967

31   The Burtons flying high – 1968

32   The Burtons' yacht, 'Odessia', in Sardinia – 1968

33   Elizabeth Taylor and servant in *Boom!* – 1968

34   The excellent Douglas Slocombe with the exquisite Taylor in his sights for *Boom!*

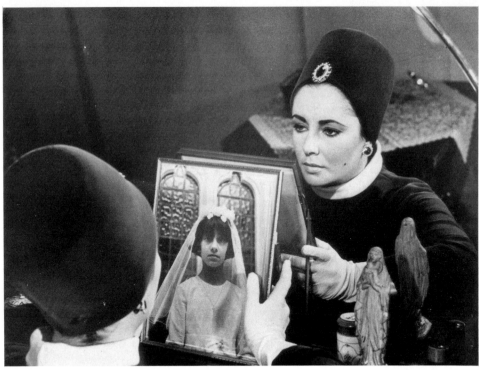

35   Elizabeth Taylor brooding over her daughter's photo in *Secret Ceremony* – 1968

36   Losey and Liz: fondest of friends – 1968

37　Joshua Losey, Patricia and friend

38　Gerry Fisher, Losey and Mia Farrow – 1968

39 George Tabori,
scriptwriter on *Secret Ceremony*
– 1968

40 Robert Shaw and Malcolm
McDowell struggling towards
their doom in *Figures in a
Landscape* – 1970

41 Dominic Guard, Margaret Leighton and Julie Christie, *The Go-Between* – 1971

42 Julie Christie contemplates her two suitors (Alan Bates and Edward Fox) during the cricket match in *The Go-Between* – 1971

43   Margaret Leighton batting, Edward Fox keeps wicket, during the making of
The Go-Between – 1971

A few critics, such as Bosley Crowther and David Thomson, took a negative view: 'Now and again,' wrote Crowther, 'one of them will say something amusing or trenchant, thanks to Mr. Pinter's dialogue. But the whole thing is such a teapot in a tempest, and it is so assiduously underplayed that it is neither strong drama nor stinging satire.' Thomson was even more scathing, referring to the 'pastoral slowness and pretension of *Accident*. The film was highly praised,' he concedes, 'whereas it should have been taken to pieces for its ingrowing artiness, its self-conscious beauty and its opting for restraint rather than urgency. It was difficult not to conclude that Losey had fallen into thinking of himself as an intellectual; whereas his best films show that he is a passionate melodramatist, torn between ideas and feelings.'

The news from California was rather more bracing, with John Springer reporting on Rex Reed's highly favourable review, and promising to send all the clippings by air mail that night. Losey, the tireless letter-writer, responded with a torrent of gratitude, thanking John Russell Taylor for his big review, Dilys Powell for her fine commendation, and dozens of friends for their invaluable support. To Harold Pinter, who was in New York at the time, he wrote that the film had opened successfully in Oxford and was drawing the crowds to the Odeon, Kensington. He was in high spirits even though he reported that despite the film's good reviews, business was poor in the provinces.

The film opened in New York in mid-April, at the prestigious Cinema II, where queues formed around the block. Donald Rugoff, the theatre's proprietor and one of the biggest distributors in America, had been more than usually enthusiastic about the film, and threw all his considerable weight behind it. From New York, Losey wrote to Bogarde, who at this juncture had only heard about the disastrous Crowther review, advising him to ignore what he had heard about unfavourable reviews like Crowther's since the film had broken box-office records at Cinema II. But the film ran into difficulties with the American censors. Writing in February 1968, Rugoff informed Losey that after its successful New York run the film had done badly out of town, and that NBC, which had wanted to acquire it, had been obliged to turn it down because of internal concerns about a story which seemed to condone adulterous relationships.

Even the French felt that *Accident* marked a return to Losey's former greatness, with *Positif* pronouncing it an 'excellent film'. *Cahiers du Cinéma* called it 'a vain and sophisticated film, with all the appearance of rigour. Each scene articulates itself through a small, significant detail, gently underlined by the zoom.' *Nouvel Observateur*, however, complained that 'Losey doesn't like women "dans l'axe de la came"' (i.e. as being central), adding 'Pinter is an imbecile, even an intelligent, cultivated one. He is incapable of bringing anyone alive, his only pleasure, asphyxiation.'

In a post-production letter to Losey, Nicholas Mosley commented observantly on the way Pinter and Losey had offset some very English scenes against a process of self-analysis that seemed far more French than Anglo Saxon. Even the *La Crosse Tribune* sprang to life again for *Accident*, if only to report on an interview which Losey had granted Joan Barthel of the *New York Times*. 'I'm an American, for God's Sake!', shouted the headline, although in La Crosse they seemed to be more interested in Losey's subsequent comment: 'My mother was a D.A.R. [Daughter of the American Revolution]; regrettable, but she was. I still have some family in my home town, and those roots don't change. But I'm totally oriented here, and can't conceive of having any other base at this point in my life. It's taken twenty years for me to get a place into which to move my things; last year I had them in storage with friends in eleven different parts of the world. It's been disastrous financially – this is the first house [in Royal Avenue] I've owned since 1948, and the first car. The only thing I've jealously preserved is the right to say "No".'

Barthel was clearly impressed by the house, taking special care to mention the convex, gold-framed mirror in the Losey drawing room, which she recognized as the one used in *The Servant*. She noted that its distorted reflections now revealed a man with exhausted eyes, sombrely dressed in brown suit, shirt and tie, his round, expressive face framed by longish, thinning grey hair. He'd been fighting all day with distributors, he explained, and felt like death.

In the publicity material for the film Losey wrote: 'Abuse, in the same way as in a marriage, is taking people for granted, which is the most hurtful thing one can do. I've been accused of this by people I've lived with and worked with. Then sometimes one grows out of people too, although I haven't had much difficulty with this. I sigh as a way of living, as a way of breathing [because of the asthma], and not because I'm mentally burdened, but it presents an image which is heavy, and makes people think of me as being weighted down with worry.'

During the course of his long interview with Ms Barthel, Losey mentions that the chief complaint in the few negative reviews emanating from the British press was that it was time Losey, Pinter, Bogarde and Baker broke up their collaboration. The critics were not the only ones to sense that a change of direction was overdue. Of the three, only Pinter would work with Losey again.

Once, when he was about to embark on *The Servant*, Dirk Bogarde and his sister, Elizabeth, had a conversation about his desire to 'put down roots', and pursue a gracious lifestyle working for low-budget artists like Joe Losey. She accused him of not having grown up: 'But I did, I think,' Bogarde writes in his autobiography. 'The four films which I made with Losey between '62 and '66 saw to that. Each one was a bitter, exhausting, desperate battle. It never got any better; only Losey's obstinacy, determination, belief, optimism and unflagging courage managed to get us through; that coupled with a crew who also believed, and a growing company, as he called it, of actors who were also prepared to put money second to career.

'The work in those years with Losey gave me the self-respect in my work which I had never dared even hope for and strengthened my somewhat shaky belief that I must never again compromise no matter what the cost. But although my belief had been strengthened all right, it did not mean, sadly, that other forces far beyond one's control would not cause it to bend; it is unrealistic to try and make films for a minority audience in a business which is geared above all things towards a mass audience. After we'd finished *Accident*, the most difficult and perhaps the most successful of our endeavours together, Losey and I found, regretfully, that the *boucle était bouclée*: we had used ourselves up; there was nothing more for us to say together; weary, drained almost, and to some extent disillusioned, we realised that we must separate for a time and go our own ways.'

Baker turned increasingly to film production and was knighted a month before he died of cancer ten years later, in 1976. Dirk Bogarde left England in 1968. The British film industry was going through a bad patch, and there was little work, even for actors of his stature. There had, however, been a flurry of tempting offers from the Continent – from Visconti, and later, Resnais and Fassbinder; he saw which way the wind was blowing, and it was pushing him towards Italy and France. Thus, without much further ado, he and Tony Forwood pulled up their English roots and planted them afresh in one of the loveliest hill-top farmhouses in the South of France, in Grasse, where the scent of the sea mingled with that of the more commercial scents for which the region is most famous. As for Losey, he chose, to the surprise and some dismay of those who knew him best, to move towards more commercial cinema. None of his future films were to live up to the achievement of *Accident*, least of all the two films with Elizabeth Taylor that followed immediately thereafter.

XII

A Financial Boom

1967 was a time when Losey needed money. The tax vultures in both Britain and America were circling, and letters were flying back and forth between Losey, Robin Fox, their lawyer Laurence Harbottle and Gerry Burke, Losey's accountant.

But help was on the way in the form of John Heyman, the person responsible for making Losey a wealthy man, if only momentarily. Heyman, the agent for Richard Burton and Elizabeth Taylor was, as president of World Film Services, also packaging films. Apart from the amiable Joseph Janni, he is one of the few producers with whom Losey remained on speaking terms after filming was completed. Losey had difficulty understanding the complications of a newly proposed business plan, and became suspicious of the whole operation, relying on the greater expertise of Heyman, who not only attempted to explain the new arrangement, but also communicated directly with Harbottle and others on Losey's behalf. Losey was appreciative and extremely fortunate to have a producer who was not only able but willing to advise him.

Heyman approached Losey to direct *Boom!*, Tennessee Williams's adaptation of *The Milk Train Doesn't Stop Here Any More*, an unsuccessful play which charts the relationship between Flora Goforth, a wealthy, dying widow, and a handsome young intruder billing himself as a poet and the angel of death. Originally Losey wanted Simone Signoret and Sean Connery in the leading roles, but his plans came to nothing. When Elizabeth Taylor, who had made two successful films based on Williams's plays, was first suggested, Losey thought James Fox would be ideal to play opposite her as the mysterious stranger. Heyman suggested that it should star the

Burtons who were then at the apogee of their extravagant marriage and preferred to work together. The idea, he admitted later, was 'a piece of sheer opportunism'.

As Losey's world expanded, and the number of people with whom he felt he was obliged to communicate multiplied, so the number of letters and telegrams, dashed off to various corners of the world, reached hundreds each month. Having first retired in '58, the devoted Pieter Rogers, who had been brought back for *Secret Ceremony* as casting assistant and general adviser, found that, in order to get Losey through the work load, he had to pitch in and help with the correspondence. The thing he apparently minded most was Losey's continuing attachment to the grotty blue dressing gown in which he would remain until lunch-time, while dictating his letters. Under normal circumstances, his own vanity would prevent him from being seen in this attire, but the mornings at home, it seems, constituted the one time when he was prepared to give aesthetics a rest.

Between the release of *Accident* in early '67 and the beginning of filming *Boom!* in August, Losey somehow found time to consider other projects, neglected but not forgotten, which still lived and grew in his imagination. One of his new 1965 passions had been for Marguerite Duras, the French feminist and intellectual, who had written a film-script called *The Chaise Longue*. They agreed to produce the film together, but, although Losey thought the script was brilliant, Duras insisted on using an actress who Losey felt was completely wrong for the part, so the project was abandoned. Duras offered Losey two other stories, *The Sailor from Gibraltar*, and *10:30 p.m. Summer*, but both were finally to be made with other directors. The former, starring Jeanne Moreau, was to have been financed by Wolfgang Reinhart, but Moreau took the idea to Tony Richardson who, pre-empting Reinhart, ultimately directed, while Jules Dassin took on the latter.

Boom! gave Losey the chance of working again with his old friend George Tabori. The pair had recently collaborated on a script entitled *The Horizontal Man*, which had been commissioned and then rejected by Carl Foreman (resulting in Losey's estrangement from Foreman, in spite of all the support he had provided during the painfully lean, early days in England). In fact, Tabori was summoned to rewrite some of Tennessee Williams's more complicated dialogue, unbeknown to Williams.

In the mid-1960s Hardy Kruger, another actor beloved by Losey, had come up with an idea based on a classic German short story, *The Man From Nowhere*. Losey's old friend and colleague, Daniel Mainwaring, worked with him on three different versions of a screenplay; the fourth and best, however, was written by Tabori, but they were still unable to get backing. With Kruger's agreement, Losey decided that the only way to obtain financing was to procure a big, bankable star such as Burton for the leading role. Losey offered it to Heyman, who agreed to produce *The Man From Nowhere* 'back to back' with *Boom!*, co-producing with Spike Priggen, and using the same actors and film crew. But Burton had been seduced into a more commercial film, *Where Eagles Dare*, which guaranteed him a fee of one million dollars plus a percentage, and so the Kruger project was scuppered.

Boom! was originally conceived as a gilt-edged film. Universal Pictures, who had set up a London office, backed it with $4 million, of which Burton and Taylor received $2 million plus expenses and percentages. The omens, however, were bad. Williams, who tried to kill himself in May, was often incapacitated by drink and drugs, or obsessed by sex, while working on the script with Losey. Meanwhile, Losey, Williams and Priggen had flown to Portofino to discuss the script with Taylor, only to discover that she had failed to return from a week's yachting holiday. When, after another week of waiting for her to arrive, she baulked at leaving the yacht, *Odessia*, Burton bought it for her for £75,000 and had it refitted at vast expense. Before filming began, the Burtons had a small party on board, which included Williams, Losey, Heyman, Rex Harrison and his wife Rachel Roberts – an occasion which proved disastrous. Burton wrote in the notebook he used as a diary: 'Rachel became stupendously drunk and was or became totally uncontrollable. The strangers, T. Williams, Losey, Bill, French, Heyman, left in disgust.'

Work began in midsummer with a search for a suitable location. 'We went for a bit of a wander down the Italian coast,' as MacDonald puts it, 'Ended up in Sardinia. I'd got up very early one foggy morning, and went for a drive, and found this extraordinary place. We both went along there after breakfast and, as the mist cleared, it just became perfect, and so we said, "Right. This is fine, let's do it here."' In June, Losey wrote to tell Elizabeth Taylor that he had discovered the perfect location for the film at Capo Caccia, where there was a suitable harbour for the Burtons' yacht. He added that he hoped she and Burton were busy getting in shape for the film.

Much to his satisfaction, Losey had been able to lure Douglas Slocombe back as lighting cameraman on the picture, and although Slocombe had been equally delighted, he too found certain aspects troubling: 'Originally, this was to have been a small sort of film, with James Fox as the Angel of Death, and Simone Signoret as Mrs Goforth – to cost something like £600,000. Then John Heyman must have suggested Elizabeth Taylor, so before we knew it, we were into a monster budget. At first Joe was a bit frightened of Elizabeth, the queen of Hollywood – it was she who had the power, even though Richard was the great actor. She's the one who insisted that he get the same fee that she did, and they got a million dollars each – because now everyone was falling over themselves to finance the film, whereas before, they were having trouble even starting.

'So now that most of the money was going to the Burtons, there was precious little for the set, and it cost a fortune to build, because everything had to be imported. In Sardinia, there's no wood, and no plaster, and they had to build a two-and-a-half kilometre road, plus the entire house, which was a sort of open-topped affair – built like that for me, really. I mean, I couldn't have sunlight coming through girders and things, casting shadows.'

Even MacDonald was experiencing difficulties. Carlo Patrono, the chief architect, whose English was very sketchy, found it so difficult to communicate with MacDonald that he wrote a long, agonized letter to Losey in hopelessly fractured English, withdrawing from the job. Jorie Pepper, Beverly Pepper's daughter, who was taken on by MacDonald as an assistant, also quit after two months, finding the hours too long and the work less glamorous than she had expected.

Another totally unexpected obstacle was that Taylor refused to wear fake jewellery in the role. In response, Priggen and Heyman managed to persuade an Italian jeweller to lend them several million dollars' worth of gems, which had to be guarded day and night. She also demanded that her brother, a marine biologist who had dropped in to visit her on the yacht, play a minor role in the film – and that he be paid a thousand dollars. Losey's secretary Philippa Drummond, who had come to Sardinia at MacDonald's request as part of the production team, vividly remembers the Burtons' heavy drinking and their angry voices floating across the water from the boat at night, although Elizabeth, a thorough professional, still managed to arrive on the set every morning looking immaculate. Burton, on the other hand, was often late, vying with Williams in the bad behaviour stakes: on the very first day's shooting, he was too ill to work.

Although she was to make another film with Losey, Elizabeth Taylor seems to have found working with him on this occasion rather unpleasant, perhaps because of the current state of her relationship with Burton, and the weather seemed to mimic her mood. One morning, as Slocombe and MacDonald were bowling along the road up to their set, they came around a bend and found that the entire roof-tower had been blown into the sea by a gale the night before. It took ten days and a great deal of money to restore. MacDonald thought 'it was terribly funny. Having got the thing up, it then blew down, because we suddenly had winds of 150 miles per hour, from God knows where. But it was frightfully good fun.'

On another day, just after Taylor had left the trailer that served as her dressing-room, a sudden gust of wind blew it over the edge of the cliff, tossing it down into the sea. Tempers frayed, then flared. Burton displayed little empathy with his fellow-drunk Tennessee Williams, calling him in his notebooks 'a self-pitying pain in the neck'. Noël Coward, who was playing the witch of Capri, was suffering from a failing memory, and had difficulty in learning his lines. He also took an inexplicable dislike to the dwarf-actor Michael Dunn, who was playing Taylor's sadistic security guard. 'It must be horrible to be a dwarf,' Coward observed at lunch one day, 'but even worse to be such a boring dwarf.'

MacDonald affirms: 'Certainly it was difficult. All sorts of people seemed to be having a terrible time. But I wasn't. I just thought it was all a great party.' Slocombe adds: 'One got the impression that there were lots of things going on behind the scenes that one wasn't supposed to know about. Noël was bitchy, not only to Michael Dunn, but to Tennessee. They were too competitive, and Joe was rather mean to him too, tending to ignore him when he was blotto.

'We'd arrive first thing in the morning to set everything up, and settle down to wait for the stars. Then suddenly you'd see a whole cavalcade of cars – something like twenty – slowly advancing through the dust, which was, of course, Elizabeth and her retinue. Once she was on the set, she was impeccable, knew her lines, the lot. Totally professional. They both were. This was the first time Joe had worked with Elizabeth, and we were all a bit in awe of her. She was nice to people, but one had to find time to get to know her. She's very demanding of everybody, not least herself.' Taylor, who was often nervous at the start of a film, developed 'psychosomatic symptoms' which delayed the start of shooting by three days. When they began work, Losey and Taylor found themselves in disagreement over the very first scene, which was eventually reshot thirteen times.

Further disagreements arose over the music. Both John Dankworth and Michel Legrand, having been summoned at various stages, were subsequently, and rather shabbily, discarded after having done a good deal of work. This was the first time it had happened to Dankworth. Having hired the entire string section of the London Symphony Orchestra at Losey's behest to record his music, Dankworth played the resulting tapes to Losey, who wrinkled his nose in displeasure, and said, 'I guess I just hate strings.' A nonplussed Dankworth accompanied Losey to the pub, where the director pronounced the score one of Dankworth's best, indicating, somewhat feebly, that the decision against it had not been entirely his own. 'You have to listen to the Money,' was Dankworth's gloomy conclusion. It seemed to some of Losey's colleagues that he was losing his creative confidence.

Losey told John Barry, who was the final choice as composer, that Universal were demanding that he use Dankworth's song for Georgie Fame in the film, but that he would make sure that it was hardly noticeable. It would not, Losey confided, detract from the impact of Barry's score. Dankworth was not alone in regretting that Losey had apparently retreated from his lofty position of artistic and financial purity. Most people understood how a highly talented director of Losey's age could be tempted to earn some decent money for a change, but not the Joe Losey who was described by one of his closest female colleagues as 'a man of large and permanent gestures – resilient and stoic'. No one had expected him to waver in his artistic resolve. Losey would have argued that he was not in retreat, but in his heart he must have known the film was conceived largely as a commercial picture, and only incidentally as a work of art. Nevertheless, he saw *Boom!* in terms of grand opera; what he liked about Williams's writing was its sound, its resonance and emotional content, not its sense.

Philippa Drummond was among those close to Losey who was saddened by this new direction in her boss's career, her profound admiration for his previous work having been what attracted her to the job initially: 'With *Boom!* and *Secret Ceremony* everything changed. He got interested in money rather than film-making. His whole mood changed, and I felt he was letting the side down – not being true to his art. I don't know too much about how he actually behaved in private with these people, because more and more, when he was with big stars, he tended to push me out of the way, so that he could have them to himself. It was his vanity and insecurity, which went hand-in-hand.'

Losey, at sixty-two, was overweight, drank an enormous amount, and was increasingly prone to bouts of asthma and other assorted health problems, many of which were genuine, while others sprang from his chronic hypochondria. The film's final indignity came when, in his enthusiasm over a scene in which Elizabeth Taylor falls prey to a disturbingly realistic fit of coughing, Losey got in the way of the camera, which ran over his foot and broke a toe.

A telegram from Losey to Dr Cooper dated 29 October 1967 marked the end of the filming, and also indicated that many of the troubles which plagued the production had to do with health. His illness was over, he told Cooper, but he felt worn out. A letter which followed reveals that the usually robust editor Reginald Beck had also been ill, which had worried Losey. After the company disbanded, Losey went into his usual frenzy of letter-writing, thanking everybody for their contribution. Giulio, the grip, was praised for his skill and sensibility and as the perfect compliment to Chick Waterson's brilliant camerawork; the two Carlos – Lastricati and his deputy – were named the perfect team; Heyman was hailed as the ideal producer, which, coming from Losey, was high praise indeed.

At least both the big stars were pleased with *Boom!*. Burton considered that his performance was one of his finest, and when he and Taylor made a list of her ten best films, they included not only *Boom!* but her later work with Losey on *Secret Ceremony*. During filming, Burton wrote in his notebook on 20 September: 'We all saw rushes and some assemblage last night. It looks perverse and interesting. I think we are due for another success, particularly E. I was worried about her being too young, but it doesn't seem to matter at all.' Tennessee Williams did not agree. He regarded Losey as a master but thought both the stars were wrong. 'The direction, the script and the sets were stunning, but Dick was too old for Chris and Liz was too young for Goforth,' he wrote in his *Memoirs*.

Having attended an early, pre-release screening, the British censor John Trevelyan wrote to tell Losey that he thought it was the best film he had ever made, choosing to ignore the various 'shits', 'bitches', 'God damns' and Taylor's sexy writhings. (Predictably, Geoffrey Shurlock, the American censor, objected to it all.) More comprehensible and rather touching was a letter from Richard Burton in which he said that he was not bothered by any critical reaction because he knew that they would all look back with pride at their work on the film. He felt it was magical.

Although Losey undoubtedly did the best that could be done in fashioning a silk purse out of this sow's ear, *Boom!* never really makes the grade. (The critics had a field day with the title, viz. '*Boom!* is a bomb', etc.) As always, Miss Taylor is quite magnificent to look at, in spite of the costume designer's apparent determination to make her look like a talking wedding cake whenever possible, and Losey, having evidently decided to treat the role as a rehearsal for *Who's Afraid of Virginia Woolf?*, does an excellent job of bringing the awful Flora Goforth to life at its most crass.

Burton, looking and sounding contrastingly mellifluous, actually succeeds in rendering some of Williams's skin-deep dialogue in such a way as to make it appear less pretentious than it is. Slocombe's photography is sublime, sneaking dazzling views through cavernous windows of the glowing whites and blues of the natural surroundings, and relishing the eternal beauty of things like robes and curtains blowing silently in an oceanic breeze. Losey himself declared that the real stars of the film were the sea and the wind. They did not receive $2 million, however; the Burtons did.

It's as well that Burton was indifferent to the critics, because they were unenthusiastic. Even in Paris, *Positif* reported that 'from beginning to end, Losey fails to find, through his own muscular *baroquisme*, how to transcend the more feeble *baroquisme* – charged with symbols, like an oriental robe floating on a skeletal figure – of his scenarist.' *Cahiers du Cinéma* decried 'one of the feeblest of Tennessee Williams's texts, clearly aired, with considerable reinforcement from gusts of wind and marine emanations – and Losey, on a slippery slope, supplying the security of excellent intellectual references, but what else?' In America most critics did not bother to review it at all.

*

Plans for *Secret Ceremony*, the second part of the production package involving Heyman and Elizabeth Taylor, had begun before the completion of *Boom!*. The story, adapted from a South American novella by Marco Denevi, had originally been brought to Losey years earlier by Ingrid Bergman's agent, but as it had not been possible to obtain the rights, the idea was momentarily shelved. When the rights did become available in the late 1960s, Losey was in Rome, monitoring the final dubbing of *Boom!*. He instantly commissioned Tabori to write a screenplay. Burton, meanwhile, had gone to make what Losey insisted on calling *Where Eagles Shit*, and Elizabeth Taylor, now convinced of Losey's genius, had wondered whether there was anything else they could do together.

With *Secret Ceremony* now possessing his imagination, Losey realized that Taylor was ideal for the leading role. '*Boom!* was self-indulgent,' Losey conceded later. 'But I very much enjoyed working with Taylor and wanted to work with her again.' The first-draft script was ordered from London, Taylor read it and approved, and George Tabori, then living in New York, was summoned to rework it.

In those days Tabori, who was also represented by Robin Fox, was often to be found typing away in the kitchen of Angela Fox's enchanting house in Sussex. Paul Scofield, another of Fox's clients, lived nearby, and often turned up looking for walking companions. It was during one of these constitutionals that Tabori had the inspiration for one of the scenes in *Secret Ceremony*. As he and Scofield strolled along past the village graveyard, a distracted young woman in a long, white dress ran past, wild-eyed, hair streaming, dodging among the tombstones before disappearing into a copse of cedars beyond. It provided Tabori with a good bit of business for Mia Farrow, who would eventually play Elizabeth's mad, adopted daughter.

Tabori had always enjoyed working with Losey, and they rarely experienced any real problems with each other until *Secret Ceremony*. 'He resented my living in New York, amidst the "barbarians",' Tabori explains. 'He thought I should be living in London and servicing him, said I was involved in all this American "psycho-shit", and here he was, an American making psycho movies and visiting his shrink regularly. We were all on a certain trip in the '60s; there was a lot of craziness, and he was getting more and more European, while I was getting more and more American.'

Given Losey's feelings about the importance of physical atmosphere in reinforcing action and psychology, the house in which much of the action takes place assumed a prime importance for him. Early on, he had told MacDonald about a building in Kensington which had enchanted him when he had passed it accompanying Gavrik to school each day. MacDonald was unenthusiastic, but when Losey insisted they go to see it, he was forced to concede that its interior was extraordinary, a romantic stew of sensual, Victorian oriental fantasy, with ceramic tiles and balconies fashioned in pierced plaster and crenellated wood. Curiously, the rooms themselves were not particularly grand, which necessitated the re-creation at Elstree Studios of the two main bedrooms used in the film. More to the point, however, the place, normally a convalescent home for the mentally ill, was empty so that Losey and his crew were able to move in.

Robert Mitchum was cast in the key role of the estranged stepfather, a decision Losey soon regretted. Robert Parrish, who was then living in London, remembers: 'One day, at ten-thirty in the morning, there was a knock on my door, and there was Bob Mitchum. He was waving a bottle of mescal around, and apparently felt like getting smashed already. I asked him what he was doing, he said, *Secret Ceremony*, and began drinking. I asked him when he was starting, and he said, "Today, somewhere between Notting Hill Gate and Shepherd's Bush. I've already done my scenes for today."'

Mitchum confided to Parrish: 'Joe's a thinker. We all go there, and we rehearse, get the scene sort of set, and the cameraman starts his lighting. Then Liz goes to her dressing room, then Mia and Joe go to theirs and discuss the scene, while we all go visiting.' Parrish had suggested that he'd better get back to the set, to which Mitchum had replied: 'No, No! It'll take Mia about an hour to say what she thinks it's about, and Joe another hour to explain what he thinks it's about. Liz and me, well, we don't give a shit about all this stuff, so we've got a lot of time on our hands.'

Cameraman Gerry Fisher thought 'Liz was super to work with. Had a ribald sense of humour, though she never liked being early. So the editing was always pre-prepared, and when she arrived she was ready. Mitchum was a problem. Joe felt he was a bit flippant. Bob's one of those characters who loves to shock people. Got upset if anyone accused him of being a good actor. Didn't want to be known as "arty".'

Mia Farrow was feeling particularly vulnerable as, not only was she miserably involved in the unpleasant breakup of her marriage to Frank Sinatra (who had deployed minders to keep an eye on her) but she was painfully insecure as an actress. Fortunately, Taylor, who was as confident as Mia was uncertain, was extraordinarily kind to the younger actress, for which Losey was eternally grateful. Apart from her therapeutic effect upon Mia Farrow, Taylor was thought to be miscast by Tabori, who reveals that Losey had wanted Vanessa Redgrave, but would not have got the money with her in the role.

'And then he met the Burtons, and Elizabeth was very keen, so what could he do?' he said. 'They couldn't cast the girl at first, and tried signing Marianne Faithfull, among other crazy ideas. I didn't want to interfere, but when he asked me if I had anyone in mind, I talked to Viveca (Lindfors, Tabori's ex-wife). She knew the script, and she said she knew this actress who was extraordinary, and who had the steel in her to work with Losey, and this was Mia Farrow.

'Nobody had any idea who she was, but Elizabeth knew the family and agreed to take a chance. So we get Mia back from India, where she'd been meditating with the Beatles, and she starts work. Joe right away became furious with me, saying Mia was absolutely hopeless, and that he shouldn't have listened to me. Then in the second week, we looked at some rushes with Elizabeth, and suddenly realized that this girl was more than good, and Joe's attitude changed. I think he resented that the picture didn't win everything, although in France and Italy it was voted the best foreign film of the year, so what's wrong with that?'

The film's score was written by Richard Rodney Bennett, who, in keeping with the theme of childhood and nostalgia for the past, made use of the tinkling, sugar-plum tones of a Victorian music box. MacDonald had unearthed a dazzling array of boxes, musical toys, clocks, and various other devices from which the music would emanate. As usual, the music is more often than not set in motion by the characters themselves, becoming part of the action as well as a reinforcing, atmospheric element. Bennett also created some wonderfully sinister sounds to underscore the darker deeds or intentions of the adult characters.

One of the most successful alliances was that between Losey and Marc Bohan (then chief designer for Christian Dior), who created Elizabeth Taylor's costumes. Slim, sleek, and ebullient, Bohan says, 'I went to London several times to see this very strange house, the colours, everything, then I made some sketches. Joe wanted a selection of these colours in the house, which were a bit bizarre, and of the peculiar atmosphere in the house.

'You know where the girl takes Elizabeth to the mother's bedroom, which is filled with pictures of the real mother in different dresses? There's one in a court dress, with the three feathers, for being presented to the Queen? Well, she wanted me to make all these dresses – just for the photograph in the silver frame! Can you imagine what this cost? I have the sketches. We did the purple because of the eyes. It was Joe's idea, but she loves purple anyway. Her eyes *are* violet.'

One night, Bohan arrived from Paris, and went straight to the Dorchester, where Taylor dragged him into her bedroom to show him some antique jewellery. She explained that they were for the film, but she hoped that Richard might give her a little present. 'She loves jewellery, but she's very generous too. At the end of the filming, she gave Joe a fabulous Cartier watch – I mean fabulous!'

Secret Ceremony is an odd, ritualistic film. A young girl, Cenci (Farrow), sees Leonora (Taylor), a prostitute, visiting the grave of her child in a cemetery. Excited by her resemblance to her own dead mother, Cenci lures Leonora to her home and installs her in her mother's old bedroom, dressing her in the dead woman's clothes. Leonora, dazzled by her new surroundings, humours the neurotic girl by adapting to her fantasies and rituals. Their private masquerade is interrupted by the appearance of Cenci's stepfather Albert (Mitchum). Eventually, the increasingly distracted Cenci claims to be pregnant by Albert, and Leonora, desperate to escape from the house's claustrophobic atmosphere, takes her away to a seaside resort, where Albert tracks them down and turns Cenci against her adopted 'mother'. Back in London, the demented girl, trapped between their conflicting wills, commits suicide. As Albert, the lethal intruder, comes to look at Cenci as she lies in her coffin, Leonora appears from the shadows and stabs him to death. Back in her own squalid flat, she recites a parable: 'Two mice fell into a bucket of milk. One yelled for help and drowned; the other paddled around all night, until in the morning, he found himself on top of butter.'

Heyman decided that the opening to the film, with its leisurely camera pans around unpeopled rooms, was boring, confusing and a bad start, and insisted on cutting the scenes, which, in Losey's view, violated his basic concept. Although it was voted best foreign film in France, the critical reaction to *Secret Ceremony* prompted Losey to comment that he had always believed in mixed breeding.

In *Secret Ceremony* Losey exercises perhaps his greatest variety of pretensions, producing a dark, sour film, overlaid with an excess of decorative nacre, as well as gratuitous nastiness. But that is not to say that he didn't have any fun in the process, or that the making of it occurred in an atmosphere of unrelieved gloom. Indeed, it was on this job that various people discovered Losey's taste for occasional ribaldry, specifically in the form of bawdy limericks, a taste he shared, surprisingly, with Trevelyan the censor, and the Burtons.

Alberto Manguel, editor of a collection of short stories which includes the novella on which *Secret Ceremony* was based, comments: '*Secret Ceremony* won the *Life Magazine* prize for best Latin-American short story in 1960 – which was then completely changed by a Joseph Losey gone haywire in his terrible film of the same name.' One of the better American reviews came from Renata Adler of the *New York Times*: '*Secret Ceremony* is Joseph Losey's best film in years – incomparably better than *Accident*. The opulent, lacquered decadence works well this time.'

The film opened in London during a heatwave, and did not attract an audience for long. Theo Cowan reported that box-office receipts for the first week at the Curzon cinema had been £4,435, which was a record. Despite the heat (it was almost 90° Fahrenheit in London), the figure for the third week was a respectable £2,437. Takings had fallen to £1,349 in the fifth week, but Losey should not be too concerned since almost every other film in the West End had been affected by the heatwave. He hoped Losey was finding the heat more productive.

Since Losey would receive more than £95,000 for his efforts, he could afford to be relatively sanguine about these reports, especially from the safety and warmth of France, to which he and Patricia had escaped for a brief respite. From St Paul de Vence he dashed off the usual spate of letters thanking and congratulating everybody and, in Peggy Ashcroft's case (she played a prying aunt), hoping to see her 'socially' after the picture was launched. To Mia Farrow he wrote that he had much to discuss with her regarding work. Pinter was busy writing *The Go-Between*, so she should not commit herself beyond June 1969.

NBC-TV in New York had paid the producers $1.5 million, according to Losey, for the television rights to *Secret Ceremony*. Without consulting either Heyman, Priggen or Losey, Universal fatally altered fourteen minutes of the film for its showing on television in September 1970. The company's editors cut some of Losey's footage to substitute a discussion between actors playing a lawyer and a psychiatrist, who analysed the motivation of the film's characters.

Losey was outraged and insisted that his name be removed from the credits of the televised version. 'The danger of setting a double standard for television and cinema is that it makes serious films virtually impossible,' he said in a statement released to the press. 'In France, where the copyright of a film belongs to the director, writer and composer, such a thing could not happen without permission of all three. The logical conclusion of all this will be that we will have serious films transmitted as a series of five-minute diluted shorts.'

The film's two producers, Heyman and Priggen, also expressed surprise at Universal's action. Said Heyman, 'This is the first time in the history of the industry that such a thing has happened. It sets a dangerous precedent, for it means that a film can reach television in an unrecognisable state but still use the title and other values of its theatrical exploitations'. Priggen added, 'The changes don't even recognise the characters. The leading lady, played by Elizabeth Taylor, was a prostitute in the original, and now works in a shop selling wigs.'

Losey was now richer than he had ever been, but possibly not as rich as he should have been, for his films were not bringing him the rewards anticipated. Bogarde was also concerned. Tony Forwood, acting on his behalf, wrote to Robin Fox in the winter of 1968 to ask whether he was satisfied that the royalty figures accurately reflected the kind of business the films had been doing.

Losey's old friend and colleague Daniel Mainwaring wrote to tell him that *The Servant* should have garnered more than $750,000 for its two prime-time showings on American television. That, he said, was the standard rate for successful films and he was sure that two showings of *Accident* would bring in at least that amount of money, since both it and *The Servant* were highly regarded. *King and Country* had not received a wide release in the States, but he was sure that a television showing should have earned no less than $250,000.

Both Losey and Pinter decided to sue, prompting Losey to remind Robin Fox that Pinter controlled the film and TV rights for *The Servant* and advising that any plan for a television version of the play should be scuppered. In order to press this suit in a serious manner, Losey approached a firm of accountants, Solomon & Finger, to conduct an investigation into the wayward royalties, for which they wanted $3,000 and a percentage of the profits. Losey, fearing that he might have to pay out more in legal expenses than he could hope to recover, decided to take no further action. He was learning that wealth and success could create almost as many aggravations as poverty and failure.

XIII

Troubled Times and Redemption

Losey was thrilled with Elizabeth Taylor's present marking the conclusion of *Secret Ceremony*. Bogarde remembers visiting his old friend at home one day and finding him lying in bed, reading Gore Vidal's latest novel. 'Before he'd practically even said "hello", he stuck his hand up in the air, and said "Look at that!", with a very florid gesture, and he had on this bloody old-gold Cartier watch. "Elizabeth gave it to me. You want to read what's on the back?" I said, "No, and listen, I knew you when you wore tin watches like a fellah", and he said, "What d'you mean by that?", but he knew damn well.' The watch never left Losey's wrist till the day he died.

With the commercial failure and disappointment of *Secret Ceremony*, Losey entered a relatively stagnant period, during which he returned to various projects languishing on the back burner, including L. P. Hartley's *The Go-Between*. He had been impressed by Nabokov's *Camera Obscura* (but didn't get far with plans to produce it) and James Kennaway's *The High Cost of Living* which, dealing with a man dying of cancer, frightened off potential backers. The project which came closest to realization was Roy Fuller's *Carnal Island*, which had materialized as a film script by Losey's old friend, David Mercer, some years before. Michael Redgrave and Alan Bates had agreed to star, with Granada producing the film, which concerned an intriguing relationship between a young poet and an older, more established writer. But this project foundered as well.

Due perhaps to advancing age, Losey had settled down with Patricia in a way that he had not managed with other lovers. Although he could still be hurtful when thwarted or impatient, he had begun to learn compassion, and where he so often failed as a lover or husband, he began to succeed as a loving friend. He spent some of the money he had earned working with Elizabeth Taylor by enlarging his home, buying the house next door at 27 Royal Avenue. He became chairman of the Royal Avenue Residents' Association and battled with the local council in an attempt to get the avenue closed off to the 'hippy haven' of Chelsea's King's Road.

Feeling thoroughly drained after the launching of *Secret Ceremony*, Losey and Patricia decided to restore their spirits with a short holiday in Venice, a city for which Losey's love had not dimmed.

Disappointed to discover that the Danieli was full up on this occasion, the couple booked in to the neighbouring Cipriani – just as grand and perhaps just as well, since few of the memories of *Eve*, so much of which was filmed at the Danieli, were happy. The decision turned out to be fortuitous, since that is where they met the handsome, refined young American, Jack Loring, who ran the Cipriani's Yves St Laurent boutique.

Loring, about the same age as Gavrik Losey, usually stayed with his mother, who had been 'watering' in Venice for years, and had recently decided to put her house on the market, placing her great friend, Peggy Guggenheim, doyenne and hoyden of *le tout Venise*, in charge of helping her find a buyer.

Loring had, in fact, first met Patricia briefly one morning when Mrs G. brought her to view her friend's house, not having the faintest idea who she was, or that her relationship with Joseph Losey had any bearing on the visit. Losey had, of course, become a follower of Peggy's – and she of his – when they met during the filming of *Eve*, agreeing with Loring's assessment that she was 'one of the few civilized people in Venice in the wintertime'. She was also quite useful, even appearing as an extra in the gambling scene in *Eve*, kitted up for the occasion in a giant hat and sunglasses.

The meeting between the two men took place a few nights later, when Peggy, stuck for a spare man for dinner, rang Loring to ask if he would come. Turning up at Angelo's at the appointed hour, he recognized Patricia at once, and was introduced to Losey, who had been a hero ever since *Boy With Green Hair*, the very first movie that young Loring had ever seen.

They hit it off immediately because they found, among other things, that they had the same understanding of and fascination with words, which made for instant communication. Loring, originally from Chicago, relished the shared mid-western background, which formed the initial bond.

'I can remember one stupid phrase,' Loring relates. 'Peggy was going on about Eleanora Duse and D'Annunzio, and I made one of those comments that were considered smart in the '60s – a clever word joke: 'Avis tries harder, but Eleanor Duse.' Joe thought this was hysterically funny, and so did Peggy. Not Patricia, who was feeling decidedly out of it.' Thereafter, they saw Jack Loring almost every day and became a threesome.

A short time after this Venetian sojourn, Loring went on a business trip to London, where he kept a small flat in the King's Road. The moment he arrived, he rang Losey and was invited over. At dinner, the Loseys suggested that he give up his flat and move in to Royal Avenue. Loring agreed, but had to wait until Mia Farrow, who had been installed there during the filming of *Secret Ceremony*, returned to Hollywood.

The singular triangular ménage mirrored many of the relationships in Losey's various films. In this case, however, rather than playing the intruder, who unbalances and destroys, Loring acted as a buffer, a companion and mediator, even a surrogate son. He also became a sort of honorary uncle to Joshua. It was a domestic arrangement similar to the one Losey had sustained all those years ago with Frances Chaney and John Barrymore, and it suited him. Once again he could bask in the devotion of not one, but two legitimate admirers, whose aim was to support, amuse, and stimulate him.

'They liked people in the house,' Loring confirms, 'but they certainly did not encourage friendships with people in general. We all continued to get on famously, and were highly entertained by each others' company. Patricia was pleased, because she had somebody to talk to and entertain her. She didn't really have much to do, what with the couple and the cleaner, and Joe having so many people around him – people like Moura Budberg, Moira Williams, and Pieter Rodgers – to read scripts and so on. Patricia always wanted to involve herself more and more in the work, it's true, and this was always a very touchy subject.

'Patricia is a remarkable woman, in a way, and Joe had great respect for her literary judgement and ability to understand things very quickly from reading scripts. I did some of that too. And "Mo" [Moira Williams] is a remarkably brilliant woman, no doubt. But at the end of the day, he wanted Patricia for his own support. He was surrounded by very good people, but not necessarily ones who could be there for him 24 hours a day. No matter how loved or famous you are, when you close the door at night in your own house, you're alone with whomever's there, and that was Patricia and, during this period, me. Life's a pretty lonely thing with all the fans and admirers outside; you need someone private, who keeps you going.

'There was a poignant scene once with Marisol [the sculptress] in France. She stopped by her mailbox one day before Christmas, and the box was crammed with cards. She said, "Isn't that interesting? All these people out there thinking so much about me – I wonder why they never telephone?" It was the same with Joe. He took solace in alcohol, for which he had an incredible capacity. Every night he'd drink Patricia and me under the table, and get up the next morning and go to work, without a hangover.'

Loring adds, 'We were incredibly close during that period, and Joe loved this kind of situation. He loved the idea of him, myself and Patricia barricaded in, as it were, where events would be played out all the time. It was the way he ran his life. We were never bored. Never. Once when Joe and Patricia were away, I had friends to stay, one in particular, David, who Patricia liked but Joe didn't, because he didn't like anybody having any other friends but him. He was horrid to David.'

Accounts vary about how Losey became involved with his next film, *Figures in a Landscape*, based on Barry England's novel about two men being relentlessly pursued across a hostile country by a sinister helicopter, controlled by dark, unspecified, authoritarian powers. (This was the second film in which a helicopter featured maliciously, the first being *The Damned*.) According to Losey he had read and hated the novel and disliked the film script, but had been persuaded to direct it by its leading actor Robert Shaw, who explained that a unit had been filming in Morocco under the direction of the producer, John Kohn, running up costs but not producing any usable footage. Shaw also offered to rewrite the script with Losey. As he admired Shaw not only as an actor, but as a playwright and novelist of considerable talent, and was offered more money than he had ever received before, Losey agreed.

Morocco proved too hot for filming, so they sought out equally suitable locations in Spain. For the first time for many years, however, he was not to have his 'repertory company' around him, being obliged to use another man's crew, none of whom knew him or bore him any allegiance. Arriving in Spain, Shaw and Losey shut themselves up in a room at the Marbella Hilton and set about producing a script, work which was to continue throughout the filming. Losey asserted that there was friction between Shaw and the film's other leading actor, Malcolm McDowell, and that he was working under intolerable conditions.

The film's producer, John Kohn, tells a different story about the genesis of the film. He insists that Losey chose his own cameraman, Henri Alekan, with whom he had worked on *Eve*, and retained his usual continuity girl, Pamela Davies. Sitting coolly in Hollywood, gazing out at his swimming pool, Kohn relates: 'It was Joe who rang me, saying, "I heard you lost your director. Can you use me?" Bob couldn't have approached him first, because I introduced them. It's true that most of the technical people were mine, but so what? They were good people. I tried to fix the script, which I rewrote in two days. I was up for an Oscar for writing *The Collector*, you know. I took it to Joe, who was amazed, and told him not to tell Bob Shaw that I wrote it, which he did. Bob, of course, said it was shit, so now *he* went to work on it, and Joe and I did amendments behind Bob's back.'

Kohn confirms that there was friction between Shaw and McDowell: 'Bob Shaw was a heavy drinker. He wasn't exactly a drunk, but drink made him dour and combative. Sitting in a cane field one day, between shoots, discussing politics or something, Malcolm put his two cents in, and Shaw says, "That's one of the stupidest things I've ever heard," and knocks his chair over. No apology, nothing. Malcolm got very upset, and Joe could have helped, but would not get involved. Just turned away, and pretended to be attending to some detail. I never forgave him for that.

'Malcolm was scared to death. It was only his second picture, and Joe and Bob sort of shut him out – always going off together for meals and little conferences. Malcolm kept saying he wasn't getting any attention from Joe, and no direction either. "Joe never takes me to lunch or dinner," he used to say, so Joe took him to lunch one day, and all he did was tell him to stop snivelling. Joe would always ally himself to the more famous actor.

'But the worst thing was what happened later when we were shooting one of the best scenes, where the two men were finally beginning to communicate, as they struggled up this mountain to freedom, supposedly. It was a two-shot, and the men had to be followed up the mountain, keeping both of them in the frame against all this mountainous space. It took two days and a lot of money to build a track up that mountain for the camera – about two football fields long; then we shoot the scene, and time it. Joe does it seven or eight times, and it's about three and a half minutes, and says, "That's it. Cut." So I said, "Don't you think we'd better do it another time, in a different way, in case the others don't work? What do we do if it goes on too long?", and Joe says, "Don't you have the courage of your convictions? Believe me, it'll work." So I said, "Look, the tracks are there, they took two days to build, what will it hurt to do a slightly different version for choice?" But nothing would move him. He absolutely refused, he was so arrogant, and stubborn. Simply impossible.'

Losey turned out to be right, however; the scene did work, but relations remained strained. Losey had shot off a scathing memo to Kohn following the second week of the projected twelve-week schedule, and another to Robin Fox saying, 'You may still have to come down here to deal with the inflexible ice cream Kohn who is in some ways worse than the Hakims.' Kohn tried to be amenable. Towards the end of the shooting he sent a handwritten letter to his director: 'Now that it is almost over, all I can say is that I wish I could have made it easier and more enjoyable for you. I value our friendship and trust it will continue despite all the problems of the past. All my love to you and Patricia.'

But Losey was not to be pacified. 'Joe wrote me a letter afterwards,' Kohn relates, 'blaming the failure of the film on me and what he called the "bad campaign" against him, and saying that I didn't support him or the picture, and I don't know what. So I wrote him back a scathing letter expressing my feelings. I mean, apart from everything else, this guy was supposed to be such an artist, an intellectual, and all that. Well, I didn't think he was so damned intelligent at all, and not that much of a genius artist either, at least not on this picture.'

Kohn's letter ended, 'Don't ever write me a letter like this again. I've had a year of your witless sarcasm, and I'm sick of it. I don't expect courtesy any longer, but I think even you, with your total lack of grace, could manage civility. On second thoughts, don't even write me civilly. I'd like to remember you as you are – as just a grumpy old man.' Seven years later in 1977, at a gathering at Joseph Janni's London flat, Kohn and Losey met again. Deciding it would be small-minded, as well as physically impossible, to pretend not to see Losey, Kohn approached his old adversary and said, 'I still think you're a shit, but Hi! I think we're both getting a bit too old to bear grudges, don't you?' Losey replied, 'I guess we are.' The two never saw each other again.

Losey's final version was rejected by the film's distributors, CBS, who recut it to try to make it into a simple action picture. Losey's contract meant that no changes could be made unless his name was taken off the film, so CBS removed his credit and distributed it as an 'abridged version'. In Italy it was shown with the words 'abridged version' in English and in very small type. 'There are always new tricks,' said Losey when he found out. CBS also changed the ending which, in Losey's version, implies that both men are captured and killed. In the CBS version the younger man escapes. 'They wanted a little hope,' Kohn explains. 'I can see their point.'

Some of the reviews were kind. 'Unrelenting, exciting toughness. Losey scores consistently in the tension he sets up in the ground-to-air hatred between the men and that cruel god that hovers in wait [the malevolent helicopter] to peck off their heads,' said Alexander Walker of the London *Evening Standard*, who placed the film among his top ten for 1970. 'Brilliantly staged, a cool, tight, utterly professional job. You would know at once that it was the work of a mature, confident artist, even if you didn't know who had directed it,' wrote John Russell Taylor in *The Times*. In France, the critics were equally enthusiastic: 'Du grand Losey,' *France Soir* avows; 'To be seen at all costs,' confirms *Combat* magazine.

One of the elements which had undoubtedly excited *Combat* was the extraordinary use of the helicopter pursuing the two men like an avenging Fury. Losey had hired Gilbert Chomat, one of France's top helicopter pilots, to fly these sequences in his Alouette, and subsequently declared that the combining of Henri Alekan's camerawork and Chomat's unique skills produced among the best aerial sequences ever filmed. Perhaps to impress Joshua, who had flown out to be on set with his father, Losey actually took to the air himself, whence he bravely directed the shots dressed as the shadowy co-pilot. He admitted that the experience had been terrifying as it was exhilarating, and indeed his fears proved justifiable: three months later Chomat was killed on another mission, and his plane destroyed.

But the audiences stayed away, which Losey blamed on inadequate publicity, especially in England where he had subjected himself to fourteen interviews in two days and received good reviews.

The more encouraging French response was largely due to the efforts of Losey's friend and PR man in Paris, Bertrand Tavernier. Losey wrote to him expressing his gratitude for his efforts, which he felt had given the film a much needed boost, and wished that the British could see the reviews of the French critics. Even so, the film failed to draw the crowds in France, which Losey felt was a result of poor advertising and the death of De Gaulle.

Instead of escaping to the sun at the conclusion of this film, Losey accepted an offer, beginning early in January 1970, to teach at Dartmouth, his old alma mater. He presided over the special preview of *Figures in a Landscape* in March at Dartmouth's Spaulding Auditorium, then visited his sister Mary Field, in Carmel, New York, where he was then persuaded to make a sentimental journey to La Crosse, his first since 1945. He found things very different from the way he remembered them. 'It certainly has changed, hasn't it,' he commented to the reporter from the *Tribune*. Disappointed, Losey returned to Dartmouth, where he indulged his abiding affection for and interest in young people.

During this sabbatical from film-making, he also wrote several articles, including one called 'Speak, Think, Stand Up', published in *Film Culture*, which addressed itself to those who appeared to be in danger of forgetting all about the McCarthy era and what it revealed about America.

'I have no brief for Senator Joe McCarthy, but I think that too much has been loaded on poor old McCarthy,' he wrote. 'Of course, he was a monstrous man and a monstrous influence, but he was only a symbol.

'I suppose that fear and abdication of responsibility produced the whole history of the past twenty or thirty years. The various kinds of betrayal, the various ways in which nations and peoples have been let down by politicians, by ideologies, by themselves. And the degree to which terror has become an instrument of policy and even an instrument of status.'

Apart from reiterating much of his personal and professional history, Losey admonished people to think, rather than rely on 'labelling' and received wisdom. As the Dartmouth idyll drew to a close, Losey received a telephone call from Stanley Kubrick, who said he was considering Malcolm McDowell for *Clockwork Orange*. When Kubrick described the role, Losey acknowledged it as perfect for McDowell, and it was due to his generous recommendation and Kubrick's admiration for Losey's film that McDowell got the part that was to bring him international fame.

While Losey was teaching at Dartmouth, Patricia journeyed to Brazil where she successfully re-claimed her two Roman children, Ghigo and Flavia, now seven and nine, and brought them back to live with her in Royal Avenue. The year was to bring another unexpected reward, for Losey was made a Knight of the Order of Arts and Letters of France, an award which he was pleased enough to accept in spite of his creeping scepticism about the excesses of Gallic analyses of his films. Though he agreed less and less with the French attitude towards directors, he accepted the award with gratitude.

Julie Christie had been Losey's first choice to play the leading role in *The Go-Between* ever since he first conceived of it as a film eight years earlier. His plans, furthermore, had developed promisingly while he taught at Dartmouth and during the unhappy period when he was filming *Figures in a Landscape*.

Losey, who once called the story 'a gentler version of *Lady Chatterley's Lover*', had first taken the idea to Pinter as soon as work had been completed on *The Servant* in 1963. Pinter had been reluctant to write the script after reading the book alone at home. 'It had such a tremendous impact on me that I actually broke down. Nothing less than tears. So I couldn't see how, feeling as I did, I could write a screenplay. Then a month or so later, Joe talked me into it.'

Within a year he had written most of the screenplay, only

stopping when Losey discovered that there was a mix-up over the rights to the story, which had originally been bought by Alexander Korda.

The film rights eventually passed to Robert Velaise, a French distributor and sometime producer, who wanted Losey to direct it; but Hartley himself had sold the dramatic rights to the book to the theatrical producers H. M. Tennant, and a television production was also being planned. Leslie Grade and Robin Fox tried to persuade Velaise to sell his tranche of the rights. 'Robin Fox could be naughty in business, as well as with women,' Velaise says. 'He said, "We will make the film, if you sell us the rights for a handsome profit." I said, "No, I won't sell them. I'm not in the business of buying and selling rights. I bought the rights to make the film," whereupon he said, "But you can't make the film," so I said, "O.K., then I won't make it, but neither will anybody else. Either it will be made by me or no one."

'Since I was being difficult as far as they were concerned, Fox tried to induce Hartley to get on with a stage version, which, if followed by TV, would have completely undermined the possible financing of a film. We were talking to EMI at the time, and they wouldn't even consider it with a TV version in the background. By this time, 20th Century was interested, Anthony Asquith was dying to do it, also Joe Janni, who'd worked with Joe already, so we had no problem finding financing in principle. People kept trying to buy these rights and I kept saying "No", till I finally was able to buy the residual rights from Tennants; I had a meeting with Grade and Fox and the same day sent my lawyer to Tennants to buy the remaining rights – tried to outsmart them. I still wanted Losey, especially after his big success with *The Servant*.'

At this point Velaise, who was too inexperienced for the financiers to trust as the film's producer, was introduced to John Heyman, who had influential connections with MGM. Luckily, the two men were able to strike a deal: Velaise would be credited as executive producer while Heyman and Spike Priggen would be joint co-producers. Half the money would come from MGM and half from EMI, provided Christie and Alan Bates agreed to star. There was no problem with Bates, but Julie Christie felt that, at 29, she was perhaps too old to play Marian, who is no more than 18 in Hartley's novel. Hartley, brimming with suggestions about virtually everything other than the script, suggested that Marian should be played by an old friend,

Vivien Heilbron or, failing that, Lizzy Spender, daughter of the poet Stephen Spender. Gently, and with great respect, Losey explained the commercial realities of casting to catch producers.

Losey consulted Gerry Fisher, who would once again work with him as cinematographer. Fisher reckoned that he could make Christie look young enough if he was given total control of the use of lenses, light filters and distance, and provided she was photographed as much as possible on her own and not with other people. 'I can't single her out within a group, and make her look younger,' he said. Luckily, this was sufficient to quieten her concern.

The search for a boy to play the crucial title role was more difficult, for Pinter and Losey agreed that it was best to use a fresh, unknown young actor. Both Daniel and James Chatto, the sons of Fox's administrator, Ros Chatto, read for the role, but Losey thought one was too young and the other too old. Finally, he chose Dominic Guard, the youngest son of a family of actors. Guard, who had played a small role at the National Theatre, was at first nervous and withdrawn, though his performance turned out to be highly satisfactory. The situation was relieved by the fact that Guard became friends with the other two boys in the company (one of whom was Richard Gibson, later Herr Flick in *'Allo, 'Allo!*), and most of the filming was done at Melton Constable Hall, a decaying stately home some twenty miles from Norwich, where the boys could play or listen to records together when they were not acting, as though part of a family – always Losey's preferred atmosphere.

Alan Bates recalls: 'Dominic was enormously shy in those days. A bit dazzled, but really just shy. His brother had started to do things, and it meant a great deal to him to do well. When he first read the script, I don't think he even knew he'd got the part. I think it was kind of Joe saying, "Now come on, let's see if you can do it, and read with everybody", which was almost a bit cruel, I thought. Not that I think of Joe in any way as cruel, but I thought it was asking a lot of the boy. But he survived it, so maybe it was the sort of challenge he needed. And he was wonderful in the end.

'But Joe did something for me which has never happened before or since, which was to write his understanding of each character in the form of an essay. I got this in the post, and it was something I didn't remotely disagree with. But what was great was that you knew before you got up there what Joe thought the character of the man, Burgess, was, and how he saw it all. And it takes away a tremendous barrier, because you don't have to then sit for hours and talk and get to know someone. It was a marvellous thing to do, enormously civilized.'

In *The Go-Between*, Losey fractures time with more force than he had employed in *Accident*, superimposing voices and images from the present onto the past, and vice-versa, until past and present become one and the same. He was faithful enough to Hartley's novel for his film to win the unqualified approval of the author. The story, set during the hot summer of 1901, deals with a series of losses: of a child's innocence, of the passion between lovers, who are defeated by the imperatives of social status, and of the certainties of class stability and immutability.

A schoolboy, Leo (Dominic Guard), known for his dabblings in magic, is invited to stay at the country house of his upper-middle class friend, Marcus, and becomes the unwitting carrier of love letters between Marcus's older sister, Marian (Julie Christie), and a local farmer Ted Burgess (Alan Bates), who is socially her inferior. The truth about his Mercurial duties is revealed on the night of his thirteenth birthday party, when the lovers are discovered together by Marian's mother, who has dragged the sobbing Leo through a thunderstorm to confront the effects of his deception. The revelation destroys Leo, who remains aloof from love throughout his adult life and from Marian, who is forced into an unwanted marriage with Lord Trimingham, an aristocratic neighbour. Burgess, whose life is in ruins, empties both barrels of his shotgun into his broken heart. The film opens as Leo (Michael Redgrave), summoned by Marian fifty years on, speaks the opening words: 'The past is a foreign country. They do things differently there.'

Losey's principal, and all-too-familiar constraint was the size of his budget. Originally, he was to be allowed $2 million, but over the eight years between the film's conception and its realization, the allowance had shrunk to less than $1 million. There were a few changes, however, in Losey's regular team. His increasing vexation with Philippa Drummond's relationship with Richard MacDonald contributed to his decision to give them both the sack. A new secretary, Celia Parker, appeared and Carmen Dillon was appointed the film's designer. Philippa was shocked and hurt, but not surprised; MacDonald felt none of these things, understanding his friend's motivations better than he did himself: Joe's supporters were supposed to be devoted to him, not to each other.

There was some local excitement when Warren Beatty, Christie's current lover, came down to stay with her, which attracted the attention of the newspaper gossip columnists. Nevertheless, filming went smoothly at Melton Constable, the huge estate offered to Losey at a peppercorn rent by the local farmer who owned it – Winston Franklin, who was thrilled to play host to the film company. The period décor was provided by the resourceful Carmen Dillon, who managed to produce original costumes, furnishings, old bicycles, even specially-made, period fire-crackers. Crumbling statuary was reproduced in plaster, and the entire place underwent costly refurbishment. Dillon was in her element, for at nearly seventy years of age, she could virtually conjure up this English *belle époque* from her own memories.

Losey believed they had got everything right, except for the farm horses, which were too small. The lawns caused a little trouble, for they had been so long neglected that when they were mown, the grass decomposed to insalubrious shades of yellow and brown, and had to be sprayed with green water-paint, which Fisher described as 'a bit dodgy, what with people wandering around in crinolines'.

Many devotees of Hartley's novel were to be upset by the changes Losey and Pinter imposed on the character of Viscount Trimingham, Marian's fiancé. Hartley's Trimingham is badly disfigured by a war wound, a scar that pulls the corners of one eye and his mouth together in a permanent, grotesque grimace; worse, he does not love Marian, seeking her hand only to regain the house, formerly his own family seat. Losey's hero, conversely, bears a rather chic scar, more reminiscent of the duelling club than the battlefield, and is genuinely in love with Marian. Pinter explains: 'You can't simply transfer a book to the screen. It doesn't work, for reasons which should be obvious. In a film, you have to go for the essence of the story, to give the film its focus, with the other elements contributing to that focus.'

The role was superbly played by Edward Fox, who described to his mother, Angela, what it was like being directed by Losey: 'We were once shooting a scene – it's very difficult to explain to you, Ma, because you're not a film actress, but he does nothing. The fact is that he's there, and he looks at you, and you catch his eye, and you know what he wants. And then he uses the camera in such a way that he gives you a chance to portray whatever it is almost by telepathy: what he's conveyed to you and knows you can do. He concentrates so hard. Once, shooting me in *The Go-Between*, a one-shot scene, which he did in one take, he was so absorbed in what he was doing, as was I, that, as he was pulling the camera back – and we were both in a sort of hypnotic trance, not saying anything at all – going back and back, he was nearly bloody killed by this huge camera squashing him against the wall. This was the way he held his actors, with his mind, and doing scenes in one take, like John Ford, without swishing his camera round in a million different directions, which is so unnerving. So he was a life-enhancer, in spite of the gloom and heaviness.'

Perhaps it was only Losey's passion for Venice which prevented him from giving his heart unconditionally to Norfolk. While most of the cast and crew were lodged within three or four miles of Melton Constable, Patricia, Loring and Losey, who had a car and driver to fetch and carry them each day, rented a cottage an hour's drive away, near the marshes reaching out to the icy North Sea. It was one of the happiest times of Losey's life, his days filled with rewarding work and his nights with buoyant camaraderie.

Marsh Barn had been a very special place to the Loseys and their friends; in fact, he had been so happy there during the filming at Melton Constable that he went on renting it for several years afterwards. He particularly adored the natural ambience – the marsh birds wheeling across that stretch of the North Sea, the friends and various children who came to stay, enjoying the warmth of home meals and open fires, the books, music, conversation, dawns and sunsets behind the orchard, and walled garden smothered in honeysuckle and rose. Driving through Thetford in the snow brought him memories of Dartmouth and home. It represented a kind of perfection.

Dominic Guard cried on the day shooting was finished on *The Go-Between*, and, indeed, everyone was saddened. Amid the congratulations, there was a personal sorrow for Edward Fox and for

Losey too: Robin Fox had developed a virulent cancer, which could no longer be ignored.

It had been a happy film, which everyone involved acknowledged to be a singular artistic achievement. Losey himself was delighted with virtually all aspects of it, including the haunting and powerful score created by Michel Legrand, sparingly used, so that the silences, employed to such chilling effect by Pinter, become as meaningful as the sound. The sound effects, which were particularly vital in capturing the rural atmosphere – skirts swishing through the riverside grass on a torrid summer's day, bees buzzing around muslined hats – were recorded by Peter Handford, whose work so delighted Losey that he was asked to join the crew on three further films.

Handford reveals that, at the outset, Losey had wanted to do the film without music, using only sound effects, but Bryan Forbes, then running Elstree Studios, insisted that no distributor would accept a film without music. Forbes said that what he always did in the circumstances was to dub some music; he thought Gilbert and Sullivan would be nice for this film, reinforcing the tone set by Ted Burgess's rendition of *Take a Pair of Sparkling Eyes* at the cricket picnic.

Handford recalls: 'Joe was aghast, rising out of his chair, declaring that the last thing he'd ever do would be to use G and S, like some high-school production. He said the only person he would allow anywhere near the music for *The Go-Between* would be Michel Legrand. Funny thing is that the music that Michel finally did come up with was splendid.'

The film was selected as the British entry for the 1971 Cannes Film Festival, although James Aubrey, then president of MGM, tried to prevent it on the grounds that it was 'the greatest still film ever made'. Aubrey had such a low opinion of the film that he sold it cheaply to Columbia Pictures for £250,000. Columbia executives did not have much confidence in it, either. But the critics disagreed and, at the 1971 Cannes Film Festival, *The Go-Between* carried off the *Palme d'Or*, beating the favourite, Visconti's *Death in Venice*, starring Dirk Bogarde. So enraged was Visconti at being spurned that the festival committee was obliged to invent a special prize to placate him.

The British premiere of *The Go-Between* took place in Norfolk, at the ABC Cinema in Norwich, on 29 October 1971, before the Queen Mother, followed by a dinner at Norwich Castle for seventy-five people. The film was an unqualified critical success, with letters and telegrams of congratulations pouring in from all around the world to swell the numbers of those received following the Cannes triumph, from admirers as disparate as Maria Callas and the Melton Constable staff who cabled: 'We knew you could do it!' Peggy Ashcroft also sent her best wishes, along with Antonioni, Fereydoun Hoveyda, Iran's Imperial Minister for Foreign Affairs, Richard MacDonald, Viveca Lindfors, Ruth Lipton, and John Van Eyssen, who sent congratulations from all at Columbia Pictures.

Losey, as always, wrote dozens of thank-you letters, including one to Bryan Forbes pointing out that the reviews had been unanimously good which, for once, was not an exaggeration. And with his customary warmth towards other people's children, Losey invited Dominic Guard to keep in touch with him, telling him that he was always ready to be of help or to listen to his problems. He also offered the boy some advice should he decide to become a professional actor, which was to view *The Go-Between* at least once a year as a permanent reminder of the talent he possessed at the age of 14 and the heights he would need to strive for in order to better his first performance.

Sadly, *The Go-Between* was to be the last picture Losey made in collaboration with Harold Pinter, although neither knew it at the time. Plans to produce a film based on Proust's *A la Recherche du Temps Perdu* were under way, and Pinter was already thinking about how to tackle the monumental task of writing the screenplay. The relationship between them was by now not only close, but also extremely generous, each man fully acknowledging, promoting, and relying on the other. Speaking to the critic Richard Roud in 1971 of his experience with other directors, Pinter champions Losey unrestrainedly in comparison with others he had worked with, such as Jack Clayton and Michael Anderson: 'I think it can objectively be said that Clayton and Anderson are, shall we say, more traditional in their approach to the writer. For them the writer ceases to matter once he's written and delivered the script. What has meant such a great deal to me, and what has taught me such an enormous amount about films, is continuing right through with Joe, participating and being welcome.'

In the months that followed, *The Go-Between* opened in New

York, Paris, Rome, and various other major European cities to unrestrained praise. In London, John Russell Taylor of *The Times* declared the film to be 'the nearest thing to a masterpiece in view', the German press promoted Losey to '*Der Meister*', while the Belgian critics referred to him as 'Un géant du cinéma mondial'. In America the critics were equally exuberant. After the opening at the 68th Street Playhouse in New York, Larry Cohen in *Show Magazine* pronounced *The Go-Between* 'A masterpiece of incredible delicacy, visual elegance and extraordinary intelligence – one of the year's perfect films', while the often waspish Judith Crist called it 'a brilliant film of classic stature'. Vincent Canby of the *New York Times* was only slightly less enthusiastic: 'While I have some reservations about *The Go-Between*, I think it's quite safe to say that it's one of the loveliest, most perfectly formed, set, and acted films we're likely to see this year.' The French were ecstatic, justifying their loyalty to a hero who, though not quite fallen, had stumbled unnervingly in the recent past. As a result, a retrospective of eight of Losey's previous films was held in Paris.

Only in Italy, where it was retitled *Messenger of Love*, was the film's reception lukewarm, and Losey was obliged to experience that at first hand, in Rome deep into preparations for his next film, *The Assassination of Trotsky*, scripted by Nicholas Mosley. Among a consistently bad batch of critiques came one from the *Rome Daily American* attacking Harold Pinter, which had outraged Losey more than anything; his summation of the matter was simply, 'merde' – a word with which he now frequently ended his more dejected letters.

L P. Hartley died in London in 1972, just before his seventy-seventh birthday, awaiting publication of his seventeenth novel, by which time it was well-known among the Hartley *cognoscenti* that the character of Leo was based on Hartley himself as a boy. Compatible with an abiding fascination with the symbology inherent in astrology and magic, he would doubtless have seen some significance in the predominance of the number seven in these circumstances.

Though a gentle and modest man, Hartley had a list of his least favourite people at the head of which stood Alexander Korda. In a combined interview with Harold Pinter given to Richard Roud in *Sight and Sound* (it was one of his last interviews), he delivered the kind of punch-line that most journalists are obliged to invent: 'You know,' he confided, 'Korda never meant to make a film of my book at all . . . He just bought it as a property, thinking it might appreciate in market value. I was so annoyed when I learned this, that I put a curse upon him. I believe he died the next morning . . .'

XIV

Treading Water

Losey's interest in filming *The Assassination of Trotsky* had begun in the '60s when Joseph Shaftel, an independent producer, brought him a script by Ian Hunter, a once blacklisted writer and Stalinist whom he had known in Hollywood. Not only did he dislike the treatment, which dealt primarily with the end of Trotsky's life, but Losey found himself rudely awakened to some of the ugly facts about Stalin and Stalinism and so accepted the commission in a spirit of 'exploration and expiation'.

He had spent the autumn and early winter of 1970 reading up on the life and writings of Trotsky, and conferring with Hunter about the script. The film was intended to deal with the last three years, the period between the two assassination attempts, when Trotsky, virtually imprisoned in a suburb of Mexico City, passed his time in making pronouncements and gestures which reached no one. But the project ran into trouble almost immediately, not only with various of Trotsky's associates and relatives still living, but with those who had been politically involved, and who expected a film that would present a larger canvas depicting Trotsky's theories, writings, and activities.

Losey's relations with Trotsky's heirs were predictably vexed. Although he and Patricia – especially Patricia – had researched the material extensively, it became apparent that to produce a commercial film which pursued a politically controversial theme was going to be virtually impossible without stirring up a hornet's nest of contention. Losey believed that the film, as planned, would present Trotsky in a straightforward manner: as the co-founder (with Lenin) of the Russian revolution, organizer of the Red Army, leader of the October movement, as well as an impressive writer and orator.

By Christmas, Losey realized that Hunter would never be able to deliver the kind of script he wanted, partly because of persistent personal problems: he was drinking very heavily, and planning to go into a clinic to dry out. Eventually Hunter did revise the script, but Losey was no happier and at last replaced him with Nicholas Mosley, in whom he had more confidence. Mosley persuaded Losey that working towards an understanding of his own father, in spite of the polarization of their views, had given him the ability to understand Trotsky.

Mosley says that Joe would often talk about his Communist and Stalinist days: 'I believed a lot of it, though he was like a schoolboy about it. He loved talking about this Russian chap he used to know in New York, who in a way was Joe's "control" in the early '40s.' With hindsight, Losey came to feel that the choice of Mosley was a mistake, for although the son shared none of his father's right-wing views, he was mistrusted from the start by Trotsky's family and followers in Mexico and Paris.

More critically, Losey was beginning to suffer an irreversible decline in both health and aspiration. In an interview with the *Daily Mail*, he bitterly revealed his disenchantment with 'the ugly world of films'. He added: 'It is more difficult for me to fight, because I'm so tired now. I've been doing it too long.' He was sixty-two and facing the death of one of his closest friends – the man who, as his agent, had guided his career.

In a last desperate effort to save the life of Robin Fox, Angela had taken him to a German clinic which claimed to have worked remarkable cures using an unorthodox approach. When it became apparent that her husband was going to die no matter what treatment was applied, Angela had brought him back to their home in the small Sussex village of Cuckfield. In the two or so weeks preceding his death, friends took turns sitting with him, holding his hand and reading to him, Paul Scofield, Dirk Bogarde, Lindsay Anderson and the journalist Godfrey Winn among them.

When death came on 20 January 1971, the loss was so painful that Losey was unable to speak of it with anyone other than those within the charmed circle. He had loved Robin Fox with a strength of emotion not often found in one man for another, and vented his pain upon the one person who was most vulnerable – Angela.

As she wrote in her autobiography, *Slightly Foxed*: 'The only person who behaved foolishly, even cruelly, towards me, was Joe

Losey, who made a hysterical scene and beat his fists against the wall, screaming at me that I was a murderer, and that if it had not been for me and my inability to be disciplined enough to stay in Germany, Robin would have been cured; I had killed him. If Joe had meant to upset me he couldn't have been more successful in his efforts.'

Many leading figures in British film, theatre and television gathered for Fox's funeral at Trinity Church, Cuckfield, but Losey was not among them; he stayed at home. Although Angela found his absence inexcusable, she knew that his presence was not one from which she was likely to gain comfort.

In his despondency, Losey's attacks of asthma became worse and more frequent, and he drank more, growing grossly fat. He was more unkind and hurtful than ever to Patricia, at home as well as in the presence of others. (Bogarde remembers an occasion when Losey reprimanded Patricia for disturbing everyone by her searching for her lost contact lens during a screening.)

But the compulsion to work drove him on, as did the need to support his increasingly luxurious life-style. There were so many films he still wanted to make: *Under the Volcano, Voss,* and Proust's *A la Recherche du Temps Perdu* – always Proust, haunting his dreams, awake and sleeping. Harold Pinter worked on the screenplay of Proust's great work for the better part of a year. For three months he read the novel every day, travelling in company with Losey and Barbara Bray, a noted authority on Proust, to Illiers, Cabourg, and Paris, steeping himself in the Proustian world. He finished during 1972, and it was to be published, to much acclaim, in 1973, although the wide availability of the script still failed to attract anyone with the money to turn it into a film.

In an interview in the *Daily Mail* on 18 November 1976, Losey boasted that he had saved the hotel at Cabourg from demolition with a view to using it for the Proust film: 'It was about to be torn down, and I appealed to the mayor, Bruno Coquatrix, who owns the Olympia Music Hall in Paris, to stop the demolition. Inside, it's all ruined for me anyway, refitted with plastic. But in the cellar, I discovered all the old fittings and the chandeliers. They're keeping it all, the hotel and the stuff in the cellars, just for me.'

In a later interview in the *International Herald Tribune* Losey added: 'We were so certain we were going to do it that Gaumont gave a celebration dinner at the Ritz at Proust's table, with Proust's menu and Proust's wines, and they even resurrected Proust's wine waiter.'

In April 1972 bitter memories were revived for Losey, when he was invited to attend the Cannes Film Festival as president of the jury. The American entry favoured to win the prize was *The Visitors*, directed by Elia Kazan. Kazan had been warned that his film had no chance of winning, as Losey had not forgotten his multiple betrayals during the last days of the blacklist, but he insisted that Losey was too big a man to let his political views cloud his artistic judgement. According to Kazan, the Swedish actress Bibi Andersson, also a jury member, told him that Losey argued vehemently against *The Visitors* in all the secret jury meetings, whilst remaining non-committal in public. She and the rest of the jury liked the film, but in the end they gave way to Losey's passion, and the prizes went elsewhere. Kazan was dismayed by Losey's attitude, particularly when he discovered that Losey later admitted to a French critic that *The Visitors* was a very good film.

Another jury member, the Swiss director Alain Tanner, remembers events slightly differently. 'Losey was firmly against giving a prize to *The Visitors*,' he says. 'As president of the jury, he had, of course, some weight. But, apart from this remark, he didn't try to impose his views on the other members. In any case, if I remember well, *The Visitors* was never proposed for any of the prizes – perhaps suggested for interpretation, but I can't be sure. But what I can be sure of is the intense dislike Mr Losey had for Kazan.'

Losey's political views were also to rebound on the *Trotsky* project and contribute to its failure, although the film was to attract no less than three bright stars: Richard Burton, Romy Schneider and Alain Delon. The subject matter, however, still provoked too many people. Criticism of the script came from Trotsky's literary executors, Marguerite Bonnet (who was a friend of Trotsky's widow, Natalya) and

Jean Malaquais, an old comrade, as well as from Trotsky's grandson, 'Seva' Volkov, who lived in and maintained the old Mexican house as a shrine to his grandfather, keeping it exactly as it was the day he died. Responding to the working script sent by Bertrand Tavernier, Losey's French publicity man, the executors wrote letters which alternated between good-natured nit-picking and more doctrinaire objections: there was too much 'blurring of political perspective', 'contradictions', and 'outright "untruthfulness"', they chorused.

Losey's response was a petulant one, complaining that Tavernier had no right to show a draft script to anyone. He tried to shift the blame away from himself, claiming that not only Tavernier but the writers had let him down. The script was not to be taken as an indication of what the film would be like, he said. He was aiming to tell the truth about Trotsky and the final script would meet their objections.

Even greater difficulties were created by the Mexican government and the revolutionary painter, David Sequeiros, who had tried to kill Trotsky in May 1940, and whose co-operation Losey believed to be essential for the success of the film. First on the list of Losey's conditions for making the film had been that it be shot on location in Mexico. The effect of using the actual settings, moreover, would rely heavily on the inclusion of murals by the great Mexican painter, Orozco, as well as those of Sequeiros. Shaftel had assured Losey that there would be no problems, but when he approached the Mexican minister in charge of cinema, he was rebuffed, and advised to shift the film to Spain, where the Mexican locations could be reproduced. But censorship problems arose there as well, and Shaftel ultimately set up the project at the Laurentiis Studios in Italy.

The extent of Losey's despair is reflected in a long memo to Shaftel saying that there was a good chance that both the Mexican government and Sequeiros would never co-operate, and that Losey wished to make it clear that he could not be responsible for failing to produce the film he had contemplated. He also stressed the fact that, should his requirements not be met, it would be impossible to guarantee the success of the project, or to fulfil his obligations to the producers, the actors, and the many technicians necessary to justify the vast expenses incurred in building sets rather than shooting on location.

The memo gives Shaftel full credit for all the hard work he had done in raising money for the film by selling distribution rights around the world, but reminds him that his own integrity is at stake, since Delon and Schneider had been wooed and won on the basis of his original concept and their personal confidence in his moral and artistic integrity.

Delon, who was to play the assassin Frank Jacson (alias Ramon Mercader, a Spanish Communist), was then among the top half-dozen male actors in Europe. It was to be his first film with Losey, and it was most important that the conditions of his acceptance were not compromised. That was also true of Romy Schneider who, in the role of Gita Samuels, Jacson's duped lover and Trotsky's secretary, was vulnerable on two counts: her lack of self-confidence, and the fact that she and Delon had recently, and unhappily, ended a much publicized love affair.

In spite of all these harassments, which were exacerbated by the fact that he had been working for the past half-year without a proper contract or financial compensation for his expenses, Losey soldiered on. While Mosley and the reinstated Richard MacDonald struggled for three days and nights to solve the problem of the murals, Losey kept doggedly after the Mexican cultural ministers and Sequeiros himself. A way simply had to be found to shoot three or four special murals in Mexico, with certain of the main actors and a skeleton crew, with the direct co-operation and consent of the artist.

Meanwhile, MacDonald undertook a covert mission to Mexico City, to see what he could discover: 'I was having a little escapade with an Israeli girlfriend, a Sabra paratrooper. I was supposed to do a "recce" of Trotsky's villa, among other things. I went on the pretence of looking for the mural painters, Rivera, Orozco, and Sequeiros, so I had something to tell taxi drivers. Looked for an English-speaking driver, who was intelligent, and we got on very well. He said, "I know Sequeiros. I used to do some work for him," so he took me out there, and I met the guy, whose wife, of course, was mixed up in the murder. Meanwhile, I was trying to get him to take me to Trotsky's villa, and we actually found it, still there, this ghastly, overgrown fortress. I arrived with my Polaroid and photographed the whole bloody place so I knew exactly what it looked like and everything.'

Near the end of June, when both time and money were running out, Losey called the cultural minister in Mexico, who now said, much to his amazement, that the government was not necessarily against the project, and suggested that Losey come to Mexico City to discuss the matter. Delighted, Losey sent him a copy of the script with a covering letter. He also wrote to Sequeiros, and managed to secure assurances of a meeting, at which Losey hoped to persuade him to participate in the film.

Alas, even these efforts ended in failure. The minister refused to co-operate, issuing instead a series of dictats to be adhered to even within the context of an Italian studio version: There was to be no depiction of drunkenness following the May Day parade planned for the opening scene; all denigrating remarks concerning President Cardeñas were to be cut; Trotsky's remarks about the Aztecs' victims as possible guinea pigs in the study of the cardiacal effects of altitude were to be cut, as well as the shanty towns on the outskirts of Mexico City.

Losey met and talked to the spell-binding Sequeiros, offering to end the film with Sequeiros standing in front of the latest of his murals, issuing a declaration and offering his own version of events, even if it meant contradicting most of what was said in the film. Although the idea appealed to the artist, his protective wife, Angelica, sabotaged the plan. Losey made one last attempt to persuade him, writing Sequeiros a long letter which the artist received just before he died. It was a complex document in which Losey tried both to assuage Angelica's fears and flatter Sequeiros as well as attempting to define his own artistic position and the place the film would have in both of their lives.

At times, the letter reads as though he were planning to make a film about Sequeiros rather than Trotsky. But Losey was still concerned by the impact of the film script on those who had read it. He wanted Sequeiros to understand that he regarded a script in much the same way that a painter might view some preliminary sketches of a mural, as the merest outline of the finished work.

He expressed some regret at ever having become involved with a film on Trotsky. It is difficult now to know whether Losey believed that, or whether he was merely trying to persuade the painter that his reluctance and his distrust of what Trotsky represented put them both on the same side: not only as revolutionary artists, but as artists who were not understood or fully appreciated by the world. As a result, both of them were trying to preserve their integrity and artistic vision in a commercial world where such aspirations counted for little.

Losey quoted Brecht's Galileo: 'A man cannot unsee what he has seen.' The film, he told Sequeiros, could explain the painter's life and work to a mass audience. That, surely, would be a revolutionary act, and one that film, especially Losey's film, was most fitted to perform. Their work, he said, was a dialectic. He wanted the film to demonstrate that by showing Sequeiros's works. He added that, if necessary, he would be prepared to cut every reference to the artist from the film. The letter ended with Losey's love and admiration for Sequeiros's life, work and wife, but it failed to have the desired effect.

Cynically, one might interpret Losey's flattery of Sequeiros as a last-ditch effort to secure the artist's co-operation, but one cannot fail to recognize the overriding sincerity of the message – even a certain poignancy in the occasional clumsiness of expression, so unexpected from a man known for his literacy and conversational grace.

Casting the film presented more problems than usual, partly because of the growing uncertainties about the quality of the script and the conditions under which it was to be shot, but also because of nationality quotas imposed by the co-producers, who included Cinetel in Paris and de Laurentiis in Rome: there could not be too many actors of a single nationality, which ruled out Simone Signoret as Trotsky's wife, Natalya, since the cast already had a majority of French actors.

It was finally decided that the role would go to Valentina Cortese, an Italian actress who, it was generally agreed, was badly miscast. According to Jack Loring, Losey kept saying, 'But who can act that part opposite Burton, with the necessary power?' Loring had no doubts: it could only be Anna Magnani. Much to Loring's amazement, for he was unaccustomed to faint-heartedness in his friend, Losey demurred, admitting that he was terrified of the great Roman actress, and feared that he would not be able to control her. Loring argued that Losey was surely much too strong a director to fear any actor, admiring, at the same time, the fact that Losey could admit to his apprehension. 'We were such good friends', Loring explains, 'that he didn't try to hide his weaknesses from me as he did from others.'

Richard Burton had not been Losey's first choice for the role of

Trotsky; even Burton admitted that 'about the only thing we have in common is our height.' Losey had asked Bogarde to play the part, but was rebuffed. Losey thought that Bogarde 'stupidly' turned the part down because the script was not good enough. He was deeply stung, feeling that, by his refusal, Bogarde had demonstrated a 'fatal' lack of confidence in him, suggesting that he would never have shot the script exactly as it was anyway. Burton's acceptance, on the other hand, indicated a faith in Losey's ability and an understanding that Losey's craft would enhance and transform the script, although, in the event, he was mistaken.

During the filming, Losey was not only off form but either so tired or drunk that he was hardly a presence at all. Burton disliked the long speeches to the camera he was given, which Losey made even longer by adding chunks of direct quotations from Trotsky's speeches; he wrote in his notebooks on 23 October, 'For the second time this week I played a scene with two people who couldn't speak a word of English and who were found to be incapable of learning, even like parrots, the few lines they had to say. It was an all-day agony of frayed nerves for everybody, including Joe, tho' we all kept our tempers and were very patient. But why did Joe cast them in the first place?'

Five days later, Burton's entry read: 'Joe is definitely not himself. He doesn't seem to know the script as well as he usually does.' Losey, drinking heavily, often had to be reminded by the continuity girl of obvious matters.

Then, halfway through shooting, Mosley, hearing by chance that Losey had cut virtually all the politics out of his script, flew to Rome to confront him. An angry row ensued between the two men, with Mosley challenging and Losey growing increasingly pompous and decreasingly plausible. Artistically, the political elements didn't work, he said; he had become worried about the validity of the statement they were making; it wasn't right to make a film sympathetic to Trotsky; art is not obliged to make a political statement.

Finally, in desperation, Losey simply handed over his files on the film for Mosley to read and the truth emerged. There were memos saying that Mosley had been the wrong choice because of his unsound politics.

'Hell,' Mosley protests, 'the whole reason he picked me in the first place over the other fellow, who'd written this ponderous thing full of Marxist jargon, was that I was apolitical, because my attitude, having survived my father, was that all politicians are loonies. When my sister saw the film, she said, "How did you ever get Richard Burton to come out exactly like Dad?"

'My script was the one that got the money, got Burton and Delon, got the whole bloody thing off the ground. The whole year he'd been saying, "This is the most wonderful script I've ever seen." Then, suddenly, I discover he's been in touch with all these damned French Marxists, who'd got to him about me and my background, and that he'd had this phone call from his old friend from the KGB, who's now a cultural attaché or something, keeping an eye, no doubt, on the old Leftists who might come in useful.

'Obviously, this guy scared the hell out of Joe. Said, "We hear you're making a film about Trotsky, and we'll be very interested to see how it comes out." Well, I said, "Come on, Joe, how can this possibly affect you?", and he became very pompous, and tried to say he'd compromised his politics, or some such rubbish. I'm not saying he thought he'd had a death threat or something like that, but I think there was a lot of paranoia – understandable – hanging over from the McCarthy era. And it's a completely gutted film. The bits about Trotsky's life in that Mexican fortress-house, with guns on the roof, and God knows what, were supposed to be intercut with political flashbacks of his life between 1917 and 1923. Now it's just a story about some old man in Mexico, waiting to be killed by some Stalinist spiv, and no one can tell who this old man is. It's a tragedy.'

Most of the reviewers thought it was tragic, too. Several French critics complained of the film's ideological insignificance. Gérard Legrand of *Le Monde* wrote: 'Stalin only appears as a celebrated effigy, who appears to encourage Sequeiros, and as a ghost floating on an artificial lake.' The Trotskyists of London were angered by Losey's ignorance of history and his lack of sympathy for their hero. The only praise was for the actors. The performances given by Burton, Schneider, and especially Delon – disarmingly handsome, insinuating himself into the doomed man's study, wielding the fatal axe – were magnificent. Burton, who had worked hard on his characterization, make-up, and gestures, managed to achieve a moving and convincing Trotsky. He had stopped drinking for the moment and was suffering from withdrawal symptoms, forgetting his lines and delivering those he remembered in an uninspired fashion. But as he dug deeper into the work, his performance grew.

The disagreement between Mosley and Losey, although it was eventually settled, was for the moment exacerbated by Losey's lack of interest in filming his novel *Impossible Object*. Mosley's understanding had been that, once he completed his script for *Trotsky*, Losey would begin preparations for filming the book. Catherine Deneuve had agreed to star, and Mosley had found a producer to put up the money. But Losey withdrew from the project, saying that he disliked the producer, and that, in any case, the money was inadequate. Whatever the reasons, Mosley was deeply disappointed. (His script was later filmed by John Frankenheimer.)

Losey's distress, following the commercial catastrophe of *The Assassination of Trotsky*, was heightened because Patricia's two children were now obliged to return to their father in Brazil. He wrote from Marsh Barn to David Davidoff, a friend and potential investor who lived in Mexico, of the enjoyment of having Patricia's children to stay over Christmas, even though he was unwell and work was proving troublesome. He told Davidoff that he expected to be visiting Mexico briefly in April, since it looked as if he would be making *Under The Volcano* there before he got round to doing *Proust*.

Losey had acquired the rights to Malcolm Lowry's novel the previous year and had phoned Bogarde in France asking him to come down to Rome so that they could talk it over. Bogarde and Tony Forwood actually went three or four times at considerable inconvenience and expense. On the last occasion, walking home from the Loseys' flat at three o'clock in the morning, Forwood had observed that it was all a bit odd; they had come to Rome several times to discuss the project, and the only person they had never talked about was Bogarde.

'Well, that's reasonable,' said Bogarde, 'since I'm playing the lead,' to which Forwood replied, 'No, I don't think you are.' Bogarde was unable to believe that his great friend would pick his brain about a film in which he was not to star. On his return to France, he rang Losey in Rome, hoping to sort the matter out. Patricia answered the phone, her tone evasive, and said that Joe had gone out. But Bogarde knew that Losey was there in the room, for in the background he could hear the rhythmic hiss of Losey's inhaler, the constant companion of his laboured, asthmatic breathing.

'This is the message,' Bogarde said. 'I know I'm not going to be involved in the film.' Just to be certain, he rang his new agent, in whom he confided his suspicions. The response was, 'Well, I guess I have to come clean; Losey may be making the film with another of my clients.' In the end, of course, Losey never made the film at all. Instead it was directed by John Huston, with Albert Finney in the starring role.

What most concerned Bogarde was Losey's betrayal. He returned to Rome not long after to discuss a film with Visconti, and rang Losey to invite him to dinner at the most luxurious restaurant in Rome. A table for twelve was organized for the party, which included Romy Schneider. Says Bogarde, 'It was a very happy dinner, though I knew we wouldn't work together again. Not after that treachery.' When it finished Romy suggested they go back to Losey's flat. Bogarde agreed, but warned that he would not go in. When they arrived, Losey asked if Dirk was coming in. Bogarde replied, 'No. Goodbye. Not goodnight – goodbye.'

In a letter Losey sent to Romy Schneider, wishing her love on her thirty-third birthday, he told her that he had been most upset by the disagreement with Bogarde. The letter also revealed a change in Losey's attitude to his leading ladies. He abandoned his usual romantic role in favour of a more paternalistic one.

One project still filled his mind. He planned to teach at Dartmouth for another term, he wrote to Davidoff before filming *Proust* in 1973.

XV

At Play with Ibsen and Brecht

While Losey continued the desperate search for a willing backer for the Proust film, other projects came and went. On a beach in Cannes, Claude Giroux, a Canadian producer, introduced himself as an old friend of Ben Barzman and suggested that Losey direct *The Story of O*, Pauline Réage's best-selling story of sex and bondage. According to Barzman, Losey replied: '"You're out of your fucking head", which isn't the way to talk to anybody.' Losey had also been in correspondence with the daughter of Zelda Fitzgerald about a film on her mother's life, but she had turned against the idea at the last minute, although she had liked the script.

Ely Landau, an American producer who had set up The American Film Theatre in 1972 to back adaptations of classic plays for television release in the States and cinema showings elsewhere in the world, suggested that Losey direct Edward Albee's *A Delicate Balance*, followed by *A Doll's House*, by Ibsen. The proposition interested him, but Landau began to have doubts about Ibsen, so Losey took the idea to John Heyman, suggesting Jane Fonda for the role of Nora. Losey had first met Fonda in Rome, having approached her to play the female lead in the ill-starred *Under the Volcano*, and had been thinking about a film in which he might involve her. Given that she was among the most bankable female stars in the world and an outspoken feminist active in political affairs, she seemed an ideal choice for Ibsen's play about the stifling effects of Victorian marriage. She accepted with pleasure and alacrity; to play the lead in a theatrical classic with Losey directing would certainly not do her career any harm.

Losey's budget, at under $1 million, was cripplingly small, which meant abandoning the star system and its lopsided salary structure.

Everyone in the cast, including David Warner, who played Nora's husband, Trevor Howard (Dr Rank), Edward Fox (Krogstad) and Delphine Seyrig (Kristine), agreed to more or less equal remuneration, such was their enthusiasm. The star herself received only slightly more than the others: $40,000 plus $1,500 per week. In addition, all would receive a small but equal percentage of the picture, with all credits (except Fonda's), including Losey's own, being listed in alphabetical order and printed in the same size.

Working on *A Doll's House*, perhaps more than on any other film since *Boy With Green Hair*, Losey was reminded of his 'Nordic' ancestry and boyhood in La Crosse. Searching for a suitable location, he had visited the place where Ibsen was born, lived and worked, but found nothing there to equal the charm and character of Røros, a small, architecturally quaint village, which at night was lit mainly by old-fashioned lamps and candles. There was only one drawback for Losey and certain other members of the cast and crew: not a drop of alcohol could be found in the town, so along with the technical equipment, crates of vodka, whisky and gin were shipped in. Filming began in November, and since there are only three or four hours of daylight in the Norwegian winter, the work was difficult and intensely concentrated, contributing to a growing tension.

Peter Handford, the sound engineer, describes the difficulties they encountered in getting equipment to Røros and, having done so, getting it to work properly in the bitter cold. Special generators and other equipment had to be imported, transported by a huge lorry, then transferred to sledges, which they pushed and pulled through the mountainous drifts. One of the happier aspects, however, was that Gerry Fisher had joined the team once again as cinematographer, producing what Losey believed to be his best work, while he bathed the little town in a perpetual, glowing twilight of pastel whites, and Handford captured the crisp, clear sounds of bells, horses' hooves and footsteps crunching on the snow. Eileen Diss, the designer, who had hitherto worked almost exclusively with the BBC, worked easily and well with her director, in spite of his disappointment in not being able to obtain the services of either Carmen Dillon or Richard MacDonald.

The play was adapted for the screen by David Mercer, whose talent Losey greatly respected; none of the projects on which they had worked together had come to fruition, so Losey was pleased to be able to offer him *A Doll's House* as a certainty. (Their most recent collaboration had been on *Voss*, based on Patrick White's novel, which was closest to Losey's heart next to Proust, and he had thought Mercer's screenplay superb.) But trouble was brewing even before filming started. Aided and abetted by Losey, Mercer opened out Ibsen's masterpiece, and radically altered the text, which outraged the female stars. It soon developed into one of the unhappiest sets on which any of them had ever worked and created schisms of an intensity that Losey had not experienced since his difficulties with the Hakim brothers. The battle was to be one between the sexes, a straight split between the men and the women, apart from Fonda's future husband, Tom Hayden, who supported the women. Seyrig and Fonda arrived in Norway already enraged by the fact that a promised period of rehearsal – in costume, on set – was cancelled due, according to Losey, to lack of time and funds.

'Now here's a funny story,' Seyrig said, conspiratorially. 'Joe saw me wearing a badge with the female symbol on it, and asked me what it was. An ex-medical student! He wondered if he could have it, so he could impress Jane when he went to fetch her at the airport in Norway. But Jane said she just burst out laughing, because he was wearing it upside down!'

Losey planned to begin with an expository scene at a skating rink, whose purpose was to establish the friendship of his two female protagonists, Nora and Kristine, before their marriages. Delphine Seyrig was horrified at the proposed changes: 'This Mercer was absolutely the wrong writer for the film. They took all the feminism out of it, which is the whole point of the play. Now, what is the point of getting two actresses like me and Jane, who are both particularly known for our views on the subject, if you're going to do that?

'At the time of *Accident*, in which I had that smallish scene with Dirk, I was asked to go and see Joe here in Paris, at the George V Hotel. I was very surprised that he wanted to see me. But this was shortly after Resnais' film, *Muriel*, came out, for which I got an award in Venice five years earlier, in 1962. I'd done some Pinter plays, but it wasn't Pinter who recommended me. If you see *Muriel* and then *Accident*, you eventually see a similarity. Joe was not so much jealous, as very impressed. He said he wanted to see if I was really an independent actress, or just a creature of Resnais. It was a funny way to approach me. Provocative. I felt he was so overcome by *Muriel* that he wanted something that belonged to Resnais – that he had used. I became a sort of status symbol – hired to create a link with another great director and not a choice for myself.'

Jane Fonda had arrived not only with her future husband, but with her own scriptwriter, Nancy Dowd, and soon decided that Mercer was 'an alcoholic, misogynist English playwright'. While the men stayed in an hotel, the women moved into rented houses nearby. Losey told Michael Freedland, one of Fonda's biographers: 'Jane Fonda seemed totally unaware of my existence, the existence of the crew or the male members of the cast, including David Warner and Trevor Howard, who felt totally isolated. For the first week, when I should have been rehearsing, they spent their time in their houses, sending in pages of notes on what should be done with the film.'

When asked what it was like to work with Jane Fonda, Trevor Howard replied, 'I wouldn't know. I never met her.' Every night the men retired to one of their rooms, which became the bar, while Fonda, Seyrig and their followers withdrew to their houses to rework the script. 'Almost daily,' Losey disclosed to *Time* magazine, 'Jane would announce to some actor, as he or she arrived on the set: "Here are some new cues for you." She never spoke to any of the men. One actor said, "Now I know what it feels like to be a nigger".' Losey told Freedland, 'I found her selfish, difficult and thoroughly unpleasant.'

In a long interview with Molly Haskell in the *Village Voice* Fonda complained, 'Most of the men were drunk all the time. And of course they interpreted anything we did as simply wanting more lines to say. They painted it as a conspiracy of dykes ganging up on "us poor men".' She added: 'Losey never had the guts to confront me. On the contrary, he wrote me love letters, but he attacked women in lower positions. He tried to set us against each other. Then when it was all over, he gave these interviews in which he attacked me, called me cruel, and said I was disrespectful to the crew.

'I was completely professional. I never came late and I always knew my lines. Losey would have preferred an Elizabeth Taylor, with tantrums and scenes. But a perfectly normal, well-disciplined actress who had some ideas about the play, that he couldn't handle. And this from a man who calls himself a progressive, a Marxist.'

The war of attrition was often destructively carried onto the set itself. Each morning there would be some new slogan to greet

Fonda as she arrived, such as 'Cleopatra needed women's lib like a hole in the head.' Losey decided that the troubles could be traced back to Seyrig's influence upon Fonda. He accused her of silly things, such as undermining Fonda's performance. And of general unprofessionalism. He never spoke to her directly during the shooting, transmitting directions by way of intermediaries. Tempers were easily lost. Losey was overheard, barking at Patricia: 'You're so stupid, you can't even find me any clean socks.' 'Is this the behaviour', muses Delphine Seyrig, 'of a man who understands women's rights? Why does he treat his wife like staff?'

Finally one night, Losey assembled the entire company, including the technicians, and announced that they were going to go through the script page by page until there was a consensus. They would then begin the shooting on the following day, and there was to be 'no more goddam talking about it, because I'm not going to be able to do this picture unless this kind of thing stops.' It did stop, and the picture was completed on schedule. Losey had many complaints about the filming, but only a few about the final result. He returned to London convinced that it was an exceptionally good film, freely admitting that some of Fonda's changes to the script had actually helped to improve it, and that her acting, in any case, was superb.

But they did not part on good terms. On the company's last night in Røros, Losey organized a party for the cast and two hundred and fifty of the townsfolk. According to *Time* magazine, Fonda appeared ninety minutes late, prompting bitter comments from one of the crew, which left Fonda in tears. Seyrig denies this story, saying that she and Fonda had arrived at the party together, not realizing that it was seated and Losey was going to make a speech.

Angered that Fonda wasn't there, and taking it as a personal slight, Losey left the party after his welcoming speech, and waited in the hall for the two women to arrive. While Seyrig went in to join the party, Losey detained Fonda and attacked her verbally. Looking back, Seyrig saw Jane standing in front of Losey like a child before the headmaster, Losey flushed with rage, bursting with vitriol and offended pride. Says Seyrig, 'Now he didn't need her any more, and had his revenge.' Jane Fonda will not discuss the matter: she does not wish to be reminded of that experience, nor does she want to heap obloquy on an admittedly great director.

*

A Doll's House was undercut, both by appearing on television in America, spoiling its chances for distribution in the cinemas, and by the appearance of a rival version of the play, starring Claire Bloom and directed by Patrick Garland, which was released at the same time. Those critics who saw both versions, however, tended to opt for Losey's, on the grounds that it was 'a real movie'. Garland had kept his characters mainly indoors, in order to reinforce both the physical and the social claustrophobia. Losey demonstrated, on the other hand, that the characters were caught in a larger trap, incorporating all the provincial society of the times: the whole village was a collection of doll's houses, and many of the dolls living in them were male.

There was talk about submitting *A Doll's House* as the British entry for the Cannes Festival, but Losey had strong reservations: *The Go-Between* had won the *Palme d'Or* only two years before, he had served as chairman of the jury in 1972, and felt that it would be tempting fate to expect his domination of the event to continue for a third year. There were other, murkier reasons. Pierre Rissient, with whom Losey had fallen out, was representing the festival in some of its preliminary selections. Losey wrote to his French co-producer, Joseph Boetie, that he would prefer not to deal with Rissient but would glad to deal with his associate, Bertrand Tavernier. Of course he would; Tavernier was his man. In addition, Jane Fonda made it known that she would not be able to make an appearance, which would have been vital for publicity, as she would then be seven months' pregnant. In the end, wisdom prevailed, and the film was shown at Cannes, but outside the competition.

A Doll's House opened in London on 5 July to very respectful reviews. John Russell Taylor in *The Times* praised much in this 'generally distinguished piece of work', singling out Losey's sharp period sense, down to details like the degree of fading we would expect to see on the paper of Torvald's drawing room walls. In his review in *The Guardian*, Richard Roud was a good deal more enthusiastic about Jane Fonda's performance than those of David Warner and Delphine Seyrig, 'who both play as though suffering from head colds.' He decided that the film 'is minor Losey perhaps, but that is measuring it against the highest standards.' The film's opening run was short. In August, Losey received a letter from John Heyman informing him that, though it was 'holding steady' in the face of daunting competition, it was not reaching house rental figures, and would be withdrawn at the end of that month.

Losey never worked again with David Mercer, which was a great pity, for Mercer at his best was a brilliant, skilful, and imaginative writer. In the late 1970s, Losey was approached by German television to direct a seven-part television series, based on Thomas Mann's *The Magic Mountain*, for which Mercer had written a superb script. Halfway into the negotiations, however, the producers decided that they wanted to make a feature film instead, which would have meant cutting the script in a manner that both Losey and Mercer found unacceptable, so the project was abandoned.

Meanwhile, Ben Barzman and his wife, Norma, still living happily in France, decided to visit London in the hopes of reviving another project: a film dealing with the assassination of the Algerian leader, Ben Barka. Barzman managed to enthuse Losey, who agreed to come to Paris to meet Barzman's prospective producer, Claude Giroux. The Barka story appealed to Losey for obvious reasons, but Barzman was unaware of the dispute that had taken place between Losey and Giroux at Cannes the previous year. The minute they met, they began bickering. 'The whole thing was up the spout in ten minutes, and Joe just flew straight back to London,' said the bemused Barzman.

A little later, an executive from Warner Brothers contacted Barzman, to say that the company wanted to film his Ben Barka script, but not with Losey. Barzman loyally responded that, in that case, they wouldn't make it. 'Listen, Ben,' said the executive, 'you're going to run into this. You won't get any American company to go with Joe, because he almost singlehandedly ruined my career, to begin with.' Barzman remembered that Losey's two pictures for Warners, *The Servant* and *King and Country*, had both lost money in the States.

Says Barzman, 'I wanted Joe because I thought he'd be wonderful with it; they wanted me because they'd seen 'Z', which I'd worked on and had been a success. But that was the general feeling at the time about Joe, and I was very much hurt by it.'

Against the odds Proust continued to dominate Losey's thoughts and plans. To Alain Delon, who was to play Swann, with Bogarde in the role of the Count, he wrote to say that the work was progressing well, and that the script was nearly completed; and to Mary Blume of the *International Herald Tribune* that the project was the hardest he had ever tackled. He had hopes that Harry Saltzman, the producer who had made a killing with James Bond movies, might back it. Fired by enthusiasm, Pinter even went as far as to suggest that Lady Antonia Fraser's daughter, Rebecca, might play the young lesbian, Albertine, with his son Daniel in a supporting role.

Then, in October, Patricia was slightly hurt in a car accident in Spain which evidently incapacitated her for several weeks, so that she was unable to assist in the tiring mechanics of raising the money for the film. This important enterprise was now largely in the hands of Nicole Stephane, whose maiden name was Rothschild, and whose contacts could prove invaluable.

Losey's next interim project was to take him back twenty-five years; at long last he was to film Brecht's *Galileo*, but, inevitably, there was a hitch: the producer Ely Landau stipulated that it had to be made for less than $1 million. It would clearly not be feasible to cleave to the original dream of filming the play on location, uncut and unabridged, since that would involve more than fifty speaking parts, hundreds of costumes, with the action fluctuating between Padua, Florence, Venice and Rome.

Losey resigned himself to a studio picture, which would be treated as a theatre piece, performed on a vast, composite set built on a revolving stage. Rather than the stage rotating around the eye, the camera would revolve around the various elements of the set, sections of which would be interchangeable, like pieces of a Lego toy, slotting in wherever needed. Once again, Losey was able to call on the talents of Richard MacDonald.

Losey described the script, which had been adapted by Barbara Bray, as a fusion of the version he had directed with Charles Laughton in Hollywood and Brecht's later German version. The original, which lasted three hours, had to be cut before it could be filmed. He worked hard on the adaptation with Barbara Bray and his old friend, George Tabori, who had become an authority on Brecht and his work. Twelve years earlier Losey had made some notes demonstrating his intentions, and these were neither compromised nor betrayed by the film which was released in 1974. His original notion had been to present a very personal view of Galileo and the significance of his life, as Brecht had represented it in relation to the problems of the modern age. Losey saw at the centre of Brecht's *Galileo* a portrait of a recognizably fallible, 'human' being, a man who liked to eat and drink, to womanize and to think. A man of animal appetites, among them the appetite for thinking.

Losey considered many actors of extraordinarily different types for the title role, including Charles Boyer and Dirk Bogarde, who wrote that he was 'sorry, but not free in July,' which is when the shooting was to begin. For a time he was obsessed by the idea of Marlon Brando as Galileo, and wrote to the actor, assuring him that, though he too was deeply concerned about the plight of the American Indians, his participation in *Galileo* would not only be wonderful for the film, but a feather in Brando's cap as well. Someone pointed out, however, that Brando was not prone to working for love, and that his fee could, in fact, gobble up the entire budget.

Then came a telegram from Otto Plaschkes, the executive producer, to the effect that he had had a brainstorm on *Galileo*: what would Losey think about Topol in the role? If there were to be no Brando, Topol would be Plaschkes's first choice. In a nice bit of irony, the last person who had admonished Losey to relax had been Brecht himself in the note which had accompanied his parting gift all those years ago. Plaschkes's suggestion fired Losey's imagination more than any other so far. Topol, fresh from his triumphs in *Fiddler on the Roof*, was delighted to accept.

Their association went back to 1968, when Losey had incongruously offered Topol the part of the Angel of Death in *Boom!* Topol had turned the offer down, since his English was virtually non-existent at the time, but later he had also been offered, and rejected, the role of Trotsky. 'I didn't like the script,' he confesses, 'and I knew he hated Trotsky. I suspect he was still a Stalinist, faithful to his youth or something like that. I didn't see how anybody was going to understand why Trotsky was killed if we didn't show him in his glorious days, as creator of the Red Army and so forth. What was the point? Then *Galileo* came, and I wanted it very much, but I thought after having crossed him twice and fought, he'd never offer me another part. Then he suddenly called, just after he found he'd got the rights from the Brecht estate.'

Inevitably, comparisons between Topol and Laughton were made, usually to the former's detriment – 'Tevye with a telescope,' as *Cue*

Magazine put it. 'Although Topol's performance captures the ordinary, animal vitality of the great scientist, the sharpness of tongue and intellect is always present.' One Ottawa newspaper declared: 'Topol Gives Life to Brecht Film,' but Vincent Canby of the all-powerful *New York Times* considered his performance was 'like *Fiddler on the Roof*: all resonant voice, calculated gestures, surface mannerisms – a lovable fellow, who at worst has moments of being crotchety.' The greatest praise was reserved for Losey: 'a man who knows more about film and more about Brecht than possibly any other film director at work today.'

While remaining faithful to Brecht's anti-illusionist, anti-realistic concept, Losey orchestrates subtle shifts in the use of the camera, in pictorial stylization, in editing rhythms, and in colour schemes, especially by contrasting the scenes involving Galileo and his pupils with those in which he confronts the Princes of the Church. MacDonald's sets glow with colour, which not only dazzles the eye, but tips off the mind as to what tone of message is about to be transmitted. The music, written by Richard Hartley and based as closely as possible on the only morsel of the original Hanns Eisler score not to have vanished, contributes an element of beauty in innocence as well as a form of punctuation to the narrative.

Losey's film follows the progression of dominant colours in the costumes of his stage production – morning tones of white, yellow and grey for the first scene, Ludovico's deep aristocratic blue, dark green for the Venetians in the second scene, increasing elegance of silver and pearl grey in the fourth scene, with scene six as a *notturno* in brown and black, the two carnivals as high points of colour and spectacle and a descent into dull greys at the end. Topol's contribution to the film went well beyond his buoyant and conscientious performance. 'Joe didn't know how to treat the ending, any more that Brecht did,' he says. 'They never really solved it, either in Hollywood or New York, but it depends on what aspect of the play's dialectic you want to emphasize, what metaphor you're going for: Reason versus Faith, the individual against authority, the responsibility of the scientist to the society he serves?

'Much to my utter amazement, he asked me to have a go at writing it, which was enormously flattering, of course. I worked on that scene most of the night, and opted for the ending in which Andrea comes to visit Galileo when he is old, and has finished the *Discorsi*, the last, great work justifying Copernicus' findings. Andrea wants to forgive his great teacher too, saying: "When you stooped to recant, we should have understood that you were about your own business – to write the book that only you could write."

'I thought Andrea should take the *Discorsi*, and smuggle it out of Italy to the more liberal, Protestant world. Next morning, Joe came in, and we did the scene for him. At the end he just said, "Shoot it." Now, you never knew with Joe when he was really pleased or if he was taking the mickey, but anyway, my version is the one we used. I had worked with Theo Otto, Brecht's designer for many years, on *Caucasian Chalk Circle*, so I was familiar with the Brecht style. Joe wrote me a beautiful letter, which I shall always cherish, saying that though it had been great working with Laughton, he had loved what I did. That meant a lot to me.

'One of the greatest contradictions in Joe was that capacity for lightning flashes of generosity – like allowing me to write that scene, to use all my talents – contrasted with bouts of awful, self-centred preoccupation. He could be just like Galileo in that scene with his daughter's suitor, where the man is so concentrated on himself and his own work that he can't be bothered to minister to his daughter, whose life is in crisis because she is about to lose her last chance to get married. And all because of him, too.'

Losey also demonstrated his gift for generosity in dealing with the singer, Mama Cass, of the Mamas and the Papas, who happened to be in London at the time, and whom Losey had recruited as an extra in the street-play scene. Virtually wrecked by booze and drugs at this stage, Cass looked a terrible mess, so Losey tactfully shot over her shoulder in order not to focus on the ruined face. She was found dead in her hotel the night before the final 'take'.

Losey was pleased with *Galileo* when it came out, writing to Daniel Mainwaring in Hollywood that it had turned out well despite the American reviews which he regarded as products of ignorant and insular critics.

Resenting his advancing age and increasing bouts of ill-health, which inhibited the full command of creative energy, Losey was becoming increasingly awkward, fussing over matters which, in earlier times, he might have let pass. When he wrote to Plaschkes to remind him of the $10,000 for his work on *Galileo* and the film which was to follow, he complained that Plaschkes's secretary had addressed him in a letter as 'Joe' which was unprofessional; he was 'Joe' only to his friends.

Even Theo Cowan had received an unusually brusque reply when he tried to sell Losey a bust of Galileo, which he had in his garden. Cowan thought that, in the full flood of his enthusiasm, Losey might be persuaded to pay £750 for the thing. Losey thanked Cowan very much, saying that at £750, he needed a nineteenth-century bust of Galileo like a hole in the head.

XVI

A Further Exile

Losey celebrated his sixty-sixth birthday in New York and, for all the momentary euphoria he experienced at the opening of *Galileo*, he was beginning to tire easily. He was still drinking heavily and growing more obese; his once-strong features were beginning to melt and dissolve so that, with his long greying hair, he began to look less patriarchal and more matronly. It was as if, like the hero of *The Go-Between*, his life was turning full circle, with Brecht's play marking the beginning of the end of his high artistic endeavours and political commitments. When he returned exhausted to England, he did so with minimal enthusiasm for his next film, despite the fact that it starred his old friend Helmut Berger and two of Britain's most admired actors, Michael Caine and Glenda Jackson.

The film was based on *The Romantic Englishwoman*, a novel by Thomas Wiseman, from which the author had produced a script that Losey found inadequate, although he was interested in its human triangle theme: the impact on a bourgeois, British marriage of an intruder – a sophisticated, handsome, young German con-man. The greater attraction, though, was that it offered work, where none of his other projects seemed likely to succeed. Losey judged the film to be about sexual anarchy and, of its three protagonists, found that he was curiously most in sympathy with the young German seducer.

Needing a fresh collaborator to work on the script, he turned, not to one of his familiar writers, but to Tom Stoppard, a young British dramatist who had established himself as a force in British theatre with his witty and intellectually provoking plays. However, Stoppard's script met with heavy-handed abuse from the film's producer Danny Angel, who had last worked with Losey on *King and Country*. Angel's memo detailing what he regarded as flaws in the plot and inadequacies in Stoppard's writing was brutally honest.

He ridiculed some of the dialogue, saying that he had never read such garbage. He also objected that one character in the script was a film producer, which he thought was a death sentence for any film. Referring to one line of dialogue in which a character calls himself a poet, Angel observed that the character's partner has no desire to know this and after reading the script nor did he. Comments such as 'rubbish' and 'stupid' and 'unbelievable' pepper his memo. He made it clear that he preferred Wiseman's script.

Losey was outraged. He wrote back that he considered Angel's remarks unworthy of his intellect and character, suggesting that he was treating Tom Stoppard as though he were some upstart who might once have written a 'B' picture for Michael Carreras. Losey pointed out that Stoppard was a major playwright and screenwriter. Angel's remarks seemed to be bad-tempered quibbles, and he was interested to know what lay behind them. The letter made it abundantly clear that he was not prepared to film Wiseman's own version. Losey's solution was to work on the script with Stoppard, then have copies sent to the actors involved to gauge their reaction. If they liked it, he told Angel, then the film should go ahead with Stoppard's script.

The finished film projects a kind of listlessness that is only partly explained by the disagreements over the script; in addition Losey did not enjoy working with Glenda Jackson, although she had been his first choice for the role. His admiration for her abilities and professionalism was unqualified, but he seemed unable to get on relaxed terms with her. He thought that, technically, she was the best actress with whom he had ever worked, but he was distressed by her reluctance to expose herself in the part. Her acting seemed to him to be brittle and superficial.

Losey saw this as both a problem and a limitation. He was always ready to give all of himself to a film, and as a director he liked talking with actors and thought actors usually liked talking to him. But Jackson had generally seemed the kind of actress who didn't want to talk much at all, and he felt there were occasions during the filming when she might have produced a better, truer performance if only she had been prepared to dig a little deeper into herself and find something beyond her own inner reserves.

Inevitably, his closest relationship was with Berger, although he was also delighted by Caine, who amazed him by being able to weep without artificial aids. On the other hand, Berger and Jackson clashed on the set, as a result of Berger's more casual approach to the film. 'She said some unpleasant things to him a couple of times; it was highly deserved,' said Losey. 'He just wasn't bothering to match up to Glenda's style of professionalism. She didn't want to waste time and, when Berger became difficult, she invariably retreated to her dressing-room. He said some very rude things about her, to which I paid no attention.'

Gerry Fisher, who served once again as director of photography, formed a good relationship with Jackson, although she otherwise kept her distance from the rest of those involved. When not filming, she sat in her dressing-room alone.

Losey, who was more used to Elizabeth Taylor's approach, where the star's dressing-room would be crowded with actors, friends and others involved in the film, seems to have found Jackson's attitude difficult to cope with. 'It's far from standard, and it's certainly rare when it happens all the time as it did with Glenda,' he told Jackson's biographer Ian Woodward. 'People were afraid of her, because once in a while she would make a crack – and the cracks could be very nasty.' Jackson, too, found Losey 'very intriguing' but the film nevertheless reflected little of that sense of fascination. Losey seemed, for example, unable to convey his purpose in the film to a larger public, confusing the critics and becoming irritated by the way his audience was determined to admire the film-couple's house, which he and MacDonald had gone to endless trouble to make as unattractively bourgeois as possible.

As a special tribute to Losey, both *Galileo* and *The Romantic Englishwoman* were shown out of competition at the 1975 Cannes Film Festival, to mixed reviews. The critic of the *Sunday Express* found Jackson's performance 'flawless'. But Pauline Kael, in the *New Yorker*, who was never an admirer of Losey's films, performed a classic hatchet job: 'Joseph Losey directed *The Romantic Englishwoman*, so it naturally has very long pauses, time in which to ask yourself why Michael Caine. . . has such awful, sticky hair. . . This may not be a big issue, but it's as big (and as clearly motivated) as anything else that you run up against in this film. . . Stoppard has given the dialogue a few Noël Cowardish bitch-nifties, but not enough to keep the blood coursing. The movie is a twist on life imitating art and vice versa; here it's life imitating pulp and vice versa – which might

44 Richard Burton as Trotsky meets his nemesis in Alain Delon in *The Assassination of Trotsky* – 1972

45 Harold Pinter, Dilys Powell, Losey and Søren Fischer after the 1973 John Player Lecture at the NFT

46 Jane Fonda struggling through the snows of Røros in *A Doll's House* – 1973

47 Jane Fonda, David Warner, Trevor Howard and Delphine Seyrig in *A Doll's House* – 1973

48   Topol looks into the future in *Galileo* – 1974

49   Galileo's words fall on deaf ears (Michel Lonsdale and Patrick Magee) – 1974

50 Glenda Jackson and
Helmut Berger in *The Romanti*
Englishwoman – 1975

51 Losey – 1977

52 Alain Delon is the fugitive in *Mr Klein* – 1976

53 Alain Delon takes tea with Jeanne Moreau in *Mr Klein* – 1976

54   Yves Montand in *Les Routes du Sud* – 1978

55   Ruggero Raimondi dressed to be killed in *Don Giovanni* – 1979

56　Dame Kiri Te Kanawa as Donna Elvira in *Don Giovanni* – 1979

57　Ruggero Raimondi flirting with Teresa Berganza in *Don Giovanni* – 1979

58　Isabelle Huppert gets some advice from Jeanne Moreau in *The Trout* – 1982

59   Vanessa Redgrave and Sarah Miles relax in *Steaming* – 1984

60   Both Losey and Diana Dors (seen here in 1984 on the set of *Steaming*) would dead by the time the film was released.

be an entertaining premise for a light comedy. In Losey's brand of mystification melodrama with leftish overtones, it's a very parched conceit. . . The floundering scenes aren't improved by pinning them on Caine's infertile imagination; besides, we recognize these screwed-up, smouldering connotations as Losey's.

'As usual, he empties everything definite out of the characters, as if that would make them richly suggestive. Themes such as women's liberation are tossed in as part of the décor. Losey is deep on the surface. . . Those who wonder why almost every sequence in the house and grounds of the bourgeois couple involves mirror reflections may be interested in Losey's explanation: "I wanted to convey their reality was totally unreal." And if you can go for that, you're ready for a Joseph Losey retrospective, to include *Boom!*, *Secret Ceremony*, *Figures in a Landscape*, *The Go-Between*, and *The Assassination of Trotsky*.'

The film did poorly at the box-office, with a few exceptions: in August the producer Danny Angel wrote that it had done £200,000 of business in Paris, while Janus Films, who distributed in Frankfurt, reported that it was having more success than either Bob Fosse's *Lenny* or Scorsese's *Alice Doesn't Live Here Any More*, which represented sobering competition. It was also a huge success at the 1975 San Sebastian Film Festival, an event which Losey nevertheless boycotted in protest against Spain's imposition of a sentence of death by garrotting, passed on a group of Basque (ETA) rebels.

The film's English opening came in October at the Odeon, Haymarket, though the reviews were somewhat stiff with respectful praise. Danny Angel as producer kept his disagreements with Losey to himself. 'I've never had an argument with him,' Angel told one astonished reporter. 'We get on because he's one hundred per cent straightforward. He doesn't tell lies and always keeps his word, same as I do. Maybe he gets a bit highbrow at times, but he has his feet on the ground.'

Losey had not yet abandoned his attempts to find financial backing for his film of Proust's novel. No other project in his life consumed so much of his time and concern: it was to be the film which would resurrect not only the events of his childhood and adolescence, but explore the ambivalence of his own identity. Through the character of Marcel, the narrator, he would examine and come to grips with his own feelings of alienation, his asthma, and the influence of his imposing (and envied) grandmother.

By now he was among the most celebrated directors in Europe, and perhaps the most highly paid in Britain. The situation was naturally gratifying; he could now almost afford his preferred life-style and rest easy in the assurance of continuing independence, although his wary accountant, Gerry Burke, was warning him that the tax-man cometh. He pointed out that Losey was liable for taxation on at least nine out of ten years he had lived in England on his earnings worldwide unless he left the country for two years, or spent no more than a total of ninety days a year in Britain.

'The bulk of my income would have been taxed at 87 per cent and there was no way I could earn enough money to sustain my way of life,' he explained. 'I don't mean it's luxurious, but simply to do my job. I lead a pressured life and I need a certain amount of money and there was no way I could sustain it. Under American law there is an automatic cut-off on taxes at 50 per cent of your earned income; and I don't have any unearned income.

'There wasn't much film industry left in Britain and even though I set up more than 20 films that were English-based, using English technicians and bringing in capital and using labour, most of those films took me outside of England. So I was living fifty or seventy-five percent of the time outside England anyway and it was ridiculous to go on paying punitive taxes.'

Socialist though he doubtless was, Losey was determined that the Inland Revenue would not be able to claim a large percentage of his recently acquired wealth. He had worked too hard and agonized too much for that. Since the filming of Proust would involve long periods of residence in France, he thought it prudent to decamp from Royal Avenue and go to live there. In March 1975, he and Patricia left their beloved house in Chelsea and moved to Paris to take up temporary residence in a flat in the Rue du Dragon, on the fashionable Rive Gauche, where Jack Loring had been its previous tenant before returning to New York to work on a series of heroic murals for the Prudential Life Assurance Company.

The landlady, Mme Aillaud, was a friend of Loring's mother and everything Losey admired though she was not a great artist. She was stylish, highly intelligent, deeply cultured, with connections to the rich and famous, including her own sister, the singer Juliette Greco.

Compatible with his contradictory nature, it did not trouble Losey that in many ways Mme Aillaud and her husband, an extremely successful businessman, exactly typified the *haute bourgeoisie* portrayed so condescendingly in many of his films.

'He was basically sado-masochistic,' Aillaud observes. 'To me he was also incredibly kind, never failing to comment on my clothes and jewels, waiting when I came back from the doctor after a nasty accident, so solicitous of my well-being. But not always to Patricia, you see. . . At one point they were both going to psychiatrists here in Paris. Patricia's was called Dr Smirnoff – seriously!'

Mme Aillaud also commented on her illustrious tenant's evolving sartorial taste: 'He admired very much the way my husband dressed, and had his tailor do some things for him. He often wore big bows at the neck. . . like a nineteenth-century artist. A complete romantic! Once the tailor left very upset, because he said Joe had kicked him up the ass. God knows what transpired between them! He probably wanted something that the tailor couldn't produce for his large figure, who knows? He was a very passionate person, and could be violent, but at the same time so lovable. . .'

In a report from the Cannes festival of May 1976, the London *Evening Standard* published a photo of Losey looking like a benign and ageing Indian over a caption which identified him as 'Victim of British Tax Law'. Losey would have preferred to stay in England. 'I detest living in Paris,' he said nineteen months after his move. 'It has become a completely depersonalized city. It was with great reluctance that I left England. After all, I have an English daughter-in-law, an English son, two English grandchildren and an English wife. I think it is the only country in the world where there is still a respect for individual freedom.'

Patricia's fluent French ensured that the role of professional helpmate that she had struggled so hard to sustain during the English years was now enhanced. Clearly, Losey would never learn to speak French, if for no other reason than that of his perfectionism; even had he possessed an ear for languages, he would not have dared to utter a word, unless he could speak perfectly, which was an impossibility.

Soon after he arrived, Losey met the French President, Giscard d'Estaing, at a social function and told him of his plans to film Proust, hoping no doubt to spark some interest or even help. Much to Losey's chagrin, however, the President responded, 'What makes you think you can adapt Proust? You come from the American Mid-West; you can't even speak French properly.' Losey explained to the bemused Giscard how he too had been politically persecuted, making him 'a Jew, so to speak'. The project was floundering, for its French backers, headed by Mme Stephane, were having second thoughts.

Losey went to Rome for a rest, where he discovered that another director, Costa-Gavras, had given up an attempt to make M. Klein, a film with Alain Delon about anti-semitism in war-wracked Paris. Keen to work again with Delon after The Assassination of Trotsky, Losey phoned the actor and, discovering that he was still interested, got hold of a copy of the script by Franco Solinas. What was also attractive was that Delon had recently formed his own production company and was prepared to invest money as well as talent, co-producing with another French company and two in Italy.

Instead of allowing himself a proper, health-restoring break in his schedule, Losey began in June 1975 to collaborate with Solinas on reworking and shortening the script of M. Klein. He then jetted off to Mexico, where he had been invited to attend a conference on the problems surrounding political cinema. Such problems were exemplified by Mexico's president, Luis Echeverria who, speaking at a Sunday brunch party held at his house to a gathering that included Sergio Leone, John Huston, Costa-Gavras, Frank Capra, Roman Polanski and Luis Buñuel, lashed out against 'the manipulation of cinema by international political tendencies, aiming to use it as an instrument to dominate developing nations.'

On his return, Losey went once more for a stint of teaching and lecturing at Dartmouth, a job he always enjoyed sufficiently to count as 'time off'. From Choate House at Dartmouth, he wrote to Danny Angel, reporting on his failure to find an American distributor for The Romantic Englishwoman, and adding that, despite the problems of noise and heat, he was glad to be in Hanover. Once more Losey's past was catching up with him. That summer, working with students at Dartmouth, he directed Clifford Odets's Waiting for Lefty, which he had staged in Moscow forty years earlier, although, from his own long perspective, he now viewed the play as blatant agit-prop.

By September he was back in Italy working with Solinas on

the script, which was taking a long time to shape successfully. The two would consult in the morning and then Solinas would spend the afternoon rewriting. Eventually, after a great deal of labour, which included some gruelling research, a strong script emerged. It helped attract one of the finest and largest casts Losey had ever assembled; even the small roles were brilliantly cast, crafted and executed. Featured were Losey's adored Jeanne Moreau as the *haute bourgeoise* doyenne of an imposing chateau, and Michel Lonsdale, who had played Cardinal Barberini in *Galileo*, as the cuckolded husband of one of Klein's mistresses.

Mr Klein, a psychological detective story, concerns a man's search for personal identity, set against a background of bureaucratic wartime horror – the *grande rafle*, or rounding up and assembling of thousands of Jews in July 1942, in a great sports stadium in Paris. Like so many of his fellow countrymen, Klein, a Catholic from Alsace, is not only indifferent to the fate of Jews under the Nazi occupation, but, as an art dealer, has learned to exploit the situation by buying, well below the market price, works of art owned by Jews forced to flee the country. Through a postal error he is confused with a Jew bearing the same name as himself, and becomes obsessed with discovering the identity of the other man.

The film's main focus is the horror manifested in the behaviour of Frenchmen towards other Frenchmen and women. Happily, Giscard d'Estaing had relaxed his attitude towards Losey's efforts to interpret the French and gave him permission to use part of a speech he had made during a commemorative ceremony some months earlier to introduce the film's theme: 'I saw them leave. The morning of July 16, 1942 we were woken by the unusual noise of the buses on the move before sunrise in the Paris streets. Some hours later, one learned that it was about Jews who had been arrested at dawn, and who were re-assembled at the *Vélodrome d'Hiver*. I had noticed that there were among them some children of our age squeezed in, unmoving, their staring look at the window during the traversing of this frozen city at an hour made for the gentleness of sleep. I think of their black-circled eyes, which became millions of stars in the night.'

Losey's continuing obsession with bisexuality is dealt with more interestingly in *Mr Klein* than in his other films, taking dramatic shape in a cabaret, performed by La Grande Eugène, a company of transvestite actors under the direction of Frantz Salieri. Filmed at the internationally famous bistro, La Coupole, it portrays various racial and national stereotypes in a vicious series of skits in which Jews and all things semitic are the satirical butt. Duality is everywhere, between Aryan and Jew, man and woman, the good of patriotism, the evil of racism. The finishing touch to this grotesque pantomime is that it is constructed around Mahler's *Kindertotenlieder*, a cycle of dramatic, emotional songs about the deaths of children.

Many people have spoken of the incredible speed and accuracy with which Losey worked, his certainty of eye and rhythm, but none was more impressed than Bertrand Tavernier by the way Losey handled the cabaret scene. Tavernier, one of Losey's more objective French admirers, as well as a director of considerable international standing himself, defines his unique talent in terms of quality that transcends creative imagination: 'It's the relationship between shots, which is exactly when Joe was at his best, the ultimate in what film direction is as an art. It's not the quality of an image, which the cameraman can control, it's much beyond that. It's the juxtaposition, the timing, the length, the almost metaphysical relationship between shots, between images. It's like the poetry of Valéry, or the painting of Picasso, where somebody is in total control of the thing, not just technically brilliant. You never know what is the balance between instinct, talent and preparation.

'There is a lot of the unconscious in everybody's talent, and that you cannot completely control. Some part of all great talent must be lodged in the unconscious. And Joe knew how to make that work for actors too, giving them the space to let their own instincts operate, not telling them what to do all the time. But the very personal was always there with Joe – his approach to the set of *M. Klein*, for example. You could feel the claustrophobia that Joe felt with his asthma; nothing is straight; every room has a door which is not level; you observe a room from another room within distorted angles, which creates a feeling of pressure and oppression. It's one of his masterpieces.'

Gerry Fisher, in a less lyrical mode, says quite simply that anyone else would have taken the whole day to do the shot, testifying to Losey's sureness of hand and the matchless understanding between the two men.

Losey, assuming that MacDonald would be busy preparing his designs for the massive and complicated Proust, turned to one of the best designers in Europe, Alexander Trauner, a Hungarian Jew who had actually lived in Paris through the ghastly times portrayed in the film, designing sets, in a clandestine fashion, for Marcel Carné. For Trauner, and many others involved in the picture, working on certain scenes became acutely painful and very upsetting: the casting director, Margot Chapellier, had lost many among her family in concentration camps, as had one of the film technicians, Claude Lyon. Losey had approached several Jewish organizations for the culminating scene at the stadium, for which he needed literally thousands of extras. Many had to abandon the task because they found it too emotionally taxing.

Jack Loring remembers receiving a letter in New York in December 1975, in which Losey did not attempt to disguise his weariness and general malaise. He and Patricia had been at the Dietetic Institute of Thalassothérapie in Quibéron, and as a result he was suffering from slimming and abstinence as well as from more usual complaints: film producers, the chill Paris winters and chest trouble aggravated by his asthma. He grumbled, too, about the reaction of critics John Simon and Pauline Kael in America and John Coleman in Britain to *The Romantic Englishwoman*. They were not calculated to make him feel any better. He added that Loring was not to bother about some money owed, but, when possible, to send some to Henry Bamburger. One cannot help but admire the tenacious loyalty with which Losey continued to honour his twenty-year debt to his Hollywood business manager, although in a slight alteration of priorities, he soon writes again saying that, although Loring was welcome to deduct the $1,000 he was owed for work on the tapestry design proposed for the opening backdrop to *M. Klein*, he really could use the rest of the money, as he must send Patricia once more to Brazil to see her children.

Losey's relationship with Trauner was very different from that which he had enjoyed with MacDonald. It was one that he, in fact, came to prefer, for Trauner, unlike MacDonald, did not argue, but noted Losey's suggestions and produced the result he wanted. Not all Losey's relationships on the film were as straightforward; a certain tension had developed between Losey and Delon, which Trauner remembers well: 'The behaviour of creative people depends on the mood, the picture, the person. Actors are always trying to impress each other. Also directors. We all try to impress the other – to surprise. Losey and Delon are both great artists, but Alain did not always take direction from Losey, which could make problems.'

Losey saw an affinity between Klein and Delon because of the complexity of the two characters, their self-destructive tendency and quest for identity. As with Losey, the contradictions in Delon's behaviour were often related to violent swings of mood. One day he could project a kind of stubborn negativism, during which he would be totally uncooperative, and the next morning he might bounce in, declaring that this was going to be the most perfect performance of his life, which, indeed, many thought it was. The problem as Trauner perceived it was that Losey, having pre-planned everything to the last detail, providing everybody with precise notes on what he expected to happen each day, applied the full force of his awesome concentration to the work, while Delon, always headstrong, would not always follow Losey's direction.

Regardless of what passed between them, each man sustained a love and respect for the other, feelings which evoked generous behaviour. On one occasion, when Losey was undergoing financial difficulties, Delon simply dispatched someone with the necessary funds, asking nothing in return. Losey was both moved and deeply appreciative, repaying the loan at the earliest opportunity. Unlike Losey, Delon was always intensely secretive about his life, but extremely bright, which was perhaps the quality that bound the two men together.

They actually got along very well until the end of the filming, when there was, to use Gerry Fisher's words, 'a rupture'. For a scene in which Klein embarks on a journey to Strasbourg, Losey had hired a train, which had to move out at a specific time on a specially reserved section of track. When the time came to shoot the scene, Fisher and his crew were on the train, cameras at the ready, Losey pacing up and down the platform in his now familiar smock and flowing scarf, thrusting back his long, whitening hair with an impatient hand. But Delon had not arrived. Any delay would mean that Losey would be obliged to renegotiate the entire set-up with the railway authorities.

Suddenly, Delon's car burst through the barriers straight on to the platform. The actor flung open the door, and dashed for the train to change his clothes. With one minute to go, Losey rushed to the star's compartment, stuck his head in and said, 'You're cutting it a bit fine, don't you think?' Delon's angry reaction was to leave the train without even putting his trousers back on, streak down the platform, climb into his waiting car and disappear, leaving Losey and his crew gawping in disbelief. It was Losey's turn to lose his temper; more than any other director working, he loathed running over time or over budget. However, Delon was found and returned, and Losey, fortunately, was able to negotiate an alternative time later in the day.

All's well that ends well, and Delon, in numerous interviews with the French press, praised Losey endlessly, calling him 'the Karajan of the camera', applauding his matchless respect for actors, his generosity, humility, and artistry. Losey too, though somewhat more restrained, testified to Delon's seriousness as an actor, his brillliance in reaching the core of a part until 'his own truth of personality engages with the truth of the character.' Delon had clearly been embraced into the bosom of the 'family'.

Somewhat surprisingly, in view of the unpopularity of the subject, *Mr Klein* was the official French entry at the Cannes Film Festival, where the *Sunday Times* described it as a film that France would prefer to forget: 'Woe betide the film maker anxious to point to the way "Le Tout Paris" continued to carry on business as usual during the German Occupation.' The newspaper reported that '*Mr Klein* received a stony reception from the smart, first-night audience at the Palais des Festivals, even though the ex-pat American director is normally a cult figure.'

The *International Herald Tribune*, which described *Mr Klein* as 'intelligent and persuasive', was astonished that the film failed to draw even an honourable mention from the jury. Losey, photographed looking tanned and relaxed in a collarless velvet suit and flowing cravat, was clearly untroubled by these reactions, secure in the knowledge that he had made a first-class film and accomplished some of the best work of his career.

Such was Losey's confidence in *Mr Klein* that he cabled Walter Mirsch of the Academy of Motion Picture Arts and Sciences three weeks before the film opened in Paris on 27 October 1976, asking what was required to qualify a film for the American Oscars. In spite of the substratum of guilt or hostility towards the film in France, it received many enviable reviews, with *France-Soir* calling it 'un coup de maître', *Cinéma*, 'un classique de demain', and *Positif*, reliably intellectual, saying that it was 'a synthesis of Losey's art, playing this Kafkaesque parable on a system of echoes'. *Positif's* October issue was devoted almost entirely to *Mr Klein*.

The film went on to win three Césars, the French equivalent of the Oscars; in February it received the award for the best film, Losey was voted the best director, and Trauner the best art director. Delon was nominated as best actor, but lost out to Robert De Niro. Its reception in the States was more muted, with Pauline Kael categorizing it as 'a classic example of his weighty emptiness'. In November, Losey was guest of honour when the film opened the London Film Festival. Losey wrote to his French distributor Raymond Danon, saying that he had spent some time talking to Sir Harold Wilson, who had introduced him and the film. He had been on television and given a number of interviews, but he did not have any faith at all in EMI, Rank or British Lion as distributors of *Mr Klein*.

Holding court at the Savoy Hotel, Losey spent the day after the opening night being interviewed by journalists to obtain as much publicity as possible for *Mr Klein*, which had still not attracted a British distributor. He was in a mellow mood, recognizing that, in the long term, he had benefited as an artist by his blacklisting and exile from America. 'I've had a much richer and better life and am much more qualified to make films than I ever would have been had I stayed in Hollywood,' he said.

The British critics were enthusiastic about the film, with Michael Billington positively raving: 'You don't want to see it twice, you *have* to see it twice, for, like all great works of art, it doesn't yield all its secrets at one sitting.' It was a comment Losey liked, for he once said, 'If a film is worth seeing, it is worth seeing twice.'

Although Losey's use of mirrors and other symbolic elements is subtler and more restrained than usual, they are all present, prompting Philip Strick to comment in *Sight and Sound*, 'It's all done, you could say, by mirrors.' He called it a 'flawless film, incorporating all Losey's talents and many preoccupations.'

By then, Losey was busy finding somewhere to live, for Loring was returning to Paris. First he and Patricia went to the Rue Monsieur, once the home of Nancy Mitford, then to a borrowed flat in the Rue du Bac, which Losey hated. Much to everyone's surprise, he acquired a dog, a long-haired dachshund, which should have exacerbated his asthma beyond endurance. But Losey was to remain besotted with his 'Tyger' until the end of his days.

XVII

Grappling with the Don

Having installed his César among his proliferating collection of trophies, Losey turned his thoughts again to *Voss*, leaving in the New Year for Australia in order to search for suitable locations, although he found the heat more than he could endure. Writing to Delon on his return to Paris, he apologized for not being in touch, explaining that he had gone to Australia for five weeks, and the intense heat had laid him low with pneumonia. The year, he felt, had begun badly. In his affectionate reply, Delon, obviously worried about Losey's health and disappointed for his sake that *Mr Klein* had been turned down for the American Oscars, cautioned him to rest and take care of his genius.

Losey had hoped that the financing for the Proust film would be in place by January, so that filming could finally begin. The money was to come from Gaumont Films and French television, and he was aware that the combination was his best and probably last chance of making the film. If this method of financing the film didn't work, he conceded, it was difficult to see what would work – barring a runaway hit when, like Bertolucci, he could make a *1900* if he felt so inclined.

But again there were hesitations and delays, and he turned to other projects. Apart from *Voss*, which was to star Maximilian Schell, he was hoping to film Brecht's *Puntila* in Finland, and he was working again with Solinas on a script about the life of Ibn Saud. He also wanted to make a film about Vietnam, but that depended on American money, which was not likely to be forthcoming. American producers, he said, might be more than willing to let him make what they called an 'entertainment' film as long as the contract stipulated that they had final cut on the film, but they would be rather less than willing to allow him to make an openly political film and they certainly would not grant him final cut.

After a brief holiday in Tunis at the end of February, the Loseys were able to move back to the Rue du Dragon, into a smaller flat, which was a little cramped for two busy adults and a lively puppy, but it was what they could afford. In March, feeling grumpier and more unwell than ever, Losey wrote to Raymond Danon, expressing his dissatisfaction with the US publicity for *Mr Klein*. In his rather tart reply, Danon pointed out that *Mr Klein* had won three Césars, and that if Losey could cast his mind back that far, not a single American company had been prepared to put money into the film, so what could he expect?

Losey sent an angry reply, demanding that the film be shown again in France in seven of the best cinemas. He added that he was coming with a gun to 'kidnap' the César which Danon had taken for Best Film, so that he could give it to someone more deserving, namely Alain Delon. In the meantime, he was kept busy with the extensive interviews being conducted for Michel Ciment's book, which he enjoyed, but which left him feeling unexpectedly exhausted.

Losey's dreams of filming Proust were fading and he was unhappy over the way Joshua was behaving, for the boy, now in his late teens, was using his energies in a manner his father disapproved of. 'We had a conflict,' Joshua admits, 'in the sense that at the time I had no passion for some of the things he did. I had my own passions that I wasn't always able to communicate, because he was thrusting, and imposing his wishes and desires for me. But he wanted me to be happy in whatever I did. He was really complaining about that adolescent thing when you're in bed till 2 p.m. every day, and not doing anything or having any direction. Unlike him, who at the age of sixteen went to university – not that he knew what he was going to do or be – but he was already motivated to make something of himself. He had ideas about me going to university, and I finally did go to Warwick for four years. I'm developing more passions now, or they're becoming more obvious to me; for acting, for instance. I'll definitely stick with that.'

A welcome distraction from the traumas of parenthood came from Jorge Semprun, the Spanish novelist and communist who had fled to France, aged sixteen, to fight with the Resistance, only to be subsequently arrested and sent to Auschwitz. Having survived,

Semprun returned to France where he fell in easily with the leftist film community headed by Yves Montand, for whom he wrote both *Z* and *La Guerre est Finie*, a film directed by Alain Resnais about an ageing revolutionary looking back to the Spanish Civil War. Now these two wanted him to direct another film, *Les Routes du Sud*, which would develop the themes of the two previous films. Losey never quite overcame his initial reluctance for the project, since he feared that it would be viewed as a rehash of the earlier works. To ease his mind, he sent the script to Resnais, who generously allowed that he saw no such danger, and the project went ahead. In September the *Sunday Times* announced: 'Joseph Losey, whose mysterious, somnambulistic, funambulistic films have made less money than stir, is about to go to work.'

Losey and Montand, both tough-minded, quarrelled during filming and many unpleasant and unfortunate things were said, which both later regretted. On the set, Montand often became argumentative and tedious, even interfering, though never with that intention or with malice; having already made *La Guerre est Finie*, he tended to believe he knew it all, something which had worried Losey from the beginning. Yet, in spite of their disagreements, Losey described Montand as kind, generous, disciplined, and professional, whilst not minimizing either the difficulties which had grown up between them or the quality and genuineness of his performance.

Only the most discerning critics managed to spot the real problems besetting *Les Routes du Sud*, which lay in the dangerous factual and psychological proximity of the creators to their material. The film is a virtual biography of Semprun – who is called Jean Larrea in the film and played by Yves Montand – about an old, exiled Spanish revolutionary living in France as a highly successful screenwriter with his wife Eve and activist son Laurent. More than that, the script, produced in collaboration with Losey and Patricia, and thrown into sharp relief by his pre-production notes, draws parallels with Losey's own life, particularly his own tortured relationship with his long-dead father who still visited him in dreams. By his bedside Losey kept a book of Kafka's letters, from which he would often reread the writer's complaint to his father of the lack of understanding between them.

Losey described, unequivocally, his view of the film as the characters' personal story, a story which involved jealousy, misunderstanding, crisis, aggression and love. At the film's centre, he saw a classical father and son conflict, the problem for a young man of asserting his own manhood while he still remains under the shadow of a powerful father. In other words, it was the Oedipus story in its most basic form. It was difficult for some young men to assert their own individuality unless their fathers had been removed completely from their own sphere of action. This might happen through the death of the father, but in that eventuality the unavoidable consequence was a sense of guilt even if the son could in no sense be considered the agent of his father's death.

Alongside this central theme was a love story, though the love between Larrea and Eve bore the marks of familiarity and was beginning to go stale as the original ecstasy of sex had waned through habit. Being much closer to his mother than to his father, Laurent had developed a jealousy of his father's relationship with his mother, and that jealousy was central to his problem. Losey saw the film's second major theme as Spain during the last year of the Franco regime, Spain after almost forty years of anti-fascist struggle. For Losey personally, the Spanish Civil War was in many respects more important than the Second World War. It was a warning, and a warning ignored. With both Losey and Semprun endeavouring to work out their own psychological problems in the film, the sharpness of dramatic focus was lost, and thus much of its artistic impact; this echoed the fate of *Eve*, another film in which Losey had worked out his own obsessions, succumbing to self-indulgence.

The relationship between father and son in the film was also reflective of Losey's attitude to Joshua. He envied the boy his youth, his sexuality, his future sparkling with choice. He had, however, the intelligence and grace to acknowledge it, not only in his mind, but to Joshua as well, with whom he discussed the notion that sons only begin to live after their fathers have died. Joshua had not been shocked or upset by that declaration, thinking that it was 'a very sensible thing to say. He was being honest, which was his way. Of all the things I feel about my father, he's primarily an honest person, who sticks up for what he was – a bundle of contradictions, yes, but he knew that as well as anybody else.' In the film, Laurent challenges his father, asking, 'What are you? Just an ex-Resistance, ex-Republican, ex-everything – an ex-man,' to which the father replies, 'All right, and what are you?'

Les Routes du Sud, which opened in Paris on 11 October 1978, prompted Joshua to write an unusually emotional letter to his father expressing joy and pride that he had undertaken the project at all. At the same time, however, he had ventured a criticism of the young girl in the film, which ignited another row. As Losey told Ciment: 'My son said that his friends thought she was a ridiculous, empty "dizzy sixties" character. I said, "What the hell do you know about the 1960s? You were aged two to twelve in that decade," and a lot of very important things happened in that time, in the arts and in politics. It is the most important decade in my life outside of the 1930s. When I taught at Dartmouth in 1970, what was left of the 1960s was still vital and interesting and creative. When I went back in 1975, there was nothing but non-commitment. And that's what is in the picture, because we are talking about the 1970s.'

The journalist Sam White reported in his *Evening Standard* column, that 'Joe Losey has had an enormous success in Paris with *Les Routes du Sud*, in spite of a turgid script.' White was not alone in thinking that Losey had been badly let down by the script, few realizing that he had written much of it himself. Even the faithful *Positif*, whose June 1978 cover story featured the film, had to concede that it was not one of Losey's great films.

One of the cruellest reviews came from David Overbey in *Paris Métro*, who called the film 'confused son of Resnais'. Overbey thought that Losey's film was a lesser work than Resnais': 'The sense of disappointment which comes after seeing *Les Routes du Sud* is partly due to having mistakenly expected an extraordinary film only to find an ordinary one. This is not so much Losey's fault as our own. In an earlier critical misapprehension and over-evaluation of his work, we led ourselves to believe that Joseph Losey was more than a conventional craftsman. Only Yves Montand survives with his reputation intact, but then it must be remembered that he's played the same role before, so his effectiveness must come in part from the memory of better days with better direction.'

Bertrand Tavernier, who always disapproved of Losey's abandonment of loyal and reliable craftsmen such as Ben Barzman in favour of more modish names, believed that in his passion to work with famous writers, Losey had been unwisely seduced by Semprun. He feels that the less glamorous Barzman would have 'got it right', and the mistake of working with Semprun led to the production of 'a very, very bad film'. Pierre Rissient dared to make this point to Losey's face, which did little to enhance their already faltering relationship. On the other hand, Tavernier recognizes that had Losey not been attracted by the idea of change and experimentation in his collaborations, he might never have worked with Pinter.

Nobody could have been more surprised than Losey when next he was offered the opportunity to direct a film of Mozart's great operatic masterpiece, *Don Giovanni*. His lack of ear for either music or languages was well-known, so what would motivate anyone to choose him for a musical project of such magnitude? Plans to film the opera resulted from a chance meeting between Rolf Liebermann, Swiss director of the Paris Opera, and Daniel Toscan du Plantier, president of Gaumont Films in France. Liebermann believed in bringing culture to the masses, in providing opportunities for people who did not necessarily dislike opera or lack interest, but who were simply not members of the élite who frequented the world's opera houses. Toscan's ideas were more related to marketing: he simply wanted to make a 'real' movie of a good story, using all the technical facilities available to the cinema, including location filming and other elements of verisimilitude.

Toscan subscribed to the French view that the essence of film-making lay in the choice of director, something alien to Liebermann, for whom musical productions, at any rate, should be under the control of musicians, and in whose country films and film directors were not quite so celebrated. Toscan wanted to choose someone who worked outside the world of opera – who was, perhaps, not even an opera buff – to create a film intended for a largely non-operatic audience, who would enjoy it as a great spectacle, a rattling good story, in an atmosphere bursting with rich and sensuous sound.

Much to Liebermann's chagrin, Losey said that he had never seen *Don Giovanni* on stage, even admitting to attacks of ennui when exposed to Verdi, and positive boredom when confronted with Wagner. Therefore, as a kind of introduction to the project, Liebermann took him to the Paris Opera one evening, during the time he was editing *Mr Klein*; Losey fell asleep as soon as the lights dimmed.

Toscan, whose company had distributed *The Romantic English-woman* in France, had met Losey on various occasions when he was in the advertising and publicity business, before he had joined

Gaumont. He had not found Losey easy, observing that day by day, Patricia was the strongest influence on him – apart from drink, which made him rude and contentious: 'Joe was in very bad shape, working night and day. Vodka is not the best friend of work, and he was starting this vodka at eleven in the morning. If you and I would drink like that, we'd be dead in three days. Then came the espressos. He was a tough man, but he treated himself badly.'

Losey explains his reasons for accepting the job as 'a combination of Mozart, the theme of *Don Giovanni*, and the architecture of Palladio,' although there were other considerations: he had not worked for nearly a year, as the negotiations for the Proust project dragged on inconclusively, and the budget needed to make it spiralled, frightening the producers; he was attracted as well by the innovative aspect – only Ingmar Bergman had tried to film an opera in similar circumstances, and he thought Bergman's *The Magic Flute*, intended mainly for television, was seriously flawed.

The theme of Mozart's opera appealed, redolent to some extent of his own youthful philanderings. Losey perceived the Don as cynical, hard, and especially cruel, but capable of being hurt, even frightened, as longing for human contact, but unable to achieve it. 'People who pursue women and sex on a one-night stand basis are running from something – from themselves, from a reality, which they perceive but can't cope with, from inadequacy, or all those things – an escape mechanism,' Losey told Ciment.

Through the filter of his personal obsessions, Losey saw the opera as a 'drama of social class'. He was quoted as saying, 'I believe it to be a very modern piece of work. Mozart could hardly have been aware of the French revolution, but I think that certain things have always been in the air simultaneously, in different places, at different times. My attitude is best explained by the quotation at the beginning of the picture, from Gramsci, a Marxist imprisoned by Mussolini: "The old is dying and the new cannot be born; in this interregnum, a great variety of morbid symptoms appears." This attitude should be reflected in the fact that only aristocrats and Leporello sing *Viva la Libertà*, while the underlings stand at feeble attention like a lot of whipped, middle-class English, standing at attention for the National Anthem at the Haymarket Theatre.

'His kind of sexuality can be seen as running away from facing homosexuality or using sex as a means to flee from social realities you can't do anything about. There is guilt in him about enjoying things which he knows he does not deserve.' Nowhere does Losey expose his puritan self so ingenuously, for there is not a hint of guilt lurking in the Da Ponte Don, but a great deal in Joseph Losey, who is not unaware of the essential point: 'Even when he (the Don) goes to hell, he refuses to repent. . .' Of course he does, for repentance represents the hope of the guilt-ridden; those unable to feel guilt have no need of it.

Don Giovanni was budgeted at twelve million francs, a sum which rose to twenty million, or six million dollars during shooting, as the schedule stretched from its original four weeks to forty-four days. Losey's explanation is that he was working under pressure, with too little money arriving only sporadically. There was insufficient time for basic preparation and the producers underestimated both the financial and temporal scope of the project.

The superb cast had been largely chosen by Liebermann for a stage production at the Paris Opera, and he simply transferred them to the film. Ruggero Raimondi starred as the Don, Kiri Te Kanawa as Donna Elvira, Edda Moser as Donna Anna, the Austrian Kenneth Reigel as her brother, Don Ottavio, John Macurdy as the Commendatore, José Van Dam as the Don's servant, Leporello, Teresa Berganza as Zerlina, with Malcolm King playing Masetto, her ill-used fiancé. The crew were also assembled under the aegis of the production team, the only members imported from Losey's 'family' being Alexander Trauner as designer, Gerry Fisher as director of photography, Frantz Salieri as assistant director, and Patricia, in her usual capacity of translator, co-ordinator, and general factotum. Most of the cast were old hands at the roles they played, and knew each other well enough to create an atmosphere of relaxed familiarity; only Teresa Berganza, new to the role of Zerlina, and nervously conscious of the fact that she was much too old to be playing it in a film, was an outsider.

In retrospect, Losey realized that one vital mistake had been made at the outset: CBS had already contracted to record the opera with the cast before it had been decided to make the film. That, he discovered, was the wrong way round, since it robbed him of much creative control. After filming had finished, he said: 'The film director and the conductor should have long, detailed conferences and decide what's interior and what's exterior before the conductor ever begins to conduct – then the result could be sold to a record company. Most of the difficulties stemmed from that one initial mistake, which was simply inexperience on the part of everybody. I didn't mind violating tradition but I didn't want to violate the music as it had been recorded, which was a mistake.'

Lorin Maazel, who directed the musical performance with the orchestra and chorus of the Paris Opera, was very impressed by Losey: 'Joe had no great formal knowledge of classical music but was very sensitive to it. We worked through the musical score and libretto note by note and word by word. We spent several days at it, and when we completed our meetings, we had a very clear idea of our vision of the work. He could "hear" my music and I could "see" his visualizations. When recording, I kept these constantly in mind.'

The singers and orchestra were recorded at the church of Notre Dame du Liban, in the Rue d'Ulm, where the nave became a studio, festooned with microphones, speakers, sound control boards and other paraphernalia.

On 22 June 1978, grey with fatigue from flying between Paris and London, where he was conducting performances of Verdi's *Luisa Miller*, Maazel arrived at the church in a jaunty blue blazer, ready to begin the session. First he had a deep discussion with Paul Myers of CBS. Singers began to emerge, happy to see old friends and colleagues. Out in the hall, perched patiently on a folding chair much too small to contain his bulk, various note-books and scores fanned out on three chairs in front of him, was Losey, a momentarily forgotten man. Having waited modestly for the show-biz buzz to subside, he called the session to order, Maazel stripped off his blazer, fished a baton from his brief-case, and two weeks of intensive work began. Curiously, Losey had an infinitely easier relationship with Maazel than with Liebermann, with whom he exchanged frequent complaining letters.

The sessions were tense, with Losey, whom the cast hardly knew, proving to be a distracting and disturbing presence, in spite of his reluctance to interfere. Paul Meyers described it as 'an uphill struggle all the way, with endless spectators, strange characters wandering in and out, and always a pervading sense of oppression – like a Fellini movie.'

The only one who appeared not to have a care in the world was Kiri Te Kanawa, who sat knitting or eating an apple while everyone else waited nervously for their cue. Two bars before her entrance, she would get up calmly and sing, her entrance bang on pitch. Of Losey, Te Kanawa said, simply: 'I'd die for him.'

When recording ended in early July, the cast heaved a communal sigh of relief and dispersed for two months, while Losey and his team installed themselves in Vicenza to plan and prepare the visual aspects, producing a dense pile of papers that included, in alphabetical categories, schedules for sound, orchestra, masks, boats and barges, vehicles, animals, in addition to the cast itself: 'Like mobilizing a regiment,' Losey pronounced, warming to the task. Losey was thrilled not to be denied his location filming, as he had been with *Galileo*. The only condition was that he confine shooting to within twenty-five miles of both Venice and Vicenza.

When shooting began in mid-September, the weather turned unseasonably cold and wet within a week, further testing the artists' nerves. There were electrical storms followed by five days of unceasing rain. Daunted, but not defeated, Losey decided simply to stop the work, and use the time till the weather cleared to sort out co-production problems vexing the project.

There were technical difficulties, with the sound engineer trying to blend live sound, mostly recorded out of doors, with the studio recording of the sung music, pre-recorded months earlier. When that was accomplished, there came the monumental task of reconciling incidental sound effects and sixteen music tracks with the *recitativi*, which comprised a third of all the music and was played live at Losey's insistence by a harpsichordist with permanently frozen fingers. Toscan displayed an unexpected insensitivity in calling Losey's insistence on the live musical accompaniment 'stupid and expensive'.

Maazel, however, defends Losey's stand, confirming that it would have been virtually impossible to pre-record the conversational musical sections, because both the words and the music move too quickly and a-rhythmically: 'Pre-recording would have hampered the action in flowing naturally as a result of the décor and lighting. In the case of a recitative, it is the action that determines nuance, tempo, dynamics, etc. and not vice-versa. Joe was right.'

Maazel also applauds Losey's expertise in drawing out cinematic interpretations from singers, who tend either to telescope emotions, or go right over the top with gestures aimed at the more removed audience in an opera house. 'Almost all the singers give a creditable account of themselves in film-theatre terms,' he assures us.

Apart from the fact that Teresa Berganza looked too old playing the teenaged Zerlina, and Kenneth Reigel was overweight ('The poor tenor,' Toscan sighs, 'He lost twenty kilos; it's a sadness he only lost them after'), Losey was obliged to modify many of his own initial theories about filming singers. At the outset, his direction was aimed at curtailing the florid and expansive gesturing to which operatic acting lends itself. Ruggero Raimondi is purported to have told Toscan that the only thing the director ever said to him on the set was, 'Don't move!' In the course of time and with the gathering of experience, Losey changed his mind: 'I found my initial desire to avoid operatic gestures was mistaken. The music carries you that way making it almost impossible, indeed, wrong, to sing some of those scenes without the grand gesture. I aimed for something in between.'

The idea of using the glass factory at Murano for the opening music and to introduce all the players resulted from a visit to the island by Losey, Trauner and Frantz Salieri, who explained that when the Palladian villas were being built, the Venetians moved inland during certain times of the year to farms and large villas designed for summer living. Within these communities embryonic industrial societies were born, concentrating on the manufacture of glass. In the course of their tour, the three noted that there was a good deal of talk about fire among the glassworkers, and an idea began to emerge in Losey's mind: why not connect Venice and the vast, flat fields of the Veneto, to show society as it expanded from trade to industry, from water to land, and to locate Don Giovanni's source of wealth in a glass factory? As the day wore on, Losey became increasingly keen on the notion of his audience meeting the Don in the place where both his wealth was born and where he would die, and by the time the launch from the hotel Cipriani reappeared through the soft, evening mist the Don's fate was sealed: the Commendatore would drag him into a hell whose foyer was a vat of molten glass.

Later, when Losey wanted a wild boar for the banquet table and was unable to obtain one, he made some calls to his old underworld acquaintances. 'Joe was fascinated by these sort of people,' confides Jack Loring. 'He always had that interest in things that had never had any place in his former life – crime, violence, wild sex, all that sort of thing. It was an obsessive curiosity – nothing whatsoever to do with his own life, because he remained basically puritanical in his own way. Still, there was that wild boar, delivered by the Mafia the next morning.'

Losey's familiar fascination with bisexuality caused speculation about the appearance in the film of a new character: the Valet in Black, a sort of *éminence grise*, who dogs the footsteps of the Don, his master. The character, played by Isabelle Adjani's brother Eric, was invented by Salieri to help resolve some of the awkward logistical problems presented by Da Ponte's text, or so Losey insisted.

Losey remained unspecific about what the valet represented. In the notes outlining his perception of the characters, he wrote: 'To me Don Giovanni is not a homosexual, though he may well be bisexual.' Losey suggested that the valet may be 'the illegitimate son of Don Giovanni, so his relations with Leporello are tense. Leporello is not as elegant or well-born as the valet, though more confident. There is resentment there. He could be the augur of Don Giovanni's death – he opens the first door at the villa, and closes the last. He should be sinister, terrifying, bitter, cold, sexual, but never effeminate, never smug. What is most important is that he is the Observer, so may represent any point of view in the piece.' The point of view of some reviewers was that the valet was homosexual. The critic of *The Guardian* referred to 'the gay Don', while *Gay News* called him the 'closeted Don'.

Directing the opera had been one of Losey's happiest experiences. 'I adored the work and it was the friendliest atmosphere of anything I had ever done,' he said. 'It's very rare that you come out of an extremely difficult work on terms of life-long friendship with nearly everybody involved. My objective was to make opera at the highest level accessible to the greatest possible audience.'

Few films could have survived the avalanche of advance publicity attracted by *Don Giovanni*. Virtually every major newspaper and glossy magazine in America, Great Britain and Europe published features on the film, together with lengthy interviews with Losey and various members of the cast. Somehow, the film was finished by late October, provoking the most excessive speculation and anticipation in France. In London the *Evening Standard* proclaimed that 'Losey is now far and away the most famous and most highly-praised foreigner in France. His latest film, *Don Giovanni*, has been acclaimed with a unanimity and a lavishness of praise that is positively dazzling.'

Kind though it was of the British press to support one of its most distinguished adopted citizens, this evaluation of French reaction was based on enthusiastic pre-release publicity.

The film's premiere was held not in France, but in America, where on 4 November it opened at the Kennedy Center in Washington D.C., and, two days later, at the Lincoln Center in New York, before moving more permanently to the Paris Theater on 58th Street. James Mazzola, president of the Lincoln Center, was struck, and not a little disturbed, by Losey's appearance and apparent bewilderment at the Washington opening. He seemed unable to work out who anybody was, confusing Roger Stevens, the theatrical producer and property entrepreneur – with George Stevens Jr., the son of the Hollywood director – or to come to grips with the burble of conversation around him. At one point when the son of one of the Italian magnates appeared, announcing 'Il Papa è morto', Losey became agitated, thinking the child's father had expired, when it was, in fact, the Pope, John Paul I, who had died.

The Paris opening came on 14 November, the reviews ranging from ecstatic to respectful, the audiences unequivocally enthusiastic. As Losey and others had feared, the sharpest criticisms centred on the sound reproduction. Maurice Fleuret of the *Nouvel Observateur*, while pronouncing the film a *'chef-d'oeuvre'*, had reservations: 'We reproach Losey for invoking de Sade when Da Ponte was only with Casanova, there to develop a sinister chant of death, when all the music of Mozart explodes with life.' *Cahiers du Cinéma*, on the whole supportive, added that 'The only problem posed by this film is that of the post-synchronization, or play-back. Losey fails here completely.'

At the end of the month, the Loseys' flew to Brazil for one of their seasonal visits with the Taluso children, returning to New York just before Christmas for interviews and meetings. Surprised by the excitement generated in Rio by the projected opening there in the New Year, Losey hoped to return to participate in it, but he was too ill to do so, and was advised to return to the Rue du Dragon and get some rest. Unable to enjoy himself doing little or nothing, Losey began writing letters, heaping praise on virtually everyone artistically involved in *Don Giovanni*, and speaking of his abiding hope that Proust could be put back on the rails. Pinter's script was already into several printings. Everyone judged it to be too long and expensive, so Losey thought that the possibility of its coming to be in his lifetime was very much dependent on *Don Giovanni*. If Mozart was a success, he felt that the money would be found for Proust.

Losey had fretted that the Italians would be the film's harshest critics, but such was not the case. Much to his annoyance and bitter disappointment, it was the American critics who were the most devastating. For the first time, Losey responded to some of them, feeling that they had been motivated by considerations which had little or nothing to do with art. The sharpest blow had come from the powerful Vincent Canby at the *New York Times*: 'This *Don Giovanni*, though marvellous to listen to, even when a singer has difficulty lip-synching his own voice, and pretty to look at, may well be utter confusion to anyone who doesn't know the score or the story. This is not a *Don Giovanni* to make converts; it sings to the committed. As the Don, Ruggero Raimondi lacks any evident charm or passion. The camera is especially unkind to Teresa Berganza, Kenneth Reigel, and Malcolm King. John Macurdy, as the Commendatore, has the easiest time of it, supposedly being made of stone. Mr Losey also adds a non-speaking character in the shape of the Valet in Black, a sort of spooky supernumerary, who turns up from time to time to clear away props and to hand the Don his mandolin. I've seen better descents into hell at our own Metropolitan Opera and in any number of Hammer horror pictures. Mr Losey and his associates haven't destroyed *Don Giovanni*, but then they haven't illuminated it either. Their film is a busy, disorienting spectacle, superbly sung.'

Losey wrote Canby a two-page letter, expressing surprise that he had so obviously misread the film and pointing out that it had been given the award for the best film of the year by the French Academy, and another for best combination of film and music. Losey's reaction was not so much personal pique as a function of his intense loyalty to the film and to everyone who had worked so hard and well on it, not to speak of the dozens of people who had loved it and written to him of their disgust with some of the reviews.

When he had thoroughly exhausted himself and his staff from typing letters of thanks, support, commiseration and encouragement to assorted cast and other colleagues, Losey rounded on the Dolby technicians responsible for the sound. He also sent rambling letters of complaint to Liebermann, receiving in reply short notes, such as 'I get the message: you're shocked, I'm wrong', or '*Cher Ami*, we are conducting a dialogue of the deaf.'

Losey's overwhelming concern was the poor quality of some of the prints that appeared in some cinemas, many of which were so bad that members of the audience were turning up at the box-office in mid-performance asking for their money back. A huge file accumulated of Losey's complaints to M. Bonnell of Gaumont, and Bonnell's apologetic replies and assurances.

In March 1980, for the first time in twenty-nine years, Losey returned to Hollywood for the Los Angeles opening of the film at the Cinerama Dome, in aid of the Opera Guild of Southern California. As one columnist remarked, the return of this prodigal son very nearly upstaged his opening. And everyone noticed that he talked as much about his hopes to make the Proust film as he did about *Don Giovanni*: 'I have yet to find the $18 million to do the Pinter play,' he conceded ('and is it any wonder?', the columnist had thought), 'but it's a great screenplay, and not an "art" film. It has every kind of sex and every kind of pageantry – all the elements for a commercial film.'

But Losey's hopes rested on the success of *Don Giovanni*. And the *Los Angeles Times'* music critic, Martin Bernheimer, was even harsher than Canby, enlisting the help of the great conductor, Carlo Maria Giulini, in his hatchet job. After asking the conductor's opinion, Bernheimer quotes his 'horrified' reaction: 'Do you wish to provoke me? The film was wrong. No one has the right to do a thing like this to the libretto and to the music. It is not allowed! If someone wants to make an interesting original film about Don Juan with just anyone's music, that is no problem. But don't say in the credits, Mozart. Don't say Da Ponte.'

Though crushed by the response to *Don Giovanni*, Losey called on old friends, many of whom he had not seen for a very long time. Norman Lloyd, who had trouped alongside him during the Depression years in New York and Boston, was saddened by the scruffily decaying appearance of his old friend, whom he hadn't seen since he visited London in 1968. He speaks with regret about some function at the Director's Guild during which Losey got unpleasantly drunk and abused people who only wished him well. Part of the problem was that Lloyd had not liked *Don Giovanni* any more than the critics. To anyone of Losey's sensitivity, his silence spoke volumes. Their parting was uneasy and left Lloyd feeling chilled.

The Barzmans, too, were dismayed by Losey's appearance – the melting features and bulging gut – and upset by the circumstances in which their reunion was taking place. But the occasion was a happy one, Ben remembers: 'Last time I saw Joe during that awful visit in April 1980 was one of the most wonderful afternoons of my life, and Norma will say the same. Joe was wonderful towards the end, mellow even. As the sun went down, I thought we might not ever see him again, and we didn't, so we're glad we had that last good afternoon.'

Norma, who was incensed that Losey had been ignored by the Americans, when he yearned so desperately for a project that would bring him home, would have been pleased to hear that he planned to go to Chicago to shoot *Silence*, a violent story of an affair between a young, uneducated black girl and a successful, middle-aged doctor. But that was to come to nothing, generating further disappointment.

His spirits were raised by the critical reaction to the film in London, which opened on 25 September at the Academy Cinema. The *Evening Standard*'s critic hailed 'A matchless Don Giovanni'. Raimondi appeared on the cover of *What's On in London*, which called it 'a spectacular and well-sung film'. John Coleman of the *New Statesman* reported that Karl Boehm had much admired it, describing it as 'a good effort at popular opera', which is all it was ever intended to be.

Though understandably biased, Lorin Maazel's view is possibly the fairest: 'I would evaluate Joe's *Don Giovanni* as a film classic – a masterpiece flawed here and there by problems beyond his control, like budget restrictions and yet-to-be-perfected sound systems. It was the first film of an opera as a film, as opposed to a filmed opera with all its opera-house conventions. As such, it was a brilliant achievement by a brilliant man.'

By November, Losey was able to write to Chris Nelson of CBS that *Don Giovanni* was enjoying a successful commercial run in London, and that the recording was a best-seller in Europe, entirely as a result of the presence of the film. More good news was on the way that month from Theo Cowan, who reported that the box-office revenue had held steady for five weeks, averaging £6,000 per week, and was rising going into the sixth. But none of this was sufficient for the film either to make a profit or to break even. It was obvious that there was now no chance of a producer raising a budget twice the size of *Don Giovanni* for Losey to film *A la Recherche du Temps Perdu*. His long imagined, endlessly desired encounter with Proust was cancelled, killed stone-dead by the Don.

XVIII

Not Waving but Drowning

Losey had enjoyed the experience of making *Don Giovanni* so much that he immediately began talking not only to Liebermann and Maazel, but also to Herbert von Karajan about filming other operas once he had finished with *Silence*. But in January 1980 he wrote to Ruggero Raimondi, with whom he hoped somehow to work again, telling him that *Silence* had been 'postponed'.

He had learned from experience, he told an interviewer, 'the better the project, the harder it is to finance. The people who do the financing become less and less knowledgeable. The older you get the more depressing it is. It's much harder now. The majors change hands every five minutes. People don't stay long enough to see a project through. You walk into Paramount and you're confronted by the people you met last week at Fox. I've given up going to the majors; it's far better to go to the independents.'

Though he was deeply disappointed, this set-back enabled Losey to work again with Raimondi and Liebermann on a production of *Boris Godunov*, to be staged at the Paris Opera marking the end of Liebermann's reign there. Although their relationship remained abrasive, Losey and Liebermann had managed to survive *Don Giovanni* with considerable mutual respect. They shared an admiration for Raimondi, who had, overnight, become an international star and domestic heart-throb as a result of the film.

Ever since he'd been introduced in Russia to the concept of the physical as well as the psychological reconciliation of audiences and actors, Losey had been antipathetic to the convention which in musical productions separated the audience from the stage. With this in mind, he had the orchestra pit covered for *Boris Godunov*, giving the singers the opportunity to play on the apron, a semi-circular extension built in front of the proscenium arch. The orchestra was arranged behind the singers in a magnificent, tiered semi-circle, or crown, with the conductor in front of them, his back to the singers. The master stroke was achieved by the conductor's control of the performers through closed-circuit television.

Seiji Ozawa, then chief conductor of the Boston Symphony, was at first excited, but soon defeated, by the concept. Television screens had been placed in strategic spots all over the stage, concealed by curtains, bits of scenery and props, so that the singers could keep an eye on Ozawa's baton and he on their faces. But the conductor proved inflexible, twisting around continuously until he developed a serious muscular spasm, which fixed his head in a backward-looking position like something out of *The Exorcist*. At the last minute, he had to retire, and his place was filled by a competent but less-known Yugoslav conductor, Rauslan Raitschoff.

Rehearsals took place six days a week for a month, with every detail of movement and set design laid out in blueprint form with architectural precision. Familiar faces turned up on the production team, such as Janine Reiss, the harpsichordist from *Don Giovanni*, as assistant musical director, and Kenneth Reigel, singing the part of Chouisky. In addition, many old friends joined the audience for the charity preview on 9 June at the Pompidou Centre, as well as the opening at the Opera three days later. These included Henry Bamburger, who had come all the way from Hollywood, Dr Barry Cooper, Jack Loring and Paloma Picasso, who contributed considerably to the glitter of the evening. Losey's first foray into the theatre for some twenty-five years was a great success, and gave a much-needed boost to his flagging spirits. The production was also filmed for French television, to Losey's satisfaction, for he regarded the result as the only good television version of an opera ever made.

Anxious then to return to film-making, Losey revived *The Trout*, a project which he had first considered in the mid-1960s, when it was to have been a big international co-production starring Brigitte Bardot, as Frédérique (the symbolic Trout), and Bogarde as her weak, homosexual husband. Returning to it more than fifteen years later, he rationalized, was a bonus, since he could now bring more experience to bear on the story.

The Trout, is possibly more heavily laden with symbolism than any of Losey's films since *Eve*. Water, with its strong sexual connotations, predominates, with aqueous sounds, images and movements framing the story. In a powerful opening image, Frédérique manipulates a female trout to release her eggs, then a male to inseminate them. Breathtaking images abound of fish swimming in their tanks, attacking each other, and defending their patch.

The Trout, based on a novel *(La Truite)* by Roger Vailland, is a tale of wickedness, corruption, and cynicism among the despots of voracious multinationals, using a trout farm in the Jura as a metaphor. (The trout is one of the most savage of game fish.)

Losey had admired Vailland, a winner of the *Prix Goncourt* and a revolutionary Marxist. He was also intrigued by the character of Frédérique, the trout-farmer's daughter, who cynically manipulates and exploits men by falsely promising them her sexual favours; she wears a T-shirt with 'peut-être' written across the bosom and 'jamais' across the back! This 'catalyst for tragedy' – as Vailland described her, was recognizable as Losey's destructive and unfeeling Eve.

In the fifteen years since *The Trout*'s conception, Roger Vailland had died and the world had changed: big corporations were even bigger, the 'players' within them were different, and Brigitte Bardot was too old, as was nearly everybody else in the original cast. Furthermore, Gaumont wanted to do the film in France, so it seemed sensible, as well as politic, to go for as many actors as possible who would not need dubbing. The character of Isaac, however – who, in the novel, was a Jewish, international financier, controlling the company in which many of the other 'trouts' fought their way upstream – was now transformed into a Japanese tycoon, Daigo, played by Isao Yamagata. Losey was happy to cast Jeanne Moreau as Lou, wife of Rampert (a French tycoon, played by Jean-Pierre Cassel), and Alexis Smith (who had been in Losey's very first English film *Sleeping Tiger*) as Gloria (a libidinous widow) who, Losey said, 'has to be played broadly, like all those Houston oil widows who control the United States.' Smith's husband, Craig Stevens, played the part of President of the company's American subsidiary; and for the first time, Losey played a small role himself, *à la* Hitchcock.

Losey kept to his usual habit of writing copious notes addressed to the cast and crew, setting forth his views on the story and its characters. In thirteen pages of 'suggestions, attitudes, and provocations', he summarizes *The Trout* as a very modern story. He saw the film as in one sense a tragedy, a story about adults who remained children and could not grow up. All these adult children were therefore the victims as well as the makers of the society they lived in.

Revealingly, Losey considered that men try to hide their childishness under a false cover of masculinity. The women in the story were, he said, far superior to the men. He was anxious to give greater validity to the social aspects of the book, and to bring what he called its 'libertine texture' into sharper focus since it was clearly more evident in society now than it had been in the mid-1960s. The key to the film, he thought, was a comment someone had once made to him, and which had been included in the script – that the distinction between heterosexuals and homosexuals no longer applied: now you were either sexual or not. The author of the remark was Jeanne Moreau, who had first introduced him to the true nature of Eve in that long-ago chateau in Brittany – and in so doing, had altered his life.

Shown at the New York Film Festival in September 1982, *The Trout* received mixed reviews, the consensus being that Huppert was miscast, and that the film contained too many symbols and psychological conundrums. One admirer, Howard Kissell of *Women's Wear Daily*, wrote that 'Huppert, whose very body has a hardness, and whose face often suggests effortless cruelty, seems perfect as the focal point for this study of non-relationships. The characters seldom connect. They circle about one another with unmasked aggression and overt sexual energy, rather like trout in a tank. One of Losey's richest, most provocative films.'

Even those who panned it found it difficult to dismiss Losey. *Vanity Fair*'s critic wrote: 'Joseph Losey has been making rotten movies for years, but he sure knows how to direct them, how to make a camera shimmy through a discotheque, fly through an airport, swim past an aquarium. He can use décor to reflect persona and persona décor; he can change his palette with each new setting; he can make elusive characters appear deep, fathomless. With the technique and control at his command, he could probably tell stories to set the imagination on fire – but he doesn't. Losey's films tend toward a sort of toney obscurantism; they strike a queasy balance between stuffiness and homiletic banality. His characters are invariably nasty, well off, and sexually disturbed, and they're always spouting gnomic sayings on life and love, like cracker-barrel philosophers who dress for dinner.'

The critic of the *Village Voice* commented that 'Huppert's performance is so cold and repellent that the movie seems less a savvy survey of the modern world than the melancholic memoir of a man who is old and loveless.'

As Losey disclosed to an American interviewer that year, 'It seems that people do need each other sexually and it's also true that even the most loyal, intelligent and loving couple can fall into the most violent and aggressive relationships. It's a common thread in my pictures.'

The time came, in 1983, when the necessary period of exile for tax purposes was over, and the Loseys could return to their home in Royal Avenue, Chelsea. Dirk Bogarde, anxious to rebuild bridges after the ten-year gap in their friendship, gave a party to welcome them back to London. 'He was very glad,' says Bogarde, 'and very sweet, and it was all very moving. We went downstairs and talked for a long time, and he apologized. He said, "Well, I'm ten years older, and I'm a washout, ruined and broke." I told him not to be silly, and he said he wanted to work with Harold again, even though Proust was kaput.'

Determined not to lose out on his desire to make a film once more in America, Losey again pursued his plans for *Silence*. He thought it 'a very shocking and profoundly disturbing book', and he had a high opinion of the screenplay written with David Rayfiel, who had scripted Bertrand Tavernier's *Death Watch*. But the subject was too downbeat for the producers to anticipate any commercial joy from the film, and Losey watched his best chance for a return to his homeland disappear once and for all.

To Adrian Hodges of *Screen International* in the UK, Losey confessed that his one abiding ambition was to make one or two films on strong, typically American subjects. 'There is a generation or two in Hollywood who don't know who I am,' he complained. 'It comes as quite a shock – particularly when you have up to ten films running permanently all over the world – to think that a lot of them think I'm either dead or retired. It's rather tough, because

I certainly don't feel old, and I'm sure my films aren't – not yet anyway.' Jack Berry, a fellow blacklisted director exiled to Europe, had returned to film-making in America in 1974 and felt sure that Losey, like him, would have found it 'a very healing experience'. But it was not to be.

Losey, at 73, was feeling his age more than ever, and his continuing disillusion with Hollywood was heightened by discovering what had gone on behind the scenes over *Silence*. John Heyman was to have produced it, but had sold the property to another Hollywood producer, Allan Carr, who, when Losey was mentioned as director, had said: 'Who is Losey? I don't even want to meet him. He's not a "name".' Bertrand Tavernier was so incensed by this turn of events that he wrote an article in *Positif* denouncing Carr as a philistine and defending Losey's honour, a gesture which so touched Patricia that she wrote to thank him.

Losey hoped for more luck with *Track 29*, written by the British playwright Dennis Potter, about a bored South Carolina housewife, whose life is overturned by a stranger claiming to be her long-lost son. Plans were well-advanced. While the crew made final preparations in Dallas, Patricia busied herself in London with arrangements for someone to look after Tyger and the house while they were away filming. Losey had flown to Mexico for a short break in which to gather energy for the task ahead. One evening, he rang, in a mood of abysmal depression, to tell Patricia that the project had been cancelled. His disappointment was shattering, not only because he had looked forward to working with Potter, but because instinct told him there would not be another opportunity to return home.

He came back to London and turned to the vodka bottle for solace, going for walks with his beloved Tyger. There seemed to be little prospect of work in the immediate future.

In the spring of 1983, there came a break in the tedium when he was invited to preside over a screening of *Don Giovanni* in Madison, Wisconsin, in aid of the Madison Art Center. He was also awarded a doctorate of Humane Letters at the University of Wisconsin. Typically, it was Dirk Bogarde who had supported and seconded Losey for the honour, knowing how much it would mean to him to receive some recognition from his own people.

On 8 June, the *Milwaukee Journal* reported that 'The movie director from La Crosse doesn't much like it here. His homecoming is full of irony. Joseph Losey's unhappiness as an adolescent came partly as a reaction against his family's conservatism. His bitterness is still evident after thirty years. "He comes as an outsider to the world of high culture," reported Russell Merritt, film professor, who first proposed giving Losey an honorary degree. "Losey is both repelled and intrigued by moral decadence, [yet] he is one of the great champions – if unwitting – of wealth for what it brings, for making it sexy."'

Back in England, and just when he thought he might die of boredom, Losey was telephoned by John Pringle, a producer who was about to make a television film, based on Graham Greene's *Dr Fischer of Geneva*, which had been scripted by John Mortimer. Pringle wanted Losey to direct it, and arranged for all three of them to meet Graham Greene in the South of France. Losey heaved himself aboard a plane, and called for a drink.

'The meeting was a disaster,' Pringle laments. 'By now Joe had become a fat, profane, drunken slob. He'd been pouring the drink down his throat all the way over on the plane, and was so drunk when I met him in Nice that he very nearly didn't make it down the steps.' Losey began a litany of complaint: Why was there no car to meet him? The hotel wasn't first class; *Dr Fischer* was a mediocre short story, not a novel at all; Mortimer was not a first-class writer either, and so on.

Greene, who was paying for dinner, remained polite, for he'd been told Losey was a genius. However, when it was all over, he told Pringle to get rid of him; nobody could be expected to work with such a character. 'I broke the news,' Pringle reports, 'saying that nobody liked the script, and offered him $100,000, half his fee. I didn't have to do that, but I thought it was right. I suppose I wanted to demonstrate that not all producers were monsters. There he was, hung over, sheepish, in this god-awful terry-cloth dressing gown. A pathetic figure. Bogarde would have played Dr Fischer, had Losey directed, and it would have been great. He was his own worst enemy – always. Totally self-destructive. In the end, Michael Lindsay-Hogg directed the picture, and I hated it. Tragic.'

Shortly after this débâcle, John Heyman approached Losey to direct a film version of a play set in a women's Turkish baths: Nell Dunn's *Steaming*, which was having a long and successful run in the West End. One of his associates had taken the Loseys to see it, and Patricia had returned so full of enthusiasm that she asked if she could write the screenplay. The advantage in this project was that it could be made on a relatively low budget of under $3,000,000, since it only required one set. Its all-female cast moreover provided half-a-dozen contrasting roles that would attract good actresses.

Losey's reasons for agreeing that Patricia should write the screenplay were complex. Although he was unaware that what was killing him was a determined cancer in his intestine, he knew that his time was growing short, and that Patricia, twenty years his junior, could have a long road to travel alone when he was gone.

Jack Loring believes that Losey wanted Patricia to write the film: 'He obviously knew he was dying, and that things could not go on as they were. I mean, he was always "dying" – of cirrhosis, or asthma, or cardiac arrest – but now he knew, and he wanted to establish Patricia in a career, so that she could go on. She had been very secure, fawned over, and pampered by all those movie stars, who were invariably her "greatest personal friends", and Joe and I would talk about this endlessly. I pointed out that there was apt to be a disaster after he died, because these people were going to leave the sinking ship, and Patricia was going to be abandoned. He knew that I was right, too.'

Patricia, in an afterword to Michel Ciment's *Conversations with Losey*, wrote that she believed the film to be important and right 'in terms of a career and a life to situate *Steaming* in the mainstream of that career and that life, death being an unforeseeable interruption at a time when major plans were being made for the future.' Although one can appreciate her sentiments, it is difficult to regard the film as other than peripheral, especially when viewed alongside the dazzling products of Losey's best years. It was doomed from the start.

Nell Dunn had been asked to write the film script herself, but she declined. She knew nothing of camera angles, lighting, lenses, long-shots or close-ups, and was frankly apprehensive of the fact that the director's wife was involved; she was shown and did not like Patricia's first version of the script, and recognized that changes needed to be made.

Patricia conceded that her relationship with Losey had been based largely upon conflict, and the work on *Steaming* was no exception; interminable arguments erupted about the female characters, their fantasies, and their views on men, which reflected the Loseys' own difficulties and preoccupations.

The finished script was delivered on 3 January 1984, to John Heyman, who rang Losey to tell him that he hated it. But time was running out. The film's set was already being built and costs were beginning to mount. Heyman wanted to call in a new writer but, after several intense meetings, Patricia was allowed to continue with the rewrites, although on one point Heyman was adamant: he wanted the film to have a happy ending. Losey bowed to the inevitable, and agreed to end the story on a note of optimism. It was his first film since *The Boy With Green Hair* to have done so, and the last he would ever make.

In spite of it all, Losey never regarded himself as a pessimist. To be an effective pessimist, he argued, you had to be aware of the worst side of human nature, and in a sense it was necessary to be a pessimist in order to be an optimist. But he made a distinction between different types of optimist. There was the kind who believed that everything was bound to turn out for the best, and the kind who said life was good if you made it good.

The message conveyed by *Steaming* cleaves to the former view. A group of women from different social backgrounds find comfort and refuge in an exclusively female Turkish baths, where they meet once or twice a week to indulge in some therapeutically plain talk. The narrative hangs on the group's determination to prevent the threatened closure of the baths which have become central to their lives, but its drama lies in the women's conversations, their fantasies and their revelations regarding the men in their lives. In Heyman's happy ending, the women's efforts succeed and the baths are saved, along with their unconventional friendships and their redeeming bond.

Unfortunately, Gerry Fisher was busy on another film, so Losey asked Douglas Slocombe to be his director of photography. Slocombe, alas, disliked everything about the project – the theme, the vulgarity of the language employed by the women – everything. But he was fortuitously saved by an attack of bronchitis, which provided him with the excuse he needed to turn down Losey's offer without offending him. 'Joe looked dreadful,' Slocombe recalls. 'He was drinking a lot. I remember saying that if we did this film, it would kill us both. I said, "You can't do this picture either, with all that steam and what-not. It'll kill you."'

Losey recruited Christopher Challis, who had been the lighting cameraman on *Blind Date* twenty-six years earlier. A strong cast had been assembled: Vanessa Redgrave, Sarah Miles, Diana Dors, Brenda Bruce, Felicity Dean and, repeating her much acclaimed stage performance, Georgina Hale.

The first indication of trouble came when Georgina Hale received the script in the post, bearing little resemblance to Nell Dunn's play. Her central role, the character of Josie, had been drastically cut, with the balance of the script now favouring two other roles – those played by Vanessa Redgrave and Sarah Miles.

She attended a preliminary reading of the script, heavy with foreboding. To add to her apprehension, Nell Dunn, to whom she had spoken about her unhappiness with the first script, had rung to apologize and to say that she would not be at the reading to support her.

Though the script she was handed at the reading had actually been rewritten, she found it only marginally better. Georgina, distressed by the way that so much of the humour had been removed from what remained of her part, fought to have the cuts restored, noticing that Losey listened attentively to suggestions made by Miles and Redgrave, but cut her off whenever she spoke. She left the reading unhappy, but willing to adjust.

A few days later Losey invited her to his home in Royal Avenue. She arrived to find him lying in wait with the film's producer, Paul Mills, in the drawing-room, where they both vehemently criticized her attitude, reducing her to tears. It was clear that they hoped she would quit the film on the spot, thus saving them the cost of her salary. But she stood her ground, forcing them to fire her and release her with a golden handshake. Patti Love was hired to take her place.

Georgina was not the only person unhappy with the script. Both Vanessa and Sarah had been promised fresh pages, Heyman having implied that Christopher Hampton, one of Britain's most admired playwrights and screenwriters, might be called in. But no new or revitalized material was forthcoming.

Filming began at Pinewood on 27 February, Losey having gathered a few familiar cohorts around him. Reginald Beck had come out of semi-retirement in the country to edit the film, Peter Handford was put in charge of sound and, as always, the excellent and indispensable Pamela Davies managed the continuity. There was virtually no one on whom Losey relied more than Pamela Davies; she managed to struggle through her work on *Steaming*, even though she had lost the use of her right arm. She assumed that the disability was caused by a trapped nerve. It was not; it was cancer.

Since Vanessa Redgrave was appearing in a West End play at the same time as *Steaming* was being filmed, her contract was necessarily specific about the hours she was available. One day, she announced that she would not be turning up the following morning, because she had to attend an important political meeting. Losey lost his temper, drawing Vanessa's attention, in language rich in invective, to the conditions of her contract, and calling on the executive producer Richard Dalton to intercede.

Vanessa attempted to get her own back when it came to filming one of the final scenes, where all the women strip off and enter a plunge-pool together. Vanessa refused. Sarah Miles recalls the off-stage drama, Losey's ripe language, and the fact that in desperation he tried to persuade her to push Vanessa into the pool at the right moment. After much wearisome haggling, Vanessa stripped and took the plunge with the others.

Under normal circumstances Losey would have taken it all in his stride, even enjoying the cut and thrust, as he had always done in the past. But he was desperately ill, and had just learned that Diana Dors had cancer as well. By all accounts, Dors was magnificent, earning the respect, admiration, and love of the entire company. Although, as filming progressed, it was obvious that she was losing the battle with her illness, she continued to give a meticulous performance, remaining cheerful and funny throughout. 'Nobody but me,' recalls Sarah Miles sadly, 'knew how bad she was, how rotten she felt. She taught me a lot about dying.'

Losey, too, went from bad to worse, falling one day on the set and smashing his knee. From then on he was obliged to operate from a wheelchair. Peter Handford, who had by now worked with Losey on four films, confirms Sarah Miles's assessment of these depressing days: 'By this time Joe was really tragic – the way he looked, as well as his mental state. It was just a very sad picture all round: Dors was dying; Pam Davies was too, but didn't know it; Joe was in such bad shape he had to be lifted by fork-lift truck up to the raised rostrum set because he couldn't climb up by himself, even without the bad knee.'

Jack Loring adds, 'Joe was in terrible pain during the making of the film. There was a doctor and two nurses, injections and massages – various things to get him together so that he could eat a little, but he had no appetite. By now he couldn't drink at all.

Then he'd be put to bed, in order to get up at five and be in the car at six to get to the set and struggle through another day's work. The atmosphere was terrible on that film, let me tell you. It's a miracle it ever got finished.' At weekends, in search of peace, Losey retreated to spend time at the nearby home of Jill Bennett, the only woman in his life with whom he had never been in conflict – not in thirty years of constant friendship.

Losey did not live to see the film's British premiere on 29 May 1985, which took place a year after his death. Its reviews were muted, *The Guardian*'s critic remarking that 'Joseph Losey is not noted for his lightness of touch, and a Losey joke book would be a slim volume indeed.' He concluded that 'the whole thing here seems less than an emotional *tour de force* and more of a striving push for significance.' On the film's Paris opening, the critic of the *International Herald Tribune* wrote, 'This film, however, can scarcely take its place with his major contributions, and one regrets that his farewell work was not of stronger substance.'

The final acts of both Dors and Losey, aimed at promoting the film, were undeniably heroic. Dors was the only person on the set who knew that she would be dead within days of finishing, and to deliver the performance that she did – one of her best and one of the film's best – represented an extraordinary act of courage. And it did not end there. Racing against time, she honoured her obligation to appear on the Johnny Carson Show in Hollywood, spoke cheerfully about the film and the genius of her director, climbed on to another plane to return to London, and died a few days afterwards.

At Heyman's behest, Losey flew to New York with the final cut of *Steaming*, although it lacked music and post-synch, so that it could be given a special showing for the distributors. Heyman, brooding about how to sell the picture, suggested they publicize it with the slogan: 'At last – a picture for women by women,' to which Losey retorted, 'and what about us males?' Heyman, tongue firmly in cheek, replied that their names might simply be dropped from the credits. Losey, unamused, vetoed the idea.

Lunching with Losey, Jack Loring found his friend so tired and ill that he was unable even to summon up the energy to order for himself. He then flew straight back to Britain, telling Loring that if he could just get his bones back to London, what was subsequently done with them was no longer of any concern to him. On his arrival he went immediately into hospital, where he was finally submitted to the various tests which he had hitherto been avoiding. Typically, he took some work tapes in with him, as he had not been well enough to sit through the music recording sessions which produced them.

Bogarde, who had come back to London in March for a brief visit, having finished a big film, had been greeted upon arrival at his hotel suite by the smell of hyacinths, an offering from Losey, accompanied by the message: 'Welcome! Next time it's with me.' Bogarde did not yet know how sick Losey actually was, but in any case they were by now both considered financial risks, and Bogarde knew that they would never again make another film together. On 6 March, Bogarde went to Royal Avenue to see his friend, finding him 'old, gross, weary and worried'. Losey said he'd been offered two probably dreadful movies; he didn't know what to do next, and he missed Paris.

'I'm a stranger again,' he'd complained. 'No one knows who I am here any more. They all do in Paris.' Bogarde revealed that he'd been offered the job of judging at the Cannes Film Festival, to which Losey had replied, 'Well, the festival has fallen on hard times. They must be scraping the bottom of the barrel. It's a terrible job, Dirkel.' Losey's laughter, Bogarde remembers sadly, was 'tired, beaten, joyless'.

It was late May when Losey went home from hospital for the last time, making plans to go to Dublin with Harold Pinter, Richard Dalton, and William Trevor on 16 July, to look for locations for a film based on Trevor's novel *Fools of Fortune*. In the month that followed Losey's release from hospital, visitors came to Royal Avenue in a continuous stream, with Patricia providing an endless flow of tea and coffee. Friends came to sit with him a while and to read to him, and Dr Cooper was on hand daily and at all hours to do what he could to make his old friend's transition less acute.

Although there was no dearth of devoted colleagues and acquaintances demonstrating their concern for Losey during this period, the jewel in the crown of his myriad friendships was surely Jill Bennett. Having helped and cherished him through the difficult early years of British exile, she now tendered her unfailing loyalty during these miserable, terminal weeks, during which the traumas of producing *Steaming* had further intensified the emotionally vexed atmosphere at home. In fact, Losey spent most of his last weekends with Jill, cocooned in her little house in Britten Street, matching her jar for jar, and talking away the night.

One of Jill's most poignant memories was of Joe sitting like a large, untidy bundle in an undersized, blue armchair, once favoured by one of her ageing dogs, now incontinent and no longer able to jump up onto it. Often Joe would himself feel so lame and feeble that he was unable to walk the few blocks home to Royal Avenue, and would stay the night or beg a lift from Jill. When he died Jill lost the last of her dearest and most supportive friends after Godfrey Tearle and her much adored mother.

Losey never did get to Dublin. His 'final cut' came at noon on 22 June, when he sighed his last sigh. A day or so before, Loring had received a call from Patricia in New York, saying that Losey was dying. He asked, 'Does that mean that Joe is continuing to die as he has been "dying" for the last ten years, or is he going in the next ten days, ten minutes, or what?' He flew straight to London, arriving at Royal Avenue shortly before Losey died. He went to Losey's room and found him agitated and occasionally raving. He did not seem to recognize his adopted son, for he had become blind.

Towards the end of his life, Losey had talked much about Gavrik to various people, including Loring. He worried about his first-born, regretted the sterility and failure of their relationship, and felt the sting of guilt accompanying the knowledge that there was much he could have done about it. Gavrik had long since put aside any thought of directing, and had 'gone over to the other side'. It is said that Losey was chagrined when Gavrik became a film producer, a Money-man, and equally furious to learn that he was extremely good at it. At the end, perhaps, Losey would have liked to wish him well, but it was too late. Gavrik's final, poignant comment came at the end of a brief, intense conversation with Loring as they sat in the garden, waiting for the end. 'What I'd love to know,' he said without rancour, 'is why you and not me?'

On the bright noon of 22 June 1984 the telephone rang at the Royal Avenue home. It was Dirk Bogarde calling from his farm-house in Provence, responding to a sudden, strange compulsion to discover how Losey was faring in his battle. Patricia had told him the day before that it was only a matter of days before the end. As a secretary asked him to hold on while she passed the phone to Patricia, he heard a sudden disturbance in the background. 'Call you back,' she said urgently. Twenty minutes later she telephoned to say, 'He's gone.' The actor's call had coincided with the moment of the director's death.

'Knowing Joe as well as I did, it would not have surprised me if, somewhere along the psychic wavelengths, he had summonsed me: and I had obeyed,' Bogarde wrote in his autobiography.

Loring, Patricia, and Gavrik had been at his bedside when Losey died. Joshua arrived shortly after, along with Dr Cooper, who told them that Losey had left his eyes to science, and that his body would be removed to a hospital so that the necessary operation could be performed.

The funeral was held at Putney Vale Crematorium, without a vicar, presumably in deference to Losey's atheism. There was music from *Don Giovanni*; Joshua read some poetry, as did Losey's secretary, Victoria Bacon. Patricia placed one red rose on the coffin before it slid from sight to be consumed by flames. Visibly upset, she returned to her seat, where she sat, immobile, until a door at the rear was flung open, and a flamboyant attendant appeared, beseeching: 'Could you all clear the room, please. The next people are waiting!' As they all filed out, Barry Cooper arrived, mumbling apologies for being late.

Feeling that this ceremony was insufficient as a fitting farewell to the man whom he had loved and hated with almost equal force for exactly thirty years, Bogarde staged a memorial gathering at Twickenham, which came to be referred to as 'Dirk's wake'. Here people came not to bury Losey but to praise him and to celebrate his life and their part in it. Robert Bolt, recovering from a stroke, had not really wanted to go, dreading the long, tiring walk across the vast sound stage to the band of thirty or forty guests who clustered at one end, but his wife, Sarah Miles, had insisted.

'When we got there,' she said, 'there was such a feeling of warmth, of love for Joe, as if he was there, knowing. The atmosphere was infused with it. Women loved him for that tragic void – that lack of inner vision of himself, to be able to see the beauty of his own spirit, not to be able to bridge that gap between his intellect and that spirit. All the chips and complexes stood in the way of his being and feeling integrated.'

Several dear friends were missing: John Heyman had been in a horrendous car crash on a motorway and had broken forty-four bones. Miraculously, he survived but was to spend more than a year in hospital. Stanley Baker had died of cancer in 1977, and Willie Fox, deeply missed, was away working on location. Very few people were closer to Losey than Heyman, or would have better understood what Losey had told Michel Ciment about his own philosophy of life, one shared by many of the characters in his films:

'There's a danger that people will get tired of struggle and want to settle down into thinking that life is pleasant. When you have to fight all the time, which I've had to do almost all my life, there comes a terrible awareness of the shortness of life. One commits oneself to a cause not only through reasoning but also through feelings. So much energy and so much time is taken up in the struggle that you begin to wonder what the hell you're on the face of the earth for, because it doesn't make much difference.'

Bibliography

Adler, Larry. *It Ain't Necessarily So*, London, Collins, 1984.

Bacall, Lauren. *Lauren Bacall, By Myself*, New York, Alfred Knopf, 1979.

Bartlett, Donald L. and James B. Steel. *Empire: The Life, Legend and Madness of Howard Hughes*, New York, Norton, 1979.

Benchley, Nathaniel. *Humphrey Bogart*, Boston, Little Brown, 1975.

Bentley, Eric. *Thirty Years of Treason*, London, Thames and Hudson, 1972.

Bessie, Alvah. *Inquisition in Eden*, New York, Macmillan, 1965.

Bogarde, Dirk. *Snakes and Ladders*, London, Chatto & Windus, 1978.

— *An Orderly Man*, London, Chatto & Windus, 1983.

Bragg, Melvyn. *Rich – The Life of Richard Burton*, London, Hodder & Stoughton, 1988.

Brecht, Bertolt. *Poems 1913–1956*, London, Methuen, 1976.

— *Life of Galileo*. Edited by John Willett and Ralph Mannheim, London, Methuen, 1980.

Callan, Michael Feeney. *Julie Christie*, London, W. H. Allen, 1984.

Callow, Simon. *Charles Laughton: A Difficult Actor*, London, Methuen, 1987.

Ciment, Michel. *Conversations with Losey*, London, Methuen, 1985.

Clurman, Harold. *The Fervent Years*, New York, Alfred Knopf, 1945.

Crowther, Bosley. *Hollywood Rajah: The Life and Times of Louis B. Mayer*, New York, Holt, Rinehart & Winston, 1970.

Esslin, Martin. *Brecht: A Choice of Evils*, London, Eyre & Spottiswoode, 1959.

Ferris, Paul. *Richard Burton*, London, Weidenfeld & Nicolson, 1981.

Fox, Angela. *Slightly Foxed*, London, Collins, 1986.

Fox, James. *Comeback*, London, Hodder & Stoughton, 1983.

French, Philip. *The Movie Moguls*, London, Penguin Books, 1971.

Friedrich, Otto. *City of Nets*, London, Headline, 1986.

Gabler, Neal. *An Empire of their Own*, London, W. H. Allen, 1988.

Goodman, Walter. *The Committee: The extraordinary story of the House*

Committee on Un-American Activities, London, Secker & Warburg, 1969.

Hart, James D. *The Oxford Companion to American Literature*, New York, Oxford University Press, 1965.

Hellman, Lillian. *Scoundrel Time*, Boston, Little Brown, 1976.

Henreid, Paul with Julius Fast. *Ladies Man*, New York, St Martin's Press, 1984.

Higham, Charles. *Orson Welles: The Rise and Fall of an American Genius*, London, New English Library, 1985.

Hirsch, Foster. *Joseph Losey*, Boston, Twayne, 1980.

Houseman, John. *Run-Through*, New York, Simon & Schuster, 1972.

—*Unfinished Business*, London, Chatto & Windus, 1986.

Junor, Penny. *Burton*, London, Sidgwick & Jackson, 1985.

Kael, Pauline. *When the Lights Go Down*, New York, Holt, Rinehart & Winston, 1975.

Kazan, Elia. *A Life*, London, André Deutsch, 1988.

Lanchester, Elsa. *Elsa Lanchester Herself*, New York, St Martin's Press, 1983.

Leahy, James. *The Cinema of Joseph Losey*, London, A. Zwemmer, 1967.

Leaming, Barbara. *Orson Welles*, New York, Viking, 1985.

Ledieu, Christien. *Joseph Losey*, Paris, E. Seghers, 1963.

Lesley, Cole. *Remembered Laughter – The Life of Noël Coward*, New York, Alfred Knopf, 1977.

Lyon, James K. *Bertolt Brecht in America*, London, Methuen, 1982.

Meredith, Scott. *George Kaufman and his friends*, New York, Doubleday, 1974.

Milne, Tom. *Losey on Losey*, London, Secker & Warburg BFI, 1967.

Nathan, George Jean. *Encyclopaedia of the Theater*, New Jersey, Associated University Presses Inc, 1970.

— *The Entertainment of a Nation*, New Jersey, Associated University Presses Inc, 1971.

— *The Theater Yearbook of The Year*, 1943–44, New Jersey, Associated University Presses Inc, 1974.

— *The Theater Yearbook of The Year*, 1945–46, New Jersey, Associated University Presses Inc, 1974.

Navasky, Victor S. *Naming Names*, New York, Viking Press, 1980.

Needle, Jan and Peter Thompson. *Brecht*, Oxford, Basil Blackwell, 1981.

Nickens, Christopher. *Elizabeth Taylor*, London, Hutchinson, 1984.

Parrish, Robert. *Growing Up In Hollywood*, London, The Bodley Head, 1976.

Pinter, Harold. *The Proust Screenplay*, London, Eyre Methuen, 1978.

Powdermaker, Hortense. *Hollywood The Dream Factory*, London, Secker & Warburg, 1951.

Schorer, Mark. *Sinclair Lewis: An American Life*, New York, 1961.
Sinclair, Andrew. *Spiegel*, London, Weidenfeld & Nicolson, 1987.
Singer, Kurt. *The Laughton Story*, Philadelphia, John C. Winston, 1954.
Spada, James. *Fonda*, New York, Doubleday, 1985.
Turnell, Martin. *The Novel in France*, New York, New Directions, 1950.
Walker, Alexander. *Hollywood England*, London, Michael Joseph, 1974.
— *National Heroes*, London, Harrap, 1985.
Woodward, Ian. *Glenda Jackson*, London, Weidenfeld & Nicolson, 1985.
Zierold, Norman. *The Hollywood Tycoons*, London, Hamish Hamilton, 1969.

Filmography

1939
Pete Roleum and His Cousins (Petroleum Industries Exhibition)

Producer, director, script: Joseph Losey
Photography: Harold Muller
Music: Hanns Eisler, Oscar Levant
Editor: Helen Van Dongen
Running time: 20 minutes

1941
A Child Went Forth (National Association of Nursery Educators)

Producers/directors: Joseph Losey, John Ferno
Script: Joseph Losey
Music: Hanns Eisler
Running time: 18 minutes

1941
Youth Gets a Break (National Youth Administration)

Director: Joseph Losey
Photography: John Ferno, Willard Van Dyke, Ralph Steiner
Running time: 20 minutes

1945
A Gun in His Hand (MGM)

Director: Joseph Losey
Script: Charles Francis Royal, from a story by Richard Landau
Photography: Jackson Rose
Music: Max Terr
Art Director: Richard Duce
Editor: Harry Komer
Leading players: Anthony Caruso, Richard Gaines, Ray Teal
Running time: 19 minutes

1948
The Boy With Green Hair (RKO-Radio)

Producer: Stephen Ames
Director: Joseph Losey
Script: Ben Barzman, Alfred Lewis Levitt, from a story by Betsy Beaton
Photography: George Barnes
Music: Leigh Harline
Art Directors: Albert d'Agostino, Ralph Berger
Editor: Frank Doyle
Leading players: Dean Stockwell, Pat O'Brien, Robert Ryan, Barbara
  Hale, Samuel S. Hinds, Walter Catlett, Richard Lyon
Running time: 82 minutes

1950
The Lawless (The Dividing Line) (Paramount)

Producers: William Pine, William Thomas
Director: Joseph Losey
Script: Geoffrey Homes [Daniel Mainwaring], from Daniel Mainwaring's novel
  The Voice of Stephen Wilder
Photography: Roy Hunt
Music: Mahlon Merrick
Art Director: Lewis H. Creber
Editor: Howard Smith
Leading players: Macdonald Carey, Gail Russell, John Sands, Lee

Patrick, John Hoyt, Lalo Rios, Maurice Jara, Walter Reed
Running time: 83 minutes

1951
The Prowler (United Artists)

Producer: S. P. Eagle [Sam Spiegel]
Director: Joseph Losey
Script: Hugo Butler, from a story by Robert Thoeren and Hans Wilhelm
Photography: Arthur Miller
Music: Lyn Murray
Art Director: Boris Leven
Editor: Paul Weatherwax
Leading players: Van Heflin, Evelyn Keyes, John Maxwell, Katherine
    Warren, Emerson Treacy, Madge Blake, Wheaton Chambers, Robert
    Osterloh
Running time: 92 minutes

M (Columbia)

Producer: Seymour Nebenzal
Director: Joseph Losey
Script: Norman Reilly Raine, Leo Katcher
Photography: Ernest Laszlo
Music: Michel Michelet
Art Director: Martin Obzina
Editor: Edward Mann
Leading players: David Wayne, Howard Da Silva, Luther Adler, Martin
    Gabel, Steve Brodie, Raymond Burr, Glenn Anders, Karen Morley,
    Norman Lloyd, John Miljan
Running time: 88 minutes

The Big Night (United Artists)

Producer: Philip A. Waxman
Director: Joseph Losey
Script: Stanley Ellin, Joseph Losey, from Stanley Ellin's novel *Dreadful
    Summit*
Photography: Hal Mohr

Music: Lyn Murray
Art Director: Nicholas Remisoff
Editor: Edward Mann
Leading players: John Barrymore Jr, Preston Foster, Howland Chamberlin, Howard St John, Philip Bourneuf, Emil Meyer, Dorothy Comingore, Joan Lorring, Mauri Lynn
Running time: 75 minutes

1952

Stranger on the Prowl (Imbarco a Mezzanotte) (United Artists)

Producer: Noel Calef
Director: Andrea Forzano (Joseph Losey)
Script: Andrea Forzano (Ben Barzman), from a story by Noël Calef
Photography: Henri Alekan
Music: C. G. Sonzogno
Art Director: Antonio Valente
Editor: Thelma Connell
Leading players: Paul Muni, Joan Lorring, Vittorio Manunta, Luisa Rossi, Aldo Silvani, Franco Balducci
Running time: 82 minutes

1954

The Sleeping Tiger (Anglo-Amalgamated)

Producer: Victor Hanbury
Director: Victor Hanbury (Joseph Losey)
Script: Derek Frye (Harold Buchman, Carl Foreman), from a novel by Maurice Moiseiwitch
Photography: Harry Waxman
Music: Malcolm Arnold
Art Director: John Stoll
Editor: Reginald Mills
Leading players: Dirk Bogarde, Alexis Smith, Alexander Knox, Hugh Griffith, Patricia McCarron, Maxine Audley, Glyn Houston, Harry Towb, Billie Whitelaw
Running time: 89 minutes

1955
A Man on the Beach (Hammer Films)

Producer: Anthony Hinds
Director: Joseph Losey
Script: Jimmy Sangster, from Victor Canning's story *Chance at the Wheel*
Photography: Wilkie Cooper
Music: John Hotchkis
Art Director: Edward Marshall
Editor: Henry Richardson
Leading players: Donald Wolfit, Michael Medwin, Michael Ripper
Running time: 29 minutes

1956
The Intimate Stranger (Anglo-Amalgamated)

Producer: Alec Snowden
Director: Joseph Walton (Joseph Losey)
Script: Peter Howard (Howard Koch)
Photography: Gerald Gibbs
Music: Trevor Duncan
Design Consultant: Richard MacDonald
Editor: Geoffrey Muller
Leading players: Richard Basehart, Mary Murphy, Constance Cummings,
    Roger Livesey, Mervyn Johns, Faith Brook, Vernon Greeves
Running time: 95 minutes

1957
Time Without Pity (Eros)

Producers: John Arnold, Anthony Simmons
Director: Joseph Losey
Script: Ben Barzman, from Emlyn Williams's play *Someone Waiting*
Photography: Freddie Francis
Music: Tristram Cary
Design Consultant: Richard MacDonald
Editor: Alan Osbiston

Leading players: Michael Redgrave, Ann Todd, Leo McKern, Peter Cushing, Alec McCowen, Renee Houston, Paul Daneman, Lois Maxwell, Richard Wordsworth, George Devine, Joan Plowright
Running time: 88 minutes

The Gypsy and the Gentleman (Rank)

Producer: Maurice Cowan
Director: Joseph Losey
Script: Janet Green, from Nina Warner Hooke's novel *Darkness I Leave You*
Photography: Jack Hildyard
Music: Hans May
Design Consultant: Richard MacDonald
Editor: Reginald Beck
Leading players: Melina Mercouri, Keith Michell, Patrick McGoohan, June Laverick, Lyndon Brook, Flora Robson, Clare Austin, Helen Haye, Newton Blick, Mervyn Johns
Running time: 107 minutes

1959

Blind Date (Rank)

Producer: David Deutsch
Director: Joseph Losey
Script: Ben Barzman, Millard Lampell, from a novel by Leigh Howard
Photography: Christopher Challis
Music: Richard Rodney Bennett
Design Consultant: Richard MacDonald
Editor: Reginald Mills
Leading players: Hardy Kruger, Stanley Baker, Micheline Presle, Robert Flemyng, Gordon Jackson, John Van Eyssen, Jack MacGowran
Running time: 95 minutes

1960
The Criminal (Anglo-Amalgamated)

Producer: Jack Greenwood
Director: Joseph Losey
Script: Alun Owen, from a story by Jimmy Sangster
Photography: Robert Krasker
Music: John Dankworth
Design Consultant: Richard MacDonald
Editor: Reginald Mills
Leading players: Stanley Baker, Sam Wanamaker, Margit Saad, Patrick Magee, Noel Willman, Grégoire Aslan, Jill Bennett, Kenneth J. Warren, Nigel Green, Kenneth Cope, Patrick Wymark, Jack Rodney, John Molloy, Brian Phelan, Murray Melvin, John Van Eyssen, Laurence Naismith, Rupert Davies, Tom Bell, Neil McCarthy
Running time: 97 minutes

1961
The Damned (BLC/Columbia)

Producer: Anthony Hinds
Director: Joseph Losey
Script: Evan Jones, from H. L. Lawrence's novel *The Children of Light*
Photography: Arthur Grant
Music: James Bernard
Production Designer: Bernard Robinson
Editor: Reginald Mills
Leading players: Macdonald Carey, Shirley Ann Field, Viveca Lindfors, Alexander Knox, Oliver Reed, Walter Gotell, James Villiers, Thomas Kempinski, Kenneth Cope, Brian Oulton
Running time: 87 minutes

1962
Eve (Gala)

Producers: Robert Hakim, Raymond Hakim
Director: Joseph Losey
Script: Hugo Butler, Evan Jones, from James Hadley Chase's novel

Photography: Gianni Di Venanzo
Music: Michel Legrand
Art Directors: Richard MacDonald, Luigi Scaccianoce
Editors: Reginald Beck, Franca Silvi
Leading players: Jeanne Moreau, Stanley Baker, Virna Lisi, Giorgio
    Albertazzi, James Villiers
Running time: 111 minutes

1963
The Servant (Warner-Pathé)

Producers: Joseph Losey, Norman Priggen
Director: Joseph Losey
Script: Harold Pinter, from Robin Maugham's novel
Photography: Douglas Slocombe
Music: John Dankworth
Production Designer: Richard MacDonald
Editor: Reginald Mills
Leading players: Dirk Bogarde, James Fox, Wendy Craig, Sarah Miles,
    Catherine Lacey, Richard Vernon, Ann Firbank, Doris Knox, Patrick
    Magee, Alun Owen, Jill Melford, Harold Pinter, Brian Phelan
Running time: 115 minutes

1964
King and Country (Warner-Pathé)

Producers: Norman Priggen, Joseph Losey
Director: Joseph Losey
Script: Evan Jones, from John Wilson's play *Hamp* and James Lansdale
    Hodson's story
Photography: Denys Coop
Music: Larry Adler
Design Consultant: Richard MacDonald
Editor: Reginald Mills
Leading players: Dirk Bogarde, Tom Courtenay, Leo McKern, Barry
    Foster, James Villiers, Peter Copley, Barry Justice, Vivian Matalon,
    Jeremy Spenser
Running time: 86 minutes

1966
Modesty Blaise (20th Century-Fox)

Producer: Joseph Janni
Director: Joseph Losey
Script: Evan Jones, based on Peter O'Donnell and Jim Holdaway's comic strip
Photography: Jack Hildyard
Music: John Dankworth
Production Designer: Richard MacDonald
Editor: Reginald Beck
Leading players: Monica Vitti, Terence Stamp, Dirk Bogarde, Harry Andrews, Michael Craig, Scilla Gabel, Tina Marquand, Clive Revill, Rossella Falk, Joe Melia, Alexander Knox
Running time: 119 minutes

1967
Accident (London Independent Producers/Monarch)

Producers: Joseph Losey, Norman Priggen
Director: Joseph Losey
Script: Harold Pinter, from Nicholas Mosley's novel
Photography: Gerry Fisher
Music: John Dankworth
Art Director: Carmen Dillon
Editor: Reginald Beck
Leading players: Dirk Bogarde, Stanley Baker, Jacqueline Sassard, Michael York, Vivien Merchant, Delphine Seyrig, Alexander Knox, Ann Firbank, Brian Phelan, Terence Rigby, Jane Hillary, Harold Pinter, Freddie Jones, Nicholas Mosley
Running time: 105 minutes

1968
Boom! (Rank)

Producers: John Heyman, Norman Priggen
Director: Joseph Losey
Script: Tennessee Williams, from his play *The Milk Train Doesn't Stop Here Anymore*
Photography: Douglas Slocombe
Music: John Barry
Production Designer: Richard MacDonald
Editor: Reginald Beck
Leading players: Elizabeth Taylor, Richard Burton, Noël Coward, Joanna Shimkus, Michael Dunn, Romolo Vallu
Running time: 113 minutes

Secret Ceremony (Universal)

Producers: John Heyman, Norman Priggen
Director: Joseph Losey
Script: George Tabori, from Marco Denevi's story
Photography: Gerry Fisher
Music: Richard Rodney Bennett
Production Designer: Richard MacDonald
Editor: Reginald Beck
Leading players: Elizabeth Taylor, Mia Farrow, Robert Mitchum, Peggy Ashcroft, Pamela Brown
Running time: 109 minutes

1970
Figures in a Landscape (20th Century-Fox)

Producer: John Kohn
Director: Joseph Losey
Script: Robert Shaw, from Barry England's novel
Photography: Henri Alekan
Music: Richard Rodney Bennett
Art Director: Ted Tester
Editor: Reginald Beck
Leading players: Robert Shaw, Malcolm McDowell, Henry Woolf,

Christopher Malcolm
Running time: 110 minutes

The Go-Between (MGM-EMI)

Producers: John Heyman, Norman Priggen
Director: Joseph Losey
Script: Harold Pinter, from L. P. Hartley's novel
Photography: Gerry Fisher
Music: Michel Legrand
Art Director: Carmen Dillon
Editor: Reginald Beck
Leading players: Julie Christie, Alan Bates, Dominic Guard, Margaret Leighton, Michael Redgrave, Michael Gough, Edward Fox, Richard Gibson
Running time: 116 minutes

1972
The Assassination of Trotsky (MGM-EMI)

Producers: Norman Priggen, Joseph Losey
Director: Joseph Losey
Script: Nicholas Mosley, Masolino d'Amico
Photography: Pasquale De Santis
Music: Egisto Macchi
Production Designer: Richard MacDonald
Editor: Reginald Beck
Leading players: Richard Burton, Alain Delon, Romy Schneider, Valentina Cortese, Giorgio Albertazzi, Luigi Vannucchi
Running time: 103 minutes

1973
A Doll's House (British Lion)

Producer: Joseph Losey
Director: Joseph Losey

Script: David Mercer, from Henrik Ibsen's play
Photography: Gerry Fisher
Music: Michel Legrand
Art Director: Eileen Diss
Editor: Reginald Beck
Leading players: Jane Fonda, David Warner, Trevor Howard, Delphine Seyrig, Edward Fox, Anna Wing, Pierre Oudrey
Running time: 106 minutes

1974

Galileo (Cinevision)

Producer: Ely Landau
Director: Joseph Losey
Script: Barbara Bray, Joseph Losey, from Bertolt Brecht's play
Photography: Michael Reed
Music: Hanns Eisler
Production Designer: Richard MacDonald
Editor: Reginald Beck
Leading players: Topol, Edward Fox, Georgia Brown, Clive Revill, Margaret Leighton, John Gielgud, Michael Gough, Michel Lonsdale, Richard O'Callaghan, Tim Woodward, Judy Parfitt, John McEnery, Patrick Magee, Tom Conti
Running time: 145 minutes

1975

The Romantic Englishwoman (20th Century-Fox/Rank)

Producer: Daniel M. Angel
Director: Joseph Losey
Script: Thomas Wiseman, Tom Stoppard, from Thomas Wiseman's novel
Photography: Gerry Fisher
Music: Richard Hartley
Art Director: Richard MacDonald
Editor: Reginald Beck
Leading players: Glenda Jackson, Michael Caine, Helmut Berger, Marcus Richardson, Kate Nelligan, René Kolldehof, Michel Lonsdale, Beatrice Romand
Running time: 116 minutes

1976
Mr Klein (Gala)

Producers: Raymond Danon, Alain Delon, Robert Kupferberg, Jean-Pierre LaBrande
Director: Joseph Losey
Script: Franco Solinas
Photography: Gerry Fisher
Art Director: Alexander Trauner
Editor: Henri Lanoë
Leading players: Alain Delon, Jeanne Moreau, Suzanne Flon, Michel Lonsdale, Juliet Berto, Francine Bergé, Jean Bouise, Louis Seigner, Michel Aumont
Running time: 123 minutes

1978
Les Routes du Sud (Trinacra Films/FR3/Profilmes)

Executive Producer: Yves Rousset-Rouard
Director: Joseph Losey
Script: Jorge Semprun, Joseph Losey, Patricia Losey
Photography: Gerry Fisher
Music: Michel Legrand
Art Director: Alexander Trauner
Editor: Reginald Beck
Leading players: Yves Montand, Miou-Miou, Laurent Malet, France Lambiotte, José Luis Gomez, Jean Bouise, Maurice Benichou, Didier Sauvegrain, Eugène Braun-Munk, Claire Bretécher, Francesco Vicens, Roger Planchon
Running time: 97 minutes

1979
Don Giovanni (Artificial Eye)

Producers: Luciano De Feo, Michel Seydoux, Robert Nador
Director: Joseph Losey
Script: Joseph Losey, Patricia Losey, Frantz Salieri, from the opera by Mozart, libretto by Lorenzo Da Ponte

Photography: Gerry Fisher, Carlo Poletti
Art Director: Alexander Trauner
Editors: Reginald Beck, Emma Menenti, Mario Castro-Vasquez
Leading players: Ruggero Raimondi, John Macurdy, Edda Moser, Kiri Te Kanawa, Kenneth Reigel, José van Dam, Teresa Berganza, Malcolm King, Eric Adjani
Running time: 176 minutes

1982

The Trout (Gaumont)

Producer: Yves Rousset-Rouard
Director: Joseph Losey
Script: Monique Lange, Joseph Losey, from Roger Vailland's novel
Photography: Henri Alekan
Music: Richard Hartley
Art Director: Alexander Trauner
Editor: Mario Castro-Vasquez
Leading players: Isabelle Huppert, Jean-Pierre Cassel, Jeanne Moreau, Daniel Olbrychski, Jacques Spiesser, Isao Yamagata, Lisette Malidor, Ruggero Raimondi, Alexis Smith
Running time: 105 minutes

1985

Steaming (Columbia)

Producer: Paul Mills
Director: Joseph Losey
Script: Patricia Losey, from Nell Dunn's play
Photography: Christopher Challis
Music: Richard Harvey
Production Designer: Maurice Fowler
Editor: Reginald Beck
Leading players: Vanessa Redgrave, Sarah Miles, Diana Dors, Patti Love, Brenda Bruce, Felicity Dean, Sally Sagoe, Anna Tzelniker
Running time: 95 minutes

Index

Abeles, Arthur 157
Accident 149, 153, 173-84, 186, 199, 211, 232
Adjani, Eric 266
Adjani, Isabelle 266
Adler, Larry 49
Adler, Luther 83
Adler, Renata 197
ahbez, eden (sic) 74
Aillaud, Mme 246, 247
Albee, Edward 230
Albertazzi, Giorgio 138
Aldrich, Robert 87-8, 136
Alekan, Henri 204, 206
Alexandra Writes a Letter (Corwin) 50
Alice Adams 46
Ambler, Eric 110
Ames, Stephen 73, 74
Anderson, John 16, 19, 33, 49
Anderson, Lindsay 219
Anderson, Maxwell 28, 29, 30
Anderson, Michael 142-3, 215
Andersson, Bibi 221
Andrews, Harry 167
Angel, Danny 163, 242-3, 245, 248
Antonioni, Michelangelo 126, 133, 134, 135, 140, 166, 168, 171, 179, 215
Archer, Eugene 113, 164
Archibald, James 106
Arent, Arthur 40, 41
Armstrong, Louis 23, 27
Ashcroft, Peggy 197, 215
Asquith, Anthony 209

Assassination of Trotsky, The 216, 218-19, 221-8, 245, 248
Atkinson, Brooks 16, 19, 62, 71
Aubrey, James 214

Bacall, Lauren 69
Bacon, Victoria 285
Baker, George P. 15, 16, 20
Baker, Stanley 111, 114-15, 116, 120, 125, 127, 129, 130, 132, 133, 139, 155, 173, 174, 177, 180, 183, 286
Bamburger, Henry 89-90, 251, 272
Bardot, Brigitte 272, 273
Barka, Ben 236
Barry, John 190
Barry, Philip 16
Barrymore, John 85
Barrymore, John, Jr 85-7, 93-4, 202
Barthel, Joan 182, 183
Barzman, Ben 73, 75, 76, 79, 84, 89, 91, 92, 104, 110, 113-14, 120, 122-3, 230, 236, 259, 269, 270
Barzman, Norma 84, 236, 269, 270
Basehart, Richard 102
Bates, Alan 200, 209, 210-11
Beatles, The 195
Beaton, Betsy 60
Beatty, Warren 212
Beck, Reginald 191, 280
Behrman, S.N. 12, 27
Bein, Albert 27, 39
Benchley, Robert 27, 28, 33
Bennett, Jill 98-101, 120, 282, 283-4

Bennett, Richard Rodney 195
Berganza, Teresa 262, 264, 268
Berger, Helmut 242, 243, 244
Bergman, Ingrid 39, 67, 193, 261
Berlau, Ruth 65
Bernheimer, Martin 269
Berry, John 109, 110, 276
Betolucci, Bernardo 255
Bessie, Alvah 68, 86
Biberman, Herbert 68, 86
Big Night, The 85-8, 91
Billington, Michael 254
Blind Date 110-14, 120-1, 149, 279
Bloom, Claire 235
Bloomgarden, Kermit 94
Boehm, Karl 270
Boetie, Joseph 235
Bogarde, Dirk 96-8, 106, 111, 129, 142-
   6, 149-54, 156, 158, 160, 162-9, 173,
   174, 176-81, 183-4, 198, 200, 214,
   219, 220, 226, 228, 229, 232, 236-7,
   238, 272, 275, 276, 277, 283, 284, 285
Bogarde, Elizabeth 183
Bogart, Humphrey 39, 69, 70
Bohan, Marc 195-6
Bolger, Ray 27
Bolt, Robert 285
Bonnell, M. 269
Bonnet, Marguerite 221
Boom! 163, 185-93, 238, 245
Boris Godunov 271-2
Botsford, Keith 78
Boulton, David 169
Bowles, Paul 43
Box, Sydney 110, 112
Boy With Green Hair, The 60, 68,
   71-7, 90, 106, 201, 231, 279
Boyer, Charles 67, 238
Brando, Marlon 82, 238
Bray, Barbara 220, 237
Brecht, Bertolt 22, 35-6, 37, 42, 46, 52,
   57, 61-5, 67, 68, 70, 71, 72, 86, 225,
   237-40, 242, 255
Bressler, Jerry 59
Bride for the Unicorn, A 29, 31
Brinton, George 29
Britten, Tony 101

Bromilley, Dorothy see Losey,
   Dorothy
Brooks, Richard 77
Browder, Earl 41, 45
Brown, Clarence 59
Brown, John Mason 16
Brown, Stephen 64
Bruce, Brenda 280
Buchman, Harold 96
Budberg, Moura 168, 202
Bunge, Jonathan 7-8, 10, 11
Buñel, Luis 248
Burgess, Fran 5, 6, 10
Burke, Gerry 185, 246
Burn, Sir Clive 102
Burn, Michael 101, 102
Burton, Richard 111, 163, 174, 185-9,
   191, 192, 193, 195, 196, 197, 221,
   225-6, 227
Butler, Hugo 81, 85, 128, 130

Cabot, Richard 30
Caine, Michael 242, 244, 245
Caldwell, Liz 131, 132
Calef, Nissim 110, 117, 165
Calef, Noël 91, 92
Callas, Maria 215
Cameron, Mary Higbee (JL's cousin)
   4, 6-7
Camus, Albert 108
Canby, Vincent 216, 239, 268
Capra, Frank 55, 248
Cardeñas, President 224
Carey, Macdonald 78
Carné, Marcel 251
Carr, Allan 276
Carreras, Michael 102, 115, 121, 122,
   124, 243
Cass, Mama 240
Cassel, Jean-Pierre 273
Cattell, Professor James McKeen 15
Cavell, Annette 169
Challis, Christopher 279
Chance Meeting see Blind Date
Chandler, Raymond 60, 131
Chaney, Frances 86, 87, 202
Chapellier, Margot 251

Chaplin, Charlie 7, 67, 68
Chase, James Hadley 125, 130
Chatto, Daniel 210
Chatto, James 210
Chatto, Ros 161, 210
Child Went Forth, A 47, 48
Chomat, Gilbert 206, 207
Christian, Charlie 21
Christie, Agatha 23
Christie, Julie 208-12
Ciment, Michel 5, 11, 12, 13, 25, 38, 51, 56, 59, 85, 121, 124, 127, 136, 155, 256, 259, 261, 278, 286
Cinetel 225
Claire, Ina 19
Clark, Petula 171
Clayton, Jack 215
Clift, Montgomery 149
Clore, Leon 104-5, 114
Clurman, Harold 25-6, 36, 46, 62
Cohen, Larry 216
Cohen, Nat 96, 102, 115
Cole, Lester 57, 68, 69, 70, 86
Coleman, John 251, 270
Collins, Richard 86
Colpi, Henri 126
Concrete Jungle, The see *Criminal, The*
Conjur Man Dies (Fisher) 39, 40
Connery, Sean 185
Coop, Denys 163
Cooper, Dr Barrington (Barry) 95, 101, 108, 151, 162, 191, 272, 283, 285
Cooper, Gary 66
Cooper, Gladys 101
Cooper, Vicky 162
Coquatrix, Bruno 220
Cornell, Katharine 30
Cortese, Valentina 225
Corwin, Norman 50
Costa-Gavras, Constantin 248
Count Basie Orchestra 21
Courtenay, Tom 163-4, 165
Cowan, Theo 158-9, 197-8, 241, 270
Coward, Noël 189, 244
Craig, Wendy 146, 149, 151, 153, 155-6
Crawford, Cheryl 26

Crime Doesn't Pay series 57
Criminal, The 115-18, 120, 149
Crist, Judith 216
Crowther, Bosley 160, 164, 181
Cushing, Peter 104

Da Ponte, Lorenzo 266, 267, 269
Da Silva, Howard 43, 83
Dalton, Richard 281, 283
Damned, The 121-5, 128, 203
Dana, Henry Longfellow 14-15, 17, 28, 29
Dana, Richard Henry 14-15
Dankworth, John 116, 137, 148, 149, 170, 176, 190
D'Annunzio, Gabriele 202
Danon, Raymond 254, 256
Danziger, Edward 95
Danziger, Harry 95
Dassin, Jules 108, 109, 168
Davidoff, David 228, 229
Davidson, Robert 62, 63
Davies, Joseph 49
Davies, Pamela 123, 179, 204, 280, 281
Davis, John 106, 107, 113
Davis, Miles 136, 137
de Laurentiis, Dino 225
De Niro, Robert 254
Dean, Felicity 280
Dearden, Basil 154, 158
Dearden, Melissa 158
Debs, Eugene 10
Delfont, Bernard 144
Delon, Alain 221, 223, 227, 236, 248, 251-6
DeMille, Cecil B. 79, 80
Deneuve, Catherine 228
Denevi, Marco 193
Deutsch, David 107, 111, 112
Di Venanzo, Gianni 133, 135, 150
Dies, Martin 45
Dieterle, William 46
Dillon, Carmen 176, 211, 212, 231
Dimes, Albert 115, 130
Dior, Christian 195
Disney, Walt 19, 64, 66
Diss, Eileen 231

Dmytryk, Edward 57, 60, 68, 73, 86
Dodds, Olive 97, 106
Doll's House, A 168, 230-5
Don Giovanni 260-72
Doran, D.A. 44, 45
Dors, Diana 280, 281, 282
Dos Passos, John 46
Dowd, Nancy 233
Downey, Senator Sheridan 58
Draper, Paul 49
Dreyfuss, Pierre 171
Drummond, Philippa 188, 190-1, 211-12
Dunn, Michael 189
Dunn, Nell 277, 278 280
Dunne, Philip 69
Duras, Marguerite 186
Duse, Eleanor 202
Dylan, Bob 21

Echeverria, Luis 248
Eisenstein, Sergei 37, 158
Eisler, Gerhart 66-7
Eisler, Hanns 22, 37, 46, 47, 57, 63, 65-8, 239
Eisler, Ruth 66
Eldridge, Florence 12
Elizabeth, Queen, the Queen Mother 116, 214
Ellin, Stanley 85
Endfield, Cy 111
England, Barry 203
Eva see Eva
Eve 21, 125-8, 130-41, 142, 146-50, 155, 157, 158, 161, 162, 175, 201, 204, 258, 273

Fabre, Michel 109, 110, 114
Fairbanks, Douglas, Snr 7
Faithfull, Marianne 195
Falk, Rossella 169
Fame, Georgie 190
Faragoh, Francis 44, 45, 57
Farrow, Mia 193-6, 197, 202
Fassbinder, Rainer Werner 184
Faulkner, William 162

Fellini, Federico 140, 263
Ferber, Edna 19
Ferno, John 47, 48
Field, Mary *see* Losey, Mary
Figures in a Landscape 203-8, 245
Finney, Albert 229
Firbank, Ann 175
First on the Road 114
Fisher, Gerry 169, 176, 180, 194, 210, 212, 231, 244, 250, 252, 262, 279
Fisher, Rudolph 39
Fitelson, Bill 94
Fitzgerald, Zelda 230
Flanagan, Hallie 25, 38, 41-2, 45, 46
Fleuret, Maurice 267
Fonda, Jane 230, 232-5
Fontaine, Joan 78
Fontanne, Lynn (Mrs Lunt) 12, 13
Forbes, Bryan 214, 215
Ford, John 66, 80, 213
Foreman, Carl 78, 82, 92-3, 95, 96, 97, 100, 110, 186
Forester, C.S. 22
Forwood, Tony 143, 146, 184, 198, 228
Forzano, Andrea 92
Fosse, Bob 245
Four Saints in Three Acts (opera) 30
Fox, Angela 143, 144, 159, 193, 212, 219-20
Fox, Edward 212-13, 231
Fox, James ('Willie') 145-6, 151-6, 159, 160, 185, 188, 286
Fox, Robin 143, 144, 145, 155, 159, 161, 165, 171, 185, 193, 198, 205, 209, 214, 219, 220
Frankenheimer, John 228
Franklin, Winston 212
Fraser, Lady Antonia 237
Fraser, Rebecca 237
Freedland, Michael 233
French, Philip 157, 187
Frink, Elisabeth 122
Fuller, Roy 200

Gabel, Martin 27, 43, 49, 83
Gabin, Jean 125
Gable, Clark 66

Galileo (film) 72, 237-40, 242, 244, 249, 264
Galileo (play) 61-5, 67-8, 70, 71, 79
Gance, Abel 171
Gang, Martin 79, 80, 84
Garfield, John 67
Garland, Judy 69
Garland, Patrick 235
Gaulle, Charles de 207
Geiger, Rod E. 71
Gershwin, Ira 69
Gibbs, Patrick 157
Gibson, Richard 210
Gilliat, Sidney 166
Gilliatt, Penelope 156, 164-5
Gimble, Elinor 50
Giroux, Claude 230, 236
Giscard d'Estaing, Valéry 247-8, 249
Giulini, Carlo Maria 269
Go-Between, The 198, 200, 208-17, 235, 242, 245
Gods of the Lightning (Anderson) 28, 29, 32, 40
Gods of the Mountain, The (Losey) 11
Goldman, Emma 39
Goodman, Benny 21
Goodman, Walter 66
Gordon, Ruth 23
Gorelik, Mordecai 27-8
Goster, Mrs Burnside 31
Grade, Leslie 144, 145, 156, 209
Grade, Lew 144
Grant, Cary 113
Great Campaign, The 62
Great God Brown, The (O'Neill) 11
Greco, Juliette 246
Green, Paul 26, 39
Greene, Graham 277
Greene, Patterson 68
Griffith, D.W. 7
Griffith, Hugh 97
Gromyko, Andrei 49
Guard, Dominic 210, 211, 213, 215
Guggenheim, Peggy 201, 202
Gun In His Hand, A 59
Gypsy and the Gentleman, The 106-8, 117, 168

Haight, George 20, 21
Hakim, Raymond 125-6, 130-3, 136-40, 146, 205, 232
Hakim, Robert 125-6, 130-3, 136-40, 146, 205, 232
Hale, Barbara 90
Hale, Georgina 280
Halifax, Lord 49
Hambledon, T. Edward 62, 70
Hammond, John Henry III 21-2, 26, 27, 28, 31, 32, 35, 36, 39
Hamp see *King and Country*
Hampton, Christopher 280
Hanbury, Victor 97
Handford, Peter 214, 231, 280, 281
Harbottle, Laurence 185
Harris, Jed 18-19, 20, 23, 27, 94
Harris, Robert 101
Harrison, Rex 187
Hartley, L.P. 200, 209-12, 216-17
Hartley, Richard 239
Haskell, Molly 233
Hawes, Elizabeth *see* Losey, Elizabeth
Hayden, Tom 232
Hayes, Helen 50
Hayward, Doug 47
Hayworth, Rita, 69
Hecht, Ben 19, 27
Heflin, Van 80, 82
Heilbron, Vivien 210
Hellman, Lillian 46
Hemingway, Ernest 13
Henreid, Paul 70
Hepburn, Katharine 46, 69
Heydrich, Reinhard 57
Heyman, John 185-8, 191, 193, 196, 198, 209, 230, 235-6, 276, 277, 279, 280, 282, 285-6
Hickerson, Harold 29
Hildyard, Jack 169
Hiller, Wendy 101
Hodges, Adrian 275
Hodson, James Lonsdale 162
Holiday, Billie 21, 126, 128, 136, 137
Hoover, Herbert 18
Hoover, J. Edgar 58, 64
Horne, Lena 77

Houseman, John 25, 26, 28, 30, 31-2, 39, 40, 41, 51, 52, 63, 65, 71, 74, 78
Hoveyda, Fereydoun 139, 215
Howard, Leigh 110
Howard, Peter 102
Howard, Sidney 12, 16, 53
Howard, Trevor 231, 233
Hubley, John 64, 79, 82
Hughes, Howard 69, 74-5, 76, 77
Hunt, Roy 79
Hunter, Ian 218, 219
Huston, John 69, 79, 80-1, 149, 229, 248
Hymn to the Rising Sun (Green) 39

Ibn Saud, Abdul Aziz 255
Ibsen, Henrik 5, 20, 230, 232
If I Had a Million 46
Imbarco a Mezzanotte see *Stranger on the Prowl*
Ingersoll, Ralph 48
Injunction Granted (play) 41-2
Intimate Stranger 102
Ivens, Joris 37, 47

Jackson, Glenda 242, 243, 244
Janni, Joseph 166, 167, 171-2, 185, 206, 209
Jayhawker (Lewis and Lewis) 32, 33, 53
Jester, Ralph 31
Johnson, Eric 73
Johnston, Dennis 29
Jones, Evan 121, 122, 128-31, 134, 135, 136, 138, 163, 166, 170-1, 175
Jones, Robert Edmund 16

Kael, Pauline 244, 251, 254
Kahn, Gordon 86
Kanin, Garson 27
Karajan, Herbert von 271
Kaye, Danny 69
Kazan, Elia 26, 33, 36, 42, 52, 62, 94, 221
Keaton, Buster 7
Keeler, Christine 157
Kelly, Gene 67, 69

Kelly, Walter C. 33
Kennaway, James 200
Keyes, Evelyn 80, 81, 82, 87
Kienzle, Ray see Ray, Nicholas
King, Malcolm 262, 268
King and Country 162-5, 177, 199, 236, 242
Kissell, Howard 274
Knox, Alexander 97, 98, 122, 123, 124, 163, 167, 175, 180
Koch, Howard 92, 102, 116, 117
Kohn, John 203-6
Komisarjevsky, Theodore 20
Korda, Alexander 209, 216
Kramer, Stanley 82, 93
Krasker, Robert 115
Kropotkin, Prince Peter 39
Kruger, Hardy 110, 111, 113, 130, 187
Kubrick, Stanley 208

La Gallienne, Eva 28
Laine, Cleo 116, 137, 148, 149
Lampell, Millard 110, 113
Lanchester, Elsa 22-5, 64, 72
Landau, Ely 164, 165, 230, 237
Lang, Fritz 82, 83, 84, 121
Langner, Lawrence 12
Lardner, Ring, Jr 57, 68, 69, 86, 87
Lasky, Jesse 76-7
Lastricati, Carlo 191
Laszlo, Ernest 83
Lattuada, Alberto 176
Laughton, Charles 22-5, 61-5, 67, 68, 70, 71-2, 237, 238
Lawless, The 77, 78-9, 109
Lawrence, H.L. 121
Lawson, John Howard 13, 57, 68, 69-70, 86
Lawson, Kate 13, 57, 63
Lawson, Wilfrid, 99, 100
Leadbelly 43
Lees, Robert 7, 10
Legrand, Gérard 160, 227
Legrand, Michel 137, 190, 214
Lehman, 'Sam' 50
Lenin, V.I. 218
Leone, Sergio 248

Leontovitch, Eugenie 20, 21, 36
Let Freedom Ring (Bein) 39
Levitt, Alfred 73
Lewis, Frank 120
Lewis, Lloyd 32-3
Lewis, Sinclair 32, 33, 53
Liebermann, Rolf 260, 263, 268, 271
Lindfors, Viveca 122, 123-4, 169, 195, 215
Lindsay-Hogg, Michael 277
Lipton, Peter 119
Lipton, Ruth 112, 117, 118, 119, 128-9, 131-2, 137, 148, 151, 161, 215
Lisi, Virna 127, 133, 138
Little Ol' Boy 27, 28
Littlewood, Joan 40, 144
Litvak, Anatole 55
Lloyd, Harold 7
Lloyd, Norman 28-31, 40, 41, 43, 63, 71, 78, 83, 269
Long Names None Could Spell (Corwin) 50
Longfellow, Edith 14, 15
Longfellow, Henry Wadsworth 14, 15
Lonsdale, Michel 249
Loring, Jack 24, 41, 201-2, 203, 213, 225, 246, 251, 265, 272, 278, 281-2, 284, 285
Lorre, Peter 50
Lorring, Joan 87, 89, 91, 92
Losey, Dorothy (JL's 3rd wife) 99, 100, 101, 103, 104, 105, 114, 117-18, 128, 131, 180
Losey, Elizabeth (JL's 1st wife) 31-2, 36-7, 38, 40, 44, 47-8, 50-1, 54, 75, 90-1, 117
Losey, Fanny (JL's aunt) 2, 9, 13, 22
Losey, Gavrik (JL's son) 44, 50, 59, 75, 86, 89-92, 103, 105, 119, 128, 129, 166, 180, 194, 201, 284, 285
Losey, Ina (née Higbee, JL's mother) 4-5, 7, 10, 14, 101, 113, 114
Losey, Joseph Walton I (JL's grandfather) 2, 3, 5
Losey, Joseph Walton II (JL's father) 2-6, 8, 9, 16, 83, 257
Losey, Joshua (JL's son) 105, 118-19,

128, 129, 131, 162, 180, 202, 206-7, 256, 258-9, 285
Losey, Luisa (JL's 2nd wife) 54, 55, 56, 60, 75, 81, 84, 87, 89-92, 116-17
Losey, Mary (JL's aunt, 'Aunt Mer') 2, 3, 5, 6, 13
Losey, Mary (JL's sister, later Field) 6, 8, 14, 101, 114, 207
Losey, Patricia (JL's 4th wife) 131, 132, 138, 148, 149, 151, 161-2, 165, 168, 198, 200-3, 205, 208, 213, 218, 220, 228, 234, 237, 247, 251, 257, 261, 262, 276, 278, 279, 284-5
Losey, Rosie (JL's aunt) 2-3
Losey, Sally (JL's daughter-in-law) 180
Love, Patti 280
Lovejoy, Alexander 16
Lowry, Malcolm 228
Lumet, Sidney 44
Lunt, Alfred 12, 62
Lyon, Claude 251
Lyons, Arthur 54

M 2-4, 133, 134
Maazel, Lorin 263-4, 264, 270, 271
MacArthur, Charles 19
McCarthy, Senator, Joseph 80, 94, 98, 207, 227
McClintic, Guthrie 30
McColl, Ewan 40
McCowen, Alec 104
MacDonald, Richard 96, 98, 102, 106-7, 108, 115, 123, 129, 131, 132, 134, 136, 147, 156, 163, 166, 167, 169, 173, 175, 187, 188, 189, 194, 195, 211, 212, 215, 223, 231, 237, 239, 244, 250, 251

McDowell, Malcolm 204, 208
McKern, Leo 104, 163
MacLeish, Archibald 46
MacLendon, Rose 25
MacMurray, Fred 46
Macurdy, John 262, 268
Magee, Patrick 115
Magnani, Anna 225
Mahler, Gustav 250

Mainwaring, Daniel 77, 78, 120, 187, 198, 240
Malaquais, Jean 222
Malraux, André 157
Malraux, Florence 157
Maltz, Albert 86, 120
Malz, Howard 68
Man On the Beach 102
Man on the Train 77
Manguel, Alberto 197
Mankiewicz, Joseph 79, 80
Mann, Thomas 236
Manunta, Vittorio 91
March, Fredric 12-13, 69
Margaret, Princess 116, 170
Marisol (sculptress) 203
Marlowe, Christopher 45-6, 143
Marx, Groucho, 53, 69
Marx, Karl 53, 68
Marx Brothers 53
Mason, James 154
Massey, Raymond 50
Matalon, Vivian 151
Matthau, Walter 154
Maugham, Robin 142, 147, 153, 154
Maugham, W. Somerset 142
May, Hans 107
Mayer, Louis B. 53-4, 60, 61
Mayersberg, Paul 160
Mazzola, James 267
Menjou, Adolphe 66
Mercer, David 200, 231-2, 233, 236
Merchant, Vivien 175, 177
Mercouri, Melina 106, 108, 168
Meredith, Burgess 27
Merin, Eda Reiss 65
Merritt, Russell 277
Meyerhold, Vsevolod 20, 36, 37, 42
Michell, Keith 106
Miles, Sarah 145, 146, 153, 155, 156, 159, 280, 281, 285
Milestone, Lewis 27, 86
Miller, Arthur 65, 94
Miller, Gilbert 22, 35
Mills, Paul 280
Mills, Reginald 147
Milne, Tom 120

Mirisch, Walter 253
Mr Klein 248-56, 260
Mitchum, Robert 194, 196
Mitford, Nancy 254
Modesty Blaise 166-72, 173
Moeller, Philip 12, 13, 16, 19
Molière 11
Molnar, Ferenc 12
Monckton, Lord 102
Montand, Yves 257, 259
Moore, Henry 102
Moreau, Jeanne 125-8, 130-4, 136, 138-41, 186, 249, 273, 274
Morris, Edmund 99
Mortimer, John 277
Moser, Edda 262
Mosley, Nicholas 173, 175, 179, 182, 216, 219, 223, 226-7, 228
Mosley, Sir Oswald 173
Moss, Jack 54, 55
Moss, Luisa *see* Losey, Luisa
Moss, Michael 54, 59, 60, 75, 86, 89
Mostel, Zero 94
Muni, Paul 50, 89, 91-2, 102
Murder at Harvard 77
Myers, Paul 263

Nabokov, Vladimir 200
Nathan, George Jean 40, 53
National Velvet 59
Navasky, Victor S. 65
Nebenzal, Seymour 82
Night of the Ball, The 101
North, Alex 62
Northumberland, Duke and Duchess of 179-80

Oakes, Philip 158
O'Brien, Pat 74, 88
Odets, Clifford 26, 36, 46, 248
Okhlopkov, Nikolai 36, 40
Olivier, Sir Laurence 19, 145, 156
O'Neill, Eugene 11, 12, 13
Ophuls, Max 109
Ornitz, Samuel 68, 86
Orozco, José 222, 223
Orpheus (Cocteau) 14

O'Toole, Peter 110-11
Otto, Theo 240
Overbey, David 259
Owen, Alun 115, 122
Ozawa, Seiji 272

Paris Opera 262
Parker, Celia 211
Parks, Larry 86
Parrish, Robert 139, 194
Partridge, Derek 165
Patrono, Carlo 188
Pepper, Beverly 134, 161, 168, 188
Pepper, Jorie 188
Perelman, S.J. 53
Pete Roleum and his Cousins 46
Phelan, Brian 117, 118, 175
Picasso, Paloma 272
Pichel, Irving 86
Pickford, Mary 7
Pine, William 77
Pins and Needles (revue) 43
Pinter, Daniel 237
Pinter, Harold 142, 143, 147, 149, 153,
    154, 156, 160n, 162, 173, 174, 175,
    179-83, 197, 199, 208, 210, 212, 214-
    17, 220, 232, 237, 260, 267, 269, 275,
    283
Pirandello, Luigi 11
Piscator, Erwin 37, 38
Plaschkes, Otto 238, 240
Plowright, Joan 104, 105
Plummer, Sir Leslie 100, 102
Polanski, Roman 248
Potter, Dennis 276
Powdermaker, Hortense 54
Powell, Dilys 181
Preminger, Otto 109, 121
Presle, Micheline 111
Priestley, J.B. 52
Priggen, Norman (Spike) 144, 163, 174,
    180, 187, 188, 198, 209
Pringle, John 277
Profumo, John 157, 160
Proust, Marcel 6, 215, 229, 221, 230,
    232, 236, 246, 247-8, 250, 255, 256,
    261, 267, 269, 270, 275

Prowler, The 81-2, 85, 90, 92, 97, 109,
    128

Ragland, Geneva 4-5
Raimondi, Ruggero 262, 265, 268, 270,
    271
Raitschoff, Rauslan 272
Rand, Ayn 66
Ratoff, Gregory 20, 21
Ray, Nicholas (né Kienzle) 1, 6, 26, 33,
    41, 42, 60, 74, 76, 80, 95, 114, 154
Rayfiel, David 275
Reagan, Ronald 230
Réage, Pauline 230
Redgrave, Michael 104, 200, 211
Redgrave, Vanessa 195, 280, 281
Reed, John 35
Reed, Oliver 122
Reed, Rex 181
Reigel, Kenneth 262, 265, 268, 272
Reilly, James 49
Reiner, Ethel Linda 101
Reinhardt, Max 22
Reinhart, Wolfgang 186
Reiss, Janine 272
Reisz, Karel 116
Resnais, Alain 140, 157, 184, 232, 233,
    257, 259
Revill, Clive 167
Reyher, Ferdinand 61, 62
Rice, Elmer 12
Richard, Cliff 144
Richardson, Tony 186
Riley, Bridget 167
Rios, Lalo 78
Rissient, Pierre 109, 110, 114, 120, 121,
    138, 165, 235, 259
Rivera, Diego 223
Rivette, Jacques 114
Roberts, Rachel 187
Robeson, Paul 49
Robson, Joan 118, 131
Rockefeller family 26
Rodin, Auguste 113
Rogers, Ginger 66, 97, 170
Rogers, Pieter 96, 101, 106, 186, 202
Rohmer, Eric 114, 120

Romantic Englishwoman, The 242-5, 251, 260
Roosevelt, Eleanor 46, 48
Roosevelt, Franklin D. 25, 43
Rosenberg, Rupert 76
Rossellini, Roberto 71
Roud, Richard 160, 215, 216, 235
Routes du Sud, Les 257-9
Rowlandson, Thomas 106
Rugoff, Donald 181
Rush, Barbara 154
Rushdie, Salman 143
Ryan, Robert 90

Sacco, Nicola 15, 29, 30
Salieri, Frantz 249, 262, 265
Salt, Waldo 86
Saltzman, Harry 237
Sangster, Jimmy 115
Santis, Pasqualino de 135
Sarton, May 16-17, 28, 29, 30
Sassard, Jacqueline 153, 175, 176, 177
Saville, Victor 117
Schaefer, Louis 42-3
Schallert, Edwin 68
Schary, Dore 60, 71, 73, 74, 76, 77-8
Schell, Maximilian 255
Schneider, Romy 221, 223, 227, 229
Schwarzkopf, Elisabeth 27
Scofield, Paul 193, 219
Scorsese, Martin 245
Scott, Adrian 60, 68, 71, 73, 86, 120
Secret Ceremony 186, 191, 193-8, 200, 201, 202, 245
Selznick, David 60
Semenenko, Serge 49
Semprun, Jorge 256-7, 259
Sequeiros, Angelica 224, 227
Sequeiros, David 222-5
Servant, The 117, 142-65, 173, 179, 182, 183, 199, 208, 209, 236
Seyrig, Delphine 168, 231-5
Shaftel, Joseph 218, 222-3
Shakespeare, William 25
Sharvan, Joe 113
Shaw, Irwin 139
Shaw, Robert 203, 204

Sherman, Vincent 62
Sherwood, Robert 16
Shivas, Mark 160
Shumlin, Herman 20
Shurlock, Geoffrey 192
Signoret, Simone 185, 188, 225
Simenon, Georges 162
Simon, John 251
Simonson, Lee 16
Sinatra, Frank 69, 195
Singer, Kurt 71-2
Sleeping Tiger, The 96-8, 102, 123, 142, 273
Slocombe, Douglas 149-50, 169, 176, 188, 189, 279
Smirnoff, Dr 247
Smith, Alexis 97-9, 273
Sokolow, Anna 62, 63, 65
Solinas, Franco 248-9, 255
Solomon & Finger 199
Spender, Lizzy 210
Spender, Stephen 210
Spiegel, Sam 81, 87, 90, 94, 173-4
Springer, John 181
Stamp, Terence 167, 168, 169
Stander, Lionel 27
Stanislavsky, Konstantin 36, 37, 62
Starnes, Joe 42, 45, 46
Steaming 277-82, 283
Stein, Gertrude 30
Stephane, Nicole 237, 248
Stevens, Craig 273
Stevens, George, Jr 267
Stevens, Roger 267
Stockwell, Dean 59, 74, 75-6, 155
Stone, Fred 33
Stoppard, Tom 242-3, 244
Strand, Paul 46-7
Stranger on the Prowl (Imbarco a Mezzanotte) 89, 91-2
Strasberg, Lee 25-6, 37
Stravinsky, Igor 63
Strick, Philip 254
Stripling, Robert E. 45, 65
Stroheim, Erich von 7
Sturges, Preston 54
Sun up to Sun down (Faragoh) 44

Sundgaard, Arnold 62

Tabori, George 59, 71, 91, 162, 186, 187, 193, 195, 237
Taluso, Flavia 208
Taluso, Ghigo 208
Taluso, Patricia *see* Losey, Patricia
Taluso, Signor 131, 161-2, 168
Tanner, Alain 221
Tavernier, Bertrand 207, 222, 235, 250, 259, 275, 276
Taylor, Elizabeth 59, 163, 184-98, 200, 201, 233, 244
Taylor, John Russell 181, 206, 216, 235
Taylor, Robert 66
Te Kanawa, Kiri 262, 263
Tearle, Godfrey 98, 99, 284
Tennant, H.M. 209
These Are The Damned see *Damned, The*
Thiess, Frank 22
Thomas J. Parnell 45, 65, 66, 67, 69, 70
Thomas, William 77, 78
Thomson, David 124, 181
Thomson, Virgil 25, 29, 30, 41
Tiger, Edith 65
Time Without Pity 104-5, 106, 114, 126
Todd, Ann 104
Todd, Mike 62
Tone, Franchot 26
Topol 238, 239
Toscan du Plantier, Daniel 260, 264, 265
Townsend, Leo 84
Townsend, Pauline 84
Trauner, Alexander 250-1, 252, 262, 265
Trevelyan, John 113, 165, 192, 197
Trevor, William 283
Triple – A Plowed Under (Arent) 41, 45
Trotsky, Leon 218, 219, 221-7
Trotsky, Natalya 221, 225
Trout, The 272-5
Truffaut, François 114
Truman, Harry S. 69, 70
Trumbo, Dalton 57, 66, 68, 81, 86

Tynan, Kenneth 103, 146

Unger, Oliver 164

Vailland, Roger 273
Van Dam, José 262
Van Dyke, Willard 48
Van Eyssen, John 215
Vanderlip, Narcissa 32
Vanzetti, Bartolomeo 15, 29, 30
Vaughan, Olwen 95-6, 98
Velaise, Robert 209
Vidal, Gore 200
Viertel, Salka 61
Villion, Emile 108, 109
Visconti, Luchino 124, 134, 140, 184, 214, 229
Vitti, Monica 126, 166, 167, 168, 172
Volkov, 'Seva' 222
Vorhaus, Bernard 89, 91
Voss 255

Waiting for Lefty (Odets) 26, 36, 248
Walker, Alexander 206
Walker, Charles 39
Wallace, Henry 49
Walsh, Raoul 121
Walton, Izaak 2
Warner, David 231, 233, 235
Waterson, Chick 191
Watson, Morris 40, 41, 42
Watts, Richard, Jr 42
Waxman, Philip 85, 88
Wayne, David 83
Wayne, John 66
Weber, John 89, 91
Weigel, Helene 64, 65, 70, 72
Weill, Kurt 22
Welles, Orson 1, 25, 28, 52, 61-2
Wells, H.G. 23
Wexley, John 56, 57, 60, 84
White, Kenneth 43, 48
White, Patrick 232
White, Sam 259
Whitman, Walt 259
Who Fights This Battle? (White) 43, 48-9

Wilder, Billy 67, 124
Wilder, Thornton 23, 27, 63
Wiley, Guildford M. 8
Williams, Emlyn 104
Williams, Moira 202
Williams, Tennessee 163, 185, 186, 187,
  189-92
Willman, Noel 115
Wilson, Dooley 39, 110
Wilson, Sir Harold 254
Wilson, John 162
Winn, Godfrey 219
Wiseman, Thomas 242, 243
Wolfit, Donald 102
Wood, Sam 65-6
Wooden Dish, The (Morris) 99-100,
  101
Woodward, Ian 244
Woolf, Virginia 17
Worlds at War (radio series) 50
Woulijoki, Hella 35-6
Wright, Frank Lloyd 67
Wyler, William 69

York, Michael 174, 176, 177
Young, Stark 28
Youth Gets a Break 48

Zinnemann, Fred 79